Thinking Machines

Machine Learning and Its Hardware Implementation

Shigeyuki Takano
Faculty of Computer Science and Engineering
Keio University
Kanagawa, Japan

ACADEMIC PRESS
An imprint of Elsevier

Academic Press is an imprint of Elsevier
125 London Wall, London EC2Y 5AS, United Kingdom
525 B Street, Suite 1650, San Diego, CA 92101, United States
50 Hampshire Street, 5th Floor, Cambridge, MA 02139, United States
The Boulevard, Langford Lane, Kidlington, Oxford OX5 1GB, United Kingdom

First Published in Japan 2017 by Impress R&D, © 2017 Shigeyuki Takano
English Language Revision Published by Elsevier Inc., © 2021 Shigeyuki Takano

Notices

Knowledge and best practice in this field are constantly changing. As new research and
experience broaden our understanding, changes in research methods, professional practices, or
medical treatment may become necessary.

Practitioners and researchers must always rely on their own experience and knowledge in
evaluating and using any information, methods, compounds, or experiments described herein. In
using such information or methods they should be mindful of their own safety and the safety of
others, including parties for whom they have a professional responsibility.

To the fullest extent of the law, neither the Publisher nor the authors, contributors, or editors,
assume any liability for any injury and/or damage to persons or property as a matter of products
liability, negligence or otherwise, or from any use or operation of any methods, products,
instructions, or ideas contained in the material herein.

Library of Congress Cataloging-in-Publication Data
A catalog record for this book is available from the Library of Congress

British Library Cataloguing-in-Publication Data
A catalogue record for this book is available from the British Library

ISBN: 978-0-12-818279-6

For information on all Academic Press publications
visit our website at https://www.elsevier.com/books-and-journals

Publisher: Mara Conner
Editorial Project Manager: Emily Thomson
Production Project Manager: Niranjan Bhaskaran
Designer: Miles Hitchen

Typeset by VTeX

Working together
to grow libraries in
developing countries

www.elsevier.com • www.bookaid.org

Thinking Machines

Machine Learning and Its Hardware Implementation

Contents

List of figures

List of tables

Biography

Shigeyuki Takano received a BEEE from Nihon University, Tokyo, Japan and an MSCE from the University of Aizu, Aizuwakamatsu, Japan. He is currently a PhD student of CSE at Keio University, Tokyo, Japan. He previously worked for a leading automotive company and, currently, he is working for a leading high-performance computing company. His research interests include computer architectures, particularly coarse-grained reconfigurable architectures, graph processors, and compiler infrastructures.

Preface

In 2012, machine learning was applied to image recognition, and it provided high inferential accuracy. In addition, a machine learning system that challenges human experts in games of chess and Go has recently been developed; this system managed to defeat world class professionals. Advances in semiconductor technology have improved the execution performance and data storage capacity required to do the deep learning task. Further, the Internet provides large amounts of data that are applied in the training of neural network models. Improvements in the research environment have led to these breakthroughs.

In addition, deep learning is increasingly used throughout the world, particularly for Internet services and the management of social infrastructure. With deep learning, a neural network model is run on an open-source infrastructure and high-performance computing system using a dedicated graphics processing unit (GPU). However, a GPU consumes a huge amount of power (300 W), thus data centers must manage the power consumption and generation of thermal heat to lower operational costs when applying a large number of GPUs. A high operational cost makes it difficult to use GPUs, even when cloud services are available. In addition, although open-source software tools are applied, machine learning platforms are controlled by specific CPU and GPU vendors. We cannot select from various products, and little diversity is available. Diversity is necessary, not only for software programs, but also for hardware devices. The year 2018 marked the dawn of domain-specific architectures (DSAs) for deep learning, and various startups developed their own deep learning processors. The same year also saw the advent of hardware diversity.

This book surveys different machine learning hardware and platforms, describes various types of hardware architecture, and provides directions for future hardware designs. Machine learning models, including neuromorphic computing and neural network models such as deep learning, are also summarized. In addition, a general cyclic design process for the development of deep learning is introduced. Moreover, studies on example products such as multi-core processors, digital signal processors (DSPs), field programmable gate arrays (FPGAs), and application-specific integrated circuits (ASICs) are described, and key points in the design of hardware architecture are summarized. Although this book primarily focuses on deep learning, a brief description of neuromorphic computing is also provided. Future direction of hardware design and perspectives on traditional microprocessors, GPUs, FPGAs, and ASICs are also considered. To demonstrate the current trends in this area, current machine learning models and their platforms are described, allowing readers to better understand modern research trends and consider future designs to create their own ideas.

To demonstrate the basic characteristics, a feed-forward neural network model as a basic deep learning approach is introduced in the Appendices, and a hardware design example is provided. In addition, advanced neural network models are also detailed, allowing readers to consider different hardware supporting such models. Finally, national research trends and social issues related to deep learning are described.

Acknowledgments

I thank Kenneth Stewart for proofreading the neuromorphic computing section of Chapter 3.

Outline

Chapter 1 provides an example of the foundation of deep learning and explains its applications. This chapter introduces training (learning), a core part of machine learning, its evaluation, and its validation methods. Industry 4.0 is one example of an application that is an advanced industry definition supporting customers with adaptation and optimization of a factory line into demand. In addition, a blockchain as an application is introduced for machine learning. A blockchain is a ledger system for tangible and intangible properties; the system will be used for various purposes with deep learning.

Chapter 2 explains basic hardware infrastructures used for machine learning. It includes microprocessors, multi-core processors, DSPs, GPUs, and FPGAs. The explanation includes microarchitecture and its programming model. This chapter also discusses the reason for the recent use of GPUs and FPGAs in general-purpose computing machines and why microprocessors meet difficulty enhancing their execution performance. Changes in market trends in terms of application perspectives are also explained. In addition, metrics for evaluation of execution performance are briefly introduced.

Chapter 3 first describes a formal neuron model and then discusses a neuromorphic computing model and a neural network model, which are recent major implementation approaches for brain-inspired computing. Neuromorphic computing includes spike timing-dependent plasticity (STDP) characteristics of our brain, which seems to play a key role in learning. In addition, address-event representation (AER) used for spike transmission is explained. Regarding neural networks, shallow neural networks and deep neural networks, sometimes called *deep learning*, are briefly explained. If you want to learn about a deep learning task, then Appendix A can support your study as an introduction.

Chapter 4 introduces ASICs and DSAs. The algorithm is described as a representation of an application that leads to software on traditional computers. After that, characteristics involved in application design (not only software development) of locality, deadlock property, dependency, and temporal and spatial mapping (the core of our computing machinery) are introduced. Good hardware architecture has good design using the factors effectively. Deadlock property and dependency are uniformly explained by general resource systems. In addition, design constraints are explained. Lastly, deep learning tasks are analyzed in cases of AlexNet on both inference and training.

Chapter 5 briefly explains a process of neural network model development and how the coded model works on a computing system through a virtual machine of Python's script language. In addition, code optimization techniques of vectorization, SIMDization, and memory access alignment are explained. These improve data-level parallelism, which is an indicator of data-intensive computing, an execution performance just like a deep neural network task. In addition, Compute Unified Device Architecture (CUDA) is introduced. CUDA is NVIDIA's common programming infrastructure for data-intensive computing including deep learning tasks. You will see how a GPU-based system works.

Chapter 6 explains methods of execution performance improvement. Six methods of model compression, numerical compression, encoding, zero- skipping, approximation, and optimization are explained. Model compression includes pruning, dropout, dropconnect, distillation, principal component analysis (PCA), tensor approximation, and weight-sharing. Numerical compression includes quantization, low-precision numerical representations, edge-cutting, and clipping. Encoding explains run-length encoding and Huffman coding. Zero-skipping includes compressed sparse row (CSR) and compressed sparse column (CSC) sparsity representations. Approximation explains approximation of activation function and the multiplication operator. We not only explain the methods themselves, but we also discuss performance improvement through these techniques in terms of data size, number of executed cycles, and energy consumption. These techniques have a constraint on use case, such as applying phase, only at training, only at inference, and/or both phases.

Chapter 7 provides case examples of major research and products. Regarding neuromorphic computing, surveys are shown briefly in this book. We discuss hardware architecture that is specialized to deep neural network tasks. In addition, a comparison between neuromorphic computing and deep neural network hardware is provided. Finally, we include tables to summarize the chapter.

Chapter 8 explains strategy planning for designing deep learning neural network hardware as discussed and explained in previous chapters. What is a factor in designing the hardware? In addition, we discuss what points should be considered for future neural network hardware designs. Chapter 9 concludes this book.

Appendix A shows the basics of neural network models represented by equations, especially linear algebra representations, and its data size is presented based on a feed-forward neural network. Appendix B shows an implementation example for deep learning supporting both inference and training. The hardware architecture can be implemented with a bidirectional bus and local memory supports. Appendix C explains basic neural network models of a convolutional neural network model, recurrent neural network model, and autoencoder model. After that, we explain a residual neural network model, which proposes a bypassing method, as a common approach to make deeper neural network models. Appendix D explains the national trends in research. Appendix E discusses social issues based on deep learning.

Chapter 1

Introduction

This chapter describes how machine learning is applied, the dawn of machine learning, and an example use case of Industry4.0 and transaction processing. In addition, this chapter introduces the types of machine learning being studied and what problems or issues they are used for. Further, previously deployed services and applications are also discussed. First, remarkable examples of machine learning are introduced. IBM's Watson AI machine, which indicated the advent of machine learning in the research domain, and Google's Go Playing machine, are introduced. Next, definitions of inference and learning are introduced, and a full perspective is provided through examples. The inference obtained from learning is then described. Before the learning of a neural network model, input data are cleaned and modified to effectively improve the learning task; the techniques used for this are also provided. In addition, a common learning method, taxonomy of learning, and its performance metrics and verifications are introduced.

Then, Industry4.0 is introduced as a use case of machine learning. Two typical example models of factory automation are applied in the explanation. Finally, the use of transaction processing is introduced. Machine learning is applied to process huge datasets, and a transaction is a procedure applied between each data processing. Although there is no direct relationship between machine learning and the transaction process, a block chain used in the transaction process can be applied anywhere and combined with machine learning. Therefore, a block chain is introduced in this chapter.

1.1 Dawn of machine learning

This section introduces remarkable events marking the dawn of machine learning. This book differentiates between machine learning and artificial intelligence (AI) to avoid confusion.

1.1.1 IBM Watson challenge on Jeopardy!

"Joepardy!" is quiz TV program in the USA. In February 2011, IBM's Watson was a challenger on the program, and won 100 million dollars (Fig. 1.1(a)). This was sensational news [256]. Jeopardy! requires an inference of intention to answer a question, and the participant needs to answer quicker than the other challengers. The Watson system requires a natural language processing perfor-

Thinking Machines. https://doi.org/10.1016/B978-0-12-818279-6.00011-6

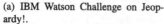

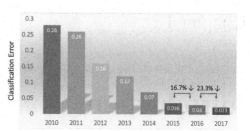

(a) IBM Watson Challenge on Jeop-   (b) Outperforming Human Recognition Performance.
ardy!.

FIGURE 1.1 IBM Watson and inference error rate [46][87].

mance (shorter latency and higher inference accuracy) to respond quickly. The system inferences meaning from a question, and uses the computer's high-speed processing power for information processing. By 2014, Watson was being applied on Linux OS using a ten-rack IBM Power 750 Server. It had a 2880 core processor and 16 TiB of memory [361]. The processor core was a POWER7 running at 3.5 GHz.

The Watson system applies a question and topic analysis, question decomposition, hypothesis generation, hypothesis and evidence scoring, synthesis, and final confidence merging and ranking. This pipeline fully composes the Watson system. IBM provides a development infrastructure for software programmers to utilize the Watson system [6].

1.1.2   ImageNet challenge

In 2012, Hinton's team entered an image recognition competition using a deep learning technique, which is currently called a convolutional neural network (CNN) [231]. The neural network used at the competition was based on LeNet [239]; it achieved an inference accuracy of 84%, while other teams achieved accuracies of 70%. After this breakthrough, the accuracy of the machine learning domain began outperforming that of human recognition, as shown in Fig. 1.1(b), which became a hot topic in this field.

1.1.3   Google AlphaGo challenge of professional Go player

In March 2016, DeepMind, which is Google's AI division entered a challenge to play Go with a professional, finally winning four out of the five games [316]. The AlphaGo system consists of a policy network and a value network. To improve the inference efficiency, it uses a Monte Carlo tree search (MCTS) [326]. See Fig. 1.2.

The learning system consists of two pipeline stages. In the first stage, the policy network consists of an SL policy achieved by learning from a teacher, and a rollout policy with a quick decision-making process. These stages roughly

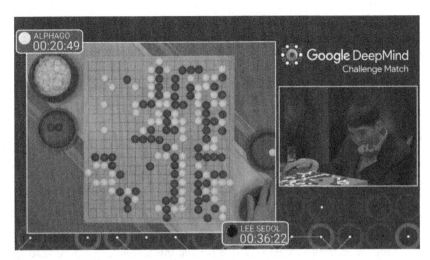

FIGURE 1.2   Google AlphaGo challenging a professional Go player [273].

determine the direct action required to win. The next stage feeds the policy network result and applies reinforcement learning (described later in this chapter),
called a value network, and then learns the details of the policy.

The policy network consists of a 13-layer deep learning model with a teacher
for learning the rules, and it applies reinforcement learning with an instance of
itself (playing with itself). It avoids an overfitting (explained later in this chapter)
through a random instance selection upon reinforcement learning. The MCTS
chooses a branch of the tree topology of the defining policy and its flow. It also
has an evaluation function to choose a branch as well as a policy extension function not only for learning the branch but also for learning the policy. AlphaGo
is implemented using the TensorFlow API (described in Chapter 5) and offloads
the task to the tensor processing unit (TPU).

1.2   Machine learning and applications

1.2.1   Definition

Machine learning is a software system on a computer that learns without requiring explicitly programming [315]. It has two typical characteristics:

- Learning/training
  This process is used to obtain temporal and or spatial features or some other
  context of the input data.
- Inference
  This process is used to infer a user-defined problem based on the result of the
  learning. An inference is applied to make elucidate any unknown matters.

Let us call an object that is the target of learning, including not only humans, cars, and animals, but also any object that can be represented through digital signal information.

1.2.2 Applications

Machine learning can be categorized as follows:

- Detection
  Machine learning recognizes near future statements from past data, and thus uses temporal series data. It detects an anomaly statement that differs from a normal statement (called anomaly detection). For example, both defect detection [378] and security [9] use this technology. In addition to the inside of robotics and a mobile object, it can be applied to a herd of any objects. In addition, setting a normal state as an object, such as a healthy person, and setting an anomalous state as a sick person, this technology can be used in medicine, for example, in cancer detection [157].
- Prediction
  Machine learning predicts a temporal statement or spatial space using a series of data. In order to predict after training for target problem, obtaining some pattern (generally called a feature) with input, such as a past data or a spatial space data is needed. Examples include weather prediction [314]; stock price prediction [263]; alternative investments [118]; mobile and communication traffic prediction [251]; infrastructure management such as electricity, gas, and oil [281]; water networks; voice prediction [284]; and predictive maintenance [343]. In addition, machine learning can be applied to video frame interpolation [206] and image inpainting for irregular holes [246], as well as for recommendations [305] such as in fashion [79]. If machine learning treats statements regarding humans, animals, or plants as input data, it can be applied to their health prediction and management.
- Estimation
  Machine learning can be used as a measurement application. Depth estimation is a typical application for estimating the depth of an environment using a camera. It takes an image as input and estimates the depth for each pixel [126]. It can be used for localization in autonomous driving. It is also applicable to distance estimations between objects and to pose estimation for detecting human joints and generating discriminated images (video) based on the pose [354].
- Planning
  Machine learning autonomously allows a plan to be created based on the learning experience. It supports autonomous systems with the most plausible plans based on future predictions. It can be used in vehicles [14], bikes [21], ships [210], drones [75], and other mobile objects, as well as in factories and plants with many objects and systems consisting of additional objects

and information, including robotics and bots involving cooperation through a plan of action.

- Generating
  Machine learning is applied to learn and obtain the features of the target information, and imitates such features. As an example, one can learn the features of a particular painter, and generate a picture with similar features [80]. Painting through machine learning has also been developed [288]. In addition, natural image [295] and music [202] generation has also been studied. Moreover, 3D object generation from images [371] can be achieved using a 3D printer or computer graphics.
- Recognition
  Such items are based on the recognition of information. Image recognition [231], multiple object detection in an image, semantic image segmentation [248], instance segmentation [189], image captioning [201], object tracking of video [372], situation recognition [360], voice recognition [373], lip reading [334], translation [114], and abstraction [312] are examples.

Detection and prediction use temporal series information, and thus there is a premise that past information affects the present information. Thus, there is a correlation among the elements of information. Recognition requires a correlation among elements in the data temporally or spatially. This technology is used for video [308] and music searches [63]. Therefore, the use of machine learning is not limited, and information that can be sampled as digital data can be applied.

1.3 Learning and its performance metrics

Fig. 1.3 shows an example of a feedforward neural network that stacks multiple layers consisting of an activation function and weighted input and output edges. Signals propagate from the input side to the output side through hidden layers. The weighted edges are summed before being fed by the activation function. The summed value is called a pre-activation. The output from the activation function is called a post-activation, or simply, an activation.

1.3.1 Preparation before learning

1.3.1.1 Preparation of dataset

We need to know whether a result is correct. To determine the result, the expected data should be prepared and used for validation regarding the execution and inference, which is used as the expected result information. The expected result information is called a label and is attached to the input data used for training. Therefore, the data label must be appended, which is extremely redundant and time consuming.

TABLE 1.1 Dataset examples.

Category	Name	Creator	Descriptions	Web Site
Image	MNIST	NYU	Handwritten Digits Images	[33]
	Fashion-MNIST	Han Xiao, et al.	Fashion version MNIST	[11]
	CIFAR10/100	Univ. of Toronto	Natural Image	[32]
	ImageNet	ImageNet.org	Object Detection in Natural Images	[87]
	Open Image Dataset	Google	Natural Images	[24]
	Google-Landmarks	Google	Landmark Images	[13]
Face	CelebA Dataset	CUHKst	200K Face Images	[18]
	MegaFace	Univ. of Washington	4.7 Million Photos and 672,057 Unique Identities	[19]
	Labeled Faces in the Wild	UMASS		[17]
Video	YouTube-8M	Google	Natural Videos	[36]
	YouTube-BoundingBoxes	Google	Object Detection (Bounding Boxes in Videos)	[37]
	Moments in Time Dataset	MIT	Captioned Videos	[20]
	Atomic Visual Actions	Google	Human Motion	[4]
	UCF101	UCF	Human's Motion Caption	[34]
	BDD100K	UC Berkeley	Driving Videos	[92]
Scene	Apollo Scape	Baidu	Driving Videos	[28]
	DeepDrive	UC Berkeley	Autonomous Driving	[29]
	KITTI	KIT	Driving Videos	[16]
	SUN Database	MIT	Object videos and its Scenes	[31]
3D Object	ShapeNet	Princeton, Stanford and TTIC	3D Object Models	[30]
	ModelNet	Princeton University	3D Object Models and Its Scenes	[26]
	Disney Animation Dataset	Disney	Disney's Character Objects	[8]
Text	20 newsgroups	Jason Rennie	classification task, mapping word occurrences to	[1]
	Reuters Corpuses	Reuters	newsgroup ID text/topic prediction	[306]
Audio	DCASE	Tampere University	Natural Sounds	[3]
	AudioSet	Google	Sounds collected from YouTube	[2]
	Freesound 4 seconds	FreeSound	FreeSound's Official Data Set	[12]
	AVSpeech dataset	Ariel Ephrat, et al.	A large collection of video clips of single speakers	[5]
	Common Voice	Mozilla	Voice Data Set	[7]

By using a standardized dataset, developers and researchers can evaluate, analyze, and share their results. Examples of labeled datasets that are open-sourced on the Internet are listed in Table 1.1.

1.3.1.2   Cleaning of training data

In this book, one training data is called a training sample, and several such training samples are called a training dataset, or simply, training data. Commonly, input data are modified before training for greater efficiency. In addition, to achieve a high accuracy of inference, a neural network structure is devised.

- Data normalization
  Data normalization averages the data for distribution to each training sample through a linear transformation [279]. Image classification often uses input data with differences between the original image and the average image composed through the dataset training.
- Data augmentation
  One way to avoid an overfitting caused by relatively fewer training data (as described later) compared to the scale of the neural network model, is to dilute the number of training data through a modification [279]. One way is to generate training data with a small shift and a small image rotation for image classification.
- Model averaging
  The output values of multiple neural networks with the same input and output layer are averaged [279]. There are several approaches, including different initializations across several of the same networks, and training using the same training dataset on different networks.

Different learning with a different initialization obtains different features through the training. Common initialization uses a pre-training, which aims to preliminarily train the features for every layer before the full training. A common method for setting the initial value is described in Appendix A.

1.3.2   Learning methods

This section describes the learning of a neural network and an evaluation of its performance. Neuromorphic computing takes a different approach.

1.3.2.1   Gradient descent method and back propagation

Training and learning are based on the viewpoint of the trainer, and learning is based on the viewpoint of the learner, and thus a training sample and the training dataset are based on such viewpoints. For a specific training sample, learning aims to narrow the difference between an inferenced result and the expected result represented as a label, and we can see and evaluate the result as the inference performance. This difference is constructed using an error function, a loss function, a cost function, and/or an objective function. In general, the learning aims to converge the function to zero by feeding the error rate back to each parameter, holding one feature while updating its value through a particular method, as shown in Fig. 1.3. This can be an iterative calculation as an example.

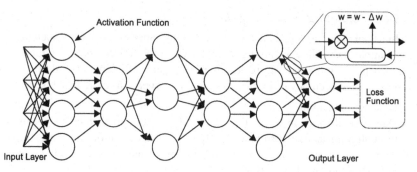

FIGURE 1.3 Feedforward neural network and back propagation.

- Gradient descent method

  The gradient descent method is used to treat the error function as having an argument of weight w, $E(w)$, making the error function value converge to the minimum absolute value with an iterative calculation. Finding the global minima is difficult in general, and instead, the method aims to find the local minima. The absolute minimum value point has a gradient of zero; for example, a convex function has a peak point with a gradient of zero, and thus it aims to calculate $\partial E(w)/\partial w$ iteratively to achieve a zero gradient.

- Online and batch learning

  Applying the gradient descent method using a training sample is called online learning, or stochastic gradient descent (SGD) because of the convergence through a probable gradient descent, just looking like a random walking on a valley. In addition, batch training aims to apply the gradient descent method to the training data [279]. In the case of larger training data, batch learning takes a longer training time and generates a larger temporal dataset. This makes the verification inefficient and a check of the intermediate results difficult, and halts or restarts the training. Such training generates a larger temporal dataset, which requires a high-performance computing system with larger memory. Therefore, by sub-dividing the training data into a subset, the training workload is reduced with a single subset. This technique is called mini-batch learning, and subset step is called an epoch.

- Back propagation

  The updated amount for each parameter representing a feature is obtained from the upper (output side) layer based on the gradient descent method. Thus, it calculates the amount of gradient descent on the output layer and propagates the value to the next lower layer by calculating the amount of gradient descent for each parameter, sending it to the next lower layer, and continuing the calculate-and-propagate process, which is achieved by its input layer. Thus, we can observe the propagation from back to front in contrast to forward propagation on the inference [311]. This back propagation is described in Appendix A.

TABLE 1.2 Combination of prediction and results.

		Expected Result	
		Positive	Negative
Predicted Result	True	True-Positive (TP)	True-Negative (TN)
	False	False-Positive (FP)	False-Negative (FN)

We call a value having a feature a "parameter." A neural network model consists of parameters, such as a weight and bias. Back propagation updates the parameters using a rule defined as an equation.

1.3.2.2 Taxonomy of learning

A learning method can be categorized into three approaches: supervised learning (SL), unsupervised learning (UL), and reinforcement learning (RL).

- Supervised learning
  SL uses training data having a label to update the parameters. The output layer is evaluated with an error function.
- Unsupervised learning
  UL uses training data without a label. It does not require an error function to update the parameters.
- Reinforcement learning
  RL aims to learn from the interference between an actor and its environment [368]. An actor receives a reward as result of its action, and it selects an action to maximize the reward. It learns a policy for the actions, a value, and/or both.

Training data can have both labeled and unlabeled data, and thus, such learning is called semi-supervised learning. Studies have been conducted to improve the inference performance by developing a training method for the learning of a neural network model. Adversarial training is a learning process used to classify input training data that are both unmodified and modified, with robustness for a modification of the data, and also an improved generalization performance (as described later) for unmodified training data [267]. Adversarial training needs labeled training data for the learning. Virtual adversarial training [267] is an extended model for a few labeled training data, and improves the generalization performance with both supervised and semi-supervised learning.

1.3.3 Performance metrics and verification

After the training, we need to evaluate and validate the results regardless of the accuracy of the inference, and the generalization performance must be acceptable in terms of the target of the customer. Table 1.2 lists the patterns between the expected and trained prediction results. We can use the table by counting how many results are categorized into each class.

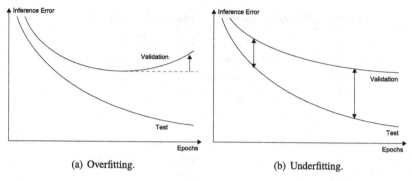

(a) Overfitting.   (b) Underfitting.

FIGURE 1.4 Generalization performance.

1.3.3.1 Inference performance metrics

An inference performance can be evaluated based on the inference accuracy, generalization performance, precision, recall, and F1 score.

- Accuracy

  This is a common metric used to show the inference performance on the trained neural network model, and is a ratio of the total number of inferences to the total number of results matched with the expected value. In addition, the inference error E is obtained as $E = 1 - A$, where A ($1 \geq A \geq 0$) is the inference accuracy shown below.

$$A = \frac{TP + FN}{TP + TN + FP + FN} \tag{1.1}$$

  Occasionally, the top-N accuracy is used for a non-mission critical problem, in which the accuracy for such an inference is among the top-N. Thus, top-1 accuracy is the same as A.

- Generalization performance

  This is a common metric of the inference accuracy or error for general input data of the trained neural network model, and not for the training data. Low generalization performance such as meeting an overfitting or an underfitting, designed neural network model is specialized for the training data or the training could not sufficiently lead to necessary features, respectively.

  - Overfitting

    The superfluous fitting of a particular dataset is called overfitting.

  - Underfitting

    An insufficient fitting to the training data is called underfitting.

  Figs. 1.4(a) and 1.4(b) show the learning curves in terms of the inference error rate for overfitting and underfitting, respectively. Both cases have a large gap between the test and validation. An overfitting often increases the error rate as the training progresses, as shown in Fig. 1.4(a). In underfitting, there is an increasing gap between the test training and validation training.

To avoid overfitting and underfitting, a regularization (as described in Appendix A) is commonly applied to an error function to adjust the back propagation.

- Recall, precision, and F1-score
  When the training data are skewed, the accuracy of the inference cannot guarantee a likelihood. The ratio of correct to incorrect results needs to be evaluated to validate the inference performance.

  - Recall
    This is a metric used to show the ratio of correct data against how many errors occur in the target data. In the case of cancer detection, it shows the number of correct detections among all patients. The recall is as follows.

$$R = \frac{TP}{TP + FN} \tag{1.2}$$

The recall shows that correct answer how much covered the patients.

  - Precision
    This is a metric used to show the likelihood of the inference, and evaluates the ratio of truly correct results. For example, in cancer detection, an inaccurate result is not allowed; however, it is difficult to achieve completely accurate results. An index is needed to indicate how much of the result are correct; precision is used for this. Precision P is as follows:

$$P = \frac{TP}{TP + FP} \tag{1.3}$$

The precision shows how much answered correctly.

  - Average precision
    We can draw a precision-recall curve (PR-curve) by plotting the recall on the x-axis and the precision on the y-axis. We then obtain the average precision with the PR-curve $p(r)$ as follows:

$$AP = \int_0^1 p(r)dr \tag{1.4}$$

The mean AP (mAP) is the mean average precision.

  - F score, F1 score
    Achieving 100% for both precision and recall at the same time is extremely difficult. We can use the harmonic mean applying both the precision and recall to fully evaluate the neural network model. The F1 score is as follows.

$$F1 = 2\frac{P \times R}{P + R} \tag{1.5}$$

- Intersection over union
  For object detection, a bounding box is used for indicating the predicted object. Representing a label box and a predicted box as TB and PB, respectively, we can estimate the accuracy, called an intersection over union (IoU), as follows.

$$IoU = \frac{TB \cap PB}{TB \cup PB} \tag{1.6}$$

If $TB \cap PB$ equals $TB \cup PB$, then the box is completely matched on the image frame.

1.3.3.2 Verification for inference

When using training data for learning to obtain the parameters for an inference performance evaluation, a statement of overfitting or underfitting is included, and thus a generalization of the performance cannot be verified. For example, in case of an overfitting, a neural network model with parameters is equivalent to a student knowing the answers to an examination and obtaining a high score. To check the generalization performance, it is necessary to prepare a dataset, called a test set, which does not include the training data for the testing. In addition, to verify the hyperparameters and the designed model, alternative training data, called a verification set, are needed. This set does not include the training data and test set, and we can evaluate the generalization performance after the verification. This validation method is called cross-validation [154]. In general, all data are divided into training data, test set, and verification set. The cross-validation is described in Chapter 5.

1.3.3.3 Learning performance metrics

Regarding the learning metrics, a way to efficiently estimate the learning progress should be considered.

- Learning curve
  The learning curve is a graph of the epoch or data size used during training against the inference accuracy. Fig. 1.4 shows the use of the inference error rate. The inference performance is improved when a certain threshold is achieved, and the curve is saturated when it achieves this threshold.
- Learning speed
  The slope or gradient of a learning curve shows the speed of learning, or how much the inference performance is improved by the amount of training data. This is not a constant value in general.
- Saturation delay
  An alternative metric is when the learning reaches a point of saturation. The training works efficiently when it quickly achieves saturation. The model architecture achieves a good training performance because it needs less training data to achieve the target inference accuracy. The training has a lower inference accuracy when it quickly achieves saturation and the model architecture

TABLE 1.3 Layer structure in Industry4.0.

Layer	Objective	Processing
Authorizing	Supporting Decision Making	Statistical analysis based on consolidation, and or planning
Consolidating	Correlation of Sampled Data, and or Planning	Detecting and Predicating
Sampling	Information Sampling	Sensoring

does not achieve a good training performance, and thus the training can be terminated at the half way mark, and the next training can be applied. This technique is called early stopping.

1.4 Examples

1.4.1 Industry4.0

The fourth industry revolution, called Industry4.0, has been researched and developed. Industry4.0 aims to dynamically change factory lines adapted to user demand, efficiently manage materials and storage, and accept requests from customers to output products specifically for them [219]. It is optimized and adapted as a highly efficient production system using information technology. In this section, the role of machine learning in Industry4.0 is described. First, the processing flow is explained, and an example of a factory model is provided.

Industry4.0 is based on information technology (IT), which aims to support autonomous decision making. Machine learning has a role of consolidating the sampled information. Users are not only individual humans but also any objects including individual animals and plants, machines, bots, and their sets. Table 1.3 presents a layer structure.

- Sampling
  A bottom layer is used to sample information through the sensor(s). Along with a physical space, an Internet is also a target for collecting information.
- Consolidating
  A middle consolidating layer is used to detect a correlation among information collected from the bottom layer, and it supports analysis and decision making.
- Authorizing
  An upper authorizing layer is used to analyze the statistics based on the detected correlation and or prediction, and to finally support decision making.

Industry4.0 can be applied to any information processing environment and domain of the past industrial revolutions. The sampling layer uses Internet of Things (IoT), Industrial Internet of Things (IIoT), and Internet of Everything (IoE), and it is equivalent to the edge devices. The consolidating layer is a machine learning layer, and the authorizing layer is equivalent to data analytics.

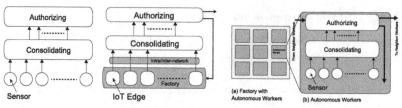

(a) Basics of Indus-   (b) Centralized Management   (c) Distributed Management Based Fac-
try4.0 Factory.   Based Factory.   tory.

FIGURE 1.5   IoT based factory examples.

Fig. 1.5(a) shows a typical factory using Industry4.0. Centralized and distributed approaches are used.

1. Centralized factory

   Fig. 1.5(b) shows a factory model based on a centralized management approach consisting of an information collection layer, information integration layer, and authorization layer. These three layers are equivalent to an IoT client (edge device), machine learning system, and authorization system, respectively, and form a hierarchy. The upper layer feeds information from the bottom layer, and acts as a player with its own role. An intranet or the Internet are present between the information collection layer and the information integration layer. For example, in the case of a pipelined factory, information is collected from each pipeline stage of the production and or processing, and the statement of each stage is evaluated based on the collected information and then predicted and/or inferred, allowing a decision to be made through an action plan. Finally, the most efficient and/or effective plan is selected based on a production schedule. Based on the decision, the parameters of each stage are determined, and fed back to each stage as cyclic optimization, similar to the back propagation used in deep learning.

2. Decentralized factory

   Fig. 1.5(c) shows a factory model with a distributed management. There are human and robot workers on the floor, and the workers can move about. An object can consist of a sampling layer, a consolidation layer, and an authorization layer. In the case of a robotics worker, information is collected on the joint of the body and the neighboring environment through sensors, the current statements are recognized, and a decision is authorized (an action plan). This can create an interference problem between neighboring workers. To suppress the interference, individual workers require a certain rule. In particular, human workers on the same floor and in the neighborhood of robotic workers may have difficulty maintaining the rules, and thus the robots must support and take care of their neighboring co-workers.

If the system uses the Internet, security becomes the most important issue, and rules for any leakage should be developed under the premise of an unsecure

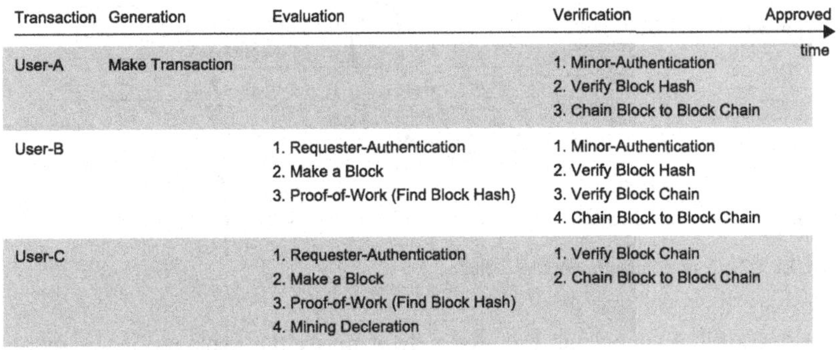

Transaction Generation	Evaluation	Verification	Approved
			time
User-A Make Transaction		1. Minor-Authentication 2. Verify Block Hash 3. Chain Block to Block Chain	
User-B	1. Requester-Authentication 2. Make a Block 3. Proof-of-Work (Find Block Hash)	1. Minor-Authentication 2. Verify Block Hash 3. Verify Block Chain 4. Chain Block to Block Chain	
User-C	1. Requester-Authentication 2. Make a Block 3. Proof-of-Work (Find Block Hash) 4. Mining Decleration	1. Verify Block Chain 2. Chain Block to Block Chain	

FIGURE 1.6 Transaction procedure using block chain.

system. Near-sensor processing aims to avoid the leakage of personal information by unsending such information to the upper layer. The security of personal information and privacy is expected.

1.4.2   Transaction (block chain)

Block chain was proposed and disclosed on the Internet by Satoshi Nakamoto in December 2010 [276], and is a mechanism for approving the use of virtual currency or "Bitcoin." It can be applied not only to physical objects but also to information. Block chain is a type of transaction processing used to approve a request and can be applied to the Byzantine Generals Problem [289], which is a problem used to establish consensus building without a centralized control, in which several generals are loosely connected. Communication for building a consensus and the generals are equivalent to trades and users, respectively. The required conditions for Bitcoin trading are as follows:

1. It should approve the user to trade using a public key system.
2. There should be a network allowing users to trade, and the network should support user communications.

Let us assume the following distributed computing environment:

1. An unspecified large number of users are connected to the network.
2. Computing nodes are loosely connected and are sometimes unconnected.

A user may fail to send a request, or can attempt a malicious act. Block chain is a consensus building mechanism for such a situation. As the consensus building, the user requests trading with an unspecified and large number of other users, other users evaluate and verify the request of a transaction, and additional users approve the transaction (as shown in Fig. 1.6).

Fig. 1.7(a) shows the basic data structure of the block chain. Several transactions are bundled into a single unit called a block, which is a processing unit. Each transaction in the block has a unique number, blocks are chained, and each

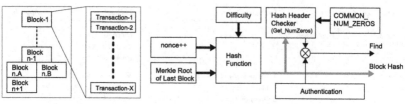

(a) Block Chain Data Structure.   (b) Proof-of-Work Architecture.

FIGURE 1.7 Core architecture of block chain.

user has a block chain and processes. To simplify the explanation, let us assume that we can know the number of blocks in the block chain, which can be represented as "NumBlocks."

- Approval and chaining
  The approval process is composed of a user authentication subsystem and a hash function. A block chain is applied through a hash function, as shown in Fig. 1.7(b). When the approval key value obtained from a hash function (HashValue) and a public key (COMMON_NUM_ZEROS) match, the trade request is true. When a trade is true and no improper activities are detected through a collation process, trading users append (chains) the block, including the transaction, to the terminal of the block chain.

- Proof-of-work
  The user performs a verification process called a proof-of-work during a pooled transaction. Fig. 1.7(b) and Algorithm 1.1 show the proof-of-work. A hash function has an argument of a Merkle root value, which can be obtained from a Get_MerkleRoot function and has a NumBlocks-th block with a different nonce value. The hash value from the hash function is represented by a binary value. By matching between the number of zeros, "NumZeros," from the most significant bit in the binary representation and the public key, "COMMON_NUM_ZEROS," shared among users, the block can be approved. Notifying the nonce value and the hash value to other users, additional users apply the approval processing, and the block is registered to the other and chained to their block chain through a collation process.

- Branch of block chain
  Several users can be used for verification concurrently by receiving the proof-of-work results from different users. When a user receives a correct notification from several different users, several blocks at the same level of block chain are appended, as shown in Fig. 1.7(a). Block chain uses a temporality of blocks, and needs to select one block from the most recent candidates. Thus, a user can have several branches of different lengths, and the block chain can form a tree topology, as shown in Fig. 1.7(a). Valid blocks on a branch should have the longest chain.

The use of a hash function and a block chain data structure composed of temporarily chained blocks makes it difficult to falsify the trade information.

Algorithm 1.1: Proof-of-work

RETRUN: Find, nonce, HashValue;
Find = 0;
MerkleRoot = Get_MerkleRoot(BlockChain, NumBlocks);
for nonce = 0; nonce $< 2^{size\_of\,(unsigned\ int)}$; nonce++ **do**
    HashValue = HashFunction(MerkleRoot, nonce);
    NumZeros = Get_NumZeros(HashValue);
    if *NumZeros == COMMON_NUM_ZEROS* **then**
        Find = 1;
        return(Find, nonce, HashValue);
    end
end
return Find, 0, 0;

Falsification requires modifying a block chain composed of records of past traded information without chaining the hash values. To do so, significant machine power is necessary.

With a virtual trading system based on block chain, as proposed by Bitcoin, rather than using machine power for fructification, a fair trade is deemed reasonable and rational. This technology can be applied to anything that can be represented through digital information. Machine learning is an information processing system, whereas block chain is a transaction processing system between the information processing. We can see that these two processes compose a pipelined processing system.

1.5 Summary of machine learning

1.5.1 Difference from artificial intelligence

Machine learning is an inductive reasoning approach in contrast to a traditional deductive reasoning approach based on a mathematical observation. Learning or training is applied to update the parameters representing a feature aiming to achieve a zero loss function. The learning process uses back propagation, in which the error information is propagated from the output layer to the input layer to calculate the amount of updation required for the parameter, such as the weight and bias. A mathematical model is called deep learning or a multi-layer perceptron. The terms "Artificial Intelligence" and "AI" are widely applied. AI includes various methods based on an inductive approach, and thus can be used as a model that is not related with the current trends of deep learning, which stacks multiple layers.

It is better to take an AI task, with the exception of deep learning, when the model can represent the user's problem at a reasonable cost. The use of deep learning should not be the aim. Thus, the sampled data are first analyzed, and what type of model is suitable for the problem is then considered; finally, what scale of the model is better for the representation and its target hardware platform specification should be considered in a step-by-step manner.

1.5.2 Hype cycle

Gartner, Inc., shows hype cycle every year, which shows trends in technology. Deep learning has peaked and has entered a phase of practicality. This indicates the end of the "Cambrian period," and customer focus is on real applications rather than experiments in a laboratory. Thus, we will meet greater demand for both the execution performance and the power consumption through training and inference for winning from competitors.

Note that a peak does not mean the end of a trend, rather it implies entrance into an actual application phase. Thus, the market can grow after such a peak, and engineering techniques for service deployment are needed.

Chapter 2

Traditional microarchitectures

Chapter 2 looks at the history of computing systems from the 1980s, with a description of the current microprocessors, graphics processing units (GPUs), and field-programmable gate arrays (FPGAs) applied to computing systems.

First, microprocessors, GPUs, and FPGAs are explained. The performance stagnation of the traditional microprocessor has created opportunities for applying GPUs and FPGAs to general-purpose computing hardware.

We look at changes to computing systems that have occurred through changes to the major applications over time. We look back on the history of the computing industry, and describe what occurred. In addition, we observe the state of machine learning hardware. Finally, we consider the metrics of the execution performance.

2.1 Microprocessors

2.1.1 Core microarchitecture

Fig. 2.1(a) shows masks of first microprocessor in the world, developed by Intel, Co., the i4004.

Fig. 2.1(b) shows the basic architecture of a recent core. Recent processors include a single instruction multiple data (SIMD) stream unit that executes the same operation on multiple operation units with different multiple data in par-

(a) i4004 Microprocessor Die Photo.

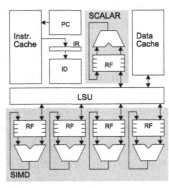

(b) Current Core Microarchitecture.

FIGURE 2.1 Microprocessors [47].

Thinking Machines. https://doi.org/10.1016/B978-0-12-818279-6.00012-8

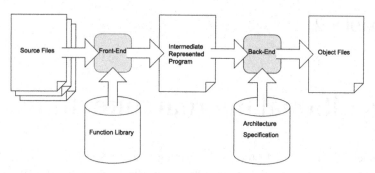

FIGURE 2.2 Compiling flow of a microprocessor.

allel to improve the data-level parallelism (DLP) in addition to a traditional operation unit that operates with scalar data [332].

Current microprocessors are based on a register-to-register architecture under the premise that the source operand(s) is already in the register file (RF) through a load/store unit (LSU) from cache or external memory.

2.1.2   Programming model of a microprocessor

2.1.2.1   Compiling-flow of a microprocessor

Fig. 2.2 shows a compiling flow. The source code references a library that maintains common functions. The front-end of the compiler compiles the source files and common functions, as well as the links among them, finally generating an intermediate representation (IR) assembly code. The IR is an architecture independent instruction set based representation. A program is divided into (multiple) basic block(s) of the control flow, in which the end of the block is a jump or branch instruction.

An IR is used for the compiler infrastructure to support various instruction set architectures (ISAs) by partitioning the architecture-dependent operation from the compilation. The IR program is fed into the back-end of the compiler, which references architecture-dependent constraints such as the ISA and resource availability (RF size, functional unit support, etc.), and finally generates an object file, which can run on a target computer system.

The back-end optimizes the transformed code (called an IR) program to fit into the target microarchitecture. The optimization includes removing unnecessary constants and address calculations, control-flow optimization such as code-reordering for branch predication and a speculative execution, and data-flow optimization such as a vectorization. The IR is then emitted to a binary code.

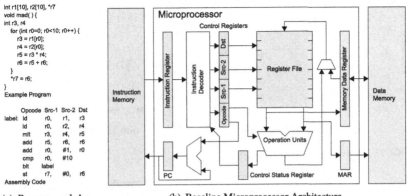

```
int r1[10], r2[10], *r7
void mad( ) {
  int r3, r4
  for (int r0=0; r0<10; r0++) {
    r3 = r1[r0];
    r4 = r2[r0];
    r5 = r3 * r4;
    r6 = r5 + r6;
  }
  *r7 = r6;
}
Example Program

      Opcode  Src-1  Src-2  Dst
label:  ld     r0,    r1,    r3
        ld     r0,    r2,    r4
        mlt    r3,    r4,    r5
        add    r5,    r6,    r6
        add    r0,    #1,    r0
        cmp    r0,    #10
        blt    label
        st     r7,    #0,    r6
Assembly Code
```

(a) Program and As-   (b) Baseline Microprocessor Architecture.
sembly Code.

FIGURE 2.3 Programming model of a microprocessor.

2.1.2.2   Concept of programming model on microprocessors

Fig. 2.3(a) shows the pseudo code of a program (upside) and its assembly code (bottom). The program uses arrays and a for-loop.

The array is translated into two index values, namely, a base address of the data memory and a position index (an offset) indicating the position from the base address. An assembly, a binary instruction, is fetched from the instruction memory to the instruction register (IR) using a program counter (PC), i.e., a Harvard architecture, which decouples the instruction and data address space to each, as shown in Fig. 2.3(b). The instruction decoder decodes the IR value to the set of control signals. The signal decides which operation should be operated, the location of the source operands in the RF, and where the destination operand is located to store its operation result.

A typical basic block has a jump or branch instruction at end of the basic block. A for-loop is translated into a repeat-time calculation, the instruction is compared to check the repeating time on the loop achieved to exit from the loop, and a conditional branch with a branch instruction is then applied, as shown at the bottom of Fig. 2.3(a). The comparison result is stored in a control status register (CSR), and the following branch instruction determines the next basic block based on the CSR value. The PC is updated with an offset value greater than 1 or less than −1 if the condition is true; thus, the branch makes a conditional branch to jump onto the instruction memory address.

2.1.3   Microprocessor meets its complexity

As the trend of logic circuit integration, Gordon Moore predicted that the number of transistors would increase twice every 1.8 years, which is called Moore's Law [271], as shown in Fig. 2.4(a). Based on this law, we can scale the logic circuit size in the unit area, and as a result, the transistor gate length is decreased,

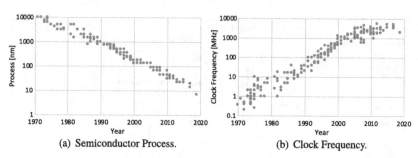

(a) Semiconductor Process.   (b) Clock Frequency.

FIGURE 2.4 History of microprocessors.

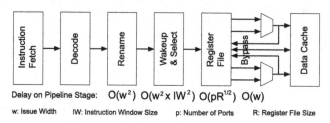

Delay on Pipeline Stage: $O(w^2)$ $O(w^2 \times IW^2)$ $O(pR^{1/2})$ $O(w)$

w: Issue Width   IW: Instruction Window Size   p: Number of Ports   R: Register File Size

FIGURE 2.5 Scaling limitation on microprocessor pipeline [347].

shortening the gate length, which reduces the clock cycle time, improving the execution performance with a performance scaling. Namely, we can predict the future specification, and thus, we can predict a wire-delay, the number of transistors, the gate length, and other factors. Therefore, we can predict the execution performance with such a scaling factor.

However, during the 1990s, the execution performance improvement rate was stagnated despite having sufficient resources (and thus, design space) with semiconductor technologies. The major reason is the difficulty of shrinking (scaling) the gate length. Thus, it is difficult to scale the clock frequency. This tends to increase the energy consumption (as described later in this chapter), and increase the design complexity. We can estimate the design complexity based on the critical path length of the logic circuit. The critical path length is the longest path length introducing the longest path delay on the logic circuit. For a pipeline consisting multiple logic circuits, the critical path determines the clock cycle time and thus, the clock frequency. Fig. 2.5 shows the order of the critical path on a pipelined microprocessor in terms of complexity. The execution time T_{exec} for scalar processors can be estimated using the following equation.

$$T_{exec} = T_{cycle} \sum_{i}^{N_{instr}} N_{cycle}^{(i)} \tag{2.1}$$

$$\approx T_{cycle} \times CPI \times N_{instr}$$

$$= T_{cycle} \frac{N_{instr}}{IPC}$$

where T_{cycle}, N_{cycle}, and N_{instr} are the clock cycle time, the number of execution cycles for each instruction, and the number of instructions executed, respectively. This equation can be simplified using the average number of clock cycles per instruction (CPI: clock cycles per instruction) or the average number of instructions per clock cycle (IPC: instructions per clock cycle).

2.1.4 Pros and cons on superscalar microprocessors

For superscalar processors that can issue and/or execute multiple instructions at the same time, the processor can dynamically analyze the instruction stream generated by the compiler, and execute multiple instructions in which a set of instructions does not break the algorithm of the application to the program (algorithm) and its result. Superscalar technology contributes to a reduction of IPC and N_{instr}. A critical path of the pipeline stage logic circuit designed for multiple executions concurrently is proportional to the squared instruction issue bandwidth w^2 and squared scale of the instruction window used for independent instruction detection (called an instruction wakeup) and selection IW^2 [285].[1]

The instruction issue bandwidth w means it is possible to issue w instructions at the same time, and therefore, IPC is improved; scaling up the IW instruction window makes it possible to find independent instructions that can be executed at the same time by widening its analysis scope in the instruction stream without damage to the program, thereby contributing to an improvement in the IPC.

2.1.5 Scaling of register file

The RF maintaining the temporal variables has a scaling complexity that is determined by the number of registers R in the RF, and the number of ports p is accessible at the same time, as shown in Fig. 4.8. Larger values of R and p can allow more register numbers represented in the instruction to be renamed, making independent instructions that can be issued and or executed at the same time, and thus, the IPC can be improved [328].

2.1.6 Branch predication and its penalty

For pipelined processors, the branch instructions generated by the compiler also determine the execution performance. The branch instruction changes the control flow, determining the branch of the flow destination. The processor decides the branch destination, called a branch target address, (BTA) based on the execution result of the preceding instruction result. Therefore, the BTA depends heavily on the preceding instruction result used for the condition of the branch.

---

[1] An instruction window is a centralized integration approach used to execute multiple instructions; instead, we can use a distributed control based on a reservation station [353], called Tomaslo's algorithm [365], with a dispatching technique for the instructions.

The branch instruction on the pipelined processors must wait for the result of the preceding instruction making the branch condition, and thus, the IPC is decreased by pipeline stall cycles making it impossible to issue the branch instruction. Therefore, typical pipelined processors predict the branch condition using a technique called branch prediction, and they speculatively issue and execute instruction(s), which is called speculative execution. Thus, it does not wait to generate the branch condition.

A larger number of predicted branch conditions makes it possible to hold a larger number of BTAs, thus making it possible to achieve a speculative execution more aggressively. In addition, to improve the prediction accuracy, a widening scope of analysis for the control flow, and a combination of a local scope and global scope, are used [318].

A missed branch prediction involves a penalty consisting of numerous clock cycles used to recover the speculative execution on the wrong control flow path. The penalty is determined by the number of pipeline stages between the issued pipeline stage and the execution (on a branch unit) pipeline stage generating the branch condition. Superpipeline aims to subdivide a basic pipeline stage into finer grained pipeline stages, and there tends to be a larger number of pipeline stages between the instruction issue and instruction commit. Thus, when scaling up the pipeline stage, larger penalties are involved, namely, a higher prediction accuracy of the branch unit is required. A lower prediction accuracy significantly degrades the IPC.

2.2 Many-core processors

The superscalar technique and its logic circuits explained here cannot provide a scaling benefit owing to the complexity. The performance is stagnated for a single program execution on current microprocessors. In addition, multiple processor cores have introduced many-core processors running multiple threads. The unit set of a microprocessor and cache memory is called a core. The minimum unit of a process is called a thread. A compiler suitable for utilizing multiple cores has yet to be developed, and therefore, a GPU and an FPGA are applied to computing systems.

2.2.1 Concept of many-core

Many-core processors are used to integrate multiple processors and cache memory on a chip, a so-called chip multi-processor (CMP). Fig. 2.6 shows a many-core processor having a 4 × 4 two-dimensional mesh topology. The core, indicated as "C" in the figure, is connected to a router, indicated as "R," through network adaptor, and the core communicates to other core(s) as well as to the external world passing through the router(s) [362]. The current core has level-2 cache memory shared with the instruction and data, and level-3 tag memory to feed data from the other cores.

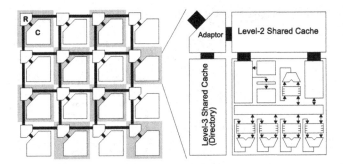

FIGURE 2.6 Many-core microprocessor.

2.2.2 Programming model

2.2.2.1 Coherency

Basically, a many-core microprocessor can use a common compiler-flow in the development tool as a single microprocessor system, although task partitioning and communication require alternative tools.

For multiple data storages, the coherence must be guaranteed. The process communication and coherency can be categorized into two groups.

1. Shared memory: implicit messaging

   Implicit messaging is a shared memory approach in which a single memory address space is shared with multiple processors. Although the development of a program with process communication is not required, exclusive control (a mechanism used to synchronize among the different processes) of the shared variables and coherence is needed. Recent processors have transactional memory that speculatively applies exclusive control (called a lock) [194].

2. Distributed memory: message passing

   Message passing is a distributed memory approach in which each processor has its own memory address space and does not share variables among the processors. It uses a message delivered between the processor cores, and message passing to communicate among them. Message passing uses the API of the message passing interface (MPI) [272] in a software program, and explicitly orders the communication. It communicates using a message and thus does not share the variables among processes, and does not need to take exclusive control or maintain coherency.

Studies on shared memory and message passing types have been conducted [226]. For many-core processors, a software program and its dataset are subdivided to fit into the core, which is called a working-set [152], and it is necessary to take care of the cache memory architecture to avoid a cache miss when accessing the external world as a penalty and creating unnecessary traffic on the chip.

(a) Texas Instruments TMS32020 DSP Die Photo.

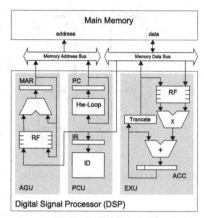

(b) Digital Signal Processor.

FIGURE 2.7 Digital signal processors [86].

2.2.2.2 Library for threading

OpenMP is used for the threading of a single process for a shared memory system. At minimum, it requires multiple cores such as simultaneous multi-threading (SMT), in which running threads have their own context storage, such as a program counter, register file, and control status register, and share functional units concurrently. For threading, the programmer needs to explicitly code using a directive, applying the threading region in the code. OpenMP consists of a set of compiler directives, library routines, and environment variables that define the threading behavior at run-time.

The MPI is mainly used for multi-process threading of a distributed memory system. The number of threads is unlimited and can vary from a single thread to a dozen or more child threads for a particular process. In addition, it does not limit the number of processes to the threading. The programmer needs to code using the MPI function to define the transmitter and receiver of the message interface. The MPI consists of a set of library routines and environment variables.

2.3 Digital signal processors (DSPs)

2.3.1 Concept of DSP

Fig. 2.7 shows the digital signal processor (DSP) architecture. A DSP consists of an execution unit (EXU), as shown in Fig. 2.7(b), which is composed using a multiply accumulate (MAC) operation, which is applied in typical digital signal processing (DSP). An accumulator register has guard bits to avoid a carry-out at the accumulation. Thus, n-bit guard can support a $2^n - 1$ fold accumulation. To store the value in the accumulator register, a truncation is used to fit the value to the width of the data word of the RF entry.

2.3.2 DSP microarchitecture

2.3.2.1 DSP functionality

The task (program) for DSP typically iterates the same operation; thus, a hardware loop function (shown as Hw-Loop in Fig. 2.7(b)) is required to repeat the execution on the program fragment composing the loop. Thus, it does not have a branch unit in general. In addition, it has memory access patterns, and therefore, the DSP has an address generation unit (AGU) to generate the memory addresses under specific patterns. Therefore, the DSP might have a very long instruction word (VLIW) ISA to issue multiple instructions and create a software pipelining.

First, the DSP has an integer and fixed-point unit and an assembly-language based development environment; the current DSP has a single precision floating-point unit and programming languages such as the C-language environment. A recent DSP has an SIMD configuration in its datapath to improve the execution performance with the DLP, which is applied in many DSP algorithms. For hardware simplicity, the microarchitecture often takes a Harvard architecture partitioning address space between the program and data. Thus, the DSP has an independent memory address bus, memory, and accessing path.

2.3.2.2 DSP addressing modes

DSP applications have typical memory access patterns. A pointer in programming language can be represented by an affine equation with a stride factor, counter, and base address (offset).

The equation can be implemented using an MAC operation or simply an accumulator. Both approaches set the base address to the accumulator as the initial value, and therefore, this approach assumes that the processor has accumulation register(s) in the AGU. The accumulator implementation has a counter and accumulates by reaching the end of the counting.

Typical addressing mode is a bit-reverse that reverses the address in a bitwise manner. Addressing mode is used for a butterfly operation such as an FFT algorithm. The DSP can have an RF in the AGU to maintain a set of three values of the equation.

2.4 Graphics processing units (GPU)

2.4.1 Concept of GPU

Before the GPU, graphics processing was implemented using a hardwired logic circuit. Two-dimensional graphics processing was a major approach during the first half of the 1990s. With the introduction of multi-media applications, three-

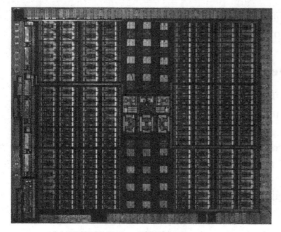

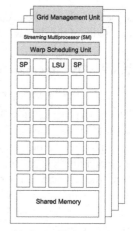

(a) NVIDIA Turing GPU Die Photo.   (b) Stream Multiprocessor.

FIGURE 2.8 GPU microarchitecture [221].

dimensional graphics with high resolution became a requirement. Programmability was applied to a logic circuit specialized for graphics processing, and graphics programming was introduced; a developer's own graphics algorithm could then be applied to the chip [269]. The architecture was then changed from a fixed graphics pipelined logic circuit to a programmable GPU [278].

Polygon based three-dimensional graphics consists of huge amounts of vertex and map data. However, the processing at the pixel unit is a large task, and thus, from the geometry calculation to the mapping of three-dimension graphics onto a two-dimensional plane for the display, the same sets of processing are repeated. Thus, DLP is easily obtained.

2.4.2 GPU microarchitecture

The GPU was considered for use in general-purpose processing with a huge DLP [167], and a general-purpose GPU (GPGPU) or GPU computing [278] was introduced. Based on this trend, today's GPU is used in high-performance computing systems, and a GPU has a double precision floating-point unit for scientific applications. Fig. 2.8 shows die photo and whole GPU structure.

The vertex and pixel processing workloads are not balanced, and thus tend to achieve inefficient processing on a chip. NVIDIA's Compute Unified Device Architecture (CUDA) parallel programming model performs vertex and pixel processing on the same processor, and thus, dynamic load balancing is supported [244]. Therefore, NVIDIA can efficiently concentrate on the development of such a processor. See Fig. 2.9.

NVIDIA's GPU consists of a stream multi-processor (SM), which consists of multiple streaming processors (SPs), which take a superscalar ar-

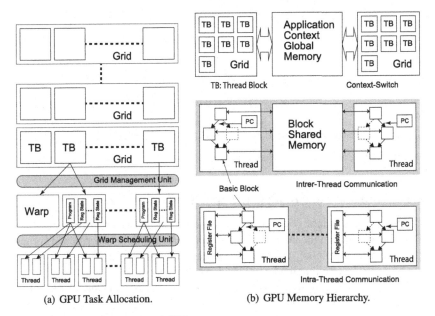

(a) GPU Task Allocation.   (b) GPU Memory Hierarchy.

FIGURE 2.9 Task allocation onto a GPU.

chitecture rather than the vector processor architecture, and applies scalar operations with a traditional compiler and tools with reasonable instruction scheduling.

The same thread is packed and managed as a single unit, called a thread block. The SM controller allocates a warp consisting of 32 threads to the SPs (a single SP has a single thread). A thread in an SM has its own PC and context, independently executing a thread program. Namely, the threads in an SM have the same program but their own context, and thus, their own control flow. A barrier instruction is also used to synchronize among the threads.

NVIDIA calls this threading technique single instruction, multiple thread (SIMT). Programmers do not need to consider the architectural parameters based on the CUDA and SIMT for their programs. The GPU manages multiple thread blocks as a single unit called a grid, one thread block is allocated to one SM, and SM allocates one context to a single SP.

This improves the cache memory and supports an out-of-order execution at the thread block level, multiple warp schedulers, and a context switching [45][48]. High bandwidth memory (HBM) has been used from 2016. It integrates half precision floating-point units, called a Pascal architecture [78].

Recent NVIDIA GPUs have a matrix calculation unit called TensorCore to improve the matrix operation in the program mainly for deep learning applications [296].

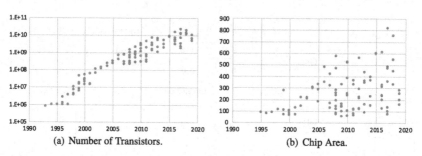

(a) Number of Transistors. (b) Chip Area.

FIGURE 2.10 History of graphics processing units.

2.4.3 Programming model on graphics processing units

CUDA C is a standard C extension. It sets a *kernel* that can be run on a GPU. To call the kernel on the host program, the program needs to describe the kernel qualified with a "global" annotation, which indicates that the function should run on a GPU. Note that the kernel can have its own name.

To set the block, a special description is used, which indicates the number of blocks and which variables are used for the kernel for compilation. In the program, we need to allocate memory resources to such a variable with CUDA memory allocation (cudaMalloc), which is comparable to Malloc in standard C. In addition, it also needs to free up allocated memory after an execution with a cudaFree function. Between the host processor and the GPU, CUDA's memory copy function is used for transfer.

2.4.4 Applying GPUs to a computing system

Fig. 2.10 shows the GPU implementation trends. Regarding the number of transistors, logarithmic scaling occurred by 2010, and after this period, its rate of increase has slightly decreased. Today, the chip area used to integrate such a huge number of transistors has reached 800 mm^2. An area of 800 mm^2 is equivalent to a 28 mm square, whereas typical chips are less than 10 mm square, which is larger than enterprise many-core processors.

2.5 Field-programmable gate arrays (FPGAs)

2.5.1 Concept of FPGA

Before FPGAs, programmable-logic devices (PLDs) and programmable-logic array (PLAs), which emulate a gate-array, were applied. The use of such a device and an FPGA was first focused on a verification of the time reduction through the development of a user logic circuit on the device, verifying the electrical behavior, similar to a test-bed.

An FPGA introduced a look-up table (LUT) based combinatorial gate emulation and interconnection network, forming a tile array, as explained in next

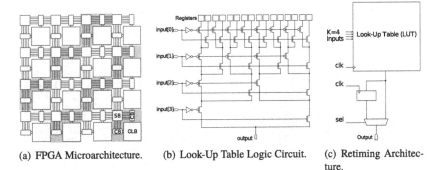

(a) FPGA Microarchitecture.   (b) Look-Up Table Logic Circuit.   (c) Retiming Architecture.

FIGURE 2.11 FPGA microarchitecture.

section. These fundamental organizations introduced a scalable architecture in contrast to PLA and PLD.

2.5.2 FPGA microarchitecture

Fig. 2.11(a) shows an FPGA based on SRAM, which holds the configuration data [122]. The configurable logic block (CLB) configures the combinatorial logic. The connection block (CB) connects between the interconnection network and the CLB. The switch block (SB) is an interchange between vertical and horizontal networks. In this book, configuration data and their configured logic circuit are called a user logic circuit (or simply, user logic) to differentiate between the user logic circuit and platform logic circuit of an FPGA. One set of CLB, CBs, and SB composes a tile that is replicated for placement on a chip.

The CLB is equivalent to a truth table having 1-bit entry and takes an LUT composed of a binary-tree of a multiplexer, as shown in Fig. 2.11(b) [137][136]. The LUT selects 1-bit data from 2^K 1-bit data with K single-bit inputs. As shown in Fig. 2.11(c), the LUT output has a retiming register to hold the data to feed back the signal to the user logic and implement a finite state machine (FSM), as an example.

A signal on the CLB passes through the CB and SW to change its direction. Multiple wires in an interconnection network are bundled into a single track, and into several tracks with different lengths; this interconnection network architecture supports an efficient mapping of the user logic on the platform and avoids a superfluous delay on the network. It also improves the utilization of network resources. This interconnection network architecture is called a channel segmentation distribution [122]. Xilinx's Virtex architecture modifies a tile-based arrangement into a column-based arrangement replicating the same logic into a single column to improve the integration density.

Fig. 2.12(a) shows the number of LUTs for Xilinx's single chip FPGA, where the left side is an XC2000, and the right-most side shows a Virtex 7. Note that this plot is not based on a timeline and does not plot low-end products

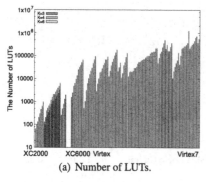

(a) Number of LUTs.

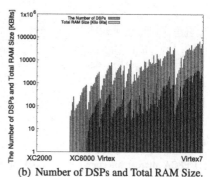

(b) Number of DSPs and Total RAM Size.

FIGURE 2.12 History of Xilinx FPGAs.

such as Spartan. Xilinx increases the number of LUTs by XC4000 to configure the random logic circuit. XC6000 does not use the LUT, but does use the multiplexer for the CLB. After a Virtex architecture, it does not increase the number of LUTs, but increases the size of the on-chip memory (called a memory block) to reduce the memory accesses to the external memory chip, and reduces the delay in accessing the data, maximizing the parallel multiple data accesses. Thus, parallel data processing is realized. In addition, as shown in Fig. 2.12(b), many DSP blocks (different from traditional digital signal processors) consisting of a multiplier and an adder are integrated on the chip to support DSP algorithms. Rather than implementing a data path, the DSP block contributes to minimizing the footprint of the user logic circuit [233]. In addition, the DSP block contributes to the timing and a high frequency is possible.

2.5.3 FPGA design flow

The hardware development flow on an FPGA is similar to the register transfer level (RTL) coding and simulation of an application-specific integrated circuit (ASIC) for verification; repeating this, after the synthesizing, placement, and routing for the target FPGA device, a bit stream of the configuration data is generated, and the FPGA downloading of the configuration data is verified. Recent tools support software programming for the development of hardware. C-language is a typical support for such tools, and the program is translated to the hardware description language (HDL) [125][35]. See Fig. 2.13.

2.5.4 Applying FPGAs to computing system

An FPGA was invented for a logic circuit verification (testing), and it was designed to configure any digital logic circuit by changing the configuration data having such configuration information; an SRAM-based FPGA can be used many times based on its reconfiguration by restoring the configuration data to the SRAM.

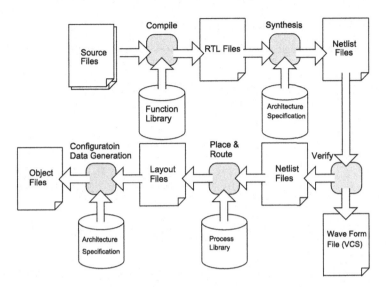

FIGURE 2.13 Compiling flow for FPGAs.

At the end of the 1990s, FPGA vendors claimed that the time from design to market (called Time-to-Market) had been shortened [39]. Current trends include a less variant production and huge nonrecurring engineering (NRE) costs on current ASICs using FPGAs to suppress the costs. The ability of reconfiguration introduces to patch updating configuration data on FPGA, little bug of user logic circuit can be fixed by the reconfiguration after release to market.

A current FPGA has many memory blocks and numerous DSP blocks consisting of a multiplier and an adder, and therefore, an FPGA can be applied to a system-on-chip (SoC). Many memory blocks placed on a chip reduce the number of external memory accesses, and thus can reduce the latency for data access; in addition, multiple memory blocks can perform multiple data accesses in parallel, and thus, an FPGA can be used for DLP applications. Through the integration of a DSP block, the user logic circuit designed for DSP can be applied with a relatively higher clock frequency. The current DSP block can perform integer and fixed-point arithmetic operations and also floating-point arithmetic operations, and thus, a variety of applications can use an FPGA [62].

An FPGA has a general purpose configuration for any user logic circuit. Therefore, compared with its implementation using an ASIC, it has a smaller equivalent number of gates, a lower clock frequency, and a higher power consumption, as shown in Table 2.1. In the case of tiny benchmark logic circuits, the equivalent number of gates, clock frequency, and power consumption on an FPGA are equivalent to those of the older third- and fourth-generation ASICs. The integration of memory blocks and a DSP block enhance the old design space. The use of an FPGA having such an older equivalent generation is supported by the higher NRE and fabrication costs of an ASIC implementation;

TABLE 2.1 Implementation gap (FPGA/ASIC) [233].

Comparison Point	Logic Only	Logic and Mem	Logic and DSP	Logic, DSP, Mem
Area	32	32	24	17
Critical-path Delay	3.4	3.5	3.5	3.0
Dynamic Power Consumption	14	14	12	7.1

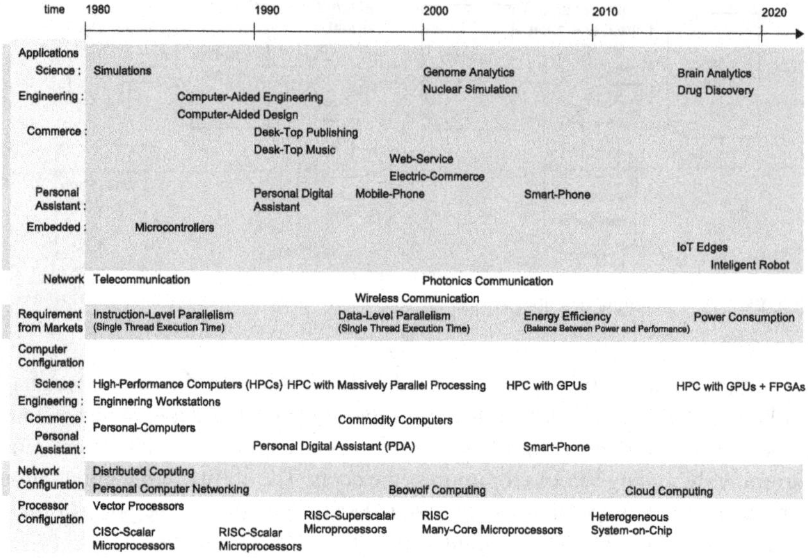

FIGURE 2.14 History of computer industry.

however, there is also a risk that bugs in the logic circuit after fabrication of an ASIC are impossible to fix. Thus, today's FPGAs are used to reduce the costs and shorten the time-to-market.

Recently, an FPGA was used for high-performance computing. Intel Co. acquired Altera (an FPGA vendor) [54] and proposed integrating an FPGA with an enterprise microprocessor [68].

2.6 Dawn of domain-specific architectures

2.6.1 Past computer industry

Fig. 2.14 shows the history of the computer industry during the past 35 years. Mass production introduced low-price chips and products, and allowed them to become a commodity. First, the application required the execution performance for a single program, and thus, the design focused on instruction-level parallelism (ILP). During the 1990s, multi-media applications such as graphics, audio processing, and games were introduced. For such applications, a high execution performance involving a huge amount of data was needed.

Processor vendors took single instruction stream and multiple data stream (SIMD) technology, which is one of the DLP processing approaches, as a subword level parallelism [241][298]. By optimizing the compiler for DLP and SIMD operations on the processor, the multi-media ASIC market was destroyed. After the second half of the 1990s, external memory access latency became an issue [124], and the design complexity of the microprocessor stagnated its execution performance. After 2000, multiple processor cores were placed on a chip, with multiple threads executed at the same time, utilizing thread-level parallelism (TLP), and promising a complete execution performance for customers. In reality, however, many cores could not be utilized owing to a lack of application development and compiler technologies suitable for a many-core system.

The past decade has seen an explosive growth in the use of mobile phones, and technology drivers have changed from personal computers to mobile devices sensitive to power consumption; thus, SoC, which integrates various logic circuits on a single chip as a system, was introduced. Processor vendors were still focusing on execution performance rather than power consumption, whereas the focus of most customers changed from personal computers to mobile devices, creating a gap between their claim and customer demand. Namely, vendors improperly predicted the specification requirements.

The architecture was unsuitable for the application characteristics, as described through Makimoto's Wave in Chapter 4, creating the opportunity to introduce GPUs and FPGAs onto the computer market. GPUs are used for applications with a huge DLP, and FPGAs are used for applications with a complex control flow and requiring a higher execution performance. FPGAs can configure the user logic circuit, reaching a performance close to that of older generation ASICs; in addition, an updating ability introduces an early deployment, allowing bug-fixing and updates after release.

Recent customer trends have changed from the need for a higher performance to energy efficiency.

2.6.2 History of machine learning hardware

Deep learning is composed of matrix operations, as described in Appendix A, machine learning hardware with a high-performance matrix operation unit, balanced bandwidth between memory and the matrix operation unit, and memory access flexibility, thereby achieving better energy efficiency.

The execution on a CPU needs a repeated execution with unnecessary executions involved in the loop part, and a scalar operation is conducted; thus, a huge DLP in a neural network model cannot be utilized. Although a CPU is suitable for executions involving a complex control flow, a neural network does not have such a complex control flow. Half of the core area is consumed by cache memory, which uses the localities of the program, for which the cache memory hierarchy architecture is not suitable for deep learning applications having different locality patterns, and thus is unnecessary.

A GPU is substantially designed for a matrix operation, and thus, a geometry calculation in graphics processing is a matrix operation: therefore, a GPU is suitable for a huge DLP in a neural network model. However, it has numerous unnecessary parts related to graphics processing a specific logic circuit. In addition, it does not have the flexible memory access functionality needed in a neural network model. Thus, execution with a die area of over 800 mm^2 and more than a 1 GHz clock frequency introduces 300 W of power consumption, which is significant. Therefore, although it has a high-performance operation capability, a mismatch in the memory access flexibility and a higher power consumption are serious problems. It has a much lower energy-efficiency than the ASIC implementation, which has a three-order of magnitude lower power consumption.

An FPGA has a compute node for a single bit operation, and can configure the user logic circuit on demand. It can be used for a straightforward implementation method, and its application is configured as a virtually hardwired logic circuit. For such a finer-grained compute node, an arithmetic operation consisting of a wide bit width on an FPGA involves an overhead both temporally (having a huge wire delay on an interconnection) and spatially (significant interconnection resources). An FPGA is equivalent to several generations of older ASICs. Thus, from the perspective of energy efficiency, it is on intermediate position on CPU, GPU, and ASIC implementations, and there were no killer applications; thus, the applications for an FPGA have been limited. However, as described in the Appendix A, a binary operation based neural network model was researched, and therefore, an FPGA has the potential to lead the machine learning hardware.

An ASIC implementation has freedom in terms of the design constraints of the resources, wire-delay, power consumption, and packaging. It can be implemented not only in a specialized logic circuit but also in a general-purpose logic circuit, and the hardware can be freely designed on demand. Thus, through a suitable implementation and design for the characteristics of machine learning models, a high execution performance, low energy-consumption, and thus, energy efficiency, can be achieved.

2.6.3 Revisiting machine learning hardware

Owing to the stagnation of the execution performance of traditional microprocessors and the higher cost and risk regarding ASIC implementation, a method for releasing an FPGA onto the market and using it to replace an ASIC after fixing the bugs and achieving the targeted market share has been developed [38][43][40]. In this case, the design requires compatibility on the logic circuit and an electronic equivalence in terms of the interface between an FPGA and ASIC.

Instead of developing a new method, there has been a trend to provide a programmable LSI fitting the characteristics of a particular application do-

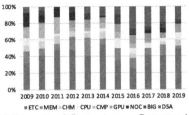

(a) International Symposium on Computer Architecture (ISCA).

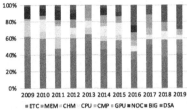

(b) International Symposium on Microarchitecture (MICRO).

FIGURE 2.15 Recent trends in computer architecture research.

main through mass production, obtaining a higher execution performance, lower power consumption, and lower cost. The development of machine learning hardware also belongs to this trend. Machine learning hardware has been researched from the 1990s; however, the advancement of a software based execution on a general-purpose microprocessor has overtaken such hardware because the application domain has been extremely narrow. Machine learning hardware has lost the opportunity to enter the market [352].

Recently, traditional computer systems have had limited improvements in execution performance and have introduced higher power consumption. In addition, application vendors can obtain huge amounts of data from the Internet by the advancement of information and communication technologies. Machine learning researchers have made a breakthrough in terms of inference accuracy, and a higher execution performance with lower power consumption is required. Owing to these demands, machine learning hardware development is being aggressively researched at present. The year 2018 was the beginning of the machine learning hardware market.

Fig. 2.15 shows research trends from the International Symposium on Computer Architecture (ISCA) and International Symposium on Microarchitecture (MICRO). Recently, studies on the processor core architecture (i.e., CPU) have decreased, and studies on machine learning hardware including accelerators and programmable LSIs (i.e., ACC) have rapidly increased, as shown in Figs. 2.15(a) and 2.15(b).

Figs. 2.16 and 2.17 show the clock frequency and power consumption on machine learning hardware. GPUs are also plotted; their power consumption is given in thermal density power (TDP).

Researchers have designed hardware architectures with various balances between the clock frequency and scale of the chip in terms of the number of transistors. Chips with an older semiconductor process tend to have a lower clock frequency. The primary reason for this trend is a longer gate length, relatively should have lower clock frequency than elder process provides. However, it can have a frequency of higher than 500 MHz. The hardware designer can probably take care of the resource utilization, thus fusing multiple arithmetic units, and introducing a longer critical path.

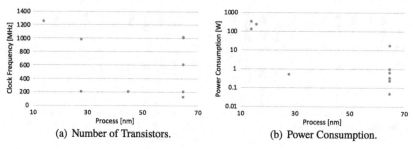

(a) Number of Transistors.   (b) Power Consumption.

FIGURE 2.16 Process vs. clock frequency and power consumption.

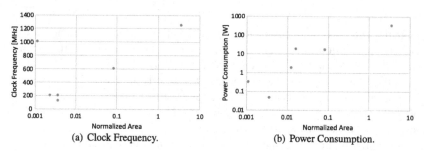

(a) Clock Frequency.   (b) Power Consumption.

FIGURE 2.17 Area vs. clock frequency and power consumption.

In addition, a larger chip probably tends to have higher clock frequency because of the ease of pipelining when applying a large design space. The power consumption is proportional to the clock frequency, and thus a larger chip having a higher clock frequency tends to have a higher power consumption.

A GPU using 12-nm process technology requires a chip area of over 800 mm^2. Regarding machine learning hardware, old process technologies such as 28-nm and 65-nm required a chip area of 50 mm^2 or less. Compared with NVIDIA TITAN X, machine learning hardware has achieved up to a dozen-times higher execution performance and a lower clock frequency (less than half), as well as a 100-times smaller power consumption. Thus, it has achieved an extremely high energy efficiency (100- to 1000-times higher than that of a GPU).

2.7 Metrics of execution performance

Architects aim to maximize the execution performance and minimize the power consumption as much as possible under certain constraints, such as the number of workers, available time, and budget. Performance modeling (an assessment of the performance) is conducted, and architects improve the architecture based on analysis results, entering a logic circuit design. The execution performance can be evaluated based on the latency and/or throughput, number of operations per second, energy and power consumption, energy efficiency, utilization, and cost.

2.7.1   Latency and throughput

The response time, i.e., latency, is important for an inference service. This metric can be calculated based on the time between a request of inference and the resulting response. Training generally takes a mini-batch (described in Chapter 1), and the time required for each epoch (explained later) is important. The latency $T_{latency}$ can be represented as follows.

$$T_{latency} = N_{cycle} \times f \qquad (2.2)$$

where N_{cycle} is the number of clock cycles taken for the execution. This metric can be applied to both inference and training. Note that some specifications of a product include the clock cycles executed for pre- and post-processing.

The throughput is an index used to consider the number of results per unit time obtained. This can be calculated as the number of inferences per second in the case of machine learning applications. For example, an image recognition can be evaluated by the number of frames per second as the frame rate. The throughput N_{th} can be represented by $T_{latency}$ as follows.

$$N_{th} = \frac{1}{T_{latency}} \qquad (2.3)$$

Note that this metric does not consider the problem scale and thus, this metric should be used carefully. For example, the image size in the object detection is not considered, and thus, the computation and storage requirements are independent metrics.

2.7.2   Number of operations per second

The number of operations per second (OPS) shows how many operations are possible to operate within the unit time.

$$OPS = N_{op} \times f \qquad (2.4)$$

where N_{op} is the number of operations in a single cycle, and thus, we obtain OPS by multiplying by the clock frequency f. In general, because the clock frequency is on the order of gigahertz, and hardware takes thousands of operations in a single cycle, we use the trillion operations per second (TOPS) as the value. Fig. 2.18 shows an estimation flow-chart for the OPS. The peak OPS can be calculated based on the number of operation units when multiplied by the clock frequency.

Here, N_{op} indicates DLP on a chip. Therefore, the number of MACs or multiply-adds (MADs), N_{mac}, is the peak DLP. Thus, N_{op} can be estimated as follows.

$$N_{op} \leq 2N_{mac} \qquad (2.5)$$

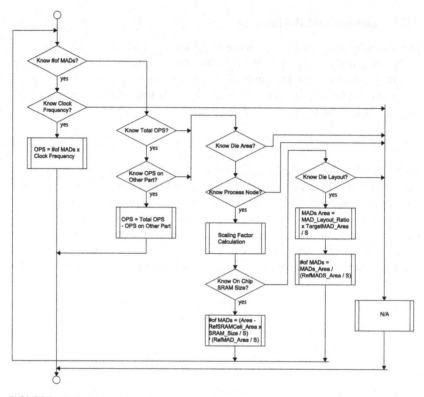

FIGURE 2.18 Estimation flow-chart for OPS.

2.7.3 Energy and power consumptions

The major energy consumption on a logic circuit is determined by the number of gates required to compose the operation. The energy consumption E can be represented as follows.

$$E \propto V_{dd}^2 \times C \times A \tag{2.6}$$

where V_{dd}, C, and A are the voltage, capacitance, and area ratio of the die area to active area, respectively. Thus, scaling of the voltage V_{dd} is effective; however, once Dennard's scaling has reached its end we can no longer expect a further decrease because of current leaks in the transistor.

Table 2.2 shows the major energy consumption on the TSMC 45 nm process node, and we can see that external memory access consumes huge amounts of energy [183]. The energy consumption E is per clock cycle in general, and therefore, the power consumption W can be obtained by the energy consumption per cycle multiplied by the clock frequency f. Fig. 2.19 shows an estimation flow-chart of the power consumption.

TABLE 2.2 Energy table for 45-nm CMOS process [183].

Data Type	Operation	Precision [Bits]	Energy [pJ]	Energy Cost	Area [μm²]	Area Cost
Integer	Add	8	0.03	1	36	1
		16	0.05	1.67	67	1.86
		32	0.1	3.33	137	3.81
	Mult	8	0.2	6.67	282	7.83
		32	3.1	103.33	3495	97.08
Floating Point	Add	16	0.4	13.33	1360	37.78
		32	0.9	30	4185	116.25
	Mult	16	1.1	36.67	1640	45.56
		32	3.7	123.33	7700	213.89
SRAM Read	(8KiB)	32	5	166.67		
DRAM Read		32	640	21333.33		

2.7.4   Energy-efficiency

This metric shows a balance between the execution performance and energy consumption for inference and training. In the case of power consumption, this is called the power efficiency. These metrics show the inherent potential of the hardware architecture. The energy efficiency EE can be obtained as follows.

$$EE = \frac{OPS}{E} \qquad (2.7)$$

Fig. 2.20 shows an estimation flow-chart for the power efficiency. As shown in Table 4.1, power consumption after the end of Dennard's Scaling, described later in Chapter 4, increases on the order of S^2. In addition, the execution performance can be enhanced by the process node on the order of S^2. Thus, the power efficiency, in terms of the TOPS divided by the power consumption shows the potential of a hardware architecture, independent from the process node.

Fig. 2.21 shows how the power-efficiency is used to consider the potential performance of the designed hardware architecture. The TOPS per power consumption is plotted on the graph.

When the architect considers the scalability of the hardware architecture, by drawing a line from zero onto the point, an architect can predict the scalability. If the line is within the sub-linear domain, it indicates difficulty in scaling the TOPS, easily increasing the power consumption in contrast to TOPS growth. For a superfluous TOPS, the architect predicts that the power consumption cannot be easily decreased, or a scaling of the wattage shows difficulty in the execution performance in terms of the TOPS.

When there are two hardware architectures, we can compare the potential based on the power-efficiency, as shown in Fig. 2.21(a) and 2.21(b) for the ex-

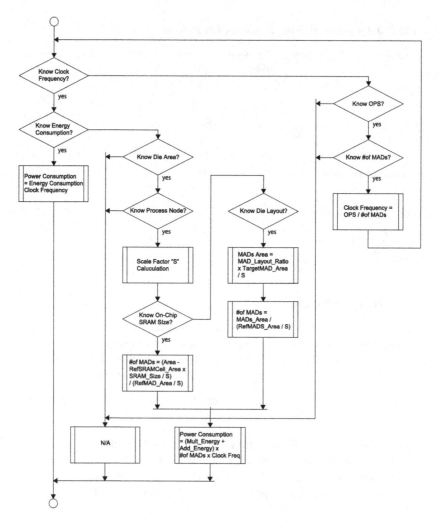

FIGURE 2.19 Estimation flow-chart of power consumption.

ecution performance and power consumption perspectives, respectively. In the case of TOPS, we look at how it is obtained under the same wattage budget. A sub-linear domain line shows a rapid growth in power consumption and a slight growth in the TOPS. By contrast, a super-linear domain line shows a rapid growth of TOPS and a slight growth of power consumption.

This implies a check of the slope of the line, and thus, the TOPS per power consumption shows the architectural potential of the execution performance. In the case of the power consumption, we can use the same scheme for the X-axis. When the execution performance, namely, TOPS, is superfluous, we can scale down the execution performance. When we consider that the power con-

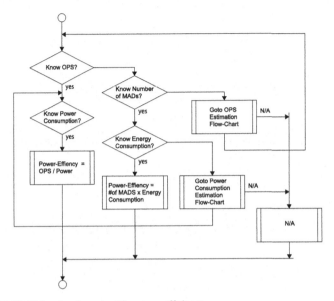

FIGURE 2.20 Estimation flow-chart for power efficiency.

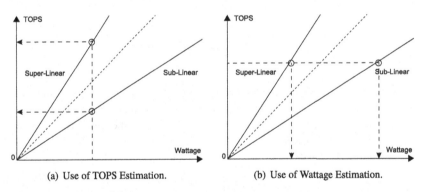

(a) Use of TOPS Estimation.   (b) Use of Wattage Estimation.

FIGURE 2.21 Power-efficiency.

sumption is too expensive, we can also scale down the execution performance. Thus, the super-linear domain cannot easily scale down the power consumption in contrast to the sub-linear domain.

Fig. 2.22(a) shows the efficiency of the studies and some products. Regarding the power efficiency, it clearly shows a linearity even it is FPGA based. The baseline is 1 TOPS/W, and the highest power-efficiency is 3.2 TOPS/W.

Fig. 2.22(b) shows the area-efficiency, which uses the normalized area with the semiconductor process. Because the peak number of operations every cycle is decided based on the number of arithmetic units on a die, chips with a higher TOPS tend to have a larger chip area.

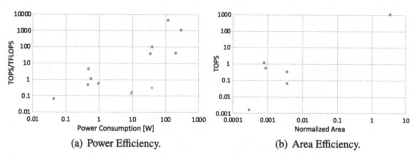

(a) Power Efficiency. (b) Area Efficiency.

FIGURE 2.22 Efficiency plot.

2.7.5 Utilization

How many computing resources are active in the total execution time is one consideration to check. Such utilization U is calculated using the following equation.

$$
\begin{aligned}
U &\geq \frac{OPS}{T_{latency}} \\
&= \frac{N_{op} \times f}{N_{cycle} \times f} \\
&= \frac{N_{op}}{N_{cycle}}
\end{aligned}
\tag{2.8}
$$

Thus, this is an average rate indicating how many operations are conducted in a single cycle. In general, it is $N_{op} < N_{cycle}$. To enhance the utilization, an extremely easy approach is to fuse multiple stages of the pipeline, and thus N_{cycle} can be easily decreased.

In addition, the utilization can be estimated using N_{th} and OPS as follows.

$$
U \approx N_{th} \times OPS
\tag{2.9}
$$

The throughput N_{th} does not include the property of the problem (input) size, and thus, the utilization does not include the problem scale. Therefore, simply observing the utilization incurs a risk of failure in terms of such consideration. The utilization is effective only for an evidence-based approach.

In addition, the utilization can be used for an effective data-level parallelism N_{op} as follows.

$$
N_{op} = 2N_{mac} \times U
\tag{2.10}
$$

Thus, to achieve a higher utilization, the number of execution cycles should be close to the number of operation units on the chip as follows.

$$
N_{cycle} \approx 2N_{mac}
\tag{2.11}
$$

2.7.6 Data-reuse

The major energy consumption is caused by a storage access, as shown in Table 2.2. By reusing the data word based on the temporal locality, the task can reduce the number of storage accesses, and thus, this technique contributes to a reduction in the energy consumption.

On a traditional microprocessor-based system, the data-reuse can be measured by the duration in terms of the number of clock cycles taken for the load for every memory address. Such a reference duration indicates a temporal locality for the data word on the address, and a value close to one cycle indicates a higher temporal locality. Data words having a lower temporal locality can be a candidate to spill out to the off-chip memory.

Regarding processing element (PE) array-based architectures, the maximum data-reuse can be approximately calculated by the critical path length of the data flow for data reuse as the life of the data on the array. Therefore, this observation implies that a longer critical path obtains a higher data reuse rate; however, it requires a longer latency. In the case of MAC based architectures, a reuse duration for the accumulator occurs at every cycle, and the critical path is the input vector length. Thus, it returns to the total number of execution clock cycles. We need to find the optimal reuse rate and critical path length.

Through a program, we obtain the data-reuse from a loop-body. Let us use the following example statement to discuss the reusability.

$$A[i] = \alpha A[i - N] + \beta \qquad (2.12)$$

where α and β are the scalar variable, and the statement references the N-distance array element. Whereas the reuse duration of vector A includes every step, the element of the vector is determined by the offset N. This state has a reference duration (liveness) N, which means the element of vector A is accessed after the step N. Therefore, the buffer needs a length of N. A line-buffer generally used in convolution engine is one example.

In the microprocessor-based system, the compiler needs to check the liveness duration for every tensor by checking the index. When N exceeds the buffering capacity, it needs to insert store and load instructions. In addition, if N is a dynamic variable, the compiler cannot know the liveness and cannot schedule the variable, and thus, we cannot use the buffering.

2.7.7 Area

The die area indicates how much silicon is necessary as a resource of the hardware architecture implementation under the implementation constraints. Fig. 2.10(a) show the number of gates for the GPUs. Fig. 2.10(b) shows the GPU die area. We can roughly estimate the area A_{die} by counting the number of transistors N_{xtor} on the die under the process node (gate length or wire-pitch)

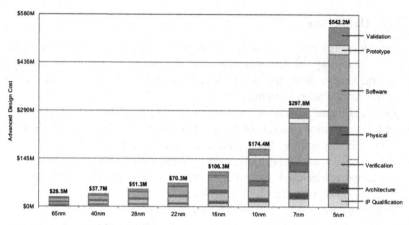

FIGURE 2.23 System design cost [115].

S_{xtor} as follows.

$$A_{die} \approx \frac{N_{xtor}}{S_{xtor}^2} \qquad (2.13)$$

However, this equation ignores the wiring on the metal layers. The wire traffic rate determines A_{die} as follows.

$$A_{die} \approx \max(\frac{N_{xtor}}{S_{xtor}^2}, \frac{N_{wire}^2}{S_{wire}^2}) \qquad (2.14)$$

where N_{wire} and S_{wire} are the number of wires on an interconnection network using a metal layer, and the wire-pitch for the metal layer, respectively.

This equation implies that, in the case of $\frac{N_{xtor}}{S_{xtor}^2} \gg \frac{N_{wire}^2}{S_{wire}^2}$, the architecture needs superfluous interconnection network resources. In addition, $\frac{N_{xtor}}{S_{xtor}^2} \ll \frac{N_{wire}^2}{S_{wire}^2}$ indicates that the local wiring traffic is huge, and thus, the critical path delay is relatively longer and cannot obtain a higher clock frequency. Thus, pipelining is necessary, which increases the power consumption on the pipeline registers.

2.7.8 Cost

This metric is used to determine how much budget is necessary for the design, implementation, and fabrication during a certain period. The design cost has a nonrecurring engineering (NRE) cost, such as a licensing fee for the design tool, intellectual property (IP), and hardware constraint library. The fabrication cost includes the chip area, yield, process node, wafer scale, and other factors. These factors determine the chip price, as described in Chapter 4.

Fig. 2.23 shows how the entire cost required to design the system has increased, and its breakdown [115]. Recent process nodes such as a 7-nm node

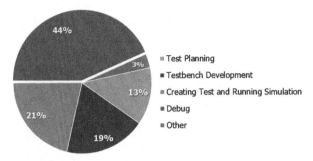

- Test Planning
- Testbench Development
- Creating Test and Running Simulation
- Debug
- Other

FIGURE 2.24 Verification time break down [274].

can require more than 290 M US dollars. The future 5-nm process will require more cost, approximately twice that of the current 7-nm process, as shown in Fig. 2.23. Remarkable points include the software design and the cost for verifying the hardware design. The system software requires approximately half of the design cost. The verification process is a major part, as shown in Fig. 2.24.

A complex hardware introduces unnecessary verifications in terms of time and budget. In addition, if a vendor wants to make a series of products, an ad-hoc extension creates more difficulty in terms of software development and hardware verification. For example, for hardware consisting of N modules, there are $O(!N)$ combinations of patterns. Thus, the required verification increases with such an order. This easily increases the debugging time for the verification process.

Chapter 3

Machine learning and its implementation

Chapter 3 describes the basic architecture of machine learning. First, a neuron composing a nerve network is explained, followed by two types of machine learning models.

The first section describes neuromorphic computing, which applies neuroscience, and along with its functionality, the structure and firing theory of the brain are also considered. Neuromorphic computing takes care of the timing of the firing (described in Section 3.2.1), and therefore its hardware takes care of the timing. The basic architecture is explained through the firing system. In addition, an address-event representation (AER), which is used for synchronization and transmission of a spike (detailed in Section 3.2.1), is also described in Section 3.2.3.

Section 3.2 discusses neural networks, which are well known as deep neural networks (DNNs) and deep learning. Three basic neural network models, namely, a CNN, a recurrent neural network (RNN), and an autoencoder (AE) are described. Next, the basic hardware architecture is explained. For readers interested in exploring the mathematical model of a basic neural network model, Appendix A provides the basics.

3.1 Neurons and their network

Fig. 3.1(a) shows cranial nerves in our brain. Neurons are connected to each other and form a network of nerves. Nerve cells in the brain are called neurons.

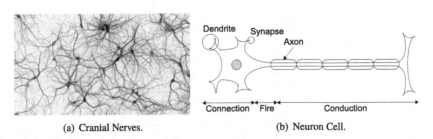

(a) Cranial Nerves.   (b) Neuron Cell.

FIGURE 3.1 Nerves and neurons in our brain [192].

Thinking Machines. https://doi.org/10.1016/B978-0-12-818279-6.00013-X

49

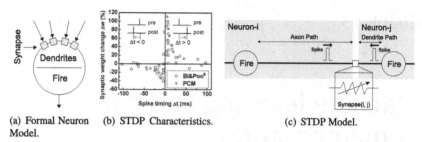

(a) Formal Neuron Model.   (b) STDP Characteristics.   (c) STDP Model.

FIGURE 3.2 Neuron model and STDP model [234].

Fig. 3.1(b) shows neurons composing the main part of our brain. Connections between neurons occur at a synapse on the tip of a dendrite. Ions[1] coming from several preceding connected neurons increase the voltage on the neurons, creating a signal spike when crossing over a threshold. This spiking is called a firing. A spike passes through an axon and reaches the synapses on the following neurons.

An ion current coming from the preceding neuron passing through a synapse is observed. The synapse changes the intensity of its connection based on the temporal difference between the spike coming from the preceding neuron and the spike coming from the neuron. This change in intensity is based on the difference in the timing of the arriving spikes, or the so-called spike-timing dependent plasticity (STDP). It seems that our brain uses the STDP characteristics to learn.

Neurons can be represented formally, as shown in Fig. 3.2(a). The intensity of the connection at the synapse can be represented as a weight coefficient; in addition, the conductance at each synapse determines the arriving ions, and thus determines the voltage at the neuron, outputting a signal, which is occasionally a spike when a neuron is fired. This is called a formal neuron model [259]. Thus, a neuron network can be represented by the weighted edges of the axon and firing node.

The machine learning proposed during the past decades includes a decision tree [294] and a self-organizing map (SOM) [229]; however, the current approach is to apply at least one function of neuroscience. An approach that considers not only the functionality but also the firing system is called brain-inspired computing.

Brain-inspired computing can be categorized into two types, neuromorphic computing systems, and systems using shallow and deep neural network hardware. The former approach applies neuronal dynamics in its hardware to achieve an efficient processing, whereas the latter approach applies statistics with non-linear activities in the neurons. Commonly, both approaches apply a non-linear function to generate an output, and the input passes through a weighted edge(s).

---

[1] These are generally called neurotransmitters. In this book, they are simply called ions when mapped onto a logic circuit (hardware architecture).

Namely, a weighted signal (a spike in neuromorphic computing or something else in a neural network) coming from the preceding neurons is summed and fired when a certain condition of the neuron is true. In the case of neuromorphic computing, a firing occurs if the membrane potential of a neuron (sum of the current on the weighted edges) exceeds a certain threshold. In the case of a DNN, typical spiking is based on a non-linear activation function such as a sigmoidal function.

3.2 Neuromorphic computing

Neuromorphic computing is also called a spiking neural network (SNN).[2] Such computing uses a Mann Marian function of the spiking and its structure to apply an inference, and the learning uses the STDP.

3.2.1 Spike timing dependent plasticity and learning

For a particular neuron, the intensity of its connection to the preceding connected neuron is related to the firing condition, and with the learning mechanism. For a synapse (effective intensity), the time of the spike arriving at the synapse from the preceding neuron, and the time of the spike arriving at the synapse from the neuron, determine the intensity of the connection to the synapse reflecting to the current in the neuron, and thus determines the firing. Namely, the difference between timings determines the STDP [257] composing the learning mechanism. When implementing the learning mechanism for neuromorphic computing, this characteristic should be implemented with hardware. This section describes learning with the STDP shown in Fig. 3.2(c).

For a spike coming from a particular neuron, before the spike arrives, the synapse is operated through a long-term potentiation (LTP), which creates a persistent strength relationship between the spike and synapse, and thus increases the connection intensity on the synapse. For a spike coming from a preceding neuron before a spike arrives from a particular neuron, the synapse is operated through long-term depression (LTD), which creates a persistent weakness between the spike and synapse, and thus decreases the connection intensity on the synapse. LTP and LTD have characteristics of a shorter timing duration with a higher effect.

For a change in the effective intensity by firing, a shorter duration between the firing on a specific neuron and the firing on a preceding connected neuron has an exponential function, and it can be obtained using an equation model. Namely, we can create a model for an effective intensity on a synapse with an exponential function by the timing duration function for the spiking.

The firing on a specific neuron after the firing on the preceding connected neuron has a positive duration (difference between timing), and thus this is the

---

[2] Neuromorphic computing, also known as neuromorphic engineering, is a popular term for brain inspired computing.

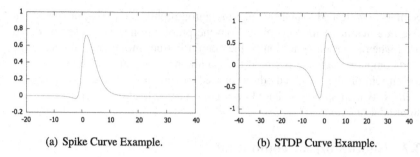

(a) Spike Curve Example.   (b) STDP Curve Example.

FIGURE 3.3 Spike and STDP curves.

LTP. Firing on a specific neuron before firing on a preceding connected neuron has negative duration, and thus this is the LTD. When the absolute duration is longer, the change in conductivity is smaller, the duration is shorter, and thus the change in conductivity is exponentially larger.

The spiking mechanism can be modeled using the equations noted in [330]. Let us assume that the timing information is not shared with the neurons, and that the firing is based on an interference of ions, which impacts the effective intensity on the synapse. Let us set voltage $V^{(j)}_{neuron}(t)$ on a particular neuron j at time t, voltage $V^{(i)}_{neuron}(t)$ on the preceding connected neuron i at time t, at the synapse between neurons i and j. We then obtain the voltages coming from the preceding connected neuron and the neuron as $V^{(j)}_{neuron}(t + \delta^{(j)}_i)$ and $V^{(i)}_{neuron}(t + \delta^{(i)}_j)$, respectively, where $\delta^{(j)}_i$ and $\delta^{(i)}_j$ are the delay time in arriving at the synapse from the firings. The spiking function $f^{(j)}(*)$ on neuron j and the effective intensity $w^{(j)}_i(t)$ can introduce the total ions $I^{(j)}(t)$ on the neuron body j as follows:

$$I^{(j)}(t) = \sum_i w^{(j)}_i(t - \delta^{(j)}_i) V^{(i)}_{neuron}(t - \delta^{(i)}_j) \tag{3.1}$$

With such ions $I^{(j)}(t)$, we can model the voltage $V^{(j)}_{neuron}(t)$ on neuron j at time t by the spiking of $f^{(j)}(*)$ as follows.

$$V^{(j)}_{neuron}(t) = f^{(j)}(I^{(j)}(t - \delta^{(j)}_i)) \tag{3.2}$$

When $V^{(j)}_{neuron}(t) \gg 0$, neuron j fires at time t and generates a spike. The spike can be represented by two sigmoid functions, as shown in Fig. 3.3(a), one for an increase in the ions and the other for diffusion. The effective intensity $w^{(j)}_i(t)$ on a synapse can be represented by a learning coefficient $1 > \epsilon > 0$ and a gradient of conductivity $\Delta I^{(j)}_i(t)$ as follows:

$$w^{(j)}_i(t + \delta_t) = w^{(j)}_i(t) + \epsilon \Delta I^{(j)}_i(t) \tag{3.3}$$

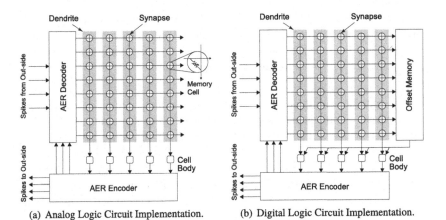

(a) Analog Logic Circuit Implementation. (b) Digital Logic Circuit Implementation.

FIGURE 3.4 Neuromorphic computing architectures.

where $\delta_t > 0$ is a minimum time tick. Therefore, learning is equivalent to updating the effective intensity, namely, weight w can be viewed as the conductivity from a hardware implementation perspective. The gradient of conductivity can be represented by the difference in current, as follows.

$$\Delta I_i^{(j)}(t) = I^{(j)}(t + \delta_i^{(j)}) - I^{(i)}(-(t + \delta_j^{(i)})) \tag{3.4}$$

The STDP characteristics are shown in Fig. 3.3(b), which assumes that intensity w is in the peak.

3.2.2 Neuromorphic computing hardware

Fig. 3.4 shows a neuromorphic computing architecture. In general, a spike is a unit pulse, and is fired by whichever voltage exceeds a threshold at a specific timing. The timing on the hardware is guaranteed by an AER, as described in Section 3.2.3. A neuron has a dendrite consisting of multiple synapses, and a firing unit. The entire cell body is called a soma. Five columns of clustered are shown in Fig. 3.4. This creates a graph with any topology under a hardware constraint. A typical approach is to have a crossbar and router in unit q and to replicate the units on the die. A spike is shared with a soma cluster, which makes it possible to compose a complex graph.

A firing unit in a neuron can be fired when the coming signal exceeds a threshold. When a neuron fires a spike, the spike is sent to the connected neuron(s), which can include itself, to update its ionic current based on the synaptic weight of the connection. The AER encoder applies the formatting to the output, and outputs to another unit or feeds back to itself. This module forms a core part and replicates the composition of the entire brain.

There are two categories for implementing neuromorphic computing hardware. The product between the spike and conductivity w on a synapse connected to a soma, and the total ions on the soma, namely, a dot-product operation, can be implemented using a digital or analog logic circuit.

1. Analog logic circuit

   A dot-product is implemented using an analog logic circuit. A synapse on a dendrite is implemented with a storage cell, which memories the effective intensity w as its conductivity, as shown in Fig. 3.4(a). A dendrite composes the memory cell array. An output wire coming from the timing synchronizer, called an AER decoder, is equivalent to an address line on a traditional memory cell array. For a specific timing, more than one input spike can be forwarded from the AER decoder to the address lines on the memory cell array, and each dendrite outputs a read-out value based on the conductivity. For each synapse on a memory cell, the voltage and conductivity of the input spike create an output current on the read line. Multiple currents are on a single read line, which is thus equivalent to multiplication on a memory cell, and the junction of these values (currents) is equivalent to the sum, and thus they compose an analog dot-product operation on a dendrite. We can use memory cells such as phase change memory (PCM), resistive RAM (ReRAM), and spin-transfer torque RAM (STT-RAM).

2. Digital logic circuit

   A synapse array on the dendrites can be implemented with a crossbar switch array, as shown in Fig. 3.4(b). At a specific timing, the AER decoder outputs one input spike to one row of the crossbar array. The spike passes the cross point, which is equivalent to a synapse when the cross point is turning on. The input spike is shared with multiple dendrites, and thus multiple outputs from the crossbar are possible. The neuron body (firing unit) inputs the spike. The accumulation of N spikes is needed to emulate the N synapses, and N spikes are input into the crossbar to achieve the total amount of ions I.

   In addition, the spiking is based on I firing and is implemented with a logic circuit. Because a synapse is made with a cross switch, conductivity on the synapse has a unit value similar to that of the spike, and needs an adjustment method for the firing conditions. The digital logic circuit model can be categorized into synchronous and asynchronous logic.

3.2.3 Address-event representation

3.2.3.1 Concept of address-event representation

Neuromorphic computing uses an AER for the representation of a spike. An AER consists of ID numbers addressing the neurons and synapses in the system. A fired spike is sequentially sent to the destination neuron with an ID represented spike. Namely, it sends spikes with time-sharing (time-multiplexing) in an interconnection network.

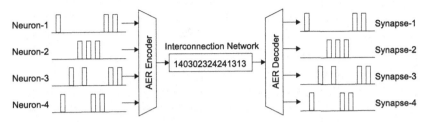

FIGURE 3.5 Spike transmission using AER method.

We can define the AER as follows.

$$AER = \{\{x_0, t_0\}, \{x_1, t_1\}, \ldots, \{x_{n-1}, t_{n-1}\}\} \tag{3.5}$$

where x_* and t_* are a neuron-ID or not a number when the neuron is fired at time t_*, respectively. The baseline model can be represented solely by the existence of a spike by encoding every time-tick, and thus is not a number, meaning a non-spiking is also encoded into the timeline.

Fig. 3.5 shows the AER-based spike transmission method. On the left side, the neurons fired generate spikes. Every neuron has its own unique ID, labeled 1 through 4 in the figure. The unit of the spike is the height, which can be fed into the encoder on the timeline. When there is no spike at the unit time, such a state can be represented as "zero," as an example. The AER code can be decoded at the destination hardware through the decoder.

In the case of a two-dimensional layout, neurons are arranged in a complete network topology. Thus, N neurons need a $2 \log_2 N$-bit address code. The address can be laid out into a $\log_2 N$-bit row address and $\log_2 N$-bit column address.

There is a possibility that the destination neuron is in a different core and/or different chip. Thus, it is necessary to identify the destination neuron, destination core, and destination chip, and therefore an addressing mechanism is needed. Multiple fires are possible at the same time. Therefore, an arbitration logic circuit is integrated, or simply treats the multiple firings as collisions [119]. It uses FIFO to buffer the spikes waiting to be sent. This requires a translation address, transfer, and inverse-translation in every Δ/n [119], where Δ and n are the duration time for firing and the maximum number of firings at the same time, respectively. Under this constraint, the architecture can be scaled out.

3.2.3.2 Router architectures for AER

There are two approaches to implementing a router for an AER packet.

One approach is to use a traditional network-on-chip (NoC), which is based on the destination address. The other approach involves using tag-based routing.

The AER packet destination address cannot have multiple destinations because the NoC architecture supports only point-to-point communication, as

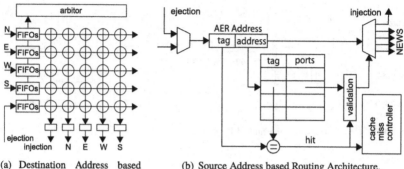

(a) Destination Address based Routing Architecture.

(b) Source Address based Routing Architecture.

FIGURE 3.6 Routers for neuromorphic computing.

shown in Fig. 3.6(a). Therefore, multiple transfers are necessary to conduct a fan-out (broadcasting one AER packet to multiple destinations). Thus, it has a hard timing constraint limited by the number of destinations. This approach can serve multiple outputs depending on the arbitration ability.

The AER packet can have a source address to indicate where it came from, and thus the router needs to hold the routing information to send to the next neighbor router. Fig. 3.6(b) shows an example of the router for this approach, which uses a cache memory approach as a look up to determine the destinations. This approach can have multiple destinations, and in the case of a two-dimensional mesh topology for the routing, it can have four destinations at most. This approach must take care of a cache miss, which means there is no information for the AER packet in the table, and thus a miss involves external memory access and stall.

3.3 Neural network

A neural network emulates the function of the mammalian brain, and applies statistical methods. A model based strongly on a statistical method is sometimes called statistical machine learning. The neuron body inputs data multiplied by the weight, and the total sum creates an activation in an activation function. Common neural network models are introduced here, after which, a common approach for hardware implementation is described.

3.3.1 Neural network models

An expected result appended to the input data is called a label or teaching data. In a neural network, a random graph structure comparable to that of neuromorphic computing is not used, and an explicit layer structure is applied, as shown in Fig. 3.7 (a). In addition, the input data are called vectors because they consist of multiple scalar elements.

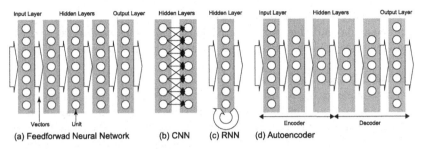

FIGURE 3.7 Neural network models.

Moreover, an output from the activation function is called an activation. An input vector from the preceding layer is an input activation on the layer, and the output activation can be input to the next layer. Conductivity on a synapse is represented as a weight, weights on the dendrite are called parameters, and each element of a weight is called an individual parameter. In the set of topologies of the graph, for the parameters, the type of activation on each layer is called a network model, or simply, a model. For a network model, the entire model, which is the target of the design, is called an architecture, including the learning mechanism and method.

The value is propagated from the input (bottom) layer to the output (upper) layer, and a neural network is sometimes called an FFN, or a multi-layer perceptron (MLP), because it consists of multiple layers. Neural networks are categorized into two types, shallow and DNNs.

3.3.1.1   Shallow neural networks

A shallow neural network has one intermediate layer (hidden layer) between the input and output layers.

- Support vector machines
  A support vector machine (SVM) is a model, including logistic regression [139]. Logistic regression is applied to create a border line in the feature distribution domain of the input vector, and the region made with a border line(s) has a particular class and creates a group. By learning, the parameters making the border line(s) are obtained, where the input data fitted into the region indicate its class at the inference.
  An SVM does not explore the optimal border lines during learning, and inferences the class for the input vector based on the nearest distance from the point of the feature map obtained from the learning. This makes a group with an indexing of the distribution of the input vectors at the learning time.
  Whereas logistic regression determines $n - 1$ dimension borders for an n dimension input vector, an SVM equivalently determines the n dimension region. For example, in the case of $n = 2$, logistic regression has only one curve, and the SVM has a margin on the curve as a region. Therefore, an SVM is

occasionally called a maximum-margin classifier because of the learning required to maximize the margin. An SVM is a commonly used model, similar to logistic regression, for structural correlation programs between information.

- Restricted Boltzmann machines
  A Boltzmann machine (BM) consists of visible neurons and hidden neurons, in which each neuron composes an input layer and a hidden layer [164]. A hidden layer represents a dependency expressing a correlation between the observed data elements held by the input layer. It learns the probability distribution [208].
  A BM is a unidirectional graph model known as a Markov random field (MRF). By using a Gibbs distribution, which represents a probability distribution having an MRF as a probability variable, a joint probability distribution is represented for a pair of visible and hidden variables. In addition, by introducing latent variables, we obtain the dependency between visible variables from the joint probability distribution. The design of the training on the BM is difficult because of the complexity of the model, and therefore tips regarding the implementation and variation are required. A restricted BM(RBM) constrains a neuron as a bipartite graph, and thus, there is no connection between neurons in the same layer [313]. This is used for a dimensionality reduction, classification, collaborative filtering, feature learning, and topic modeling, among other factors.

3.3.1.2 Deep neural networks

A neural network with more than one intermediate layer (called a hidden layer) between the input layer and output layer is called a DNN, or deep learning.

- Convolutional neural networks
  A CNN consists of a convolution layer and a pooling layer [279]. A convolution is a filter operation commonly used in image processing. In the case of an image recognition task, the convolution layer extracts the feature. A CNN learns the filter coefficient as a weight. Pooling is an interpolation layer, guaranteeing a difference in the object positions in an image.
  By stacking the convolution and pooling, and by replicating such a stack, the output layer side obtains a high context, meaning particular features are obtained in each layer, and the output side layer achieves a high context, and finally recognizes the object as a classification problem.
  A convolution operates a filtering with specific elements on two-dimensional input data, which can be represented in a linear dimension. The node then connects to the following nodes with particular patterns, and it does not connect to all following nodes, as shown in Fig. 3.7(b). In addition, a normalization layer can be added to compensate such a contrast.
- Recurrent neural networks
  An RNN is used for sequenced data [279]. The sequenced data have an order between elements of information, and the order constructs a correlation

among the elements. The length of the sequence is variable. An RNN extracts the features from inside the sequenced data, and it can be used for audio recommissioning, video recognition, and text data consisting of sequenced data.

An RNN has cyclic edges on a layer, as shown in Fig. 3.7(c), and functions as a memory of the preceding weighted inputs (feature). To support a long duration of the memory in a unit, long short-term memory (LSTM) is used. Such a memory unit has several gates on a node, such as an input gate, an output gate, and reset gates. Each gate consists of weighted edges and an activation function similar to a dot-product operation.

- Autoencoders
An AE is not a recurrent network, and a particular network model has an inverted order, with the inversion network appended to the original network model [310]. An M-layer network model is inverted in its order (excepting and removing the M-th layer), and this model is appended to the original, as shown in Fig. 3.7(d). For an AE consisting of $2(M-1)$ layers, the M-th and $2(M-1)$-th layers are equivalent to the output and input layers, respectively. Training makes no difference between the input and output layers of the AE. The original model without an output layer is called an encoder, and an inverted model is called a decoder. The encoder outputs an inference. This means we obtain the inference and learned parameters without a teacher. An AE can be used to obtain the initial value of the parameters, which is called pretraining [279].

A CNN, an RNN, and an AE are described here. Most deep learning models combine or modify these to design a user defined model. For example, a deep brief network (DBN) is a model for the stacking of RBMs [195], which is used for recognition and generative models, such as in image, video sequence, and motion-capture data, among the different data types [151].

The most interesting point of the design is to obtain superior parameters that provide highly accurate performance in the design of the hyperparameters, which include the learning rate and regularization coefficient (as described in Appendix A). These are involved in the design of the model, in addition to the epoch (number of repeated learning in a batch), batch size, and other factors (described in Appendix A). Numerous studies have been conducted in this area.

- Bayesian optimization
Adjusting the hyperparameters involved in obtaining good parameters accurately representing a feature, the experience and exploration of the design space are needed for introducing a high inference accuracy. Studies have applied the Gaussian process (GP) to optimize the hyperparameters, and a parameter update has been used for experiments involved in a sensitivity analysis, consistency adjustment, and prediction [331].

Bayesian optimization is used to find the minimum structure by constructing the probability model for the function, and the next step references the current evaluation of the function. A non-convex function having the minimum structure can be found with a relatively small number of retries.

• Learning of optimization
Optimization algorithms have been proposed to obtain better parameters updated at the learning stage, such as an algorithm based on manual handling. To reduce the workload, an automatic algorithm for obtaining such parameters using machine learning has been devised [111].
By preparing the network model to optimize the parameters, the parameters are updated using the error information of the target network model. Cyclic parameter updating is applied between the optimization network model and the target optimization network model.

• Deep generative models
A generative model generates a dataset by using a probability model. In general, this is used for generating input data for learning and/or obtaining the learned parameters with specific features. In particular, a generative model constructed with a DNN model is called a deep generative model (DGM) [224].
A DGM consists of labeled (M2) and unlabeled (M2) generative models. Unlabeled data are treated as incomplete data, and a probability density function is used. A DGM can combine with deep learning, can efficiently learn with a few labeled data, and achieves a higher accuracy than common deep learning models.

3.3.2 Previous and current neural networks

A neural network can be represented as a graph. A graph can be represented by a matrix, and it is natural to represent it as a matrix operation for a neural network. In addition, it takes more than a 2-rank tensor, and thus a tensor operation has a neural network representation. A graph consists of nodes and edges connecting among nodes.

In a neural network, a node is an activation function, and an edge is a weighted link. The weighted edge is used to multiply a weight to a signal coming from a preceding node. The weighted edges are fed into the node and sum the inputs, and the result is used for the activation function. The inputs to the activation function are represented by a dot-product operation in a matrix (2-rank). An edge connection is not random (except for a dropout, described in Chapter 6), and has certain patterns and composes a particular topology. A topology can be a fractal [236]. In addition, there are several utilization layers such as in a residual network, an added output of several sub-networks, and a concatenation of the preceding sub-networks. Namely, a fork and a join are used in a graph representation.

There is question regarding which is better at a constant number of activation functions, i.e., a larger number of layers and a smaller number of activation functions in a layer to obtain a high context, or a smaller number of layers and a larger number of activation functions in a layer to obtain the representation capability in the layer. We should simply choose the best number of layers and the best number of activation functions in each layer. Regarding the training, back propagation can be represented using a weighted routing. Thus, if a deep learning processor architecture also considers the training, it is necessary to consider such routing.

There are two types of deep learning models based on such a framework: a static model and a dynamic model. A static model cannot change the graph structure at runtime, but a dynamic model can. Chainer, PyTorch, and the recent TensorFlow support a dynamic model.

A static model executes in a sequential manner, and under a control flow there is no branching of the flow. A loop is represented using a static address calculation. Thus, we do not need a branch prediction unit in such a processor for deep learning tasks. In addition, the address calculation can be analyzed at the compilation time, and a useful data structure is prepared; thus, we do not require cache memory. We can achieve a trade-off between the address calculation and data structure, resulting in an optimization. In its entirety, a traditional computing architecture does not fit into the characteristics of deep learning tasks. We can remove an unnecessary logic circuit unit and add a new unit to improve the execution performance.

The previous method to achieving an architecture for a neural network was to approach the primal issue of an external memory access, and to reduce the number of memory accesses and their transfer traffic. However, we must consider an eager execution supporting a dynamic graph composition, and thus a previous static graph execution approach will no longer work well in the near future. In addition, various activation functions have been proposed, and the hardwire implementation requires some complexity. Moreover, with pipelined machine learning, in which multiple machine learning jobs are chained and operated as a pipeline, support for future neural networks with unknown task characteristics will be important.

TensorFlow, PyTorch, Caffe2, Chainer, and various other frameworks have been developed, and researchers and architects can choose their preferred framework. Each framework has its own pros and cons. By choosing an appropriate framework that fits the design requirement of a neural network model, the user can achieve better performance on the designed neural network model. A cross platform will soon be supported. By using ONNX [99], a neural network with a specific framework can migrate to another framework. In addition, a neural network model can be mapped onto various devices by supporting its own compiler back-end. The TVM [95] of an NNVM is a specialized compiler back-end for deep learning tasks. These tools are briefly described in Chapter 5.

3.3.3 Neural network hardware

There are two types of implementation approaches, as shown in Fig. 3.8: a logic circuit and an analog logic circuit. A digital logic circuit implementation is

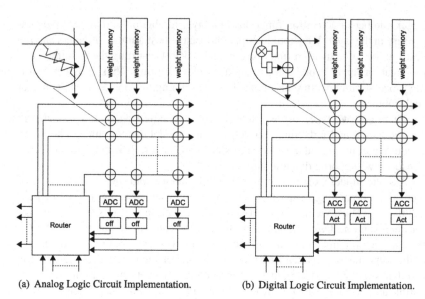

(a) Analog Logic Circuit Implementation.   (b) Digital Logic Circuit Implementation.

FIGURE 3.8 Neural network computing architectures.

described here. A dot-product used in analog processing is similar to a neuromorphic computing approach.

3.3.3.1 Dot-product implementation

The hardware structure for a neural network is shown in Fig. 3.8.

An analog implementation takes a non-volatile memory cell to conduct a multiplication. Its outputs are summed on the output line, and they form a dot-product operation on the soma block. In general, an analog-digital converter (ADC) is used to create a digital value, which is fed into the offset ("off" in Fig. 3.8(a)) to support a negative value and create an activation based on its activation function.

A digital implementation applies an array of arithmetic units, as shown in Fig. 3.8(b), and conducts an MAD; a series of MADs on soma realize a dot-product operation. The output is accumulated (ACC) to support a large-scale dot-product, and the accumulator can have an initial bias value. The product is fed into the activation function (Act) logic circuit.

There are three approaches to conduct a dot-product operation:

1. MAC method

   As one approach, a multiply-accumulate (MAC) approach takes n steps for an n-length vector operand operation. To improve the performance, by subdividing the vector and preparing multiple MACs, MACs are applied in parallel, and the partial sums are finally added.

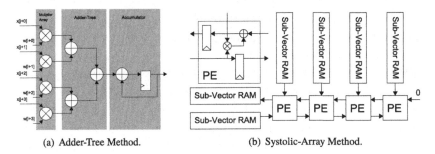

(a) Adder-Tree Method.   (b) Systolic-Array Method.

FIGURE 3.9 Dot-product operation methods.

2. Adder-tree method

This approach does not replicate multiple MAC units, but replicates multipliers for multiplication between activations and parameters; the results are fed into an adder-tree, as shown in Fig. 3.9(a). An adder-tree has a tree topology and a particular radix and performs a partial sum. In the case of a large-scale tensor, the operands are subdivided and the sub-tensors are transferred to the multipliers; finally, the accumulator is applied in the last stage.

3. Systolic-array method

Multiple processing elements (PEs) are connected using the same pattern, and the connection uses the data dependency, or a projection mapping function is coordinated, and the dependency graph is mapped onto a grid space to make a connection. Data are fed in, and the result is output to the outside or maintained in each PE, and an execution is systemically conducted. This paradigm is called systolic array processing [232]. In general, the loop part in a program is applied to this architecture, and thus a matrix operation and a convolution operation are typical applications. Fig. 3.9(b) shows a one-dimension mapping of a matrix multiplication. For a larger-scale design space than a physical space, a partition and scheduling of the fragments are needed.

The MAC approach is applied in the temporal processing domain, and an adder-tree approach uses the spatial domain. A systolic array approach can coordinate between the temporal and spatial processing domains [268]. Thus, the user can project a portion of the loop program into both the temporal and spatial domains freely, and can achieve a trade-off between resources and the execution cycles. In general, hardware having a systolic array has a fixed (static) coordination. Reconfigurable computing (RC) hardware has the possibility of a coordination, a typical example of which is an FPGA. FPGAs have a 1-bit operation node of a configurable logic block (CLB), and a coarse-grained reconfigurable architecture (CGRA) has a mid-sized or larger node granularity [186].

Table 3.1 summarizes the three implementation methods for a dot-product operation. To compare simply between an adder-tree and a systolic array, let us

TABLE 3.1 Comparison of three approaches.

Approach	Steps	Multipliers	Adders
MAC	$O(M(N+1))$	$O(1)$	$O(1)$
Adder-Tree	$O(M\lfloor \log_r N \rfloor)$	$O(N)$	$O(r^{\lceil \log_r N \rceil} - \lfloor \log_r (N - r^{\lfloor \log_r N \rfloor}) \rfloor - 1)$
1D Systolic	$O(M(N+1))$	$O(N)$	$O(N)$
2D Systolic	$O(M+2N+1)$	$O(MN)$	$O(MN)$

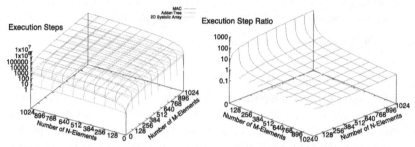

(a) Execution Steps for Matrix-Vector Multiplication   (b) Step Ratio of Adder-Tree to Systolic Array.

FIGURE 3.10 Execution steps with different dot-product implementations.

consider $N = r^n$ and $M = r^m$. Regarding the number of steps, the break-even point between them can be as follows.

$$M \log_r r^n = M + 2r^n + 1 \tag{3.6}$$

Thus,

$$n = 1 + 2r^{n-m} + r^{-m} \tag{3.7}$$
$$\approx 1 + 2r^{n-m}$$

We therefore obtain a breakeven point, creating approximately the same number of steps between the adder-tree and the systolic array methods as follows.

$$m \approx \log_r \frac{2r^n}{n-1} \tag{3.8}$$
$$\approx n - \log_r (n-1)$$

Thus, more than $n - \log_r (n-1) < m$ units need to achieve the same execution performance for the adder-tree method. However, in the case of a systolic array, the scale must be within $n - \log_r (n-1) > m$.

Fig. 3.10(a) shows how many steps are required for a matrix-vector multiplication based on Tables 3.1 and 2.2, where the matrix shape is $M \times N$. Note that an adder-tree requires radix-2. For the MAC approach, the number of steps is

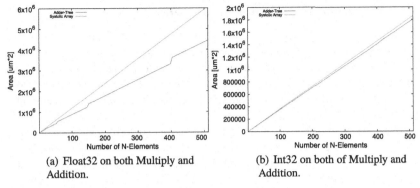

(a) Float32 on both Multiply and Addition.

(b) Int32 on both of Multiply and Addition.

FIGURE 3.11 Dot-product Area-I: baseline precisions.

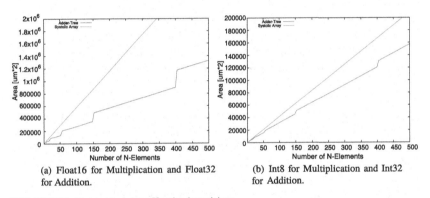

(a) Float16 for Multiplication and Float32 for Addition.

(b) Int8 for Multiplication and Int32 for Addition.

FIGURE 3.12 Dot-product Area-II: mixed precisions.

linearly increased. The MAC approach always requires many steps. An adder-tree is superior for a small-scale matrix; however, a systolic array outperforms a large-scale matrix, as shown in Fig. 3.10(b), which demonstrates the steps in the ratio between an adder-tree and a systolic array.

Fig. 3.11(a) shows the area requirement for a dot product with a single precision floating-point on a 45-nm process node using Table 2.2. Compared with the single precision floating-point shown in Fig. 3.11(a), a 32-bit integer or value equivalent to a fixed-point numerical representation requires less than one-third the area. Fig. 3.11 shows that an adder-tree always requires a smaller area than a systolic array.

Fig. 3.12(a) shows the area requirement for a dot product with a half-precision floating-point for a multiplier and a single-precision floating-point for an adder. Compared with an 8-bit integer for multiplication and 32-bit integer for addition, as shown in Fig. 3.12(b), an adder-tree approach requires the same range of area as shown in Fig. 3.12(a).

3.4 Memory cell for analog implementation

An analog logic circuit for several dot-products in parallel is implemented using a memory cell array configuration with several dendrites forming an array.

A memory cell stores a weight using a specific technique, and the cell outputs a current through the weight resistance; finally, the junctional currents are the dot-product value. In the read-out from every bit-line, the junctional currents have a pre-activation value.

Thus, by composing a crossbar with a memory cell corresponding to a cross point, a matrix-vector operation can be conducted on the crossbar. However, a negative value cannot be used, and therefore, the pre-activation requires an offset to adjust to achieve a correct value, or a preprocessing must be applied before conducting a spiking function.

- Phase change memory
  PCM uses the changing property between an amorphous phase and a crystal phase. By quickly decreasing the electric pulse in the memory cell, the cell is changed into an amorphous phase having a higher resistance. This phase can be changed by slowly decreasing the pulse to a crystal phase having a lower resistance.
- Resistive RAM
  ReRAM has an insulating layer between the metal layers, a conductive filament forms a conductive path in the insulating layer, and the path rates a lower resistive memory cell. Memorization uses the changing resistance value in the memory cell with the applied voltage.
- Spin-transfer torque RAM
  STT-RAM uses the STT effect (a phenomenon in which the spin of the impurity ions occurs with a magnetic to polarization effect) on the magnetic tunnel junction (MTJ). It memorizes the value of the tunnel-barrier states with a reversible ferroelectric polarization of the thin-film insulating layer.

STT-RAM achieves a lesser decline in the materials caused by repeated phase changes, as seen in other memories, and has a higher switching speed. PCM has a smaller memory cell area. An analog logic circuit implementation for neuromorphic computing is summarized in [297], and thus our survey briefly introduces this domain.

Chapter 4

Applications, ASICs, and domain-specific architectures

ASICs, which integrate logic circuits designed for a specific application, are introduced in this chapter. Herein, an application is represented as an algorithm. An algorithm is implemented as software, hardware, or a combination of the two, and has locality and dependence, which are also introduced and described. Hardware having a good architecture utilizing such localities and dependencies improves the execution performance and energy consumption, and thus improves the energy efficiency.

4.1 Applications

This section describes an application through a comparison between the software and hardware development.

An application with the objective to solve a user's problem can be represented as an algorithm. An algorithm consists of three components, namely, variables, operators referencing the variables, and a substitution of the result into the variable. Hardware implementing an algorithm also involves a signal transfer between storage holding the variables passing through the operation logic circuit.

4.1.1 Concept of applications

Today, software programs, which are one approach to representing an algorithm, use such components in a single state, and such states are described from top down in a program file under the premise of a sequential execution.

A software program is translated into an instruction stream and stored in the instruction memory before its execution. An instruction is loaded (called an instruction fetch) sequentially, from the beginning of the instruction stream to the end. A fetching instruction is addressed by a PC. The fetched instruction is decoded into a set of control signals and executed on a functional unit(s). In general, a variable determining the BTA as a changing path of the control flow is stored in a CSR hidden from the user programs, and the user program cannot be directly stored into the register. Instead, a programming language has a grammar representing the control flow. A compare-instruction updates the CSR,

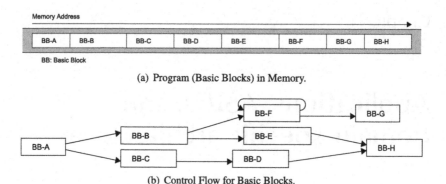

(a) Program (Basic Blocks) in Memory.

(b) Control Flow for Basic Blocks.

FIGURE 4.1   Program in memory and control flow at execution.

and the conditional branch instruction then reads the CSR and branches toward the correct path to change the flow of the instruction stream.

For hardware, an application is represented by an HDL such as Verilog-HDL or VHDL. In a logic circuit, the signal flow does not occur sequentially, and therefore, all substitutions can be achieved at the same time. Of course, writing to a single register has a priority to avoid multiple writings into the register.

4.2   Application characteristics

This section describes a locality, a deadlock property, and a dependency, which appear upon an implementation with both software and hardware. Good software utilizes the localities and dependencies by optimizing these properties to fit into a specific hardware architecture. Good hardware also utilizes the localities and dependencies by minimizing the signal-flow distance and its frequency, and obtaining a high energy efficiency, and thus these factors are the most important.

In the case of software, the program is stored to memory having a single address space and, generally, a specific execution pattern. The instruction and data streams make up the behavior of the program, and each instruction has a dependency whose characteristics are related with variable access to the execution order among the statements, and a locality whose characteristics are temporally and spatially related with the signal propagation as shown in the memory address patterns of the memory access, for example.

4.2.1   Locality

4.2.1.1   Concept of locality

Each instruction composing the instruction stream can be identified by a memory address, which is a mapping address of the instruction stored in memory, as shown in Fig. 4.1(a). Similarly, all data or variables can also be identified by the memory address, which is a mapping address of the data stored in data memory. Regarding the control flow, the instruction stream fragment typically has a branch instruction at the end of the fragment, with the branch updating the BTA. The fragment is called a basic block, as shown in Fig. 4.1(b). A loop part of "BB-F" exists. A program execution has a pointer, called a PC, addressing the next fetching instruction. A PC is incremented every cycle on the basic block. When an instruction decoder detects a branch instruction at the end of the fragment, it updates the PC by selecting the BTA or next instruction.

The next instruction is on the next instruction memory address based on the assumption of a sequential execution within the basic block. For the instruction memory address space, the characteristics of the address pattern based on the increment are called a spatial locality. Data also have a spatial locality when multiple data are composed into an array, and when accessing the array with a particular pattern, in a next-to-next manner based on an increase in the data memory address, as an example.

When a particular basic block such as a loop part in a program is repeatedly executed, this basic block having repeated executions has access to the same addresses with a temporal pattern, which is called a temporal locality. When highly repeating the execution and accessing a specific memory address region, a highly temporal locality occurs.

Similar to an instruction, data having a temporal locality based on the memory access pattern can be seen as addresses on a timeline. Therefore, the program has its own unique locality. Changing the control flow, this is based on a special register (CSR) holding the branch condition, and has similar characteristics as the data, as described in Section 4.2.3. Instruction and data cache memories are typical examples utilizing the spatial locality and temporal locality based on a contiguous memory address space and on mapping onto such a memory region.

4.2.1.2 Hardware perspective for locality

For an electrical logic circuit, a signal propagating through the logic circuit involves a signal propagation delay and energy consumption. Similar to software, hardware has locality characteristics and should be considered highly local.

Repeatedly or frequently accessed datasets should be located closely in the same domain to shorten the distance and suppress the delay, as well as to suppress the energy consumption. The spatial placement creates both temporal and spatial locality. Frequent access is determined by scheduling a signal propagation mainly through a data flow in the circuit. Such a temporal placement on the timeline should be arranged such that a set of correlated signals are closely within the same time domain.

The reuse of data means having both temporal and spatial localities in a certain domain. The easiest way to implement a high locality is to create a bandwidth hierarchy through storage between interconnected networks having a high bandwidth on the nearby operational logic circuit.

4.2.2 Deadlock

4.2.2.1 System model

Let us use general resource systems [199] to construct a management and scheduling model. This is represented as a general resource graph, i.e., a bipartite directed graph. This graph consists of disjointed sets of a process $\Pi = \{P_1, P_2, \cdots, P_n\}$ and sets of memory resources $M = \{M_1, M_2, \cdots, M_l\}$. An edge at a system state of $S \in \Sigma = \{\cdots, S, T, \cdots\}$ represents a request or assignment. For individual system states, S and T, management is achieved through three operations as follows:

1. **Request**

   A request edge directed from a process to a resource of M means that the process requests the resource. In state S, if no request edges are directed from node P_i to each identical resource of M, then the state becomes $S \xrightarrow{i} T$.

2. **Acquirement**

   An assignment edge directed from the resource of M to the process means that the resource requested by the process is acquired. In state S, if there are request edges directed from node P_i to each identical resource of M, then $S \xrightarrow{i} T$. The request edges are replaced with assignment edges directed from identical reusable resources of M to P_i.

3. **Release**

   The acquired reusable resources are used for the process P_i. Reusable resources are released when the process does not need reusable resources or information produced that may be requested for communication. During state S, if no request edges are detected from P_i to reusable resources of M and some assignment edges are directed to P_i, then $S \xrightarrow{i} T$.

   More details can be found in [199].

   In a traditional system, a deadlock is a considerable problem. Let us use the following expressions to describe the resource allocation operations of a request, acquirement, and release at time t.

1. **Request operation**

   A set of addresses of identical memory resources requested by $P_i \in \Pi$ is represented as $Req\_addr(i, t)$.

2. **Acquirement operation**

   A set of addresses of identical memory resources acquired by $P_i \in \Pi$ is represented as $Acq\_addr(i, t)$.

3. **Release operation**

   A set of addresses of identical memory resources released by $P_i \in \Pi$ is represented as $Rls\_addr(i, t)$.

   Note that resources are represented by a set of memory addresses. In addition to a collection of such addresses, the number of memory resources related to process P_i by an operation is represented as $|Req\_addr(i, t)|$, as an example.

4.2.2.2 Deadlock property

A deadlock does not occur in a system that only supports statistical scheduling. Memory resources are mutually exclusive. A deadlock occurs when the system state holds sufficient and necessary conditions [199] as follows:

Theorem 4.1. *A cycle in a general resource graph is a necessary condition. If the graph is expedient, a knot is a sufficient condition.*

A necessary condition can be detected by checking the sets of requests and acquirements. Resources in a knock under an expedient state are blocked for all processes with requests and cannot be assigned to such processes. The processes in a knock are in a state of deadlock. The deadlock management can serve as memory protection, and thus is a subset mechanism for accessing the memory resources. Theorem 4.1 provides the following fundamental aspects to the system model with a previously proposed expression showing a set of addresses:

Corollary 4.1. *A deadlock occurs during a system state having $Block(t) \cap Arbit(t) \neq \phi$.*

$$Block(t) = Req\_addr(i, t) \cap Acq\_addr(j, t) \neq \phi,$$
$$Arbit(t) = Req\_addr(j, t) \cap Acq\_addr(i, t) \neq \phi,$$

where $i \in \{0 \leq i < C, P_i \in \Pi\}$ and $j \in \{i \neq j, \forall j, P_j \in \Pi\}$.

Theorem 4.2. *Process $P_i \in \Pi$ is in a blocked state if are no states T such that $S \xrightarrow{i} T$.*

Corollary 4.2. *Blocking occurs in system state having $Block(t) \neq \phi$.*

$$Block(t) = Req\_addr(i, t) \cap Acq\_addr(j, t),$$

where $i \in \{0 \leq i < C\}$ and $j = \{i \neq j, \forall j, P_j \in \Pi\}$.

Blocking occurs when the process requests the acquired memory resources. The process waits for an acquirement, and thus it should clearly have an alternative state to avoid a blocking.

Corollary 4.3. *Arbitration is needed in a system state having $Arbit(t) \neq \phi$.*

$$Arbit(t) = Req\_addr(j, t) \cap Acq\_addr(i, t),$$

where $i \in \{0 \leq i < C\}$ and $j = \{i \neq j, \forall j, P_j \in \Pi\}$.

Corollary 4.3 derives a requirement of arbitration to release the memory resources or block certain processes.

Statement-1: A = B + C;	Statement-1: A = B + C;	Statement-1: A = B + C;	Statement-1: A = B + C;
Statement-2: B = E * A;	Statement-2: B = E * A	Statement-2: B = E * A;	Statement-2: B = E * A
Statement-3: A = B - F;	Statement-3: A = B - F;	Statement-3: A = B - F;	Statement-3: A = B - F;
(a) Program Fragment.	(b) True Data Dependency.	(c) Output Data Dependency.	(d) Anti-Data Dependency.

FIGURE 4.2 Algorithm example and its data dependencies.

4.2.3 Dependency

4.2.3.1 Concept of data dependency

A software program is presumed to have a sequential description written from top to bottom in the program file, namely, it has sequential execution characteristics, and when its multiple instructions are executed concurrently, it will fail to execute the program. Fig. 4.2(a) shows a program fragment consisting of three statements, i.e., addition, multiplication, and finally subtraction. This fragment is used for a description of the relationship between the algorithm and its sequential execution. The program is generally executed from the top line to the bottom line, and the three statements in the program fragment are equivalent to three instructions generated by the compiler, which should be sequentially executed to avoid breaking the algorithm.

4.2.3.2 Data dependency representation

Before a substitution of the (writing to a) variable, it tries to reference (read from) the variable; its operation fails, and it cannot output the correct result. This data flow (equivalent to a signal flow on a logic circuit) forms an algorithm. The data flow of a specific variable between statements has dependency, which is called the true data dependency. A logic circuit including the ASICs is composed of such true data dependency.

In Fig. 4.2(c), multiple operations try to write into the same variable. For a logic circuit, a specific register-write is defined in one block with priority, generally described in "if-else" statements. Thus, a writing conflict does not occur. Unfortunately, in the case of a software program, the last writing has the highest priority at the end of the basic block execution. Therefore, it cannot guarantee the correctness of the sequential execution when the processor simply tries to execute multiple instructions at the same time. Multiple writings into a single variable between statements is also a characteristic of a dependency, which is called the output data dependency.

In Fig. 4.2(d), before referencing (reading) a variable, one statement tries to write into the variable, and thus it fails the operation and violates the rule of sequential execution. This inverse flow must be avoided, which is also a characteristic of dependency, called anti-data dependency.

Deadlock management can serve such dependency, and the results may be used for scheduling. The observation shows that the dependency may be analyzed and managed as a deadlock problem.

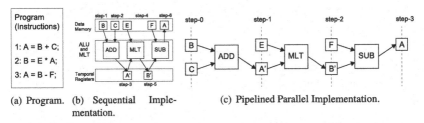

(a) Program. (b) Sequential Implementation.   (c) Pipelined Parallel Implementation.

FIGURE 4.3 Algorithm example and its implementation approaches.

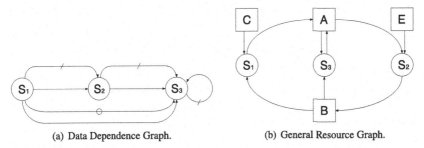

(a) Data Dependence Graph.   (b) General Resource Graph.

FIGURE 4.4 Example of data dependency.

Let us consider the following example, consisting of three operations that are identified by the labels S_1, S_2, and S_3.

1. $A = B + C$
2. $B = A + E$
3. $A = A + B$

A data dependence graph (DDG) shows the possibility of parallel processing of three operations. Fig. 4.4(a) shows a DDG as an example. It shows the need of a sequential execution and a difficulty of improving the performance. If the microarchitecture does not support a forwarding path, three operations are sequentially executed. This consideration has the premise of an execution flow, in which three operations are, in order from top to bottom, statements S_1, S_2, and S_3. The premise introduces the need of hardware or software support for scheduling.

There is an alternative viewpoint to the above example. When a microprocessor tries to simultaneously issue three operations, the general resource graph is helpful in considering the dependency. Fig. 4.4(b) shows a partial general resource graph for the example. There are three circles, namely, $\{(S_1, A), (A, S_2), (S_2, B), (B, S_1)\}$, $\{(S_2, B), (B, S_3), (S_3, A), (A, S_2)\}$, and $\{(S_3, A), (A, S_3)\}$. The system state is in a deadlock, and the results cannot be guaranteed.

Data-flow dependence. *Data-flow dependence occurs for a resource with a request edge and an assignment edge. This is represented as $\{(S_{t'}, M), (M, S_t)\}$,* *where $t' < t$. The data flow directed to the resources of $Block(t) \neq \phi$ must be guaranteed.*

Resources having at least two different edges of requests and assignments must be used in the order represented by the data flow. The data flow represents the *data flow path* between operations, and the resources may be used for the retiming in a synchronous system.

Data anti-dependence. *Data anti-dependence occurs for a resource having a request edge and an assignment edge. This is represented as $\{(S_t, M), (M, S_{t'})\}$, where $t' < t$. The data flow directed from the resources of $Block(t) \neq \phi$ must be blocked.*

The directed edge represents a violation of the data flow.

Output dependence. *Output dependence occurs for a resource having several request edges. This is represented as edges to the same memory resources $(S_{t'}, M)$ and (S_t, M), where $t' < t$. Processes having requests for resources of $Block(t) \neq \phi$ have conflicts for the resources.*

The output dependence clearly indicates that a general resource graph must be temporally partitioned to create an in-order comparable to the states. Thus, processes having a request for a memory resource of $|Req\_addr(*, t)| > 1$ must be scheduled for sequential access based on priority.

A data flow can be represented by a general resource graph. The properties of the data dependence based on the deadlock property indicate the order of execution of a temporal partition of the graph into several system states, and make scheduling a necessity. The order defines the data flow, and its inverse flow must be blocked. The need for a temporal partition implies the need of a priority to schedule and manage the data flows through the resource allocation. Defining the order eliminates the possibility of dependencies, as well as remaining dependencies that construct the algorithm. Data anti-dependence consists of a single process such as $\{(S_3, A), (A, S_3)\}$, which in the example is clearly a sequence of requests and acquirement operations.

Control dependency. *The control dependency can be represented by a data dependency in which the CSR can be a resource, and general resource systems can steer the allocation. The control flow determines the next data flow path, and thus the node of the control flow (CSR) resource becomes a computational bottleneck. Thus, the node is a partitioning node used to effectively map onto the timeline.*

4.2.4 Temporal and spatial operations

Fig. 4.3 shows a temporal mapping and spatial mapping of three statements (Fig. 4.3(a)). Fig. 4.3(b) shows the aim of suppressing the amount of processing resources, which can be performed at the same time, and which is equivalent to executing a software program on the microprocessor. Fig. 4.3(c) shows that each statement is mapped onto a chip as an instance, and as an ASIC implementation, is a straightforward approach. Intermediate results are stored in the pipeline registers or simply on a wire propagating to the next arithmetic units.

Fig. 4.3(b) shows a sequential implementation using a temporal register to remove data memory accesses. When variables B and C are located on the same memory bank, two sequential memory accesses are considered. Even if the hardware system supports multiple storage to memory, a conflict may occur. A conflict means that the possible number of accesses to the memory bank at the same time is physically limited by the design. Thus, multiple accesses to one bank create a delay for un-granted requests. This is called a memory access conflict, or simply a conflict. A sequential execution takes a total of six steps to finish an execution.

In the case of spatial mapping, we can freely map the variables on a chip. In addition, all variables can be placed on a chip and can create a pipelined datapath, as shown in Fig. 4.3(c), requiring a total of three steps to finish the execution. We design an architecture with coordination between temporal and spatial mappings to balance the amount of resources and the number of execution cycles.

Therefore, we can create a taxonomy by mapping the approaches of the temporal computing and spatial computing based on the mapping orientation.

1. Temporal computing
   To share resources, the approach requires a time-multiplexing of the execution. Such an approach can suppress the resource requirements; however, the timeline requires a long execution time.
2. Spatial computing
   This is an execution with a mapping of the data flow onto a spatial space. This approach maximizes the parallelism and obtains a short execution time; however, it requires a relatively large amount of resources.

Resources such as memory and arithmetic units on a chip are finite. Thus, when sequentially executing a program fitting the number of resources, and/or a parallel execution as a spatial mapping, we need to coordinate the architecture design to utilize the finite number of resources. For high-performance microprocessors, a binary instruction stream is generated by a compiler from the software program, applying a register renaming method to resolve the dependencies between the instructions and the issued instructions in the processor core, and finding multiple independent instructions to issue at the same time, thereby selecting issuable instructions from a pool of candidates, and executing on out-of-order execution with avoiding breaking the program. The issue is the bandwidth, and the instruction window is scaled based on the number of resources, creating an out-of-order execution. In the case of an ASIC implementation, the chip area is a physical limitation. Within this limitation, a finite state machine (FSM) is used when the sequential execution is sufficient, and

TABLE 4.1 Dennardian vs. post-Dennardian (leakage-limited) [351].

Property	Dennardian	Post-Dennardian
ΔQuantity	S^2	S^2
ΔFrequency	S	S
ΔCapacitance	$1/S$	$1/S$
ΔV_{dd}^2	$1/S^2$	1
ΔPower	1	S^2
ΔUtilization	1	$1/S^2$

a parallel datapath is designed when a parallel data execution is required. The architecture design involves such an optimization.

For machine learning hardware, the hardware resources on a chip limit the scale of the machine learning model. DNN models require a huge number of parameters, which cannot all be placed on a chip. Thus, partitioning of the data is required, and loading the subset data from external memory and storing the intermediate results in external memory are necessary. The loading and storage of data imply an access latency and power consumption. A portion of most power consumption comes from external memory access, which also requires a latency of hundreds of cycles, as well as a higher energy consumption than that required by signal propagation on a chip.

These facts introduce the need for minimizing the amount of data transfer and its frequency for the partitioned dataset.

4.3 Application-specific integrated circuit

4.3.1 Design constraints

We can predict the future scale of the area, clock frequency, capacitance, voltage, power, and utilization based on scaling factor S, which is defined as follows.

$$S = \frac{S_{node}}{S_{node}^{Scaled}} \tag{4.1}$$

where S_{node} and S_{node}^{Scaled} are the process nodes of the older and elder, respectively. The future scale of the factors can then be predicted, as shown in Table 4.1. The term Dennardian indicates the age at which Dennard's scaling works well. The scaling of the voltage V_{dd} is completed after Dennard's scaling is applied. Therefore, the power consumption easily increases, and the resource utilization is easily decreased.

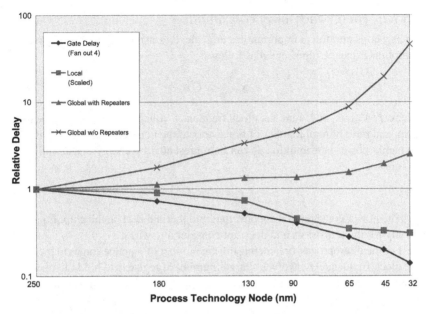

FIGURE 4.5 Relative wire delays [41].

4.3.1.1 Wire-delay

Advanced semiconductor technologies require a wider design space based on a shrinkage of the semiconductor process and a minimization of the wire width, and its pitch creates a larger wire resistance. Thus, the aspect ratio of the intersection of the wire has a higher height to suppress the resistance.

During the first half of the 1990s, a delay on a transistor was determined by the signal propagation delay, and thus the gate length of the transistor was an important factor for enhancing the clock cycle time. Currently, however, a wire-delay determines the critical path delay [258]. Since the second half of the 1990s, a longer signal transmission has required a lower resistance, and therefore a copper wire is used now instead of aluminum. Fig. 4.5 shows the relative delay for metal wires used locally and globally. Although the gate delay is scaled down well by shortening the gate length, a global wire results in a relative increase in the delay.

A wider design space introduces a larger number of logic circuits in the space, introducing a greater number of wires to connect among them, and this trend tends to make a longer wire delay based on the logic circuit. Therefore, rather than direct wiring among the modules, packet routing on a chip was considered [146]. Today, this is called an NoC and is a commonly used technique.

4.3.1.2 Energy and power consumption

Energy consumption is important for edge devices using a battery. Energy consumption E can be represented as follows.

$$E \propto V_{dd}^2 \times C \times A \qquad (4.2)$$

where f, V_{dd}, C, and A are the clock frequency, voltage, static capacitance on a chip, and ratio of total number of transistors to the number of active transistors. Dynamic power consumption P can be represented by energy consumption E as follows.

$$P = E \times f \qquad (4.3)$$

The power consumption is converted into thermal heat on the chip. Eq. (4.3) is only for the transistors and does not consider any wires.

For the microprocessors, increasing the number of pipeline stages to increase the clock frequency f involves a larger number of registers to hold the intermediate data, resulting in higher power consumption [321]. A larger number of pipeline stages introduces a higher penalty for a mis-prediction of the branches, and therefore, a superpipeline requires a higher accuracy for the branch prediction [335].

Eq. (4.3) scales the semiconductor process, called Dennard's scaling [120]; after applying a 90-nm process, the current leakage on the transistor is increased, and the voltage cannot be easily scaled down. A shrinkage of the semiconductor process does not contribute to a scale down of voltage V_{dd}.

Thus, we must either decrease the clock frequency f or the active transistor rate A. As shown in Fig. 2.4(b), after the year 2000, difficulties in increasing the clock frequency were caused by a thermal issue, increasing the power consumption. To deal with the problem between semiconductor process scaling and design space scaling, called the dark silicon problem [158], we need to design a logic circuit to balance the design complexity with a wire delay and the power consumption; thus, the execution performance and energy consumption should be balanced. This index is called the energy efficiency.

4.3.1.3 Number of transistors and I/Os

Fig. 4.6 shows the physical resource constraints for the number of transistors and the number of I/O pins on a package. The number of transistors on a chip is for the microprocessors, as shown in Fig. 4.6(a). This shows that the scaling of the number of transistors is done according to Moore's Law.

However, this law is no longer be applicable because the atomic size has been reached. Today, a Fin-FET transistor is used instead of a planer transistor, and applies a fin to make the depletion-layer more effective. The number of fins is slightly increased to maintain the performance of a FIN-FET. Thus, we cannot expect a linear scaling of the number of transistors in the unit area.

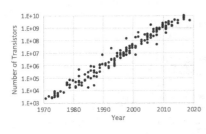

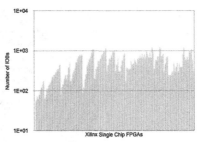

(a) Number of Transistors in the Microproces- (b) Number of IOBs in Xilinx Single Chip FP-
sors.   GAs.

FIGURE 4.6 History of composition.

Regarding the number of I/Os on a chip, the number of configurable user
I/O blocks (IOBs) on an FPGA chip, except for low-end products, is as shown
in Fig. 4.6(b). Note that the plot is not a timeline. The rate of increase has been
stagnated by the packaging technology.

4.3.1.4 Bandwidth hierarchy

Numerous accesses may occur on a specific memory holding multiple variables.
Numerous accesses for writing (called a fan-in), and numerous accesses for
reading (called a fan-out) can also occur, which incur a memory access conflict. Therefore, a hierarchical memory structure was introduced. A traditional
computing system uses the memory hierarchy not only to reduce memory access
latency [124] but also for such conflicts.

An on-chip design can coordinate the resource allocation, and thus a wire-
delay oriented bandwidth hierarchy can be considered to obtain the cost-
performance of the interconnection networks. A higher bandwidth consisting
of a significantly large number of wires can be used for an interconnection network near the functional unit, and creates a tradeoff for a lower level network
having a narrower bandwidth. Between networks, storage is applied to maintain
data reuse, and thus we can see a memory hierarchy.

The peak bandwidth B_{peak} can be calculated using the following equation.

$$B_{peak} = N_{wire} \times f \tag{4.4}$$

where N_{wire} is the number of wires on the interconnection network, which is
observed for estimating the bandwidth. Instead of such a peak bandwidth, we
should take care of the effective bandwidth B_{effect} with overhead C_{ov} for transmission at the start and end. In terms of the number of clock cycles, and the
transmission data size L_{data} in terms of the number of bits in the data, B_{effect}
can be estimated as follows.

$$B_{effect} = \frac{L_{data}}{N_{wire}} \times f \times (C_{ov} + \frac{L_{data}}{N_{wire}})^{-1} \tag{4.5}$$

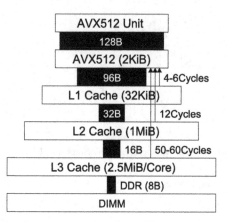

FIGURE 4.7 Bandwidth hierarchy.

$$
= \frac{L_{data}}{C_{ov} \times N_{wire} + L_{data}} f
$$

$$
= \frac{C_{data}}{C_{ov} + C_{data}} N_{wire} \times f
$$

$$
= \frac{C_{data}}{C_{ov} + C_{data}} B_{peak}
$$

where C_{data} is the number of clock cycles used to transmit the data, $C_{data} = L_{data}/N_{wire}$. Here, B_{effect} is always $B_{effect} \leq B_{peak}$. Therefore, overhead C_{ov} and/or N_{wire} determine the effective bandwidth B_{effect}. Namely, large data cancel the effect of the overhead with a large C_{data}, and thus the data streaming is effective.

Fig. 4.7 shows the bandwidth hierarchy in recent traditional computers, in terms of the path width N_{wire}. The figure shows the path from the AVX512 SIMD datapath to the DIMM of the external memory. The path near the datapath has a wider path, and at a longer distance has a narrower path width.

Between the last level cache and the AVX512 register file, a transfer takes more than 50 clock cycles. DIMM access takes hundreds of clock cycles. Storage near the datapath has a smaller size, and at a longer distance has a larger size.

4.3.2 Modular structure and mass production

In early decades, computers were an application-specific machine, such as a differential machine, used to calculate an electricity network. IBM introduced a block called a module, which is a common unit used by computers. This approach brought about regulations of the module, and created a general-purpose computer system with a stored program paradigm.

By coding a module for the design hardware, it can be treated as an instance similar to that supported by object-oriented software programming language. Similar to a software program, using not only an interface as an argument but also the return value, the hardware can be modularized by defining the timing of the interface. Today, we can use the IP of the hardware.

The same logic circuit, such as memory, can be mass-produced. The mass production reduces the effect of the NRE cost, and the effect can set the price lower, and a lower price makes widespread use of memory. Such a market growth introduces a greater mass production and a lower price, and creates a positive spiral. This commoditization makes such a spiral and contributes to mass production, a lower price, and market growth.

Estimating the effect of mass production, the number of dies N_{die} obtained from a wafer having a diameter R_{wafer} can be represented as follows [193]:

$$N_{die} = \frac{\pi \times (R_{wafer}/2)^2}{A_{die}} - \frac{\pi \times R_{wafer}}{\sqrt{2} \times A_{die}} \tag{4.6}$$

$$< \lfloor \frac{A_{wafer}}{A_{die}} \rfloor$$

where $A_{wafer} = \pi \times (R_{wafer}/2)^2$ and A_{die} are the wafer area and die area on process node S_{node}, respectively. The die yield β_{die} can be defined by the wafer yield β_{wafer} and the number of defects in unit area N_{defect} as follows:

$$\beta_{die} = \beta_{wafer} (\frac{1}{1 + N_{defect} \times A_{die}})^N \tag{4.7}$$

where N is a parameter called the process-complexity factor, and has a value of 10 to 14 for a 16-nm process [193].

We must consider the defects in a failed die. The actual available number of dies N_{die}^{yield} is then as follows.

$$N_{die}^{yield} = \beta_{die} \times N_{die} \tag{4.8}$$

In addition to the available number of dies, we must consider the production rate N_{fab} at fabrication. The number of chips that can be shipped to market, N_{chip}^{ship}, can therefore be represented as follows.

$$N_{chip}^{ship} = \min(N_{die}^{yield}, N_{fab}) \tag{4.9}$$

Therefore, we cannot ship at a rate greater than the fabrication throughput N_{fab}. This equation implies that a production adjustment close to the fabrication throughput N_{fab} is necessary; thus we need to maximize the yield β. The gross profit P_{gross} can therefore be as follows.

$$P_{gross} = P_{chip} \times N_{chip}^{ship} \times \gamma - (C_{fab} + C_{NRE}) \tag{4.10}$$

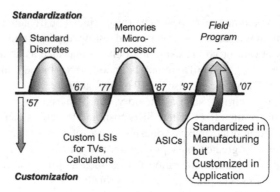

FIGURE 4.8 Makimoto's wave [255].

where P_{chip}, γ, C_{fab}, and C_{NRE} are the price per chip, sales rate, fabrication cost including the test and packaging costs, and NRE cost, respectively. Therefore, the price per chip can be represented as follows.

$$P_{chip} = \frac{P_{gross} + (C_{fab} + C_{NRE})}{\gamma N_{chip}^{ship}} \qquad (4.11)$$

Thus, by setting a reasonable target price per chip, the cost can be a minor factor. In addition, the greater number of chips shipped can lower the price per chip. To increase N_{chip}^{ship}, the die area A_{die} directly affects the price. Therefore, improving the process node, we obtain more dies N_{die} by enlarging the scale factor S, and thus achieving an advanced semiconductor process technology. Note that the NRE cost C_{NRE} and fabrication cost C_{fab} are functions with the scaling, and their value is increased by an advanced process node.

4.3.3 Makimoto's wave

Referring to Makimoto's wave [255], the performance on a general-purpose processor is insufficient for new applications; the trends turned toward an ASIC implementation, after which the microprocessors caught up with the performance requirement. Hence, the trends turned again toward general-purpose processors with a usability oriented generalization capability. This changing trend can be represented as a pendulum between generalization and specialization. See Fig. 4.8.

Originally, an application is an algorithm used to solve a user problem and is a different vector from the generalization and specialization. The generalization and specialization are a tradeoff problem when implementing an application, and within a constraint, function in the design of an application. A general-purpose processor based system cannot be responsible for kick starting the marketing phase for new applications because of a mismatch between the processor specifications and applications. GPUs are a specialized programmable

LSI for huge DLP applications, and FPGAs are a specialized programmable LSI for logic circuit optimization. Based on their stagnated execution, and by advancing for general-purpose use, microprocessors cannot contribute to customer demand. This has created the opportunity to apply GPUs and FPGAs to computing systems.

4.3.4 Design flow

The design flow for an ASIC is almost the same as the flow of an FPGA, as shown in Fig. 2.13, except for the last phases, which involve physical information of the transistor's placement and routing.

Although an FPGA has a building block on a chip, and such devices are used as IPs in HDL, ASIC has a freedom of design, and thus there are few coding constraints. Thus, FPGAs and ASICs have their own coding options.

An NRE cost is a fixed cost for the modeling, design, and development. Such cost includes fees for the tool, library, and IP licensing and worker salaries.

4.4 Domain-specific architecture

4.4.1 Introduction to domain-specific architecture

4.4.1.1 Concept of domain-specific architecture

A traditional computing system faces a stagnation of the execution performance and a significant power consumption. Such problems are caused by a generalization of the microarchitecture used for any workload on the system. One solution is to apply a domain-specific architecture (DSA).

The term "domain-specific" means to target onto a particular application domain, such as deep learning or web-analytics. In addition, the specialization has a certain range. For example, regarding deep learning, targeting onto the inference or training is one specialization, whereas targeting onto the CNN or RNN is another. A DSA is hardware and/or a hardware system targeting a specific application domain.

To develop such an architecture, we first need to know the characteristics of the application, and decide what type of operation and memory access pattern are most frequently used; namely, we need to find the higher priority operations and memory access patterns. This might be quite different from traditional computing systems, or mostly similar, depending on the characteristics. The difference indicates the need for optimization of the application domain.

Chapter 6 introduces methods for improving the execution performance and energy consumption. As described in Chapter 6, most of the execution performance comes from a reduction of the MAC operation workloads. In addition, most of the reduction in energy consumption comes from a reduction of the external memory accesses. A common point of a bottleneck between the execution performance and the energy consumption is a sparsity of the tensor. Therefore, how to obtain the sparsity and how to utilize it are the main theme of a deep learning hardware.

4.4.1.2 Guidelines of domain-specific architecture

In [193], guidelines of a DSA are described, which can be summarized as follows.

1. Reduce traffic and frequency of access to external memory
   A specific application domain has its own datum transfer traffic patterns and frequency of access to external memory. It might include control data such as an instruction and/or data operated by a datapath.
   Therefore, using dedicated memory, as found in the on-chip memory blocks of an FPGA, not only an enhancement of both of the latency and energy consumption but also parallelism of the instruction-level and/or data-level can be enhanced. In addition, particular access patterns can be found. Thus, by specializing the address generation, there is a chance to minimize the traffic and frequency. Moreover, by reducing the amount of normal and/or control data, the data traffic can be reduced. Regarding the deep learning task, the sparsity of the data is the most important point for such a reduction.

2. Invest resources into part specialization
   Traditional microprocessors invest resources into control and memory access, ILP such as a branch prediction and speculative execution, out-of-order execution, superscalar architecture, and cache memory.
   Similarly, DSAs can invest their own enhancement point. For example, DLP is focused on specialized address generation, and a huge amount of on-chip memory and distributed dedicated memory on a chip help in the execution performance and energy consumption.

3. Specialized parallelism matching the domain
   There are three types of parallelism, namely, instruction-, data-, and TLP. A specific application domain has its own parallelisms and balance. By specializing the parallelism to the domain, the architecture obtains a boost in the execution performance.

4. Use of domain-specific programming languages
   A DSA has its own control characteristics, and therefore, a traditional programming language has a relatively large semantic gap between the architecture and language. By preparing a specific programming language for the target domain, the gap is filled, and it becomes easy to control the architecture and steer the data through the architecture. This easily reduces overhead through programming language specialization.

4.4.2 Domain-specific languages

Both hardware and languages are specialized to a particular application domain. Most of such domain-specific languages are based on a rich DLP in the application, which includes the opportunity to enhance both the execution performance and the energy consumption.

4.4.2.1 Halide

Halide is an API-based DSL for standard C, starting from the image processing application domain. Recently, it has also focused on deep learning tasks because image processing tasks have similar characteristics as CNN models.

A program has into two components, one is the computation and the other is storage. The computation part describes a computing kernel representing the operation of the algorithm. The storage part describes a scheduling of the input and output of the kernel. A nested loop in the kernel, the nesting order of which is determined by the schedule, is lowered for easier optimization. The smaller loop is inferred to find its boundary based on a bound inference.

Next, Halide tries to compose a sliding window and fold the storage to minimize the resources needed for the kernel and its interface storage. The code is flattened by the loop, vectorized, and/or unrolled. The flattening results in an array index for access to the linear memory. Finally, the code is emitted to the object code, which can run on the target device.

Halide proposes a domain order, which determines the granularity of the computations and storage using the traditional loop transformation concepts of sequentialization and parallelization, vectorization and unrolling of the loop, loop nest reordering, and finally, recursively splitting the dimensions of the loop to be more easily optimized. First, the splitting is equivalent to vectorization and/or unrolling.

4.5 Machine learning hardware

Machine learning hardware is a DSA specialized for machine learning. Chapter 7 describes a case study of the machine learning hardware including neuromorphic computing and a DNN.

There are several types of machine learning hardware. Using a hardwired neural network model implemented as a logic circuit is a straightforward approach, as shown in Fig. 4.9(a). A programmed neural network model is executed on a logic circuit, and a programmable machine learning hardware is another approach, as shown in Fig. 4.9(b).

Early in the decade, the use of accelerators, which feed the parameters, input the data, and output the inference result, was a major approach. Rather than a hardwired logic circuit, using programmable accelerators with flexibility is currently a major approach. In addition, a programmable deep learning processor has been introduced. In general, programmable machine learning hardware is called a machine learning processor, and it includes a deep learning processor. Research and development on many-core processors, GPUs, and certain types of ASICs have applied a machine learning processor approach. There is a gap between a neural network model and the specifications required for a hardware

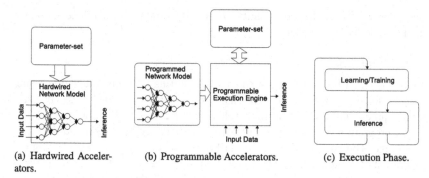

(a) Hardwired Accelerators.   (b) Programmable Accelerators.   (c) Execution Phase.

FIGURE 4.9 Accelerators and execution phase.

implementation, such as IoT and edge devices, and therefore, an optimization fitting the model onto the hardware architecture is needed. IoT and edge devices are application specific and are sufficient for use in a particular neural network model, tending to apply development as an accelerator. Although it depends on their production amount, FPGAs can be a major platform for such devices owing to their reconfigurability, which can allow the user logic circuit to be updated numerous times, and thus after its release, support the ability to fix even minor bugs.

Most machine learning hardware apply two phases: training to obtain the parameters, and an inference to use the parameters, as shown in Fig. 4.9(c). The parameters described in Chapter 6 make up a considerable number of parameters, and not all parameters can be generally applied on a chip, and it may be necessary to load the parameters from external memory. For example, AlexNet described in Chapter 1, which was the winner of the ImageNet Challenge in 2012, has 240 MiB parameters, followed by the neural network model of VGG-16, which has 552 MiB parameters [184]. Other temporal variables also have huge amounts during training, which requires a relatively larger memory size and more memory accesses. Training requires loading, storing, and updating the parameters, as well as inference loads. Therefore, such a memory access is the most influential key to the execution performance and its energy consumption, and thus is a key to the energy efficiency. Most studies to date have focused on this point.

4.6 Analysis of inference and training on deep learning

Let us consider the workload of AlexNet in terms of the scale of the parameters and the activations, the number of operations, the number of execution cycles, and the energy consumption. Regarding the workload, we use a very simple computer system, as shown in Table 4.2, because a simpler system can show inherent characteristics of the neural network model execution, and our purpose of analysis is not for a specific hardware architecture. The processor

TABLE 4.2 System configuration parameters.

Parameters	Unit	Number	Description
Memory Access Overhead	Cycles	8	External Memory Access
Memory Clock Frequency	MHz	400.0	Clock Frequency on Memory Interface
Memory I/O Width	bits	256	
Instruction Issue Width	Instr.	1	
Core Clock Frequency	MHz	400.0	Clock Frequency on Processor
Number of Multipliers	Units	1	
Mlt Operand Width	bits	32/8	
Pipeline Depth of Mlt	Stages	1	
Number of Adders	Units	1	
Add Operand Width	bits	32	
Pipeline Depth of Add	Stages	1	
Number of Dividers	Units	1	
Pipeline Depth of Div	Stages	32	
Operand Width	bits	32	No-Bypassing Path

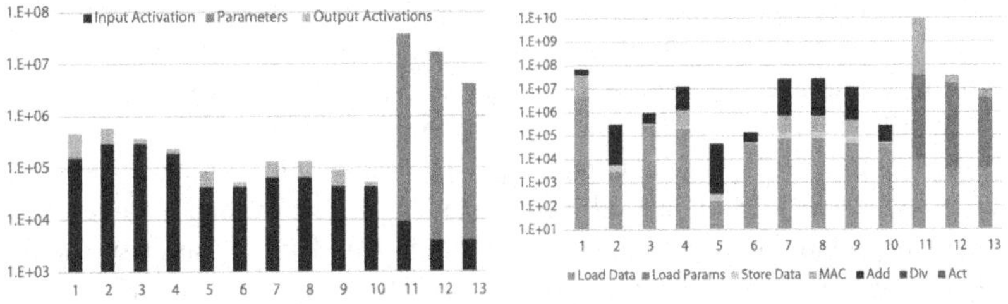

(a) Number of Words.   (b) Number of Operations on the Layers.

FIGURE 4.10 AlexNet profile-I: word size and number of operations on the baseline.

core is pipelined on the EXU, and thus, the number of operations per cycle on the multiplier and adder exceeds 0.5.

4.6.1 Analysis of inference on deep learning

4.6.1.1 Scale of parameters and activations

Fig. 4.10(a) shows the number of words in AlexNet at the log-scale. Output activation is fed into the next layer as an input activation. Thus, the output and input activation words on the next layer are the same. The number of activation words in AlexNet is greater than 8 M. Therefore, we can predict that the workload of the memory accesses for the activation will create a bottleneck of the execution. Most layers, except for fully connected layers, have many activations.

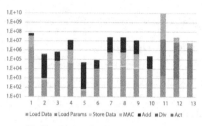
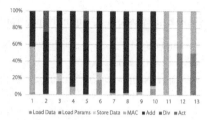

(a) Execution Cycles on the Layers.   (b) Execution Cycle Break Down on the Layers.

FIGURE 4.11 AlexNet profile-II: execution cycles on the baseline.

Fully connected layers consist of matrix-vector multiplication, and therefore, the number of parameters affects the loading of the parameters. We can predict that this introduces many execution cycles on the layer.

4.6.1.2 Operations and execution cycles

Fig. 4.10(b) shows the number of operations on each layer. The trend is similar to the number of words in the AlexNet model, implying that the number of words, namely, memory accesses has a huge impact on the operations.

Fig. 4.11(a) shows the number of execution cycles on AlexNet model. The first layer of a convolution has an impact on the execution cycles because the image flame size and the number of channels create a huge data size; however, most impactful layers are first fully connected requiring huge MACs.

Fig. 4.11(b) shows a breakdown of the execution cycles. Most layers require many execution cycles for memory access of the activation, although the parameters also have an impact on a fully connected layer. The loading parameters for a convolution have a major part in the execution. An MAC operation on the first fully connected layer is also impactful because the scale of the matrix is large, as shown in Fig. 4.11(a). It also shows the importance of an addition required to add elements between channels.

4.6.1.3 Energy consumption

Fig. 4.12(a) shows that most layers require energy for activations and parameters. In particular, a large-scale matrix operation on a fully connected layer requires a large number of parameters, which has an impact on both of the execution cycles and the energy consumption. The trend of the power consumption is directly affected by the number of execution cycles. All layers having parameters incur a significant energy consumption caused by the loading of the parameters from external memory.

The number of inputs coming from the previous layer and the number of outputs from this layer create an extremely large matrix for the parameters, as shown in Fig. 4.10(a). As shown in Fig. 4.12(b), the 11th layer of a fully connected layer consumes a huge amount of energy on the multiplier because of the huge number of MAC operations, as shown in Fig. 4.10(b). Most layers, except

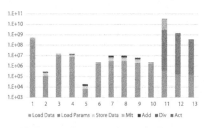

(a) Energy Consumption on the Layers.

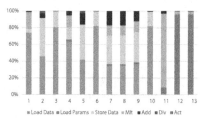

(b) Energy Consumption Breakdown on the Layers.

FIGURE 4.12 AlexNet profile-III: energy consumption on the baseline.

for a fully connected layer, are affected by the adder, and thus the adder is used not only for the addition but also for a comparison of the pooling and a reduction operation on the normalization.

4.6.1.4   Energy efficiency

In its entirety, the hardware requires 2.22 GOPS and 11.3 mW, and thus the power efficiency and energy efficiency are approximately 196.78 GOPS/W and 78.71 EOPS/J, respectively. These numbers are the minimum requirement for a hardware design targeting AlexNet and its variant models.

A convolution requires a huge number of additions based on the number of channels, contributing to a major part of the execution cycles and energy consumption. A fully connected layer requires 90% of the MAC cycles and 90% of the parameter-read energy consumption. The parameters are always an issue regarding the energy consumption.

4.6.2   Analysis of training on deep learning

Let us look into details into the workload for training on AlexNet. At current statement, batch normalization has yet to be analyzed, the operation of which is set to the same level as the inference although the data traffic on the training is correct.

4.6.2.1   Data amount and computation

Fig. 4.13(a) shows the number of words. The fully connected layers have a significant number of data words, particularly gradients to calculate δ (as described in Appendix A), the parameters of which come from the neighbor output layer side. The derivatives of the activation coming from the neighbor input side layer are continuously constructing a portion of the words for the fully connected and convolution layers. Specifically, the number of words for the derivative is a major part in the convolution layer.

Fig. 4.13(b) shows the number of arithmetic operations on every layer. The MAC operation for updating the number of calculations for the parameters is a

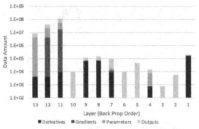

(a) Number of Words for Training.

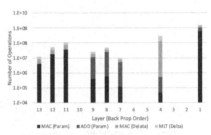

(b) Number of Operations for Training.

FIGURE 4.13   Back propagation characteristics-I on AlexNet.

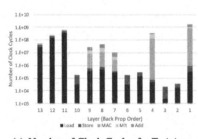

(a) Number of Clock Cycles for Training.

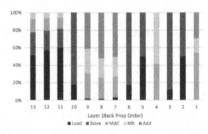

(b) Break-Down for Number of Clock Cycles for Training.

FIGURE 4.14   Back propagation characteristics-II on AlexNet.

major part in both the fully connected and convolution layers. In the case of the convolution layer, the channel-wise addition used to calculate the update amount is also a major part of the operation. An MAC operation and multiplication for a δ calculation are also major parts of the operation for both fully connected and convolution layers.

4.6.2.2   Execution cycles

In fully connected layers, which consist of a significant number of parameters, the number of clock cycles for loading, such as the parameter used to calculate the update amount, is a major part of the layer. The number of clock cycles used to store the temporal variables and the updated parameters for external memory also have an impact on the fully connected layer. The convolution layer also has extremely large parameters depending on the channel depth. The MAC takes a significant number of clock cycles in the convolution layers. A channel-wise addition is also a major part of the convolution layer, as shown in Fig. 4.14(b).

4.6.2.3   Energy consumption

Although the arithmetic has an impact on the number of executed clock cycles, memory access is a major aspect of the energy consumption. The memory access consists of parameters in the layer, parameters (gradient) from the neigh-

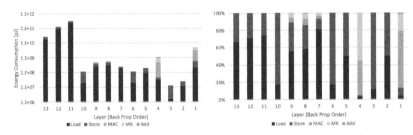

(a) Energy Consumption during Training.   (b) Breakdown for Energy Consumption during Training.

FIGURE 4.15 Back propagation characteristics-III on AlexNet.

bor output side layer, and derivatives from the neighbor input side layers. The convolution layers on the input layer side have no effect on the parameters of the fully connected layer, and thus the MAC can be a major part of the energy consumption. See Fig. 4.15.

Chapter 5

Machine learning model development

Chapter 5 focuses on the development of neural network models. The common development process and software stacks in a GPU environment are first described. Next, to rapidly apply a neural network model, the common method for optimizing the code under a particular platform is described. In general, vectorization and SIMD speed up the operations, and the key to practical coding is to achieve an efficient memory access, and thus memory access optimization is also described. In addition, a common script language used in the development of neural network models, Python, and its virtual machine (VM) are introduced. Finally, CUDA, which is a common computing system using a GPU, is described.

5.1 Development process

This section details the development process used by a machine learning model.

5.1.1 Development cycle

The development of machine learning consists of the design of the neural network model, programming (coding), training, and verification and evaluation. These phases make up the development cycle through which the network model architect performs these processes and provides feedback on the evaluation and verification for the design of a neural network model. This composes the cycle for achieving the required inference accuracy [339], as shown in Fig. 5.1(a).

1. Design
   In the design of a network topology along with its scale, the number of activation functions in each layer and the layer types, the input vector size, the dimensions of the output layer, and the type of training including a loss function should be suitable for the designed neural network model. The output is a specification of the neural network model.
2. Programming (coding)
   The coding of the neural network model is based on the specifications. In general, we can use application programming interfaces (APIs), or a framework, as described in Section 5.1.3, to shorten the development time.

Thinking Machines. https://doi.org/10.1016/B978-0-12-818279-6.00015-3

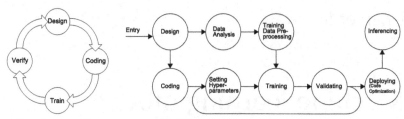

(a) Development Cycle.   (b) Lifecycle of Neural Network Architecture.

FIGURE 5.1 Development cycle and its lifecycle [339].

3. Training

   Training is conducted for the developed neural network model using the training data set, test set, and validation test set. The hyperparameters are adjusted based on the results of the evaluation of the previous cycle.

4. Verification

   The execution is correctly verified based on specifications and validation test set. A performance verification to check the execution and achieve the required inference accuracy as a generalization performance, and/or the response time with test set, is applied. The execution can be further optimized by adjusting the hyperparameters and/or optimizing the neural network model, finally providing feedback to the design phase.

   Details of the lifecycle of the deep learning model are shown in Fig. 5.1(b). The design involves not only a consideration of the architecture of a neural network but also a consideration of the dataset used for training. To achieve a high accuracy of inference and consider the architecture, data must be cleaned and analyzed based on how the sampling data were constructed. After the validation, the prototype code must be reprogrammed for deployment, and thus, this phase involves optimizing the code for the target hardware platform.

5.1.2   Cross-validation

5.1.2.1   Hold-out method

In Section 1.3.3.2, we describe a baseline validation used to split the training dataset into three subsets of training data, namely, validation data, and test data, to avoid combining the training with the evaluation. The mixing of the training data and the validation and test data means revealing the answers to the validation and testing, and thus the accuracy of the inference of the validation and testing can be closed to the training, and vice versa.

   However, such an *overfitting* lacks evidence of the training result. This type of mixing is called a *leakage* [214]. To avoid a leakage, the splitting of the training data is necessary, which is called a *hold-out* method.

5.1.2.2   Cross-validation

A hold-out method simply splits the training dataset into sub-sets, and therefore, can achieve small validation and test data when the training dataset itself is small.

By splitting the dataset into multiple groups, and by assigning one group to a validation and the other groups to training, all datasets can be used for both training and validation [214]. For example, training and validation can be applied four times when splitting the training dataset into four groups. This method is called a *cross-validation* [154].

5.1.2.3   Validation for sequential data

Data consisting of a sequence, such as a timeline, should maintain the order. A simple approach is to make the validation and test data closed to the present data using a hold-out method.

To conduct a cross-validation, for example, let us consider four folds. The cross-validation chunks the dataset into four subsets. The entire procedure consists of four trainings. Initially, the first, second, and third subsets are used for training, and last is used for validation. Next, for the training, the second, third, and fourth subsets are used for training, and first is used for validation. For this third training, the third, fourth, and first subsets are used for training, and the second subset is used for validation. For the last training, the fourth, first, and second subsets are used for training, and third subset is used for validation [214].

5.1.3   Software stacks

A common language used to develop a machine learning model is Python scripting language, as described later. Software stacks are prepared and supported for development, making it possible to achieve high-level coding and portability.

A software stack, from the upper layer to the bottom layer, consists of an API (framework) that provides primitives, which is a commonly used functionality, and supports a graph representation; a library such as NVIDIA's cuDNN, which is optimized to execute on a particular platform hardware; and a numerical operation library such as BLAS for the matrix and vector operations.

Development support such as the Software Design Kit (SDK) is provided.

1. API (framework)

   The application programming interface (API) is a library consisting of functionalities and program routines frequently used in coding. It defines the processing, input and output, data type, and routine. Table 5.1 lists typical open-source APIs.

2. Library

   The library is used for the execution of the API primitives optimized for a specific hardware architecture. By separating the API and library, the framework can be updated for a specific library, and the library can be optimized

TABLE 5.1 Comparison of open source deep learning APIs.

API	Creator	Written in	Interface	Pretrained Models	Web Site
PyTorch	Facebook	C++, Python	C/C++, Python	Yes	[27]
TensorFlow	Google Brain Team	C++, Python	C/C++, Python	No	[174]

for a particular hardware architecture isolated from the framework. Platform hardware development can focus on the development of optimal kernels belonging to the specifications of the API, which can provide a high performance for each hardware platform [133].

- cuDNN
  The cuDNN uses graphics memory on a graphics card and aims to speed up tensor operations such as convolution and linear algebra operations [133].
  Common methods include lowering the degree of dimension, applying a fast Fourier transform (FFT) to a convolution, and directly applying a matrix operation on it, among approaches. The lowering of the degree of dimension from a GPU increases the on-chip memory consumption, and limits the DLP on the GPU, finally increasing traffic for external memory access. In addition, a cuDNN is unsuitable for small tensor operations used in current neural network models such as a CNN. FFT consumes relatively large on-chip memory. To provide a high-performance, a direct matrix operation tends to be optimized for a particular size, and thus is unsuitable for general use. A cuDNN combines a lowering and tiling to improve the memory footprint issue and execution performance for convolutions.
- BLAS
  Basic linear algebra subprograms (BLAS) are used as a library for basic linear algebra operations [238]. These include the vector, matrix-vector, and matrix operations.

Fig. 5.2 shows a flow from the Python program. It invokes an API for a particular part of a common execution, which invokes a library for execution on a particular hardware architecture, and execution on the hardware. The result(s) are returned to a neural network model coded using the Python program.

A lower level software stack invokes an API, and an API invokes a library if it is possible to execute on the GPU, and after the execution is conducted on a GPU, arguments are succeeded from the top layer to the bottom layer. The execution results are returned to the instance of the neural network model program through the API.

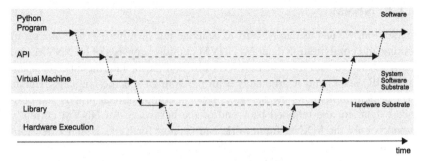

FIGURE 5.2 Program execution through software stack.

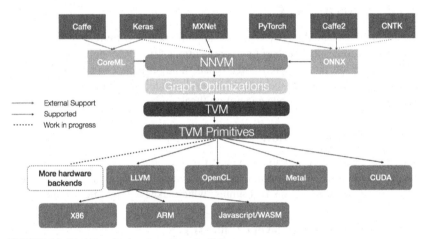

FIGURE 5.3 Tool-flow for deep learning tasks [95].

5.2   Compilers

Various frameworks are available, and users might want to use their preferred framework for such purposes. The framework should be selectable by the user. See Fig. 5.3.

5.2.1   ONNX

Thus, ONNX, which translates among frameworks, is one such choice. Network models described by one specific framework can migrate to another framework.

ONNX is open format, allowing deep learning models to be represented [99]. ONNX models are currently supported by Caffe2, Microsoft Cognitive Toolkit, MXNet, Chainer, PyTorch, and TensorFlow. Any tools exporting ONNX models can benefit from ONNX-compatible runtimes and libraries designed to maximize the performance on some of the best hardware in the industry.

5.2.2 NNVM

In addition, we can use an NNVM to generate our own binary code of a set of routing and configuration data. An NNVM compiler consists of an NNVM, and the result is fed into a TVM [95]. A TVM is a tensor intermediate representation (IR) stack, and it originates from the domain-specific language, Halide [97], which implements the operators used in computational graphs and optimizes them for the targeted back-end of the hardware. An NNVM currently supports only the MXNet framework, and support for Keras is under development; however, we can use the NNVM compiler by applying ONNX, and simply translating the Caffe2 model into an MXNet model as an example.

5.2.3 TensorFlow XLA

Accelerated Linear Algebra (XLA) is a domain-specific compiler for linear algebra that optimizes the TensorFlow computations [100]. Currently, XLA targets both TensorFlow and PyTorch, and consists of target-independent optimizations and analyses, after which it conducts target-dependent optimizations and analyses and a target-specific code generation (back-end).

5.3 Code optimization

Through a code modification applied to fit the characteristics of a particular hardware platform, the program can be executed with a shortened execution time; thus, we can speed up the training, which takes a long time in general.

5.3.1 Extracting data-level parallelism

On a CPU and/or GPU platform, a control flow instruction is executed speculatively, and therefore, a miss-prediction caused by a speculative execution involves large penalties consisting of numerous clock cycles. We can decrease the number of such penalties caused by the speculative executions, by packing several scalar data into a single block, just like a vector, matrix, and/or tensor, which reduce the number of executions for the control flow instruction creating the loop.

5.3.1.1 Vectorization

When the platform supports vector and matrix operations, a compiler generates the vector and/or matrix instructions or routine, and the processor executes using such data block in parallel.

Therefore, we can expect an improved performance with the support. A remarkable performance improvement can be obtained with a small investment, adding a fraction of a logic circuit to support such an execution. Thus, rather than the use of many scalar data for the same execution pattern, to obtain a short execution time, we should use such support of the data-level parallel execution, which takes the array data structure in a program that can be translated into a vector, matrix, and/or tensor, with the appropriate memory allocation, freeing up the memory conflict.

In general, a loop body has two types of data dependency. The loop part consists of a control flow execution such as a loop index calculation, a comparison to exit from the loop, and a branch for a loop-back or the next instruction (basic block). One type is an intra-iteration dependency, which is a data dependency in one iteration of the loop body. The other is an inter-iteration dependency, which is a data dependency across multiple iterations of the loop body. Vectorization must take care of such dependencies, and thus, the opportunity to apply the vectorization is limited. Coding must achieve an easy vectorization by the compiler back-end.

Vectorization removes several instructions composing the control flow and makes repeated executions in the loop; therefore, we cannot expect an improvement when a fraction of the vectorized part in a loop is smaller than the size of the loop (the number of repetitions in the loop part).

5.3.1.2 SIMDization

When an element in packed data has no data dependency, such independent data can be executed at the same time as DLP.

We can expect an $O(N_{par})$-fold speedup if the subdividing of a vector into N_{par} sub-vectors is executed in parallel. Single instruction stream multiple data stream (SIMD) focuses on DLP with multiple independent data and is applied using the same operation at the same time. Such vectorization and SIMD require support by not only hardware applying a parallel execution but also a compiler interpreting the parallel executable instruction stream fragment (a basic block).

SIMDization typically focuses on a part of a loop in the program. When the inner-most loop is able to be unrolled in an N way, we can map $N \leq N_{max}$ lanes of an SIMD operation unit, where N_{max} is the maximum number of lanes in the datapath owing to its data word width. The SIMD assumes that multiple operations at a time do not have intra-iteration dependency in the loop, which needs to chain between statements in the iteration loop body.

5.3.2 Memory access optimization

5.3.2.1 Data structure

Using vectorization and the SIMD of a code describing a neural network model, we obtain a speedup upon execution. However, a realistic execution involves a variable load from and storage to external memory. This also involves a substitution of the operation result with a specific variable before and after the operation. Thus, we need consider the data movement and its data structure on the hardware as a code optimization.

Memory storage is applied by several memory banks, several accesses to the same memory bank at the same time is limited as a logic circuit design, and data allocation onto memory can degrade the performance. For a dataset stored in a memory bank, the program tries to read or achieve write access to several data in the dataset in parallel, and the memory access can then create a bank conflict. This generates a wait delay for sequential access to the memory bank, degrading the performance. We need to maximize the DLP in the program. If such a memory conflict occurs for scalar data, simply adding extra scalar data slot resolves and avoids the issue as a memory map adjustment.

Such phenomena can typically occur on traditional cache memory in a processor. The overhead caused by a memory conflict for a particular element in a tensor variable can be multiple times the number of elements in the tensor variable.[1] To avoid a memory conflict for storage data, the architecture has a buffer; however, if the number of memory write events exceeds the buffer size, it easily degrades the performance from the long delay by the sequential access.

5.3.2.2 Memory allocation

Therefore, we must consider the allocation variables for the memory space. However, we must note that directly allocating the variables onto a memory space eliminates the portability. There is a trade-off between portability and the performance degradation caused by the memory conflict, and we must consider the data structure to suppress such overhead on the memory access for the target hardware. In addition, for a loop in a program, a particular memory access pattern is generally considered, and thus a tiling method [369] can be applied, such as a code part dealing with the inter-iteration data dependency.

5.3.2.3 Data word alignment on memory and cache space

A memory address space is based on byte addressing, in which one address is assigned to one byte, and contiguous addresses arrange contiguous byte-data memory. The memory address space in a traditional computing system is linear. In general, the data type such as char (8-bit), short (16-bit), int (32-bit), and long (64-bit) are aligned onto a linear address space. For example, int is aligned by 4-bytes, and thus, the address from 0x00000004 to 0x00000007 in a 32-bit address space is one data word.

If the computing system has a cache memory for a deep learning task, we must consider the alignment for the cache line in addition to the data type alignment. For example, if the cache memory has a direct mapped cache architecture, and takes a 64-byte cache line and 256 lines, it treats a 32-bit address space as the least significant 6-bit address for mapping to the bytes in the cache line, and the next 8-bits are used for mapping the corresponding data block size to the cache line onto that of a 256-entry. Thus, the upper 18-bits are used for mapping an ID (called a tag), and these 2^{18} blocks compete with one entry of the cache line. In addition, if the unit access of the data block is not on the cache line alignment, the cache memory behavior can be more complex.

---

[1] In fact, it can be multiple times the number of data in the cache memory line (cache line size).

5.4 Python script language and virtual machine

5.4.1 Python and optimizations

C language cannot change the data type because of the type declaration at the beginning of the function description. Dynamic language (called a script language) such as Python does not declare the data type [250]. Python is a simple language, and its code footprint is relatively small. In addition, Python and its environment are open-source and free of charge.

An optimization should be applied through the following steps; however, they tend to be neglected, so we should keep them in mind [175].

1. Profiling what occurs in the code,
2. Improve the slow parts of a code, and
3. Check the updated part with profiling

There are three major reasons for a lower execution performance and high resource consumption [175].

- CPU bound
  This state is a highly computationally demanding workload on a processor. Vectorization and SIMD can relax the pressure. A low workload is related to the memory bound issue, and we need to check the memory bank conflict for operands.
- Memory bound
  A mismatch between the data structure and the algorithm is a state of unnecessary memory accesses and thus creates memory conflicts. We can check this state by calculating the ratio of the total memory accesses to the real number of memory accesses. In terms of operation, this concerns the data structure, and it is important to use the correct structure.
- I/O bound
  This state is a waiting time for the I/O processing. Asynchronous processing is used to eliminate the waiting time, or kick to another task during this state. Multi-threading creates this state.

Optimization on Python has a difficulty of vectorization and SIMDizing owing to its following specifications [175].

1. A Python object does not guarantee an optimal memory allocation
   Python supports garbage collection, an automatic reservation, and its release, and thus a memory fragmentation[2] easily occurs with it.
2. Python applies an auto type setting, and not a compiler, which creates certain issues
   The order of the code execution can be changed dynamically, thus making code (algorithm) optimization difficult.

---

[2] Memory in a computer is managed at a unit size called a page. Memory allocation and release on the virtual memory creates an allocation of several noncontiguous regions in virtual memory. This creates a lower hit rate of the cache memory and degrades the performance.

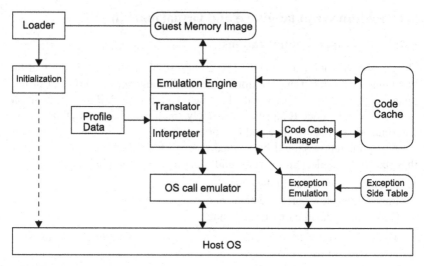

FIGURE 5.4 Process virtual machine block diagram [329].

5.4.2 Virtual machine

Python language is a script language running on a VM. The VM emulates a computer system, particularly a processor and memory system. A processor in Python VM takes a stack type rather than an R-R type, of which all operands are in an RF.[3]

Python VM interprets a Python script as a byte code (instruction set) on the operating software. An emulator engine executes the interpreted instruction fragments. In detail, the emulator engine executes the program corresponding to the byte code.

A VM system constructs a memory image consisting of a running source code, and in the VM, the processor fetches from memory and executes the byte codes. Thus, similar to a traditional computer, it has context information.[4] By switching contexts, several processes can be run on the VM. In addition, a dispatch type (decode and dispatch method) emulator engine executes the interpreted routine corresponding to the byte code implemented with the mechanism of the dispatcher used in a traditional processor.

Fig. 5.4 shows a common block diagram used in a VM [329]. The loader composes a memory image of the source code to execute. It is efficient to interpret from the source code to the byte code during the composition. Read composed byte code from memory image, or interpreting to bytecode when the reading one line of source code which is not yet interpreted to byte code, and

---

[3] An R-R type, i.e., a register-register type, assumes that all operand variables are ready in the RF before use of the variables and/or constants.

[4] The context is the information of the registers in the processor, which maintains the processor status.

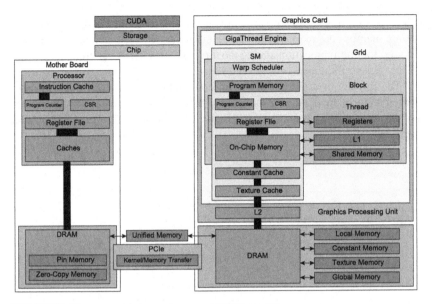

FIGURE 5.5 Memory map between storage and CUDA concept.

VM executes a program corresponding to the byte code. It references the context upon execution and emulates the mechanism of a stack-type processor.

A different platform for a specific VM has different memory addressing modes, and therefore the memory address translation is important. For example, it checks for a small endian (the byte data order is based on the elder address) or a big endian (the byte data order is based on the older address), and fetches the byte data from memory in the VM.

5.5 Compute unified device architecture

Fig. 5.5 shows a mapping between the storage and CUDA concept. The microprocessor and GPU are on the left and right, respectively.

The processor and GPU are connected to each other by a PCIe interconnection network. Communication between them is based on a data transfer in the unified memory address space shared between them. DRAM on both sides is treated as a unified memory. A data transfer passes through the external memory (DRAM) on both sides by the transfer task of CUDA with a memory copy function.

Because the GPU has a DSA, it is specialized for graphics processing. Therefore, it has special storage caches for different tasks. A constant cache and a texture cache in the GPU are mapped to specific regions in the DRAM. Such caches load the constants and textures, respectively, when a cache miss occurs.

A Giga thread engine steers the grids, which are allocated to the SMPs. The selected grid is scheduled and allocated using a warp scheduler. Every thread is allocated to a specific processor, which has a dedicated PC. Level-1 cache and shared memory are mapped onto an on-chip memory. The shared memory can be used for communication among the threads. The CUDA can treat the storage of the register file, level-1 cache, and shared memory.

The threads in a thread block can communicate with each other through shared memory mapped onto the on-chip memory. A thread has a context comparable to that of a traditional processor. The RF is visible on CUDA (as a register).

Chapter 6

Performance improvement
methods

Deeper pipelining, a popular approach for improving the performance, consumes more power by subdividing the module to achieve a higher clock frequency, or the pipeline registers introduce greater power consumption. This chapter introduces techniques that do not consider the use of a deeper pipelining.

Larger amounts of data movement introduce a larger amount of energy consumption on a chip, as well as more external memory access owing to the greater amount of energy consumption and higher latency; thus, the energy efficiency easily decreases from the low performance of the external memory access. CPUs and GPUs have the same problem. However, they do not focus on an external memory access and simply apply a high-performance external memory regulation. They also do not find a way to reduce the energy consumption, and simply apply a quantization with an 8-bit or 16-bit data width. This chapter introduces methods for improving the hardware performance or energy consumption that are commonly used in machine learning hardware.

6.1 Model compression

We call a method that aims to reduce the number of parameters composing a neural network model, a *model compression*. This technique reduces the external memory accesses, thus reducing its traffic and waiting time; thus, the execution time and energy consumption can also be enhanced.

6.1.1 Pruning

When a neural network model has a superfluous representation capability rather than the given training data set, it introduces a superfluous dimension in the input vector, and an overfitting might easily occur. When a neural network model has unnecessary units or edges, one approach is to set the parameters to zero by pruning the edges that do not contribute any output in terms of the accuracy of the inference. This results in a pruned neural network model having only units and edges contributing to the accuracy. However, as the baseline of the pruning, the aim is to simply replace non-impactful parameters with zeros. By optimizing such a sparse neural network using a zero-skipping approach, as explained in Section 6.4, the network model size itself, namely, the footprint, can be reduced.

Thinking Machines. https://doi.org/10.1016/B978-0-12-818279-6.00016-5

105

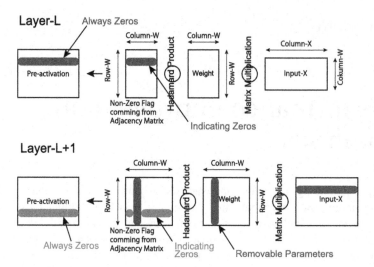

FIGURE 6.1 Domino phenomenon on pruning.

6.1.1.1 Concept of pruning

The edge pruning is achieved when the updated weight is lower than a specific threshold. A value is added as a constant to the bias term when all weights of the original neural network model have been pruned. Pruning can be applied during the training phase. The unit is pruned when all edges connected to the unit are pruned.

Thus, there is the possibility of a domino reduction effect in which the pruning of a unit in a layer introduces zero activation in the next layer, as shown in Fig. 6.1. Therefore, this can create a pruning of the unit in the layer, and the reduction is repeated until the end of the domino effect. Therefore, the pruning creates a sparse tensor of the parameters. The sparse tensor can be composed through an encoding to remove such zeros with CSR or CSC coding, as explained in Section 6.4.2, or a neural network model can be optimized to a smaller scale when the units are removed.

Pruning with zero-skipping resulting in a relatively smaller neural network model has a small parameter set and thus external memory access can be reduced; however, extra data traffic on the chip incurs a waiting time, and the memory size requirement can be reduced.

A granularity of the pruning occurs, as shown in Fig. 6.2. Fine grained pruning aims to prune the random position of an element in a tensor. When a data structure has a row-first order on the tensor, the next coarser-grained level is to prune on the column elements, which takes a constant offset of the position equivalent to the number of columns in the tensor. The next level is to prune the row elements, which are contiguous on the row-first order. These two levels are one-dimension pruning. The fourth level is to prune multiple dimensions as coarse-grained pruning. The fifth level is to prune the tensor itself. Finally, the

Unstructured   Structured

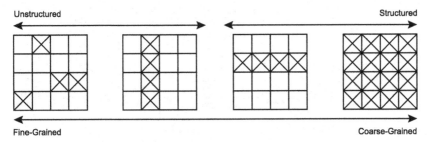

Fine-Grained   Coarse-Grained

FIGURE 6.2 Pruning granularity in tensor.

last level is to prune the neural network model in the case of parallel training, which takes multiple network models having different initial parameters or a different architecture among them.

6.1.1.2 Pruning methods

There are two major methods for pruning [304], namely, a sensitivity method that estimates the sensitivity of the error function on removable elements, and a penalty-term method that adds terms to the objection function, which rewards the network for choosing an efficient solution. The common aspect of both methods is finding weights that do not contribute to the forward propagation. Thus, it is sufficient to find a nearly zero weight during the training, and a certain threshold is used to filter the removable weights.

1. Sensitivity method

   With this method, the contribution of the parameters on the output of the network model is estimated by checking the behavior of the error function. The sensitivity can be estimated based on the behavior of the error function; thus, we can use the derivative of the error function. One approach is to apply the activity of the weight, and the derivative is for the activity. The usual sum of squared errors is used for training. Another approach is to use the sum of the derivative through epochs, and the derivative is for the sum. After training, each weight has an estimated sensitivity, and the lowest sensitivity weights can be deleted. An alternative approach measures the "saliency" of a weight by estimating the second derivative of the error with respect to the weight. This approach uses a Hessian matrix element to represent a derivative of the gradient of the error function E. Pruning is conducted iteratively, i.e., a reasonable error level is trained, the saliences are computed, low saliency weights are deleted, and training is resumed [304].

2. Penalty-term method

   With this method, a cost term is added to the error function. Instead of actually removing the weight and calculating $E(0)$ directly, sensitivity S is approximated by monitoring the sum of all changes experienced by the weight during training. The "energy" expended by a unit, i.e., "how much its activity varies over the training patterns," is an indication of its importance

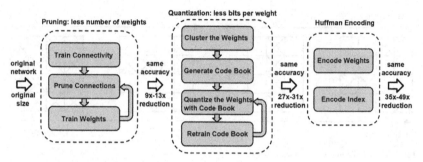

FIGURE 6.3 Pruning example: deep compression [184].

TABLE 6.1 How pruning reduces the number of weights on LeNet-5 [184].

	Conv1	Conv2	ip1	ip2	Total
#Weights [K]	0.5	25	400	5	431
Pruned Weights [%]	66	12	8	19	8

[304]. If the unit changes significantly, it probably encodes significant information. If it does not change significantly, it probably does not carry much information. One approach uses an energy-term to represent the penalty. No overtraining effect was observed despite the long training times, demonstrating that the network was reduced to the optimal number of hidden units. Another approach uses the term of the network complexity, which is represented by the sum of all connection complexities. The error function is modified to minimize the number of hidden units and the magnitudes of the weights. Both require alternative hyperparameters to adjust the effect of the additional cost terms.

6.1.1.3 Example of pruning: deep compression

Fig. 6.3 shows an example of the pruning [184]. The pruning starts from learning the connectivity in the neural network through ordinary training. A sparse structure is obtained. The sparseness is used to prune the connection having a small weight. This pruning is based on a threshold. It finally retrains the neural network to obtain parameters usable for the inference. Non-zero numbers are treated through CSR or CSC coding as described in Section 6.4.2.

Table 6.1 summarizes the effect of the deep compression on the LeNet-5 image classification model. As the table indicates, the convolution layers are reduced by 66% and 12%, respectively. In addition, the total weights after pruning are remarkable, achieving 8% of the original model weight.

6.1.1.4 Unstructured and structured pruning

Elements having a zero value are training-dependent, and we cannot predict where the non-zero elements will be. Thus, the randomness of the position of a non-zero element makes it difficult to compress the model.

To make the compression easier, structural pruning has been studied. Structured pruning aims to prune the specific position to be easily create a group of zeros and non-zeros in the tensor. Structured pruning reduces the overhead of indexing the non-zero position described in Section 6.1.1.4, and thus helps simplify the hardware.

6.1.1.5 Difference from dropout and DropConnect

Dropout and DropConnect conduct a pruning based on a probability that every epoch has a different pruning rather than a contribution metric and a certain threshold; these randomly remove the units or edges as described in Section 6.1.2 and Section 6.1.3.1 when the training phase is conducted. In addition, these techniques apply a reconstruction using the removed units and edges because the purpose is to enhance the parameter value to achieve a greater feature representation to finally obtain a high inference accuracy. During the inference phase, these techniques do not contribute to the number of parameters and unit reductions, although pruning does contribute to this purpose. Thus, pruning contributes to a reduction of the computational complexity, on-chip memory size, on-chip traffic, and finally, an improved energy-efficiency.

6.1.2 Dropout

Large networks are also slow to use, making it difficult to deal with an overfitting by combining the predictions of many different large neural nets at test time [336]. A dropout is a technique for used to address this problem.

6.1.2.1 Concept of a dropout

A dropout is used to invalidate an activation function in an MLP network during training. Which activation function in a layer is dropped is determined based on the probability. One epoch of training can reduce the number of activation functions, and thus its input edges, namely, weights connected to the function, can be removed. In addition, this method does not require holding the activations and outputs of the derivative of the activation function. Thus, it creates a relatively smaller footprint for a temporal dataset. For example, the use of a sparse representation for a parameter tensor with an artificial masking of the weight is effective at reducing the footprint while maintaining the original tensor.

6.1.2.2 Dropout method

Fig. 6.4(a) and Fig. 6.4(b) show a dropout on a different epoch. For a dropout, the activation function(s) is randomly selected based on the probability, which is

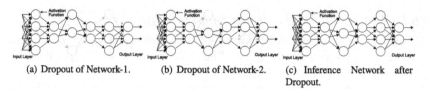

(a) Dropout of Network-1. (b) Dropout of Network-2. (c) Inference Network after Dropout.

FIGURE 6.4 Dropout method.

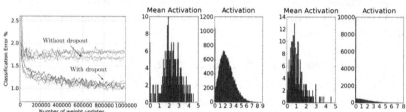

(a) Error Rate without and with Dropout. (b) Sparsity without Dropout. (c) Sparsity with Dropout $(p = 0.5)$.

FIGURE 6.5 Error rate and sparsity with dropout [336].

the rate of how many nodes are dropped. At testing and after deployment of the neural network, every weight is multiplied by the probability of being dropped on the layer to adjust the value of the activation because the number of dropped nodes is equivalent to the probability.

In [336], the characteristics of a dropout are noted. Because a dropout can be viewed as a stochastic regularization technique, it is natural to consider its deterministic counterpart, which is obtained by marginalizing the noise. In this study [336], we show that, in a simple case, a dropout can be analytically marginalized to obtain a deterministic regularization method. A dropout can be interpreted as a method to regularize a neural network by adding noise to its hidden units. During a dropout, we minimize the loss function stochastically under a noise distribution. This can be viewed as minimizing an expected loss function.

By using a Bernoulli distribution to select the nodes to drop, the pre-activation $z_i^{(l)}$ can be represented as follows.

$$r_j^{(l-1)} \sim Bernoulli(p) \tag{6.1}$$

$$z_i^{(l)} = w_i^{(l)}(r_j^{(l)} \circledast x_j^{(l-1)}) + b_i^{(l)} \tag{6.2}$$

where $r^{(l)}$ operates as a mask for the node. This method is effective at reducing the units in a fully connected layer at training time. A dropout patent was recently activated by Google [197].

Fig. 6.5(a) shows the error rate without and with a dropout on various neural network models. Clearly, applying a dropout enhances the accuracy of the inference. The sparsity is changed from poor in terms of activation, shown in

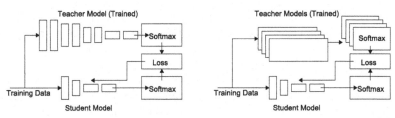

(a) Distilling using Large-scale Teacher Model. (b) Distilling using Ensemble of Teacher Models.

FIGURE 6.6 Distillation method.

Fig. 6.5(b), to rich, as shown in Fig. 6.5(c). Most activations are close to zero, and there are only a few high values.

6.1.3 DropConnect

6.1.3.1 Concept of DropConnect

A dropout invalidates the activation functions with the probability on each layer; similarly, DropConnect invalidates edges with a probability [363]. Thus, this technique is a generalized model of a dropout. Namely, DropConnect is equivalent to a dropout when all edges for one activation function are removed. Similar to a dropout, this method is effective at reducing the edges in a fully connected layer.

6.1.3.2 DropConnect method

DropConnect requires the probability p and an invalidation of each edge on each layer for an effective drop. A set of validation flags can be obtained as follows [363].

$$M_{i,j}^{(l-1)} \sim Bernoulli(p) \qquad (6.3)$$

The M is equivalent to a masking matrix for the weight matrix. A pre-activation can then be applied as follows [363].

$$z_i^{(l)} = M_{i,j}^{(l-1)} \circledast w_i^{(l)} x_j^{(l-1)} + b_i^{(l)} \qquad (6.4)$$

6.1.4 Distillation

6.1.4.1 Concept of distillation

This approach focuses on the training of a small-scale neural network model distilled from a trained neural network model. After the training of the small-scale neural network, it succeeds in the trained neural network's inference performance. See Fig. 6.6.

Therefore, it operates with a smaller number of parameters on a smaller scale neural network because a small scale has a smaller number of parameters, a smaller number of units in every layer, and a smaller number of layers than a trained neural network model. Thus, the loading parameters are relatively smaller in number, and are executed with a small computational complexity and thus a lower latency on a smaller network topology.

The ordinary-scale trained neural network teaches a small-scale network model as a student. Therefore, a trained neural network model and a small-scale neural network are called the teacher and student models, respectively. As the original idea, knowledge is distilled from the teacher model to the student model [196]. In general, outputs before the softmax model is applied have common features across classes, and the distillation focuses on correctly recognizing the unknown data when using the outputs.

The student model can use the teacher's prediction and labels, and a loss of the use of a label is called a hard-target loss; otherwise, a loss of the use of the teacher's prediction is called a soft-target loss.

6.1.4.2 Distillation method

The distillation focuses on the classification problem, which uses the softmax function, which is represented as follows.

$$softmax(x_i) = \frac{e^{x_i}}{\sum_j e^{x_j}} \tag{6.5}$$

This function shows the probability for each class. The original approach uses temperature T in softmax as follows [196].

$$softmax_{distil}(x_i) = \frac{e^{\frac{x_i}{T}}}{\sum_j e^{\frac{x_j}{T}}} \tag{6.6}$$

A larger T makes a softer output distribution. The hyperparameter T makes it possible to efficiently transfer knowledge from the teacher model to the student model. The teacher and student models apply the modified softmax, and the student applies a loss function of the cross-entropy as follows [196].

$$Loss_{student} = -\sum_i softmax(i)_{distil}^{teacher} \log(softmax(i)_{distil}^{student}) \tag{6.7}$$

Note that the modified softmax has hyperparameter T, which makes its derivative $1/T^2$ times smaller, and therefore, amplification by T^2 is necessary for use of the soft-target loss.

Another study [113] used the L2 norm for the loss in the student model as follows.

$$Loss_{student} = \frac{1}{2}||z - v||_2^2 \tag{6.8}$$

where v and z are the outputs before softmax is applied on the teacher and student models, respectively.

TABLE 6.2 Number of parameters and inference errors through distillation [143].

Model	Parameters	MADs	Top-1 [%]	Top-5 [%]
ResNet34(T)	28.1 [M]	3.669 [G]	26.73	8.57
ResNet18(S)	11.7 [M]	1.818 [G]	30.36	11.02
ResNet34G(S)	8.1 [M]	1.395 [G]	26.61	8.62

6.1.4.3   Effect of distillation

Table 6.2 shows the effect of the distillation on the ResNet models. The first row shows the teacher model (labeled as T), which has 28.1 million parameters and an error rate of 26.73 and 8.57%, respectively. The second and third rows show the student model; the smaller scale model has less than half the number of parameters and approximately a 3 point drop inference accuracy. In addition, the total number of multiply-adds (MADs) is also reduced by half. It should be noted that, although the same scale model as used in the tuning technique has fewer parameters, the accuracy of the inference is improved.

6.1.5   Principal component analysis

6.1.5.1   Concept of PCA

A principal component analysis (PCA) is a method for linearly transforming from the original input data to a space having a non-correlation among the elements of the input data and thus having a small number of elements.

We can see that the input vector has its own dispersion in the plotting, and can be mapped onto the axis after its rotation. This is applied to map the dispersion of D-dimensions onto lower dimensions such as $(D - 1)$-dimensions. Repeating this process, lower dimensions have less information, and thus the PCA is a lossy approximation method. A smaller input vector can potentially achieve a relatively smaller neural network model. It trains with a lowered training dataset, and it needs a lowering of the input vector and a reconstruction of the output on the output layer when applied to the inference.

6.1.5.2   PCA method

Let us set input vector x having m elements (m-dimension) and a two-dimensional space. By plotting the elements, it will show its own dispersion. First, we need to calculate a covariance matrix Σ [25].

$$\Sigma = \frac{1}{m} \sum_{i=1}^{m} (x^{(i)})(x^{(i)})^{\top} \tag{6.9}$$

We can then calculate eigenvectors u_1, u_2, and finally u_n. Matrix U can be formed by setting the eigenvectors to the column of U. The input vector can be rotated to x_{rot} through the following equation [25].

$$x_{rot} = U^\top x = [u_1^\top x \quad u_2^\top x]^\top \tag{6.10}$$

Of course, the inverse rotation is $U x_{rot} = x$ $(UU^\top = I)$. The rotated input data can be mapped to lower dimensions $\tilde{x}^{(i)}$ as follows.

$$\tilde{x}^{(i)} = x_{rot,1}^{(i)} = u_1^\top x^{(i)} \tag{6.11}$$

In $1 \le i \le n$, for $k \in i$, after k reaches zero, it can achieve a light weight. We then obtain the lowered input vector for n-lowering.

6.1.6 Weight-sharing

Note that this weight-sharing is different from a weight-sharing applied to train.

6.1.6.1 Concept of weight-sharing

The number of weights in the parameter set in each layer is determined by the dimensions of the input activation and the number of activation functions in the layer. By sharing the weights, in an intra-layer, or in an inter-layer, this approach reduces the total number of weights. This technique is called weight-sharing. By preparing a mechanism to share the weights having the same value, the total number of weights can be reduced. An edge-cutting, described in Section 6.2.3, can be applied to create a common value.

6.1.6.2 Example weight-sharing method

Fig. 6.7 shows the method of weight-sharing with an approximation [183]. The upper part shows how the indexes are used for the sharing. One index is an identification for an approximation. The values of the weight within the same range have the same index. In this example, the weight-sharing makes four groups.

The complexity of this method is based on how to create a set of indexes in the parameter tensor. It is necessary to determine every range of indexing and to seek one in a specific index in the tensor. In addition, it is also necessary to create a set of indexes from the tensor, which requires other storage resources proportional to the maximum scale of the supported tensor.

The bottom part shows the gradients, which are grouped by the indexes; one group is summed (reduced), but is not divided by 4 to generate the average value because we want to make "four" gradient values. The summed value is used for the weight-updating.

Fig. 6.8(a) shows the data size applied with the weight-sharing. The X- and Y-axes are the total tensor size in terms of the number of elements, and the quantized word width in terms of the bits, respectively. The word width grows by the log-scale because of an equivalent cluster index based on the number of classes for the quantization, although the total tensor size increases linearly. The

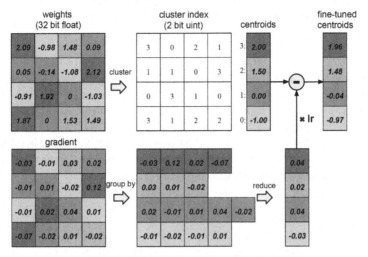

FIGURE 6.7 Weight-sharing and weight-updating with approximation [183].

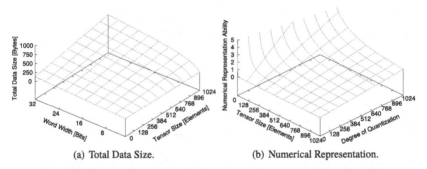

(a) Total Data Size.   (b) Numerical Representation.

FIGURE 6.8 Effect of weight-sharing.

weight-sharing is suitable for a small-scale tensor, which can have a relatively adequate number of quantized values, as shown in Fig. 6.8(b). This implies that the probability of sharing or the appearance of a common value should be set relatively large in the tensor; however, this will probably introduce a difficulty in terms of efficient training.

6.1.6.3 Tensor approximation

An alternate way to reduce the number of elements in the parameter tensor is to approximate the tensor by composing a set of lower-rank tensors. Before approximating this, we need to factorize the tensor. Let us assume that tensor A having $n \times n$ dimensions has an eigenvalue of λ and an eigenvector x as follows.

$$Ax = \lambda x \tag{6.12}$$

The equation can be reformed as follows.

$$(A - \lambda I)x = 0 \tag{6.13}$$

where I is an identity tensor. Its determination then equals zero. Thus, we obtain a factorized tensor of A by factorizing the determination. In addition, we obtain the eigenvectors using Eq. (6.13). The number of eigenvectors we obtain reaches n.

Eigenvalue decomposition is the first step to factorize the tensor in a special case of a symmetric tensor. Tensor A can be represented by diagonal tensor D, the off-diagonal elements of which are zero.

$$A = PDP^{-1} \tag{6.14}$$

where the diagonal elements of D are the eigenvalue of the tensor A. By calculating tensor P after obtaining the eigenvalues, we obtain the diagonal tensor D, and thus we finally obtain a decomposed tensor, which is represented through Eq. (6.14).

We can extend the decomposition into an ordinary tensor having an asymmetric shape, which is called a singular value decomposition (SVD), which is represented as follows.

$$A = U\Sigma V^\top \tag{6.15}$$

Tensor U and V are symmetric tensors, and Σ is an asymmetric tensor equivalent to diagonal tensor D shown in Eq. (6.14). The asymmetric tensor, called a singular value matrix Σ, needs a padding with zero. The singular value matrix has a non-zero diagonal element equal to the square root of an eigenvalue. The right singular matrix V is obtained by calculating the eigenvalue decomposition of $A^\top A$. At that time, we also obtain Σ by calculating the square root of the eigenvalue. After the calculation, we can calculate the left singular matrix U, whose column vector u_i is as follows.

$$u_i = \frac{1}{\sqrt{\lambda_i}} A v_i \tag{6.16}$$

where v_i is the i-th column vector of the right singular tensor V. We can then reform Eq. (6.16). The column vector A_i of tensor A can be defined as follows.

$$A_i = u_i v_i^\top \tag{6.17}$$

Finally, we obtain an approximated tensor A composed with r-rank lower tensors as follows.

$$A = \sum_{i}^{r} \sqrt{\lambda_i} A_i \tag{6.18}$$

6.2 Numerical compression

We call techniques for removing or reducing the size of each element composing a tensor parameter compression.

6.2.1 Quantization and numerical precision

6.2.1.1 Direct quantization

Quantization is used to make a discrete numerical representation under a data word constraint of the word width in terms of the number of bits representing a single word.

Direct quantization $DQ(*)$ for an unsigned integer representation is calculated using the following equation.

$$DQ(x) = \lfloor \frac{2^Q - 1}{2^W - 1} x \rceil \tag{6.19}$$

where Q and W are the bit width after the quantization and before the quantization, or $2^W - 1$ is an absolute maximum number of numerical representations, respectively. The input x and output of $DQ(x)$ has a numerical gap, which is called a quantization error or quantization noise. If W is larger, then the error is not correlative to the input x; however, when W is smaller, then the error is correlative to the input x and creates distortion [348].

6.2.1.2 Linear quantization

In the case of quantization from a floating-point number, it takes a wider range for the representation, and therefore the quantization cannot be effectively covered or a sparse number representation created. Thus, such a quantization needs a clipping, which makes the maximum and minimum numbers of input that x can have as $Clip(x) = \min(MIN, \max(MAX, x))$. We can make such a linear quantization $LQ(*)$ as follows.

$$LQ(x) = Clip(\lfloor S \times x \rceil) \tag{6.20}$$

where S^x is the quantization scaling-factor, which is determined as follows. The clip function takes MIN and MAX as $2^{Q-1} - 1$ with a signed flag bit.

$$S = \frac{MAX}{2^{W-1} - 1} \tag{6.21}$$

where the W-bit is also assumed to take a signed flag.

6.2.1.3 Lower numerical precision

Because a numerical representation of a single precision floating-point has a common representation, there have been several reports demonstrating no need

TABLE 6.3 Numerical representation of number.

Format	Representation of x
FP32	$-1^{x[31]}2^{x[30:23]-128}\{1.x[22:0]\}$
FP16	$-1^{x[15]}2^{x[14:10]-16}\{1.x[9:0]\}$
BF16	$-1^{x[15]}2^{x[14:7]-128}\{1.x[6:0]\}$
FX32	$-1^{x[31]}\{(x[31])\ ?\ \tilde{x}[30:30-Q].x[30-Q-1:0]+1:x[30:30-Q].x[30-Q-1:0]\}$
FX16	$-1^{x[15]}\{(x[15])\ ?\ \tilde{x}[14:14-Q].x[14-Q-1:0]+1:x[14:14-Q].x[14-Q-1:0]\}$
Int8	$-1^{x[7]}\{(x[7])?\ \tilde{x}[6:0]+1:x[6:0]\}$
Ternary	$\{-1,0,+1\}$
Binary	$\{-1,+1\}$

for such a highly numerical representation [317]. This started from a 16-bit fixed-point representation in the year 2017, which achieved a binary representation taking only a value of -1 or $+1$. Table 6.3 shows a summary of the numerical representation. FP, BF, and FX are the floating-point, BFloat, and fixed-point, respectively.

First, these are applied to the parameters; currently, they are also applied to activation. In addition, for not only inference, but also training, a gradient calculation is also considered to take a binary calculation.

A single precision floating-point arithmetic operation has a common data precision, and research on the relationship between the inference accuracy and data precision has shown that a lower precision is sufficient for the inference [317]. A necessary numerical precision on a layer seems to be related to the preceding and following layers. A multiplier on a multiply-add (MAD) can have a lower precision and can take an integer and/or a fixed-point representation; however, the sum of such products cannot be lower because the bit width of the integer representation determines how many synapses, namely, how many weights, are treated on a particular neuron (activation function). Such a limitation can easily be achieved, and a saturation is needed; however, this often creates a saturation on a large-scale neural network model. For example, the Xilinx report [166] shows an 8-bit integer, which might be on the multiplier of the MAD configured on the DSP block.

1. BFloat16 [93][215]

    BFloat16 is equivalent to the most significant 16-bit part of a single precision floating-point representation (FP32) with a round to nearest even (RNE) for conversion from FP32. Therefore, it can be simply converted from FP32 into BFloat16 by cutting-off the least significant 16-bit mantissa part in the FP32 number and calculating the RNE number using this part. It supports NaNs, similar to FP32.

    There are two advantages of such a representation. One advantage is the simple conversion to/from FP32. Another advantage is the range of BFloat16 being the same as that of FP32 (they have the same exponent range). This advantage eliminates the need for hyper parameter tuning, which is required for other numerical representations to enhance the convergence. The mixing of BFloat16 on the multiplication and FP32 on the addition (accumulation) achieves a training result near the full FP32, meaning nearly the same convergence occurs between the full FP32 training and mixed training.

2. 16-bit fixed-point number [177]

For a narrow width fixed-point representation, a carry-out from a limited width must be considered, which results in an unexpected smaller number. Studies have reported that even if a 16-bit fixed-point representation is taken, a similar accuracy of the inference as the single precision floating-point arithmetic can be obtained by applying appropriate rounding to the fixed-point.

Two approaches for rounding have been proposed, round-to-nearest and stochastic rounding. The stochastic round approach obtains an inference accuracy comparable to that of a single precision floating-point.

3. Dynamic precision [140]

For a fixed-point representation, although a fraction requires a shift operation for the multiplication and division, addition and subtraction can be applied using ordinary integer arithmetic. Studies have assumed that an integer has the same width across parameters and input activation on a particular layer, and a dynamically changing width of the fraction has been proposed. This approach checks the overflow rate, which increases the fraction width when the rate is smaller than that of the parameters and input activation, and decreases the fraction width when the rate is twice that of the parameters and input activation. Forward and backward propagations set a 10-bit and 12-bit fraction when updating the parameters, achieving a similar inference error rate as a single precision floating-point arithmetic.

4. BinaryConnect [142]

Stochastic binarization has also been studied. A parameter is a real number, and parameters are fed into a hard-sigmoid for the inference and training, and binarizing to $+1$ or -1 using a threshold of 0.5. If the hard-sigmoid ($H\_sigmoid(x) = max(0, min(1, \frac{x+1}{2}))$) is less than or equal to 0.5 then -1 is set as the parameter, and if it is greater than 0.5, then $+1$ is set. When updating the parameter, a parameter having an original real number is clipped. Using this approach, a multiplier is unnecessary for the inference and training, and simply checking the sign flag for the addition and subtraction on an adder is sufficient.

5. BinaryNet [141]

The approach on BinaryNet for binarization is different from that of BinaryConnect. Only a sign flag is checked. By setting a positive or zero value to $+1$, and a negative value to -1, a multiplication can be replaced with an XNOR operation. Thus, this approach can remove multipliers, and can improve the integration and achieve a higher parallel operation. At inference, the input vector on the input layer needs an XNOR operation with its bit field width, and the following layers can apply the XNOR-based dot-product.

Both inference and training use batch normalization. Within the benchmarks, although a larger test error rate than that of BinaryConnect occurs, the learning speed is rapid.

6. **Binary-weight-networks [301]**
A binary-weight-network has binary (a single bit) parameters. The convolution can be $I W \approx \alpha(I B)$, where I and B are the input and $\{-1, +1\}$, respectively. Thus, a represented by 1-bit, α is the scaling coefficient for the approximation. Here, -1 is set as the parameter when B has a sign flag assertion; otherwise, $+1$ is set as the parameter. Here, α has the following average norm-1:

$$\frac{||W||_{l1}}{n} = \frac{||W||_{l1}}{c \times w \times h} \qquad (6.22)$$

where c, w, and h are the number of channels, filter (kernel) width, and filter (kernel) height, respectively. Thus, each row on $\alpha(I B)$ can be obtained by scaling with α after adding or subtracting each I row with B. Binarization is applied at inference and training, but not when updating the parameters, similar to BinaryNet.

7. **XNOR-Nets [301]**
XNOR-Net binarizes not only parameters but also the input vector. A sign flag of the element in the input vector is also checked, and the assertion is set as -1; otherwise $+1$ is set, and thus we obtain input $I = \{-1, +1\}$. The convolution can be as follows.

$$I W \approx [sign(I) \circledast sign(W)] \odot K \odot \alpha \qquad (6.23)$$

where K is a filter (kernel), and $sign(I)$ is a binarization function by checking the sign flag of I, where $\circledast$ is a dot-product between the row-element in $sign(I)$ and the column-element in $sign(W)$. The dot-product can be implemented using XNOR and a population counter. Similar to BinaryNet, the dot-product is not used for updating the parameters.

8. **Quantized neural networks [203]**
A gradient calculation on BinaryNet and XNOR-Net uses a real number. A quantized neural network uses binarization for the gradient descent calculation. This method uses an approximation. Quantization with a logarithmic quantization [266]. *Logarithmic_quantization*(x, *bitwidth*) equals the following equation:

$$Logarithmic\_quantization(x, bitwidth) = Clip(AP2(x), minV, maxV).$$
$$(6.24)$$

where $AP2(x)$, $minV$, and $maxV$ are a power of 2 and are close to the x value, and the minimum and maximum quantization range, respectively. Batch normalization also uses an approximation based on a shift operation. The input vector element s can be obtained using the equation $s = \sum_{n=1}^{m} 2^{n-1}(x^n \cdot w^b)$, where m and w^b are the bit-field width of the input

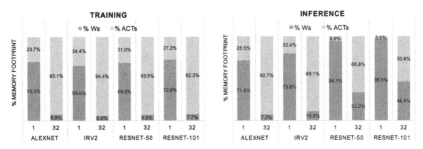

FIGURE 6.9 Memory footprint of activations (ACTs) and weights (W) [265].

vector element and 1-bit weight vector having k elements, respectively. The dot-product is applied using an XOR operation and accumulates through a population counter. Finally, the m-bit accumulation result is batch normalized, and finally the input vector is obtained. It can be scaled from a binary to a multi-bit representation.

6.2.2 Impact on memory footprint and inference accuracy

Let us consider several methods to make a numerical representation having a lower precision. Such methods have a trade-off between the representation and accuracy of the inference, which decreases when less numerical information is provided.

6.2.2.1 Memory footprint

A lower precision directly contributes to the amount of data for the activations and parameters used in storage because of the small total data size.

Fig. 6.9 shows the memory footprint of the activations and weight on batch sizes of 1 and 32 for training and inference [265]. A large mini-batch size has a relatively large number of activations for both training and inference. The activation can be more than 90% of the total data in some neural network models. Therefore, compression for the activation can be effective, especially when an ReLU activation function having the potential of halving the number of activations can reach zero on average. In addition, inference has slightly higher weights or relatively fewer activations in the evaluated neural network models.

Fig. 6.10 shows the ECR, which is calculated based on the effective uncompressed size divided by the compressed size. Direct quantization cannot effectively reduce the footprint. A 5-bit quantization shows the best ECR except for the other approaches after retraining in which the superfluous quantization (e.g., 2-bit) is more efficient in terms of memory usage for weights on larger network models. Retrained quantization has a greater effect on a reduction of the footprint for the weights. A superfluous and lower quantization also achieves a better ECR.

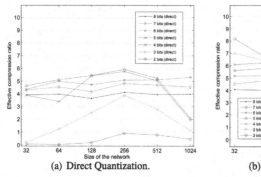

FIGURE 6.10 Effective compression ratio [342].

TABLE 6.4 Impact of fixed-point computations on error rate [129].

Inference	Training	Error [%]
Floating-Point	Floating-Point	0.82
Fixed-Point (16 bits)	Floating-Point	0.83
Fixed-Point (32 bits)	Floating-Point	0.83
Fixed-Point (16 bits)	Fixed-Point (16 bits)	(no convergence)
Fixed-Point (16 bits)	Fixed-Point (32 bits)	0.91

XNOR-Net [301] has 16, 1.5, and 7.4 MB memory footprints for VGG-19, ResNet-18, and AlexNet, respectively. While doubling the precision at 1 GB, 100 MB, and 475 MB, respectively, the binarization dramatically decreases the memory footprint through the smallest representation.

6.2.2.2 Side-effect on inference accuracy

Table 6.4 [129] shows the error rates under a fixed-point precision with different combinations of numerical representation on the inference and training. Under non-convergence at a 16-bit fixed-point used for training, a 16-bit numerical representation is insufficient for training because of the small fraction of gradient parameters used in the calculation. In addition, the need for floating-point precision for training is demonstrated, and a fixed-point precision for training increases the error. This result supports a mixed precision architecture.

Table 6.5 [179] shows the accuracy of the inference on several neural network models with different fixed-point precision levels ranging from 2-bit to 8-bit combinations of activations, and the parameters of the convolution layer and fully connected layer. A decrease in accuracy of the inference ranging from 0.1 to 2.3 points is shown. This is a serious problem of the quantization. It seems that a neural network model having a relatively lower complexity does not have

TABLE 6.5 CNN models with fixed-point precision [179].

Neural Network Model	Layer Outputs [Bits]	Conv Params [Bits]	FC Params [Bits]	FP32 Baseline Accuracy [%]	Fixed-Point Accuracy [%]
LeNet (Exp1)	4	4	4	99.1	99.0 (98.7)
LeNet (Exp2)	4	2	2	99.1	98.8 (98.0)
Full CIFAR-10	8	8	8	81.7	81.4 (80.6)
SqueezeNet (top-1)	8	8	8	57.7	57.1 (55.2)
CaffeNet (top-1)	8	8	8	56.9	56.0 (55.8)
GoogLeNet (top-1)	8	8	8	68.9	66.6 (66.1)

TABLE 6.6 AlexNet top-1 validation accuracy [265].

	32b A	8b A	4b A	2b A	1b A [%]
32b W	57.2	54.3	54.4	52.7	–
8b W	–	54.5	53.2	51.5	–
4b W	–	54.2	54.4	52.4	–
2b W	57.5	50.2	50.5	51.3	–
1b W	56.8	–	–	–	44.2

an impact on the inference accuracy when changing to an architecture with a lower numerical precision.

Table 6.6 shows the inference accuracy for AlexNet with a combination of activation (A) and weight (W) [265]. The top-1 accuracy is decreased by a superfluous quantization, such as a 1-bit activation and weight. At lower than a 4-bit quantization, the accuracy of the inference is easily decreased. This indicates that more quantization on the weight rather than on the activation has a greater impact on the inference accuracy. This means that a quantization of the parameters should be careful applied to suppress errors in the inference, implying that the training needs a quantization error interpolation as a regularization term of the cost function.

Fig. 6.11 shows the accuracy against the average codeword length per network parameter after network quantization for a 32-layer ResNet [135]. A codeword is equivalent to the bit width for the parameter. By quantizing more aggressively, i.e., less than 7-bit, the accuracy of the inference decreases. In addition, an aggressive quantization for the activation rather than the parameters introduces more errors. Both with and without fine-tuning show that a Hessian-weighted k-means quantization method achieves the best accuracy for the observed network model. The fine-tuning can suppress the decrease in accuracy under a lower numerical precision.

Fig. 6.12 shows an error with a floating-point, 2-bit direct quantization of all weights, and 2-bit direct quantization only on the weight groups "In-h1," "In-h2," and "In-h4," on different network sizes [342]. A trend in which a large-scale

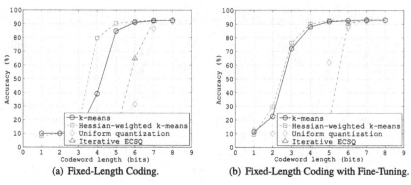

FIGURE 6.11 Accuracy vs. average codeword length [135].

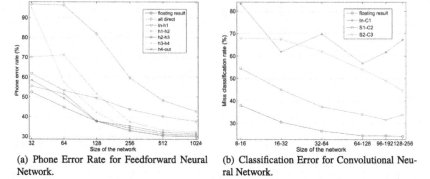

(a) Phone Error Rate for Feedforward Neural Network.

(b) Classification Error for Convolutional Neural Network.

FIGURE 6.12 Sensitivity analysis of direct quantization [342].

network can achieve high accuracy is shown. This fact seems to indicate that quantization can be interpolated through deeper networking. The decrease in the accuracy of the inference can be recovered through fine-tuning. Obviously, a network model for a mission critical task cannot have a smaller numerical precision.

Fig. 6.13 shows the effect of a dynamic fixed-point representation on permutation-invariant MNIST, MNIST, and CIFAR-10. Note that the final test errors are normalized, which means that they are divided by the single float test error of the dataset. Fig. 6.13(a) shows the test error rate along with how many bits (excluding the sign) are used for the propagation. It shows that 7-bits (plus the sign-bit) are sufficient for the test evaluations. Fig. 6.13(b) shows a case of parameters updating the weight, in which a dynamic fixed-point needs a relatively narrower bit-width than a traditional fixed-point, at just 11-bits (plus the sign-bit). This approach is also effective in a traditional fixed-point representation.

Research was conducted regarding the inference accuracy of XNOR-Net with weight binarization and both weight and input binarization as the training

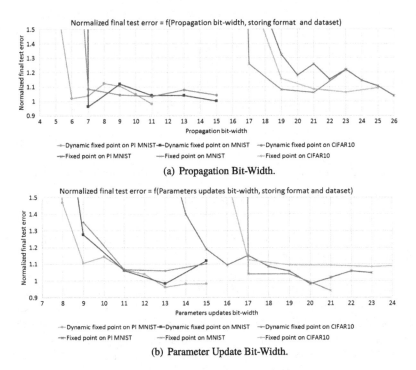

(a) Propagation Bit-Width.

(b) Parameter Update Bit-Width.

FIGURE 6.13 Test error on dynamic fixed-point representation [140].

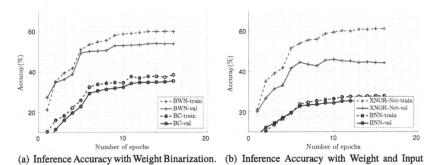

(a) Inference Accuracy with Weight Binarization. (b) Inference Accuracy with Weight and Input Binarization.

FIGURE 6.14 Top inference accuracy with XNOR-Net [301].

curve on ImageNet (ILSVRC2012), as shown in Fig. 6.14. The results show that XNOR-Net outperforms a binary connect (BC) and BinaryNeuralNet (BNN), respectively. However, the authors did not compare models having a higher precision, such as a single precision floating-point.

To summarize, superfluous quantization introduces a remarkable decrease in the accuracy of the inference. We must consider not only a quantization method but also a decrease in the inference accuracy on a neural network model. We

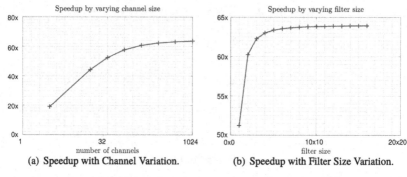

(a) Speedup with Channel Variation. (b) Speedup with Filter Size Variation.

FIGURE 6.15 Speedup with XNOR-Net [301].

should consider which method is better for the targeted neural network model in the case of an embedded solution.

6.2.2.3 Effect on execution performance

A binary representation of $\{-1, +1\}$ is assigned to values of zero and 1, respectively. Then, the multiplication is equivalent to an XNOR operation. In addition, a reduction can be achieved through population counting (called a pop-count). Therefore, the multiplication can be a bitwise XNOR; for example, a 32-bit word can have 32 XNOR operations for 32 multiplications. A two-input single-bit XNOR gate consists of three inverters, two NOR gates, and one AND gate, and thus is composed of a total of four gates, in terms of the equivalent number of NAND gates.

Thus, it introduces a much higher execution performance, as shown in Fig. 6.15. The speedup varies by changing the channel and filter sizes, as shown in Figs. 6.15(a) and 6.15(b), respectively. Because the number of channels is less than 300 in a typical convolution, we obtain a sufficient speedup by increasing the number of channels; however, a superfluous number cannot increase the speed as much. In addition, we can also state that a small-scale filter can obtain a sufficient speedup; however, increasing the scale does not benefit the binarization in terms of the filter size. The results show that increasing the number of channels is more effective than increasing the filter size because the pop-count is increased.

6.2.2.4 Effect on reduction of energy consumption

Fig. 6.16 shows the effect on the reduction in energy consumption by the lower numerical precision, with an 8-bit integer on the multiplier's operands, on the AlexNet model. These graphs include a compression of the parameters and activations, as well as zero-skipping operations. Thus, Fig. 6.16 shows the current trend regarding the architecture of an inference accelerator. The energy consumption is reduced by at least 4-fold. For a significantly large matrix operation

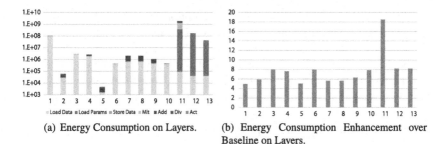

(a) Energy Consumption on Layers.

(b) Energy Consumption Enhancement over Baseline on Layers.

FIGURE 6.16 Energy consumption with Int8 multiplication for AlexNet.

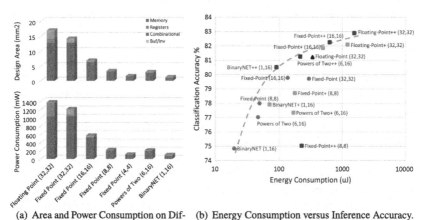

(a) Area and Power Consumption on Different Precision Levels.

(b) Energy Consumption versus Inference Accuracy.

FIGURE 6.17 Effect of lower precision on the area, power, and accuracy [187].

on the 11th layer, it dramatically reduces the energy consumption by greater than 18-times the baseline.

In addition, Fig. 6.16(a) implies that we need more techniques to reduce the memory accesses, particularly for activations that are always used.

Fig. 6.17(a) shows the design area and power consumption at different precision levels. The first and second values in the braces show the precision of the weight and input, respectively. As a remarkable point, a logic circuit is one of the major parts in the design area; however, it is a relatively small fraction in terms of power consumption. We can see how much energy on external memory access and on-chip SRAM access consume in Fig. 6.17(a).

Fig. 6.17(b) shows the energy consumption versus inference accuracy for the CIFAR-10 classification problem [187]. The black point indicates the initial single-precision floating-point baseline. The blue (mid gray in print version) points indicate the quantized models. The red and green (dark gray and light gray in print version) points are the results from the larger networks. If the system architect considers a trade-off between the energy consumption and inference accuracy, a lower precision is one option for lowering the cost of a hardware implementation. In addition, Fig. 6.17(b) also shows that a decrease in the accuracy of the inference can be recovered by a larger-scale network model, although this approach loses the purpose of a lower precision for a relatively small number of parameters when deceasing the external memory access and its power consumption.

6.2.3 Edge-cutting and clipping

Edge-cutting is used to cut off a small fraction, which can be an approximate value with a cutting-off of the lower bits, such as Bfloat16 of a half-precision floating-point number, or can be zeros in a lower bit-field in a fixed-point number. This approach directly reduces the total data size required for the parameters and/or activations.

Clipping is applied to achieve a saturation when setting the lower and upper boundaries. An ReLU6 is a typical example of clipping with zeros and 6s. This approach avoids a carry-out through accumulation and can reduce the accumulator width.

By edge-cutting and/or clipping in a numerical representation, an opportunity of applying common values for the parameters can be introduced. This effect can be used for weight-sharing. In addition, increasing the number of zero values can take techniques of encoding and zero-skipping and easily obtain such an effect, contributing to both fewer idling cycles for memory access and less energy consumption. On-chip memory requirements and external memory accesses can also be suppressed.

6.3 Encoding

A traditional encoding approach, such as a run-length compression and Huffman coding, can be applied when the data have a particular pattern or distribution. Through these techniques, a larger number of weights can be easily applied to a chip, and can therefore reduce the frequency and number of external memory excesses; thus, the latency and energy consumption are easily suppressed, thereby improving the energy efficiency. However, decoding (decompression) is required prior to the operation. Effective coding is to focus onto reduce or remove zeros, zeros are in the parameters, and opportunity to reduce external memory access as shown in Fig. 6.18.

6.3.1 Run-length coding

6.3.1.1 Concept of run-length coding

Run-Length coding uses a redundancy in the data stream. The same contiguous values are treated as single data with a header indicating the number of same contiguous data as the length. A major run-length implementation method is a switched run-length having two phases of non-redundant block encoding and re-

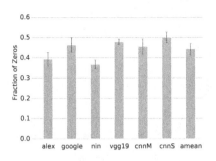

(a) Fraction of Zeros in Network Models.

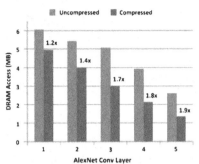

(b) DRAM Access Transaction Reduction by Run-Length Compression.

FIGURE 6.18 Zero availability and effect of run-length compressions [109][130].

dundant block encoding. It switches between non-redundant block encoding and redundant block encoding, both having a header representing the block length. As an extremely simple approach, non-zero elements are not contiguously in the tensor, and it is assumed that a redundant value, such as zero, is known.

6.3.1.2   Implementation of run-length coding

Switched run-length algorithm taking care of two corner cases. One case deals with a limitation on the length representation; for example, if 8-bits are considered, then more than 256 contiguous words must be partitioned into several blocks. However, this requires switching to a non-redundant block between redundant blocks. The other case deals with a limitation on the buffer length because the header has to be added before the encoded data stream (thus, it requires a buffer). The buffer length limits the length of a non-redundant block, and thus requires partitioning to several non-redundant blocks and switching to redundant blocks between the non-redundant blocks. Both cases have an issue in that in a switched-then-single-word, the next switched block has only one word. The decoding is extremely simple, and generates the same value when it is a redundant block.

6.3.1.3   Effect of run-length coding

Fig. 6.19 shows the effect of the run-length coding for both switched and simple run-length algorithms. Both algorithms have a different data structure, and therefore, a comparison between them is impossible. The X-axis shows the frequency of zeros in the input data stream. Regarding the switched run-length takes a huge number of headers, and thus an input stream having approximately 50% sparseness cannot be compressed. A simple run-length can compress to 20% of the input data having more than 90% sparseness.

Fig. 6.19(b) shows the compression rate by the run-length coding, which assumes that the non-zero elements are not contiguously laid out in the tensor.

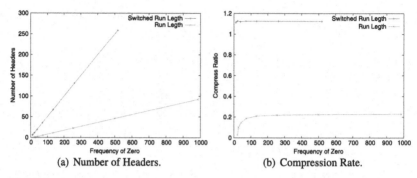

(a) Number of Headers. (b) Compression Rate.

FIGURE 6.19 Run-length compression.

The run-length coding for a vector having a random number is limited to 20%; however, a highly ranked operation on the convolution layer having such a 2D kernel with a channel depth achieves a good compression.

6.3.2 Huffman coding

Huffman coding is generally used in video compression. By combining with a binary and a ternary numerical representation, a zero-bit can be used for the compression through such coding.

6.3.2.1 Concept of Huffman coding

Huffman coding uses the assumption that the frequency of appearance is known for every datum in the stream.

It first composes a frequency table. After that it constructs a binary tree, called a Huffman tree, using the frequency table. To construct a Huffman tree, it first needs to seek the most infrequent datum, followed by the infrequent datum, which can be leaves of the Huffman tree. The frequencies of two nodes are summed and used to create a knot value for the two nodes. This is repeated to seek and create a knot except for the table entry already used for the knot.

After the tree construction, a binary is assigned to every edge, where the left edge is zero and the right edge is 1, as an example. From the terminal of the tree, the code for every datum is composed by reading the binaries. The code is used for pattern matching to translate from the original datum to the code.

6.3.2.2 Implementation of Huffman coding

As described in the earlier section, Huffman coding needs to reveal the frequency of all datum, implying that the counting is needed to create the frequency, a table is required for the frequencies, and buffers must hold the segment of the datum stream to make a pipeline of the frequency composition, Huffman tree composition, and reading binary code.

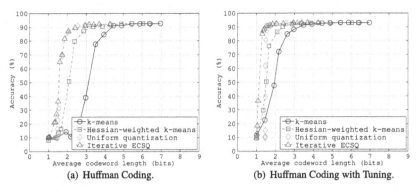

FIGURE 6.20 Huffman coding vs. inference accuracy [135].

When the pipeline consists of three stages, a triple-buffer can be applied. One buffer consists of a table and compression buffer. This works for every pipeline stage, and the frequency table and Huffman tree can be integrated into a single storage. The sequence of this is as follows: One entry from the table is read based on priority encoding to find the entry closest to the knot value. An addition is applied between the knot value and the frequency sought to update the knot value. Encoding using the Huffman code is then applied. When using this encoding only for the parameters, it is sufficient to do so offline.

Before the encoding using pattern matching, the Huffman code table should be stored to memory on or off the chip. A pattern match can be implemented using a lookup table when the datum size is sufficiently small.

Fig. 6.20 shows the side effect of compression with Huffman coding. The horizontal axis is the average bit width because the Huffman coding takes a variable length code for every datum. Fig. 6.11 shows the original effect of the lower precision in terms of the inference accuracy under the same conditions [135]. Huffman coding can reduce the effective datum by a width of 3-4 bits, whereas the original approach requires an 8-bit width.

6.3.3 Effect of compression

6.3.3.1 Compression of the parameters

Fig. 6.21 shows the effect of the parameter compression when set to 50% compression on every layer. It shows that the trend of the execution cycles is similar to the baseline. Figs. 6.21(b) and 6.23(a) show that parameter compression works well on executing a cycle reduction. The method contributes to a speedup over the baseline only at the fully connected layers, because the other layers have a relatively smaller number of parameters.

Regarding the 11th layer, the first fully connected layer requires huge MAC cycles, as shown in Fig. 6.21(a), and therefore the parameter compression cannot contribute well to a reduction of both the execution cycles and the energy

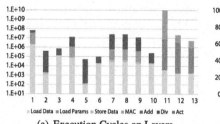

(a) Execution Cycles on Layers.

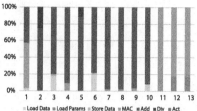

(b) Execution Cycle Breakdown on Layers.

FIGURE 6.21 Execution cycle reduction with parameter compression on AlexNet.

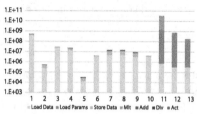

(a) Energy Consumption with Parameter Compression.

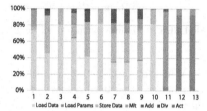

(b) Energy Consumption Breakdown on Layers.

FIGURE 6.22 Energy consumption with parameter compression for AlexNet.

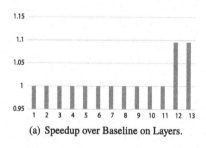

(a) Speedup over Baseline on Layers.

(b) Energy Consumption Enhancement over Baseline on Layers.

FIGURE 6.23 Speedup and energy consumption enhancement by parameter compression for AlexNet.

consumption, as shown in Fig. 6.22. As shown in Fig. 6.21(b), a convolution takes not only an MAC execution but also an addition between kernels (channel-direction).

Fig. 6.23 shows the energy consumption with parameter compression on the AlexNet model. The parameter loading on fully connected layers is reduced well. Therefore, the last two layers are a nearly theoretical enhancement of 2.0 because the loading parameters are a major workload, as shown in Fig. 6.21(b). Regarding the 11th layer of a fully connected layer, most of the execution cycles are taken for the MAC, as shown in Fig. 6.21(b); therefore, the parameter compression cannot contribute to a reduction of the energy consumption on the layer.

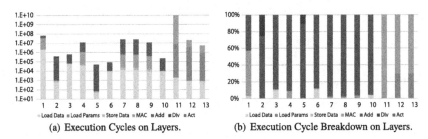

(a) Execution Cycles on Layers. (b) Execution Cycle Breakdown on Layers.

FIGURE 6.24 Execution cycle reduction by activation compression.

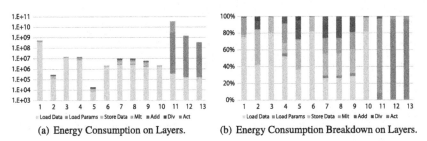

(a) Energy Consumption on Layers. (b) Energy Consumption Breakdown on Layers.

FIGURE 6.25 Energy consumption by activation compression for AlexNet.

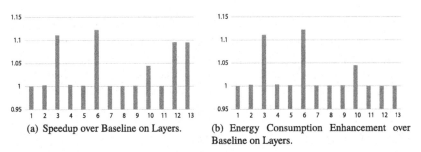

(a) Speedup over Baseline on Layers. (b) Energy Consumption Enhancement over Baseline on Layers.

FIGURE 6.26 Speedup and energy consumption enhancement with activation compression for AlexNet.

6.3.3.2 Compression for activations

Fig. 6.24 shows the effect of the activation compression, which is set to 50% compression on every layer. Fig. 6.24(a) shows that the number of execution cycles on the layers not having parameters can be reduced well by the activation compression. Such a layer can improve the execution based on the compression ratio, as shown in Fig. 6.26(a).

Similar to parameter compression, an addition is a major part in the execution cycles except for a fully connected layer. Figs. 6.24(a) and 6.26(a) show that the number of execution cycles on such non-parameter layers can be reduced. As shown in Fig. 6.24(b), normalization of the second and fifth layers requires a high rate of division, as shown in Fig. 6.24(b). See also Fig. 6.25.

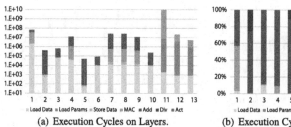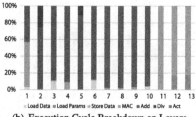

(a) Execution Cycles on Layers.   (b) Execution Cycle Breakdown on Layers.

FIGURE 6.27 Execution cycle reduction by compression.

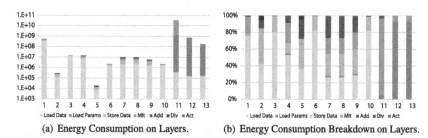

(a) Energy Consumption on Layers.   (b) Energy Consumption Breakdown on Layers.

FIGURE 6.28 Energy consumption with compression for AlexNet.

Fig. 6.26(a) shows a speedup over the baseline. A slight improvement in the pooling layers and fully connected layers is achieved. Fig. 6.26(b) shows an enhancement of the energy consumption over the baseline. The energy consumption on the pooling layer is slightly reduced; however, differing from a speedup, it does not contribute to the fully connected layers because a major factor is the MAC execution on the layer.

6.3.3.3 Compression for both parameters and activations

Fig. 6.27 shows the effect of both the parameter and activation compression, which is set to 50% compression on every layer. Fig. 6.27(a) shows that the number of execution cycles on both the convolution and fully connected layers can be reduced well. As shown in Fig. 6.27(b), such a layer can improve the execution by the compression ratio; in particular, the 1st, 12th, and 13th layers achieve a speedup close to the theoretical rate of 2.0. In addition, the number of execution cycles on layers not having any parameters can be reduced through a compression of the activation.

Fig. 6.28 shows the energy consumption break down on the AlexNet model. The parameters are still a major factor of the energy consumption at a 50% compression rate. However, compressing both the activation and the parameters improves the execution performance, as shown in Fig. 6.29(a). Fig. 6.28(b) shows that a division is a major factor in the normalization of the layers because the other factors of the memory accesses are reduced well. Most of the layers except for the 1st and 11th layers achieve a nearly theoretical enhancement of

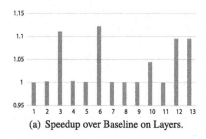
(a) Speedup over Baseline on Layers.

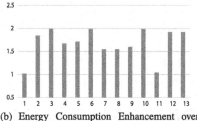
(b) Energy Consumption Enhancement over Baseline on Layers.

FIGURE 6.29 Energy efficiency with compression for AlexNet.

2.0 because of the major energy consumption, and the memory accesses are reduced well through the compression.

6.4 Zero-skipping

6.4.1 Concept of zero-skipping

A part of the parameter set is made up of zeros because the ReLU activation function generates such zeros in general. It was reported that 40% of the parameters in a fully connected layer are zeros.

We do not need to operate with zero values on multiply and addition operations because doing so consumes unnecessary energy. Multiplication with zeros can be skipped, and addition with zeros can be passed through or skipped as well. By checking for zero values before the operation, the output of zeros or the through value with operation skipping results in an efficient operation, and the latency required to operate the layer task can be reduced by the number of skips. Such skipping of zero values is called zero-skipping.

6.4.2 CSR and CSC sparsity representations

For a sparse tensor having numerous zeros, a tensor with only non-zero values can be reconstructed, which can reduce the necessary memory size on the chip. For example, this technique can be applied after pruning. Memory access can also be skipped if we know that the dataset consists of zeros. This requires a set of indexes for recording to guarantee the position of non-zero values. Thus, an index memory is needed, along with tensor and index memory access controls.

6.4.2.1 Concept of CSR and CSC encoding

There are two methods used to represent a sparse tensor, compressed sparse row (CSR) encoding and compressed sparse column (CSC) encoding, as shown in Fig. 6.30. Both encoding types use two index data for compression. CSR and CSC representations are used for row-first order and column-first order data structures, respectively.

$$\begin{bmatrix} 0 & 8 & 2 & 5 & 0 \\ 1 & 0 & 7 & 0 & 0 \\ 6 & 0 & 0 & 0 & 0 \\ 0 & 3 & 0 & 4 & 0 \end{bmatrix}$$

A_CSR = [8 2 5 1 7 6 3 4]   A_CSC = [1 6 8 3 2 7 5 4]

N_CSR = [0 3 5 6 8]   N_CSC = [0 2 4 6 8]

I_CSR = [1 2 3 0 2 0 1 3]   I_CSC = [1 2 0 3 0 1 0 3]

(a) Example of Sparse   (b) CSR Coding.   (c) CSC Coding.
Tensor.

FIGURE 6.30 Example of CSR and CSC codings.

Algorithm 6.1: CSR encoding

RETURN: indx_a, indx_n, A_CSR, N_CSR, I_CSR;
indx_a = 0;
indx_n = 0;
N_CSR[0] = 0;
for indx_row = 0; indx_row < N_{row}; indx_row++ **do**
  N_cnt = 0;
  for indx_column = 0; indx_column < N_{column}; indx_column++ **do**
    if A[indx_row][indx_column] != 0 **then**
      A_CSR[indx_a] = A[indx_row][indx_column];
      I_CSR[indx_a] = indx_column;
      indx_a++;
      N_cnt++;
    end
  end
  N_CSR[++indx_n] = N_cnt + N_CSR[indx_n - 1];
end
return $indx\_a, indx\_n, A\_CSR, N\_CSR, I\_CSR$;

6.4.2.2 Encoding algorithm

Algorithm 6.1 shows CSR encoding using two counters, "indx_a" and "indx_n," in order to check the position on the original matrix. The encoding is extremely simple, and the hardware implementation is friendly. There are constraints to its implementation as hardware, however; one constraint is the widths index words "indx_a" and "indx_n." Another constraint is the vector length limitation of A_CSR, N_CSR, and I_CSR. Regarding the CSC encoding, it is simple to exchange the loops of the rows and columns.

6.4.2.3 Decoding algorithm

Algorithm 6.2 shows the CSR decoding, which uses two counters of "indx_column" and "indx_row." First, it flushes the array "A" with zero initialization. To embedding non-zero values into the array "A," N_CSR and I_CSR are used. If streaming is applied, then it is sufficient to output zeros only when the element in the sparse tensor is not in the indexes. Regarding CSC encoding, it is also simple to exchange the loops of the rows and columns.

Algorithm 6.2: CSR decoding

RETURN: A;
$A[N_{row}][N_{column}] = \{0\}$;
indx_column = 0;
indx_row = 0;
for cnt_row = 0; cnt_row < indx_a; cnt_row++ **do**
   for cnt_column = 0; cnt_column < indx_column; cnt_column++ **do**
      indx_column = N_CSR[++indx_row] - indx_column;
      A[cnt_row][I_CSR[indx_column]] = A_CSR[cnt_row×
      N_CSR[indx_row] + cnt_column]
   end
end
return A;

6.4.2.4 Effect of CSR and CSC codings

Let us set the matrix shape as $M \times N$ and set the datum width and sparseness rate as W_{data} and R_{sparse}, respectively.

The numbers of elements N_{elem} in A_CSR and I_CSR are equivalent to the following:

$$N_{elem} = \lceil (1 - R_{sparse})MN \rceil \tag{6.25}$$

Let us assume that M_{max} and N_{max} are the architectural row and column sizes. The I_CSR datum size W_I is as follows.

$$W_I = \log_2 N_{max} \tag{6.26}$$

The maximum number of elements N_N in N_CSR and its datum size W_N are M_{max} and $\log_2 M_{max}N_{max}$, respectively. Therefore, we obtain the total data size W_{CSR} for a $M \times N$ matrix as follows:

$$W_{CSR} = (W_{data} + W_I)N_{elem} + W_N N_N \tag{6.27}$$
$$= (W_{data} + \log_2 N_{max})\lceil (1 - R_{sparse})MN \rceil + M_{max} \log_2 M_{max}N_{max}$$

The values of M, N, and R_{sparse} can be dynamically changed, whereas the others are architectural hardware parameters. Thus, the first and second terms are dynamic architectural parameters depending on the number of non-zeros and the offset, respectively.

Before the encoding, the total data size is $W_{data}MN$, and thus the compression ratio can be as follows:

$$R_{CSR} = \frac{W_{CSR}}{W_{data}MN} \tag{6.28}$$

$$\approx (1 + \frac{\log_2 N_{max}}{W_{data}})(1 - R_{sparse}) + \frac{M_{max}}{W_{data} M N} \log_2 M_{max} N_{max}$$

To be effective, R_{CSR} should be less than 1. Thus, we obtain the following condition for how the sparseness R_{sparse} should be achieved:

$$R_{sparse} \approx \frac{1 + \frac{M_{max}}{W_{data} M N} \log_2 M_{max} N_{max} - \frac{1}{1 + \frac{\log_2 N_{max}}{W_{data}}}}{1 + \frac{\log_2 N_{max}}{W_{data}}} \tag{6.29}$$

$$= \frac{W_{data}}{W_{data} + \log_2 N_{max}} \times$$

$$\{1 - (\frac{W_{data}}{W_{data} + \log_2 N_{max}} - \frac{M_{max}}{W_{data} M N} \log_2 M_{max} N_{max})\}$$

$$> \frac{M_{max}}{W_{data} M N} \log_2 M_{max} N_{max}$$

We obtain the following condition of the matrix composition:

$$M N > \frac{M_{max}}{W_{data}} \log_2 M_{max} N_{max} \tag{6.30}$$

We must take care of the tensor size, M and N, under the condition of the right side of the equation. In addition, we also obtain the following architectural condition.

$$M_{max} \log_2 M_{max} N_{max} > W_{data} \tag{6.31}$$

If the word width of the data is set to W_{data} then the hardware should be under the constraint of the left size of the equation.

6.4.3 Use case of zero-skipping

There are two types of use cases, suppressing the execution cycles and suppressing the energy consumption.

6.4.3.1 Zero-skipping for suppressing the execution cycles

One use-case is to remove unnecessary multiplication and addition operations. When an operation has operands having a zero value, a multiplication is unnecessary, and it is adequate to output a zero. In the case of addition, it is sufficient to output a non-zero operand value when one of the operands is a zero.

Fig. 6.31(a) shows the effect of the use-case in terms of the execution cycles with a zero-skipping operation applied to the AlexNet model. If zero-skipping is supported only on the multiplier, the execution is still on the adder, and the number of execution cycles is not reduced by the structural hazard between multiplication and addition in which the addition requires full execution cycles.

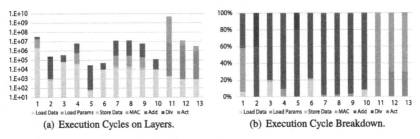

(a) Execution Cycles on Layers.

(b) Execution Cycle Breakdown.

FIGURE 6.31 Execution cycles with zero-skipping operation for AlexNet.

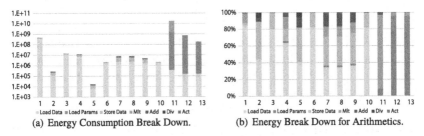

(a) Energy Consumption Break Down.

(b) Energy Break Down for Arithmetics.

FIGURE 6.32 Energy consumption break down for AlexNet.

Fig. 6.31 shows the number of execution cycles on every layer of the AlexNet model. Fig. 6.31(b) shows that the division of the normalization layers can be a major factor by removing other arithmetic operations. The seventh through the ninth layers of the convolution still require a huge addition between kernels (channels); otherwise, the other factors are reduced well. Channel pruning can reduce this workload, as discussed in Appendix B.

Fig. 6.33(a) shows the speedup over the baseline with a sparsity of 0.5 (50%). This reduces the number of cycles on the loading of both the activations and parameters through a compression technique, such as CSR encoding. In addition, zero-skipping for the execution can reduce the number of cycles of an operation well, and nearly achieves a theoretical speedup rate of 2.0 in most of the layers.

6.4.3.2 Zero-skipping for suppressing the energy-consumption

The other use-case is to reduce the footprint of the data, which reduces the requirement of the memory size, and results in a reduction of the memory access, and thus the energy consumption.

The evaluation considered the compression for the parameters and activations. The loading of both the parameters and activations is reduced well by the compression, and it therefore enlarges the factor of the activation storage, as shown in Fig. 6.32(a). Loading and storing of the activation can still reduce the energy consumption because the memory access is still a major factor of such consumption. The same ratio of compression on both the parameters and activations occurs, as shown in Fig. 6.33(b), and most of the layers achieve a

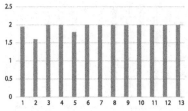
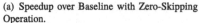
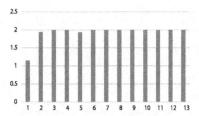

(a) Speedup over Baseline with Zero-Skipping Operation.

(b) Energy Consumption Enhancement over Baseline.

FIGURE 6.33 Energy efficiency over baseline with zero-skipping operation for AlexNet model.

nearly theoretical number of 2.0 because of the skipping of the additions. The second and fifth layers have a slightly lower enhancement because a division with a huge latency is taken. The first layer has a huge input vector that cannot be compressed, and thus the energy consumption is not reduced much.

6.5 Approximation

A neural network has robustness generated by the characteristics of its application. Therefore, we can apply more approximations into a neural network architecture.

6.5.1 Concept of approximation

An approximation can be achieved at the level of the probability function, loss function, activation function, and operators to simplify the logic circuit and improve the implementation density (the number of functions for parallelism) and lower the energy-consumption. A simplification of the logic circuit can introduce a shorter critical path, introduce a high clock frequency, and shorten the verification time for the hardware development.

Based on the approximation, an error between the original and approximated values is introduced, and this technique requires an interpolation for the parameter calculation upon a gradient descent and/or a loss function during training.

6.5.2 Activation function approximation

An approximation of the major activation functions are made through a clipping as follows.

$$Clip(x, MIN, MAX) = \min(MIN, \max(MAX, x)) \qquad (6.32)$$

where MAX and MIN are the maximum and minimum values, respectively. Within this range, the approximation function takes x.

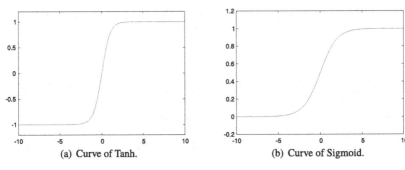

(a) Curve of Tanh.   (b) Curve of Sigmoid.

FIGURE 6.34 Typical example of activation function.

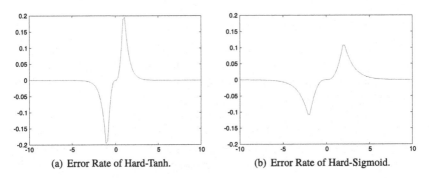

(a) Error Rate of Hard-Tanh.   (b) Error Rate of Hard-Sigmoid.

FIGURE 6.35 Precision error rate of activation functions.

6.5.2.1   Hard-tanh

Fig. 6.34(a) shows a curve of the hyperbolic tangent. An approximation of tanh can be represented as follows.

$$Hard\_Tanh(x) = Clip(x, -1, 1) \qquad (6.33)$$

Fig. 6.35(a) shows the precision error rate based on the approximation calculated by the difference between them. At a high rate, the second derivative of tanh incurs a large error.

6.5.2.2   Hard-sigmoid

Fig. 6.34(b) shows a curve of the sigmoid. The approximation of the sigmoid can be represented as follows.

$$Hard\_Sigmoid(x) = Clip(\frac{x/2 + 1}{2}, 0, 1) \qquad (6.34)$$

Fig. 6.35(b) shows the precision error rate by the approximation calculated by the difference between them. At a high rate, the second derivative of tanh incurs a large error; however, based on its relatively smaller second derivative on the sigmoid, it incurs a relatively smaller error.

6.5.2.3 ReLU6

ReLU is not a bounded function. Therefore, it can achieve the upper limit of the numerical representation on the accumulation. ReLU6 is generally used to suppress an unnecessary saturation decreasing the accuracy of the inference.

$$ReLU6(x) = Clip(x, 0, 6) \qquad (6.35)$$

Clipping with a value of 6 is an empirical hyperparameter.

6.5.3 Multiplier approximation

As we explore the energy consumption on the AlexNet model, the multiplier consumes a significant amount of energy for the MAC operations. Therefore, we can expect a reduced energy consumption through an approximation of the multiplication.

6.5.3.1 Shifter representation

A multiplier can be approximated through the use of a left-shifter in the case of a fixed-point or integer numerical representation. We can obtain an index of the approximated source operand $src2$ as follows.

$$src2 \geq \arg\max_i(2^i) \qquad (6.36)$$

Thus, we can use a left-shifter for multiplication $Mult(*)$ as follows.

$$Mult(src1, src2) \leq \min(MAX, src1 \ll i) \qquad (6.37)$$

where MAX is the available maximum value in the numerical representation. Thus, the maximum error is approximately $MAX/2$.

A simple multiplier for M-bits, $\times$ N-bits, consists of an $M \times N$ AND gate array and N $(M+1)$-bit adders. Then, an NAND2 equivalent number of gates for the multiplier A_{mult} is as follows:

$$A_{mult} = 1.5 \times MN + 4 \times (M+1)N \qquad (6.38)$$

where an AND gate and a single-bit full-adder take a 1.5 and 4.0 NAND2 equivalent numbers of gates.

The shifter can consist of M 2-operand 1-bit multiplexers on one stage and on N stages. An NAND2 equivalent number of gates for the shifter A_{shift} is as follows.

$$A_{shift} = 3.5 \times \log_2 M \times \log_2 M \qquad (6.39)$$

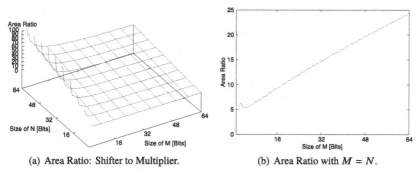

(a) Area Ratio: Shifter to Multiplier.

(b) Area Ratio with $M = N$.

FIGURE 6.36 Advantage of shifter-based multiplication in terms of area.

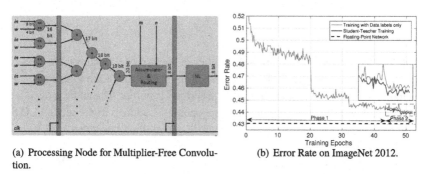

(a) Processing Node for Multiplier-Free Convolution.

(b) Error Rate on ImageNet 2012.

FIGURE 6.37 Multiplier-free convolution architecture and its inference performance [350].

The maximum shift amount N is equal to $\log_2 M$, and the shifter has $\log_2 M$ levels of selectors at most. Therefore, the area ratio R can be represented as follows.

$$R = \frac{A_{mult}}{A_{shift}} \quad (6.40)$$
$$= \frac{5.5M^2(1 + 4.0/(5.5M))}{3.5(\log_2 M)^2}$$
$$> \frac{5.5M^2}{3.5(\log_2 M)^2}$$

in which it is assumed that N is equal to M. Fig. 6.36(a) shows the area ratio from the shifter approximation to a simple multiplier in terms of the equivalent number of NAND2 gates. The multiplier can easily increase its area by the multiplicand N. A shifter approximation has at least a 5-times smaller area, and a 6-times smaller area for a 16-bit datapath, as shown in Fig. 6.36(b).

Fig. 6.37 shows a multiplier-free architecture [350]. The authors proposed an algorithm to convert from a floating-point to a fixed-point numerical representation consisting of three phases. The first phase quantizes to 8-bits until achieving convergence of the parameter updates after the network model training. The second phase uses a student-teacher learning to improve the inference accuracy, which is degraded by the quantization. The last phase uses an ensemble learning in which multiple training is conducted for the same network architecture and model ensembles.

Fig. 6.37(a) shows a processing node with a shifter on the first pipeline stage replacing the need for multipliers. This architecture uses an adder-tree method to accumulate the set of multiplications. Fig. 6.37(b) shows the error rate on the ImageNet 2012 classification problem. There is gap between the floating-point and the proposed fixed-point errors; however, training with phase-1 decreases this gap, and phase-2 obtains a lower error rate with a similar range as the floating-point approach.

6.5.3.2 LUT representation

Another approach to replacing a multiplier is the use of a lookup table (LUT) [302]. In [302], a two-stage LUT composition is applied. In the first stage, the value of the operands is searched, and the address is output. The address decoder is between two stages, which decodes the operands' address to the second LUT. The first stage is similar to a cache memory, which then generates a hit signal on the entry.

This approach can have a smaller first LUT, which can have $x \geq argmax_i(2^i - 1)$, where the bit width of i can be smaller than $\log(MAX_x)$-bit. If the multiplication has two operands of i_x and i_y, then the complexity of the address decoder is $O(i_x \times i_y)$.

6.6 Optimization

Without a loss of throughput, response time, or inference accuracy, or achieving their requirements, approaches to achieving a trade-off between the losses and the amount of data have been developed. These techniques are called a model optimization.

6.6.1 Model optimization

6.6.1.1 Combined optimization

By combining several of the previously described methods, the optimization obtains the maximal performance. By setting the target inference accuracy, the optimization can be achieved by maintaining the target. With this method, a hardware performance with the necessary inference accuracy is achieved. For SqueezeNet, the AlexNet variant neural network model has 1/510th the number of parameters, and an optimized network model with the 0.5 MB parameters can run on the edge devices.

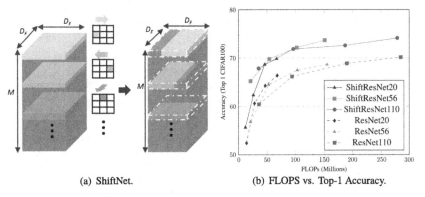

(a) ShiftNet.

(b) FLOPS vs. Top-1 Accuracy.

FIGURE 6.38 ShiftNet [370].

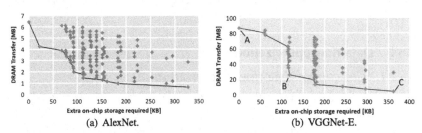

(a) AlexNet.

(b) VGGNet-E.

FIGURE 6.39 Relationship between off-chip data transfer required and additional on-chip storage needed for fused-layer [110].

6.6.1.2 Memory access optimization

In [370], the authors propose that shifting the kernels improves the inference accuracy over the baseline, as shown in Fig. 6.38(b). Thus, this technique seems to be applicable to the quantization as a supplement. The shifting shown in Fig. 6.38(a) can be achieved by an offset of the memory accesses to load the kernels. A static neural network model has static memory access patterns, and thus we can make an affine equation including an offset shifting. The loading considers this equation.

6.6.1.3 Fused layer

Activations of a specific layer should be fed into the next layer. Therefore, by fusing multiple layers into one block of layers, intermediate activations can be located in the datapath [110]. Thus, access to external memory to spill and fill the activation is not needed. This introduces a data reuse as quickly as possible. Thus, it also introduces a local memory hierarchy.

Fig. 6.39 shows the effect of fusing the layers. Amount of DRAM transfer needed is decreased by the fusion with an increase in the extra on-chip memory size to store the intermediate data locally. This also shows that there is an opti-

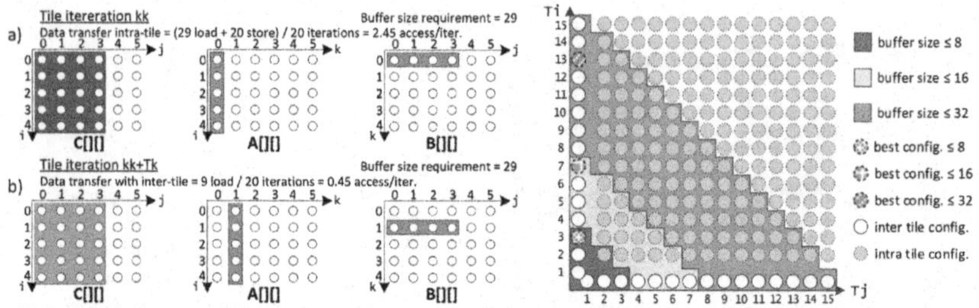

(a) Inter-tile Optimized Data Access Patterns for Matrix Multiply.

(b) Design Space for Tiling Configurations.

FIGURE 6.40 Data reuse example-I [290].

mal on-chip memory size that contributes highly to the external memory access reduction.

6.6.2   Data-flow optimization

6.6.2.1   Concept of data-flow optimization

In general, the data size for the parameter set in a neural network model is greater than the memory capacity on a chip. In addition, for the temporal data generation of the training phase, general neural network models need external memory accesses to spill and fill the data on the chip memory.

Namely, we need to consider the data flow of the neural network model to avoid an inefficient use of on-chip memory to highly improve the execution performance and energy efficiency. Data-flow optimization aims to optimize the dataflow of the neural network model on a chip.

In general, for a DSA used in deep learning, it must be noted that the neural network model cannot be placed on the chip. Thus, it is necessary to partition the model, the parameters, and the path for the activations. Namely, a scheduling of the partitioned fragments is required to achieve an efficient order of mapping onto the chip.

6.6.2.2   Data-reuse

Fig. 6.40(a) shows an example of a reuse effect on a Matrix-Matrix Multiplication, $C = A \times B$. This example is based on the technique of tiling. The multiplication takes a three-level nested loop, i, j, and k, to perform an MAC operation for every element of the result C. The tile factor is depicted as T_i as an example.

As shown in the upper part of Fig. 6.40(a), the production of 20 ($= T_i \times T_j$) elements of C is attempted. The partial product C is restored, the sequence of which requires a storage size of 20. This takes a buffer size equivalent to the colored area shown in Fig. 6.40(a), and thus requires a size of 29. Regarding the operands, A and B take five and four elements for the buffer, respectively.

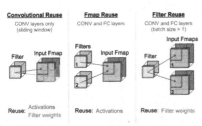

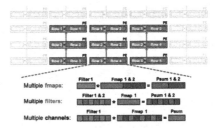

(a) Data Reuse Examples for 2D Tensor.   (b) Row Stationary Reuse.

FIGURE 6.41 Data reuse examples-II [345].

In addition, A and B move in direction k for the loading. Thus, A and B take 20/4 and 20/5 loads, namely, 4 and 5 reuses, respectively. This is achieved with $T_i \times T_j$ iterations, and thus a size of 20 is required. Therefore, this approach takes 2.45 accesses per iteration with a 29-element buffer.

Fig. 6.40(a) shows the bottom part, which tries to produce 20 ($= T_i \times T_j$) elements of C, but keeps the partial product C on the chip. This approach applies the loading of A and B, and the same number of iterations. Thus, this approach requires 0.45 accesses per iteration with a 29-element buffer. Both approaches require the same buffer size and numbers of iterations, but at a different communication cost (the number of accesses per iteration).

Fig. 6.40(b) shows the design space for the tiling, where the axes are the tile factor. A large buffer size is capable of a larger number of matrix elements. The boundary of $i = j = 1$ requires an inter-tile configuration to communicate between neighbor tiles. For inter-tile reuse optimization, one of the tile factors must equal 1, which prunes the space [290]. Therefore, the best configurations are for $T_j = 1$, as an example.

In [345], an example of a data reuse, shown in Fig. 6.41, is described. The figure shows three types of reuse, a convolutional reuse, feature map reuse, and filter reuse. The authors also proposed their own approach to the row stationary reuse, in which a row of the feature map is reused and propagated, as shown in Fig. 6.41(b).

6.6.2.3 Constraint by reuse

A data-reuse requires control of the operation order and its data preparation order. Thus, it requires a high-quality scheduling. In addition, the case of superfluous and sticks to the data-reuse, requiring a large investment in hardware resources and returns a high energy consumption. We must balance the data-reuse and its hardware cost.

For a convolution having K_d, $d \in D$, and a D-dimension kernel, the maximum number of reuses, $\max(K_d)$, is applied. A reuse is indicated on a timeline, and thus a large-scale tensor has the potential for a high data reuse; however, it also requires such a large scale of the execution steps.

TABLE 6.7 Summary of hardware performance improvement methods.

Method	Description		Applied Phase	Applying Target	Purpose, etc
Model Compression	Reduction in the total number of parameters and/or activation functions				
	Pruning	Pruning edges and units that do not contribute to accuracy	Training	Activations, Parameters	Computation complexity and data reductions
	Dropout	Invalidating Activation by probability	Training	Activations	Computation complexity and data reductions
	DropConnect	Invalidating edges by probability	Training	Parameters	Computation complexity and data reductions
	PCA	Lowering input vector by finding uncorrelated elements	Inference	Input Data (Vector)	Data reduction
	Distillation	Knowledge Distillation from Larger Model to Smaller Model	Training	Parameters	Computation complexity and data reductions
	Tensor Factorization	Tensor Approximation with Low-Rank Tensors	Training	Parameters	Computation complexity and data reductions
	Weight-sharing	Sharing the weights intra-layer and/or inter layer	After training	Parameters	Data reduction
Numerical Compression	Parameter size reduction				
	Quantization	Quantizing numerical representation	Inference Training	Activations, Parameters	Interpolation term needed for loss function (option)
	Edge-cutting	Value cutting under threshold value	Inference	After training	Computation complexity and data reduction with zero-skipping
Encoding	Compression/Decompression by data-encoding		Inference Training	Activations, Parameters Temporal Variables	Data reduction
Zero-Skipping	Operation skipping when operand has zero		Inference and Training	Operation	Computation complexity and data reductions
Approximation	Approximate functions and operators		Inference	Activations, Parameters	Interpolation term is needed for loss function
Optimization	Model Optimization	Constraining to model topology	After training	Topology	Computation complexity and Data reductions
	Data-Flow Optimization	Use of Data Recycling and or Locality	Inference and Training	All Data-Flows	Memory Access Optimization

6.7 Summary of performance improvement methods

Cache memory in traditional CPUs and GPUs is unsuitable for deep learning tasks. There is a mismatch between the locality of the data and the locality handling on the cache memory architecture. In addition, cache memory does not support exclusive storage in each level of memory hierarchy, which means a multiple copying data blocks is required across each level, which is an inefficient storage hierarchy.

Table 6.7 summarizes the hardware performance improvement methods, excluding a deeper pipelining for the logic circuit. The applied phase is categorized into three phases of inference, training, and a combination of both. In addition, the target applied is categorized into the parameters, activations, input vector, and any data used. For the quantization, a quantization error is an issue regarding the accuracy of the inference phase. There are several propositions used to add an interpolating term to the loss function to obtain the parameters, including the quantization error. The approximation must also add an interpolation term to the loss function because it directly affects the inference error. A co-design of the hardware and software is one recent trend.

Chapter 7

Case study of hardware implementation

Chapter 7 surveys case studies on neuromorphic computing and neural network hardware. Specifically, we focus on DNNs rather than shallow neural networks such as an SVM. Regarding neuromorphic computing hardware, previous survey papers are already available, and we therefore provide only a brief introduction. We describe this type of hardware using classes of many-core processors, DSPs, FPGAs, and ASICs (described in Chapter 2), based on analog and digital logic circuit categories.

7.1 Neuromorphic computing

7.1.1 Analog logic circuit

- University of Zurich and ETH Zurich: cxQuad and ROLLS
  These institutions designed two types of chips for image recognition [204]. One is called cxQuad used for pooling and convolution, and the other is called Reconfigurable On-Line Learning Spiking (ROLLS), and is a neuromorphic processor used mainly for classification, applying nine cxQuad chips.
  A cxQuad chip consists of four cores having a 16×16 neuron array with an analog logic circuit implementation. It has 1K neurons and 64K synapses, where each synapse block connected to a neuron is composed of 12-bit wide 64-entry content addressable memory (CAM) cells. A neuron uses an adaptive-exponential integrate-and fire method. CxQuad has three types of router (intra-core, on-chip inter-core, and chip-to-chip) and operates using an AER [119] based spike transmission. A spike is routed using a 3-level hierarchical routing method, with local-to-global communication. A cxQuad chip is fabricated using a 180-nm semiconductor process, has a 43.8 mm^2 area, and consumes 945 μW of power at 1.8 V.
  ROLLS has 256 neurons and a total of 133,120 synapses. A neuron has the same configuration as cxQuad. It has three types of synapses: linear time-multiplexed, short-time plasticity, and long-term potentiation. STP synapses have analog circuits that can reproduce short-term adaptation dynamics, and digital circuits that can set and change the programmable weights [204]. The LTP synapses contain analog learning circuits and digital state-holding logic [204]. ROLLS is fabricated using a 180-nm semiconductor process, has an area of 51.4 mm^2, and consumes 4 mW of power at 1.8 V.

Thinking Machines. https://doi.org/10.1016/B978-0-12-818279-6.00017-7
Copyright © 2021 Shigeyuki Takano. Published by Elsevier Inc. All rights reserved.

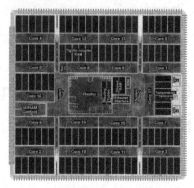

(a) SpiNNaker Node Block Diagram.   (b) SpiNNaker Die Photo.

FIGURE 7.1 SpiNNaker chip [220].

7.1.2 Digital logic circuit

7.1.2.1 Many-core

Many-core is used to make a software program emulate the neuroscience field rather than conduct a direct evaluation through a hardware implementation.

- The University of Manchester

  - SpiNNaker

    SpiNNaker is a massively parallel processing (MPP) system based on a many-core chip [220]. Fig. 7.1(a) shows a single-chip node diagram, in which the processor cores are connected through a central NoC system. The number of processor cores is an implementation constraint. A many-core processor is based on 18 ARM cores and designed using a globally asynchronous and locally synchronous (GALS) approach. Fig. 7.1(b) shows a die photograph showing 18 cores with an NoC router at the center. AER [119] is used for the routing of a generated spike [357]. An AER packet consists of a time stamp indicating the generation time and a neuron ID created at the spike.

    A simulation model is composed using a library coded in Python, called sPyNNAker. This library consists of a board SW and a host SW, as well as a tool chain to generate a configuration file on the system. The board SW is used for configuring the simulation model on a board composed of 48 SpiNNaker chips. The host SW is a library for describing a neural network without considering the use of the actual board. It defines the entire model through a graph description called a population graph, which is converted into a graph called a neuron graph defining all neurons and their synapses, which is itself partitioned into multiple subtasks (called a part-population graph) that can run on an ARM core and are finally executable on the board.

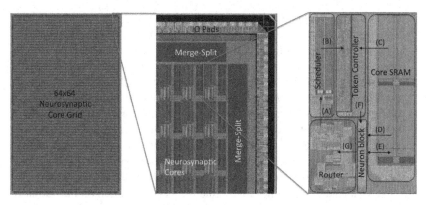

FIGURE 7.2 TrueNorth chip [107].

- SpiNNaker-2

  SpiNNaker-2 [262] is the follow-up project of SpiNNaker. It focuses on an exponential function consisting of a lookup table (LUT) and multiplications, and this function therefore considers 60–100 cycles in general. The SpiNNaker compiler first pre-calculates a range of values of the exponential decay fitting into the LUTs, which takes a high level description of the network dynamics specified by the user. The LUTs are then copied into the local memory of each core and used at run-time. This approach has two limitations: 1) A limited number of time constants and a range of exponential functions can be used owing to limited on-chip memory, and 2) if someone wants to model a learning rule that requires the timing constants to be dynamic, a regeneration of the LUTs on-the-fly or a pause in the simulation will be required, both of which are major performance bottlenecks. For SpiNNaker, the exponential function requires 95 cycles. SpiNNaker-2 integrates a fully pipelined exponential function limited to a fixed-point in a s16.15 format. The challenge is to replace the multipliers with a shifter in the exponential function, where the multiplication is a major energy consumer in an arithmetic logic circuit. The architecture is based on an iterative approach, and the loop is unrolled with a factor-four. The exponential function takes 0.16–0.39 nJ on 5928 square micro-millimeter at 22 nm process.

7.1.2.2 ASIC

- IBM: TrueNorth

  TrueNorth is a neuromorphic computing hardware for inference purposes [261]. Its core has 256 neurons, and it has a scalable architecture with a maximum of 4096 cores (64 × 64 layout) [261]. Fig. 7.2 shows a breakdown of the chip. The left side image is a 64 × 64 core array, the center shows the top-right corner of the array, and the image on the right shows one of the cores. A neuron supports a maximum of 1024 synapses. A synapse (weight) is a signed 9-bit weight and supports 256 thresholds. A spike is fed into a crossbar switch, passes the cross-point(s), and is transferred to the neuron(s). A spike is used for reading the weight from memory. Upon the transmission of a spike to a crossbar, the spike addresses the weight memory. A neuron receives, and accumulates the weight addressed by, the spike. On the side of the input image, the core shows a large weight memory on the right side of the core. The output of the spike from the scheduler enters the crossbar and addresses the core SRAM, both signals are fed into the neuron block, and the weight is accumulated by the upcoming spike assertion.

Because a TrueNorth core is a digital logic circuit and has a crossbar-based synapse, it cannot take a negative value for a pre-activation on the output of the column (soma) of the cross-points. Therefore, to take a negative weight having numerical precision, it uses the weight memory, and the value is fed into the neuron body for accumulation.

When the accumulation is greater than the threshold, it creates a firing and generates a spike. The generated spike is treated as an AER packet [119], which is transferred to itself or another core as a destination [260]. Thus, to transfer a generated spike to a specific core, the core has an AGU. The logic circuits except for the core are asynchronous, and to synchronize them entirely, a 10-KHz signal corresponding to the clock is used.

It is necessary to download the parameters trained on TrueNorth for its inference, and a back propagation for neuromorphic computing was recently proposed [159]. On the MNIST dataset, a 64-core configuration achieves an accuracy of 99.42% and consumes 121 μJ of energy.

- Tsinghua University: Tianji

  It consists of multiple cores, with each core composed of a router to interface between the cores for a spike; a synapse array; a synchronizer used for inputting the spike into the array; a neuron block creating the firing using signals coming from the synapse array; and a parameter manager. A neuron operates through time-multiplexing, and is fabricated using a 120-nm semiconductor process, and a chip with six cores.

  A tool-chain called NEUTRAMS was also developed [205]. The tool-chain consists of a four-layer development process. The highest layer is used for coding the neural network. The next layer below converts a coded network model based on the learning result, and adds a sparse connection, a numerical representation with a lower precision, and a new layer appendage. The third layer is used for mapping to a physical platform. The last layer is a simulation based on the settings.

- Zhejiang University: Darwin

  This processor has eight neurons on a chip and supports up to 2048 neurons using time-multiplexing with a factor of 256 [322]. It applies an AER [119] for a routing spike. It sets the destination neuron using the neuron ID held by its AER packet, and loads the weights and delay time from external memory.

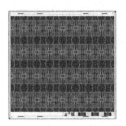

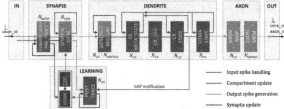

(a) Loihi Die Photo.   (b) Loihi Neuromorphic Core Architecture.

FIGURE 7.3 Intel Loihi [148].

It stores a spike into a delay queue composed of a 15-slot ring buffer based on the delay time. Weighed spikes are summed, and the result is fed into a neuron and output based on the firing condition. This architecture supports 4,194,304 synapses. For a hand-written number recognition at 25 MHz, it applies a 0.16 s delay and achieves an accuracy of 93.8%. Electroencephalogram (EEG) decoding achieves an accuracy of 92.7%, and was designed using a 180-nm semiconductor process, and has an area of 25 mm². In addition, it consumes 58.8 mW of power at 70 MHz and 1.8 V (0.84 mW/MHz).

- Intel: Loihi

  Loihi supports programmability for the synaptic learning process. It supports spike-traces corresponding to filtered presynaptic and postsynaptic spike trains with configurable time constraints, multiple-spike traces for a given spike train filter with different time constraints, two additional state variables per synapse, which in addition to the normal weight used to provide more flexibility for learning, reward traces that correspond to special reward spikes carrying signed impulse values to represent reward or punishment signals for reinforcement learning [148].

  A Loihi chip includes 128 neuromorphic cores, in which 1024 primitive spiking neural units are grouped into sets of trees constituting neurons [148]. It also includes three embedded x86 processor cores and off-chip communication interfaces. Neuromorphic cores are connected with a two-dimensional mesh topology NoC with an asynchronous implementation similar to that of other chips. The mesh's ary is four. The protocol of the mesh supports 4096 neuromorphic cores on a chip, and supports hierarchical addressing for up to 16383 chips.

  The learning rule is STDP based. The neuromorphic core has 2-M bit SRAM with an ECC. Fig. 7.3(b) shows the neuromorphic core architecture. The input spike passes through synapse, dendrite, and axon modules. The synapse unit reads the weights corresponding to the input spike from memory. The dendrite unit updates the state of the neurons. The axon unit generates spikes. The learning unit updates the weights using the programmed learning rules at the epoch boundaries [148].

Loihi is a 60 mm^2 chip fabricated using a 14-nm process and implemented with 2.07 billion transistors and 33 MB of SRAM for 128 neuromorphic cores and three x86 cores. It can operate within a range of 0.50–1.25 V. The chip was evaluated based on a convolutional sparse coding problem on a 52 × 52 image with a 224-atom dictionary.

7.2 Deep neural network

7.2.1 Analog logic circuit

- University of Utah: ISAAC
  They target a higher throughput and buffer size reduction by taking a deeper pipelining of the datapath [319]. DaDianNao is used as the baseline architecture, and multiple tiles are interconnected through a cauterized mesh topology. A tile consists of an embedded DRAM (eDRAM) buffer for the input data, an MAC unit called In-situ Multiply-Accumulate (IMA), and an output register, which are interconnected with a shared bus. In addition, a sigmoid functional unit (FU) and a max-pool unit are included.
  An IMA unit consists of four crossbar arrays, four analog-digital converters (ADCs), and a shift and add unit working as the neurons, and these five units are shared among the arrays. Here, 2^{16} resistance levels are needed to conduct a 16-bit multiplication; in addition, a DAC before the array, and an ADC after the array, are also needed, which consume the die area and generate calculation errors (precision limitation). To reduce the ADC size, an encoding is used in which every w-bit synaptic weight in a column is stored in its original form, or in its "flipped" form. The flipped form of w-bit weight W is represented as $W = 2^w - 1 - W$ [319].
  Thus, a multiplication is applied for the dot-product on the cross-point, and every product is accumulated at the output stage. Namely, a dot-product with 16-bit precision takes at least 16 steps. Bias is always added to the weight, and the result is stored in each cell; therefore, the total biases must be subtracted after the dot-product. For example, a 16-bit signed fixed-point requires a subtraction with 2^{15}, for which a shift and add unit are applied. Similar to DaDianNao, a layer-by-layer operation is applied, and the following layer operation starts after the prior layer has finished its operation. This implies that the architecture is specialized for a sequential neural network model not having a folk and join of the layer(s).
  It was designed using a 32-nm semiconductor process and CACTI 6.5, and models the energy consumption and necessary area. It was found that 74 KB is sufficient for the buffer size of the temporal data between layers, and a small-scale eDRAM was shown to be sufficient to hold the data. Such a small memory contributes to the computational efficiency and memory utilization. The interconnection network between tiles requires 3.2 GB/s, and therefore, a 32-bit network configuration is applied at 1 GHz. By pipelining, 65.8 W of power is consumed, meaning of that more power is used than DaDianNao,

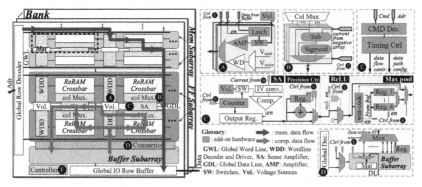

FIGURE 7.4 PRIME architecture [173].

which requires 20.1 W of power. Similar to DaDianNao, a CNN task has been targeted, although it is not yet supported for learning tasks.

- University of California at Santa Barbara (UCSB): PRIME
  PRIME focuses on a processing-in-memory (PIM) computing model [173], and considers three domains of a logic circuit, hardware architecture, and software interface [134]. See Fig. 7.4.
  A uniform PIM architecture was proposed for deep learning tasks. The resources in an ReRAM array can be dynamically reconfigured to the accelerator for such tasks. ReRAM has two modes, one is to function as a traditional memory (memory mode), and the other is to function as an accelerator (computation mode). ReRAM banks are partitioned into three domains: memory, full function (FF), and buffer subarrays.
  A memory subarray and buffer subarray operate as a data buffer. An FF subarray is used for both computations and memory and has an ReLU unit for computation mode. After compiling a neural network model, it optimizes the mapping of the model for bridging between the scales of the ReRAM bank and the model. Regarding the optimization used for execution, the OS determines the memory resource allocation and deallocation based on the memory page miss rate and utilization of a subarray. Thus, a redesign or extension to a common OS is needed.
- Gyrfalcon
  Here, a CNN was developed, namely a DSA (CNN-DSA) [341]. The CNN-DSA engine (CE) is shown in Fig. 7.5(a).
  It consists of an input-router, output-router, SRAM banks, and ALU array. The ALU array is between the input-router and output-router, and SRAM banks have a multicast-network as a row-based communication to send the parameters. The array is formed into a 42×42 arrangement and applies a 3×3 filter convolution and 2×2 pooling. CNN-DSA has a 4×4 array of CE, and 9 MB of SRAM. It operates at 9.3 TOPS/W with a peak power of less than 300 mW.

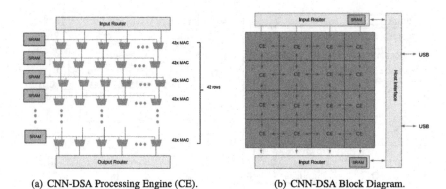

(a) CNN-DSA Processing Engine (CE). (b) CNN-DSA Block Diagram.

FIGURE 7.5 Gyrfalcon convolutional neural network domain-specific architecture [341].

An accelerator with non-volatile memory, STT-MRAM, called a CNN matrix processing engine (MPE) was also developed [340]. An MPE has a similar architecture as a CNN-DSA.

An activation uses a 9-bit domain specific floating-point (DSFP), and the model coefficients use a 15-bit DSFP [340]. This MRAM parameter memory based MPE achieves a rate of 9.9 TOPS/W.

- Mythic
  An inference accelerator was developed using embedded Flash memory technology which operates as the analog crossbar equivalent to the synapses. Flash memory is applied between the DAC and ADC. The processing node has Flash memory embedded with DA/ADC and an RISC-V host processor. The processing node is replicated on a chip and forms an array of nodes. Mythic uses a Fujitsu 40-nm embedded-flash cell [150]. The DAC has an 8-bit resolution. The power-efficiency is 2TMAC/W (4TOPS/W).

7.2.2 DSPs

A deep learning task is a dot-product composing a matrix-vector multiplication, and therefore DSP optimized to an MAC operation is a suitable architecture for such learning.

- CEVA
  - XM Series
    An XM4 DSP has two vector processing units (VPUs) performing 64 MAC operations in parallel on each unit [180]. It can conduct 8-, 16-, and 32-bit fixed-point arithmetic operations and a single precision floating-point operation. A VPU shares a large-scale vector RF. It also has four scalar processing units and two load/store units. Users can integrate a user-defined coprocessor and its instruction set. It has two 256-bit memory interfaces, supporting Caffe and TensorFlow APIs, and can convert

(a) Myriad-1 Die Photo.

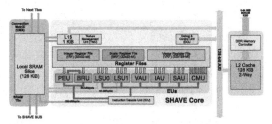

(b) SHAVE v2 Core Block Diagram.

FIGURE 7.6 Myriad-1 architecture [101].

a coded neural network model into a running binary. It was designed for a 28-nm TSMC high-performance mobile (HPM) semiconductor process and runs at 1.2 GHz.

An XM6 has a similar architecture as an XM4, but with a dedicated vector floating-point unit. It has three VPUs and shares a vector RF.

- NeuPro-S
  NeuPro-S is an imaging and computer vision inferencing processor [102]. It has a neural network processing engine called a NeuPro-S Engine specialized for convolutional neural networking tasks including a convolution and pooling. The NeuPro-S Engine consists of a convolution array performing the convolution, a pooling unit, an activation unit, and a scaling unit. The XM core and NeuPro-S are connected through the AXI bus, which supports 8- and 16-bit quantization mixed operations. The number of MACs (8 × 8-bit) ranges from 1000 to 4096 units. A single chip also has an XM processor.

- Movidius (Intel): Myriad Series
  Myriad-2 integrates 12 VLIW vector processors, one of which is called SHAVE [82]. Fig. 7.6(a) shows a photograph of a Myriad-1 die with eight SHAVE v2 cores. The vector processor supports half- and single-precision floating-point operations. A drone was developed with a chip that the drone can track by object recognition and autonomous driving [75]. They were acquired by Intel in September 2016 [74].
  Fig. 7.6(b) shows a block diagram of a SHAVE v2 core. The core consists of scalar and vector RFs, one vector arithmetic unit, one integer unit, two load/store units, a branch unit, and a comparator unit, among others. These units are controlled using the VLIW ISA. They run at 180 MHz, and achieve 17.28 GOPS with a power consumption of 0.35 W, and 181 GOPS/W for an 8-bit integer [147].

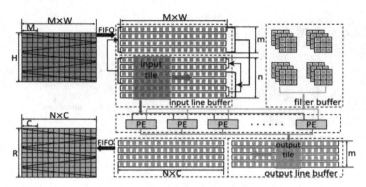

FIGURE 7.7 Peking University's architecture on FPGA [380].

7.2.3 FPGAs

- New York University: neuFlow

  A neuFlow is a processor for object recognition [160]. It focuses on image processing tasks and takes a modular approach.

  Off-chip memory is connected to every module through a DMA unit. Focus is on a high throughput rather than a low latency. A two-dimensional mesh configuration is composed by connecting an NoC to a processing tile (PT) performing the operations, which can allow dynamically reconfiguring the routing between the PTs and the PT operations. A FIFO interface allows the operator to maintain a high throughput. An image pixel is stored in Q8.8 format in external memory, and is scaled to 32 bits at the operator.

  The designed neural network model is compiled using a special compiler called a LuaFlow API to generate a binary running on the neuFlow. The neuFlow hardware achieves execution throughput of 12 fps for 20 classes each having a 500×375 image size. The peak performance is at 160 GOPS (147 GOPS, measured), with a 10 W power consumption for a Xilinx Virtex-6 VLX240T operating at 200 MHz and 10 W.

- Peking University

  Another study proposed an implementation method for a CNN on an FPGA using Winograd [380]. Fig. 7.7 shows the architecture applied. The input and output buffers are composed of line buffers because the target is a CNN model having two-dimensional input and output activations. The convolution reuses the input activation elements because of a two-dimensional window sliding, and therefore line buffers are used.

  A CNN basically has a four-level nested loop consisting of rows and columns, input channels, and output channels. These loops can be parallelized using loop-unrolling, and the loop order can change. The researchers assessed the resource requirements for the accelerator design on FPGAs. They modeled the DSP, LUT, and BRAM resource requirements, and modeled the execution time and bandwidth assessment models. The operations in fully connected layers can be treated as an element-wise multiplication by filling the input neurons and the corresponding weights into a matrix [380].

The researchers also introduced the use of a roofline model [367] to explore the best architecture, which is now a standard approach. The computation engine reads the weights from the buffer, and a multiplication between the weight and activation is conducted at the sub-unit, and the multiplication results are summed using an adder-tree. An operation takes a single precision floating-point unit. It uses a double buffer, and avoids having to wait to access the external memory through a ping-pong buffer. The authors also designed an automatic tool flow to automate the mapping onto the FPGAs, which is synthesized on a Xilinx Virtex7 FPGA with an HLS design. Using AlexNet, a convolution is performed at an average throughput of 61.62–1006.7 GOPS, and achieves 72.4–854.6 GOPS overall. On a VGG16, the throughput is 354–2940.7 GOPS overall, with a 9.4-W power consumption, and achieves 72.3 GOPS/W at 166 MHz.

- University of Pittsburgh

A study on the implementation of an FPGA for an RNN-based language model (RNNLM) was conducted [243].

The authors considered a two-stage pipelined RNN structure. Usually, the V nodes in the input and output layers are related to the vocabulary, and can easily reach up to a size of 10–200 K, whereas H nodes in a hidden layer can maintain a much smaller scale such as 0.1–1 K [243]. Therefore, the latency during the second stage is much longer than that during the first stage. To enhance the second stage, more PEs of the output layer are duplicated.

The platform is a Convey HC^{ex} computing system using a Xilinx Virtex6 LX760. It applies multi-threading to reduce the idling time for an efficient execution. The computation engine (CE) has a thread management unit (TMU) that manages to read the row of the matrix, create and allocate threads to the PE, and kick start or terminate the process. Multiple PEs are in the CE, and each PE applies a dot-product for the row and vector, as well as an activation function. The CE aims to accelerate the execution with multiple output layers and a single hidden recursive layer. The hidden and output layers run at 150 MHz, with a throughput of 2.4 and 9.6 GOPS, respectively, resulting in 46.2% accuracy and a 25-W (TDP) power consumption.

- Tsinghua University

An accelerator for image recognition was also implemented [293].

This system has an architecture combining a CPU and an FPGA. The processing system implemented on the CPU manages to access the external memory. It supports pruning and a dynamic quantization, and therefore compresses and decompresses the parameters and input data, and contributes to a reduction in the memory access traffic on a fully connected layer. The weights and data (activations) are quantized.

A convolver complex implemented on an FPGA consists of several PEs. A PE has a data buffer and a weight buffer when considering the access order by

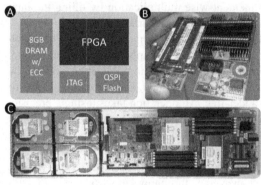
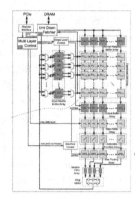

(a) Catapult Platform.

(b) CNN Accelerator Block Diagram.

FIGURE 7.8 CNN accelerator on Catapult platform [283].

a line buffer configuration. It reads several data from each buffer, applies several multiplications on a multiplier array, feeds the results into an adder-tree to sum the products, and finally applies activation and pooling. Under the constraint of the on-chip memory size, it suppresses the amount of data on the chip as much as possible by reusing data with a tiling system using a Xilinx Zynq 706. The processing of VGG16-SVD is conducted at 150 MHz, and executed with a throughput of 136.97 GOPS, and a power consumption of 9.63 W.

- Microsoft Research

  - Catapult

    The authors implemented an image recognition accelerator on a Catapult server [282] developed for a data center [282]. Catapult has an Altera Stratix-V D5 FPGA, and FPGAs are connected with a two-dimensional 6×8 torus network on a server rack, as shown in Fig. 7.8(b). The datapath for CNN processing has a systolic array configuration [283], as shown in Fig. 7.8(b). The data flow from top to bottom and are fed into the activation function through the addition of biases.

    On a system with a Stratix-V D5, CIFAR-10, ImageNet 1K, and ImageNet 22K are processed with throughputs of 2318, 134, and 91 fps, respectively, at 25 W [282]. In addition, a new version of the system, which consists of an Altera Arria-10 GX1150 applies ImageNet 1K with a throughput of 369 fps with a peak power consumption of 25 W [283].

  - BrainWave

    Similar to Amazon's F1-instance, Microsoft supports a cloud service with FPGA(s) [138]. A DNN model is mapped onto the FPGA resources configured with a neural FU (NFU). A Caffe, CNTK, or TensorFlow model is

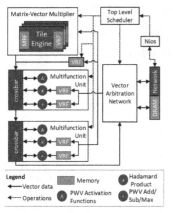

(a) Accelerator Block Diagram.

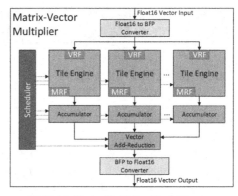

(b) Matrix-Vector Multiplier Block Diagram.

FIGURE 7.9 Accelerator on BrainWave platform [165].

fed into the frontend, which generates an IR. The IR is used to generate a bit stream of configuration data through the tool pipeline as the back-end. NFU consists of multiple Matrix-Vector Units which one operates matrix-vector multiply. The results are summed through an adder-tree, which can configure an 8-bit fixed-point as well as an 8-bit floating-point and a 9-bit floating-point. The authors claim that these narrow floating-points are sufficient for their deep learning tasks with sufficient inference accuracy. See Fig. 7.9.

- Ehime University: NRNS

  The authors proposed a matrix operation suitable for an FPGA architecture; note, however, that they did not propose an accelerator architecture [275]. The system uses a residue number system (RNS) [169] to numerically represent a remainder obtained when decomposing from an integer to a relative prime integer. Whereas an FPGA has numerous DSP blocks, a relatively larger number of LUTs are on the chip. By contrast, deep learning requires a significant number of MACs to conduct dot-product operations.

  Facing this gap, all data are decomposed into multiple smaller data using an RNS, and thus are mapped to a massive number of LUTs for multiplication with the weight and to sum the products, thereby realizing a higher parallel processing than the DSP blocks. A decomposition into nonuniform logic circuits is required to implement an RNS, and to solve this issue, the authors proposed a recursive method called a nested RNS (NRNS). Preprocessing is applied to convert an integer into an RNS, and post-processing converts the RNS after a matrix operation in such a numerical domain into an integer. A synthesis on a Xilinx Virtex7 VC485T shows that it runs at 400 MHz and performs a matrix operation at 132.2 GOPS.

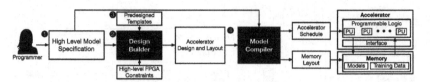

FIGURE 7.10 Work flow on Tabla [254].

- Georgia Institute of Technology
  - Tabla
    Tabla is a framework used to generate an accelerator [254]. The objective of the solution is to devise the necessary programming abstractions and automated frameworks that are uniform across a range of machine learning algorithms [254]. See Fig. 7.10.

    Tabla has a template-based design flow. As its template, the SGD is uniform across a range of ML algorithms, and this programming abstraction requires the programmer to only provide the gradient of the objective function [254]. The first step is to describe the cost function with a high-level language by looking into the gradient descent method. Common parts in the neural network model are detected, and therefore a high-level development environment can be provided. The development of the framework requires four steps.

    After a design using a template, the design builder automatically generates the accelerator and its interfacing logic, which is generated from a predesigned template. The second step is to automatically generate code of the accelerator using the cost function obtained during the first step, the high-level specifications of the target FPGA, and the design template of the machine learning accelerator. In addition, this step adds an interface used for external memory access. The third step is to construct better settings through an exploration between a specific network model and the FPGA specifications.

    The model compiler statically generates an execution schedule for the accelerator. Statically generating a schedule for the accelerator significantly simplifies the hardware [254]. The fourth step is to convert the accelerator structure into a dataflow graph using a tool called a model compiler.
  - DNNWeaver
    DNNWeaver is an updated version of Tabla, and is a framework used to generate a similar accelerator, the major difference being the fully automatic process applied [320]. The development on DNNWeaver also requires four steps.

    As the first step, the translator translates the DNN specifications into a macro dataflow ISA. The accelerator does not execute using an ISA. The control flow instruction is mapped as a control signal in the accelerator. It also creates an execution schedule. This abstraction aims to provide a unified hardware-software interface and enable layer-specific optimization in the accelerator microarchitecture without exposure to the software.

The second step uses a template resource optimization algorithm to optimize the hardware templates for the target FPGA platform. This is used to partition the DNN execution to fit the size of the accelerator for parallel processing, resource-sharing, and data-recycling. The tool used is called a design planner. The template resource optimization algorithm aims to strike a balance between parallel operations and data reuse by slicing the computations and configuring the accelerator to best match the constraints of the FPGA (on-chip memory and external memory bandwidth) [320]. The accelerator changes to the next processing after writing back the partitioned process data.

The third step is to translate the schedule for a finite state machine (FSM), and perform resource allocation and optimization based on the results of the design planner with a manually designed template. The tool used is called Design Weaver. Design Weaver uses a series of hand-optimized design templates and customizes them in accordance with the resource allocation and hardware organization provided by the planner [320]. These templates provide a highly customizable, modular, and scalable implementation for Design Weaver that automatically specialize the templates to accommodate a variety of DNNs that are translated to our macro dataflow ISA [320].

The fourth step is to add a memory interface to the previously generated code, and finally generate code for the target FPGA. A Verilog code is ready to be synthesized on the target FPGA to accelerate the specified DNN [320].

- Stanford University: ESE
  To speed up the prediction on the LSTM model and make it energy efficient, we first propose a load-balance-aware pruning method that can compress the LSTM model size by 20-fold (10-fold from pruning and 2-fold from quantization) with negligible loss in prediction accuracy [182].

  The authors proposed a pruning method called load balance aware pruning. This method forces the use of approximately the same number of elements in each interleaved CSC encoder applied in the EIE. The original interleaved CSC encoding creates idling cycles caused by varying the number of elements. The encoded weight has both index and weight values. One non-zero weight has its value followed by the index.

  The PE has a similar configuration as the EIE. Multiple PEs are composed on the channel processing cluster. The output of the PEs is fed into the LSTM-specific operation datapath. The proposed ESE hardware system is built on an XCKU060 FPGA running at 200 MHz [182]. The load balance aware pruning improves the speed from a 5.5- to 6.2-times smaller footprint. It achieves a throughput of 282.2 GOPS and requires 41 W of power consumption. Thus, it has a power efficiency of 6.9 GOPS/W.

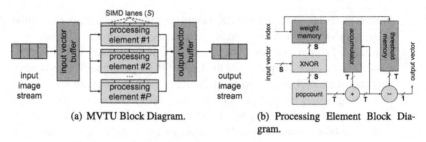

(a) MVTU Block Diagram.

(b) Processing Element Block Diagram.

FIGURE 7.11 Matrix vector threshold unit (MVTU) [356].

- Xilinx Research Labs
  - FINN

    The authors proposed FINN, a framework for building scalable and fast BNN inference accelerators on FPGAs [356].

    Finn implements a binary neural network model on an FPGA targeting a CNN model [356]. Here, "−1" and "+1" are assigned to a binary of zero and 1, respectively. A dot-product can be applied using a bitwise XOR logic operation and its population count (simply called a pop count). When the pre-activation value is greater than a threshold value, the output is 1; otherwise, the output is zero for the ReLU activation function. The above were studied in [141] [301].

    The authors claim that they observed an FPGA compute-bound performance of 66 TOPS for binary operations, which is approximately 16-times higher compared to 8-bit fixed-point operations and 53-times higher compared to 16-bit fixed-point operations [356]. However, reaching a compute-bound peak is only possible if the application is not memory-bound [356].

    The authors also pointed out a pooling implementation. Max pooling is used to apply a logical OR when comparing between the activation element and the threshold. Min pooling aims to apply a logical AND for the result of the comparison. Average pooling aims to output a zero when the number of zeros is greater than the number of 1s; otherwise, it outputs a value of 1.

    The matrix-vector-threshold unit (MVTU) conducts a matrix operation (shown in Fig. 7.11(a)). To better cater to the SIMD parallelism of the MVTU and minimize the buffering requirements, we interleave the feature maps such that each pixel contains all of the input feature map (IFM) channel data for that position [356].

    The authors also consider the effect of the binary quantization on the accuracy of the inference. By increasing the number of neurons, the error in the inference is decreased. This can also be seen in a floating-point numerical representation as a deeper neural network configuration. The difference in the error rate between the approaches ranges from 3.8 to 0.26 points.

A small-scale neural network model cannot recover from a decrease in the accuracy of the inference.

It has a control for operating under the target throughput. The authors used a Xilinx Zynq-7000 All Programmable SoC ZC706 Evaluation Kit, which was developed using a Xilinx Vivado high-level synthesis (HLS) tool targeting a 200-MHz implementation. This tool has a 283 μs latency, and runs at 2121 K-fps under an inference accuracy of 95.8% with a power consumption of 22 W.

- Arizona State University (ASU)
  In this case, the authors considered and analyzed a nested loop configuration method composing a convolution in a CNN with a high-level language-based design [252]. In a convolution task, a four-level nested loop is used, where the inner most loop is an MAC, the second loop is an input feature map, the third loop is for scan window sliding, and the outer most loop is an output feature map. The authors analyzed the effect of a loop-unrolling, a loop-tiling, and a loop-interchange to achieve an efficient architecture.

  Loop-unrolling is a factor in determining the parallelism in the convolution, deciding the number of arithmetic units for the implementation, and in deciding the data reusability. In addition, the latency for a computation is also determined by the loop-unrolling, and thus it also decides the off-chip memory accesses based on the on-chip buffer size and the data reusability.

  Loop-tiling determines the block size in the iteration of the loop, and therefore determines the necessary on-chip buffer size, as well as the off-chip memory accesses. The number of off-chip memory accesses is determined by the on-chip buffer size, and therefore depends on how the loop-tiling is constructed.

  The loop-interchange determines the order of the operation because it interchanges the order of nested loops, and decides on the number of registers used for holding the temporal results, such as a partial sum.

  Thus, it determines how the construction of the loop-unrolling and the loop-tiling changes the necessary hardware resources. These analysis results of the architecture-based design on an Arria 10 FPGA show a 3-fold greater inference throughput and a short latency compared with traditional experiment results on a VGG-16.

7.2.4 ASICs

- Chinese Academy of Sciences (CAS)
  - DianNao
    In this case, focus is on a huge amount of memory access traffic when applying deep learning [128].

    The authors analyzed the data locality and design based on the results. They also focused on a data reuse method to suppress the energy consumption by reducing the amount of traffic. To keep a partial sum after

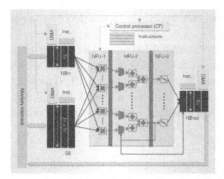

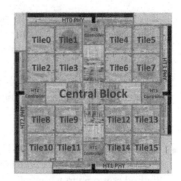

(a) DianNao Block Diagram.   (b) DaDianNao Die Layout.

FIGURE 7.12 DianNao and DaDianNao [128].

the multiplication of the activation and parameters, a register is used. In addition, the activations between the layers are buffered.

The PE has an input buffer, an output buffer, and a weight buffer, which are connected to an NFU. The inputs, synaptic weights, and outputs are time-shared by different algorithmic blocks of neurons. The NFU executes on three stages, as shown in Fig. 7.12(a). The first stage is multiplication, the second stage is an adder-tree used to make a partial sum, and the third stage is an activation function. To enhance the execution, loop-tiling is used to distribute data to each NFU effectively.

DianNao takes a VLIW instruction set to control the loop, classification, convolution, and other factors. It uses a code generator tool designed for three main modules rather than a compiler. It applies 16-bit fixed-point arithmetic with truncation. DianNao can conduct 496 operations every cycle. It runs at 980 MHz, and therefore achieves a throughput of 452 GOPS. It was designed with a 65-nm semiconductor process, and has an area of 3 mm^2. It also runs at 980 MHz with a power consumption of 485 mW. Thus, its power efficiency is 932.0 GOPS/W.

- DaDianNao
  Here, an architecture for a large-scale neural network based on the Dian-Nao architecture is considered [129]. It uses DianNao as a node, and takes a distributed architecture supporting both inference and learning.
  It does not have a main memory, and each node has four embedded DRAMs (eDRAMs); in addition, the architecture transfers activations between nodes. To apply eDRAM and learning, multiple input and output modes are applied on the node pipeline. Nodes are interconnected with a 4-ary tree. A worm-hole router connecting between chips with a two-dimensional mesh topology is also used. Each node has two controlling modes, one is for a processing, and the other is for a batch. Communication between adjacent feature maps divided into a unit fitting on the node,

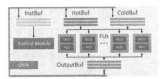 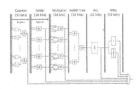 

(a) PuDianNao Block Diagram. (b) PuDianNao Machine Learning Unit (MLU). (c) PuDianNao Die Layout.

FIGURE 7.13 PuDianNao [245].

convolution layer, and pooling layer is necessary. Classification requires communication on a complete network topology.

It is designed using 28-nm ST Technology LP. In addition, eRAM and NFU operate at 606 MHz with 0.9 V, and their power consumption is 15.9 W. The chip has an area of 67.7 mm^2, integrating a 512 KB eDRAM for each node, with 16 nodes placed on the chip.

- PuDianNao

  In general, machine learning hardware tends to support a narrow domain of applications in a neural network model family such as a CNN with a hyperparameter constraint. An architectural method has been considered to support various machine learning models [245]. To evaluate the architecture, the researchers used seven machine learning approaches, i.e., K-Means, k-nearest neighbors (k-NN), naive Bayes (NB), an SVM, a linear regression (LR), a classification tree (CT), and a DNN. They concluded that the tiling method is effective for the k-NN, k-Means, DNN, LR, and SVM by utilizing its data locality; however, it is ineffective for the NB or CT because they cannot be used to predict the locality. See Fig. 7.13.

  A machine learning unit (MLU) consists of three data buffers, one instruction buffer, one controller module, one RAM, and multiple FUs (FUs). Each FU has an MLU and an ALU. The first stage is used to accelerate the counting operations through a naive Bayes and a classification tree [245]. The third through the fifth stages have a similar configuration as DianNao. MLU supports a common dot-product operation and an activation function, and it applies an adder-tree.

  The Misc stage integrates two modules, a linear interpolation module and a k-sorter module, as follows [245]. The linear interpolation module is used to approximate the non-linear functions involved in the ML techniques. Different non-linear functions correspond to different interpolation tables. The k-sorter module is used to find the smallest k values from the outputs of the ACC stage, which is a common operation in k-Means and a k-NN.

  An ALU supports not only four arithmetic operations but also conversion between an integer numerical representation, and a logarithm function, which contains an adder, a multiplier, and a divider, as well as the con-

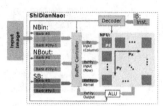
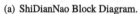

(a) ShiDianNao Block Diagram.

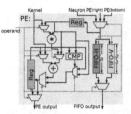

(b) ShiDianNao Processing Element.

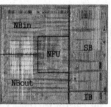

(c) ShiDianNao Die Layout.

FIGURE 7.14   ShiDianNao [156].

version of a 32-bit float into a 16-bit float and a 16-bit float into a 32-bit float.

It is designed using a 65-nm TSMC GP semiconductor process and has an area of 3.51 mm^2 when 16 FUs are integrated. It achieves a throughput of 1056 GOPS at 1.01 GHz and consumes 596 mW of power. Thus, its DLP is 1045 operations per cycle, and the power-efficiency is 1771.8 GOPS/W.

- ShiDianNao

  We studied an energy-efficient design of a visual recognition accelerator for direct embedding into any CMOS or CCD sensor, which is fast enough to process images in real time, and is used as an accelerator for image recognition [156].

  The design consists of an input buffer, an output buffer, a buffer for activation, an NFU, an ALU operating activation function, an instruction buffer, and a decoder, as shown in Fig. 7.14(a). The NFU is designed for efficiently processing two-dimensionally arranged data, and has multiple PEs with a two-dimensional layout, and applies a systolic-array method. NFU conducts a convolution, classification, normalization, and comparison for pooling purposes. Each PE has a FIFO to send data to the left neighbor PE and bottom neighbor PE and support data reuse, as shown in Fig. 7.14(b). The PE supports 16-bit fixed-point arithmetic.

  The NFU can apply a convolution, pooling, and classification. The convolution takes four cycles as follows [156]: In the first cycle, the operand data are input and a multiplication is applied. In the second cycle, the required data from the FIFO-Hs are read, and all PEs share the kernel value read from the SB. In the third cycle, each PE is processed in the first row of the corresponding convolutional window and will move to the second row of the convolutional window during the next cycle. In the fourth cycle, all PEs share a kernel value of k0,1 as read from the SB. In addition, each PE collects its received input neuron in its FIFO-H and FIFO-V for future inter-PE data propagation [156].

  It is presumed that all data can be on a chip. Each buffer has a multi-bank configuration and supports multiple access mode. The authors propose a two-level control method consisting of an FSM. A higher-level FSM de-

 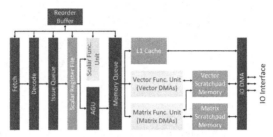

(a) Cambricon-ACC Die Lay-out.   (b) Cambricon-ACC Block Diagram.

FIGURE 7.15 Cambricon-ACC [247].

fines a layer-transition for the processing, and a lower-level FSM defines the details of the control for operation on the layer. These combinations also define the data flow control on each layer. This is designed using a 65-nm TSMC with an area of 4.86 mm^2. The device runs at 1 GHz and consumes 320.1 mW of power.

- Cambricon-ACC
  Cambricon-ACC has an ISA called Cambricon, specialized for neural network models [247]. Based on a traditional ISA, the authors proposed three primitive operations, namely, scalar, vector, and matrix operations, which require a load-storage architecture. In addition, scaling for a vector and matrix is supported, and the exponent function ($f(x) = e^x$) is used in the activation function. Instead of a vector RF, a scratch-pad memory composed of a bank configuration is applied.

  The instruction set includes computational, logical, control, and data transfer instructions as follows [247]. The instruction length is fixed at 64-bits for the memory alignment and design simplicity of the load/storage/decoding logic. Two types of control-flow instruction, jump and conditional branch, are supported. Data transfer instructions used by Cambricon support variable data sizes to flexibly support matrix and vector computational/logical instructions.

  In addition, each vector and matrix can use a direct memory access (DMA) unit supporting a variable sized vector and matrix. Cambricon-ACC embeds a Cambricon ISA into a traditional RISC microarchitecture. On ten neural network models, it demonstrated 6.41-, 9.86-, and 13.38-fold improvements in its footprint as compared with a GPU (NVIDIA K40M), x86, and MIPS, respectively.

  Fig. 7.15(b) shows a Cambricon-ACC microarchitecture consisting of seven pipeline stages, namely, instruction fetch, instruction decode, issue, register read, execution, write back, and commit stages. This is an in-order issue. For the data transfer instructions, vector/matrix computational instructions and vector logical instructions, which may access the L1 cache

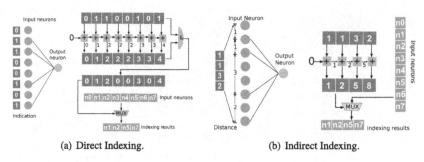

(a) Direct Indexing.   (b) Indirect Indexing.

FIGURE 7.16 Cambricon-X zero-skipping on sparse tensor [382].

or scratchpad memories, are sent to the AGU [247]. Such instructions need to wait in an in-order memory queue to resolve the potential memory dependencies with earlier instructions in the memory queue [247].

Compared with a x86-CPU and a GPU, a 91.72- and 3.09-fold higher execution performance is achieved, respectively. Compared with DaDianNao, which can apply only three neural network models, a 4.5% decrease in the execution performance occurs with its DSA. The energy consumption is 130.53- and 0.916-times superior than a GPU and DaDianNao, respectively. For a design with a 65-nm TSMC GP standard VT library, a 56.241 mm^2 area is applied. Although its clock frequency and driving voltage are unknown, it consumes 1.6956 W of power.

- Cambricon-X

  Here, the authors focus on an effective sparse tensor execution. This approach also uses an index (offset) similar to that of other studies; however, two alternative methods were considered and evaluated.

  An accelerator for sparse machine learning is used [382]. We cannot know where the zero values are in the vectors and matrices before the learning process because such values are randomly placed in the tensor as a learning result. In addition, there is a possibility of having an invalid activation function based on the sparseness.

  It is necessary to efficiently read the data, except for the zero values randomly placed in the sparse tensor. An inference is executed for the user-designed neural network model, in which data with zero values are removed. Thus, it is necessary to address the position of an element that should be read next with the present read element. The authors proposed two indexing methods to read out the parameters, namely, direct and indirect indexing.

  With direct indexing, a flag matrix addressing the existence of a parameter in the parameter matrix is prepared, as shown in Fig. 7.16(a). When a flag is "1," its corresponding non-zero parameter is in the corresponding position. It uses an index register, and if the flag in the register is asserted

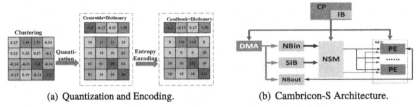

(a) Quantization and Encoding.   (b) Cambricon-S Architecture.

FIGURE 7.17 Compression and architecture of Cambricon-S [384].

onto the sequential reading, then it increases the index register, and its value minus 1 addresses the non-zero value placed in the memory (buffer). Indirect indexing uses other memory applied to relatively address the elements of a parameter in a sparse matrix, as shown in Fig. 7.16(b). Similar to a direct indexing approach, it also uses an index register, and the relative value of the index is added to the register when it reads the next element of the parameter, and its value minus 1 indicates an address of the next element.

The device has an area of 6.38 mm^2 and consumes 954 mW of power at a clock frequency of 1 GHz. Compared with DaDianNao, it achieves a 7.23-fold higher execution performance and a 6.43-fold lower energy consumption. Compared with a GPU platform using cuSPASE, which is a library for a sparse matrix, it achieves a 10.60-fold higher execution performance and a 29.43-fold lower energy consumption. The authors did not describe the learning process or how the indexes are generated after the learning.

- Cambricon-S

  Cambricon-S focuses on a cooperative software/hardware approach to efficiently address the irregularity of sparse neural networks [384]. The behavior of the training is also focused on a sparse neural network of larger weights that tend to gather into small clusters. A software-based coarse-grained pruning technique was proposed to drastically reduce the irregularity of sparse synapses with a local quantization.

  Cooperation between the software and hardware was considered to obtain sparseness. For the software, focus is on pruning, and thus static sparseness is obtained. For the hardware, the ReLU creates zeros, and thus by implementing a dynamic sparseness handler dynamic sparseness is obtained. These techniques reduce unnecessary data traffic and calculations.

  The sparsity compression flow is from normal training, iterative coarse-grained pruning and re-training, local quantization, and finally, entropy encoding. In coarse-grained pruning several synapses are first pruned together, and then grouped into blocks. Blocks of synapses are permanently removed from the network topology if they meet specific criteria. Fig. 7.17(a) shows compression with quantization and entropy encoding. The quantization uses a dictionary, which is a centroid of tensor elements,

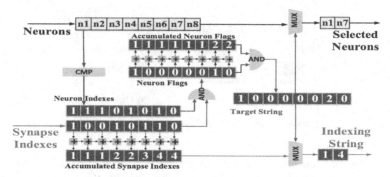

FIGURE 7.18 Indexing approach on Cambricon-S [384].

one of which addresses the dictionary element. After that, the address (index) is encoded.

The local quantization works with weight-sharing in the local domains of the neural network. Weights are encoded into a codebook and a dictionary with 1-bit per weight. Entropy encoding is lossless data-compression that adds a unique prefix-free code to each unique symbol such as Huffmann coding.

Fig. 7.18 shows the indexing method on Cambricon-S. It treats both nodes (neurons) and edges (synapses) of a neural network topology for the ReLU activations and zero-weights, respectively. When both the neuron and edge are non-zero, a calculation should be applied, and thus, the neuron and synapse indexes are applied with logic AND. The AND flags are used for generating the addresses of the neuron in the buffer, which are generated through accumulation. At the same time, it generates addresses of the synapses in the buffer, which are generated through accumulation.

An accelerator consists of a neuron selector module (NSM) and a neural functional unit (NFU). The NSM processes static sparsity with shared indexes. The NFU consists of multiple PEs consisting of a local synapse selector module (SSM) to process the dynamic sparsity. NBin and NBout is neural buffers with a synapse index buffer (SIB). It has a VLIW-style instruction set.

It has an area of 6.73 mm^2 with 798.55 mW implemented using a 65-nm process, and achieves a 512 GOPS, and thus it is 1.0 TOPS/W.

- Cambricon-F

Cambricon-F focuses on the productivity, aiming to make a homogeneous instruction set on a many-core with a structuring of the neural network operations into a fractal to make it easy to map the neural network model onto the hardware, and returns to a state of high efficiency [383]. It does not need a re-compilation for different scales of hardware.

The operations, such as a vector multiplying matrix and a matrix multiplying vector, are aggregated into a matrix multiplying matrix, and op-

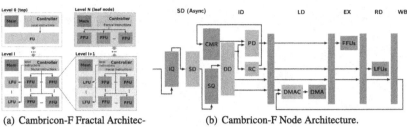

(a) Cambricon-F Fractal Architecture.   (b) Cambricon-F Node Architecture.

FIGURE 7.19 Cambricon-F architecture [383].

erations such as a matrix adding/subtracting matrix, a matrix multiplying scalar, and a vector elementary arithmetic are aggregated into an element-wise operation. The operations are refactored into seven major computing primitives after decomposition, including a convolution (CONV), pooling (POOL), matrix multiplying matrix (MMM), element-wise operation (ELTW), sorting (SORT), and counting (COUNT).

For the hierarchical topology hardware with a static pattern, as shown in Fig. 7.19(a), the input data must be shared or distributed to the lowest level nodes; for example, one activation must be shared among the nodes for a matrix-vector multiplication. Although such a fan-in is required, it is claimed that a fan-out on the hierarchical topology is minor and thus the communication cost among nodes across different clusters of nodes can be removed.

A fractal instruction-set architecture (FISA) was proposed in which the instruction is replicated as a multi-level fractal operation to map the fractal hardware, such that the instruction has a bit-field indicating the scale. The node of Cambricon-F, shown in Fig. 7.19(b), has an architecture consisting of six pipeline stages. To steer the fractal mapping, different stages are compared with a traditional pipelined processor before the execution stage. A parallel decomposer (PD) decomposes the instruction hierarchically. The reduction controller works to control the reduction communication (fan-out communication). See Fig. 7.20.

Thus, the amount of execution time spent on the pipeline is determined by the ratio of the total number of pipeline stages to the number of execution pipeline stages and the level hierarchy. For example, Cambricon-F has two execution stages with six pipeline stages, and thus the execution requires $(1/3)^i$ at the i-level. Therefore, this implies that at least 3^i nodes are necessary to cancel the execution overhead.

Cambricon-F is implemented using a 45-nm process with an embedded DRAM of 16 and 448 MB, achieving 14.9 TOPS and 119 TOPS in an area of 29 mm^2 and 415 mm^2 for Cambricon-F1 and Cambricon-F100 having 3.02 TOPS/W and 2.78 TOPS/W, respectively.

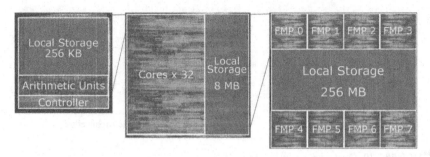

FIGURE 7.20 Cambricon-F die photo [383].

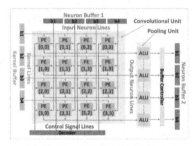

(a) FlexFlow's Entire Architecture.

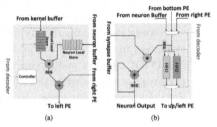

(b) FlexFlow's PE Architecture.

FIGURE 7.21 FlexFlow architecture [249].

- FlexFlow

  The authors focused on a resource utilization enhancement required by a mismatch in the DLP between the designed accelerator architecture and the designed neural network model [249]. They proposed a data-flow processing architecture to support full parallelism.

  They summarized a typical accelerator architecture, which has a fixed data direction, fixed data type, and fixed data stride. These fix the usable hyperparameters of the neural network models, and network models having different hyperparameters cannot be mapped onto the fixed architecture.

  Fig. 7.21(a) shows the entire architecture, where the PE forms an array, and there are buffers for the input features, filters, and output features. A buffer is connected to all PEs in a row or column to unicast the data of the input features and filter. In addition, a dedicated pooling unit is used as a vertical linear array of the ALU. The PE has a local storage to maintain the reuse of the data and for data routing, as shown in Fig. 7.21(b).

  Fig. 7.22(a) shows the flexible multicasting used by the local interconnection for two cases. One unicast line is shared with the buffers. Fig. 7.22(b) shows the die layout, which has a 3.89 mm^2 area with a 65-nm process and the implementation of 256 PEs. On six benchmark neural network models, it achieves more than 80% resource utilization. The unicasting

(a) FlexFlow's Complementaly Parallelism.   (b) FlexFlow's Layout.

FIGURE 7.22 FlexFlow's parallel diagram and die layout [249].

interconnection network might contribute to the enhancement of the utilization owing to its small data distribution latency. The power-efficiency is more than 400 GOPS/W on the five benchmarks applied. Thus, it seems that the running clock frequency is 1 GHz.

- Korea Advanced Institute of Science and Technology (KAIST)
  - K-Brain
    K-Brain [286] is a processor for image recognition, and consists of three major units, DNLE, DNIE, and TRNG. The deep neural learning engine (DNLE) has a 4-stage task-level pipeline configuration and supports a dual-threading execution. A deep neural inference engine (DNIE) is a dynamically reconfigurable systolic array architecture. The true random number generator (TRNG) generates a random number. These units take a two-dimensional mesh configuration based on NoC. Inference is applied for up to a 640×480 sized image. At 200 MHz and 1.2 V, an operation requires a throughput of 11.8 Gbps, 213.1 mW of power, and an energy efficiency of 19.3 TOPS/W.
  - Natural UI/UX processor with deep-learning core
    This is a UI/UX processor supporting voice recognition and a gesture for a head mounted display (HMD) [287]. The chip has a deep learning core called NINEX, which consists of a 5-stage pipelined hand-segmentation core (PHSC) for stereo-vision processing, a user-voice-activated speech-segmentation core (USSC) to detect the user's voice, an embedded dropout deep learning core (DDLC) supporting a dropout, and three deep inference cores (DICs), which are connected using NoC. A dropout is achieved using a drop-connect decider (DCD) to determine which neurons are dropped out with a true random number generator used to generate the random number. With a DCD, it controls a clock-gating for registers used for parameters corresponding to inactivated neurons. When 10% of the neurons are inactivated, the power consumption of the DDLC decreases to 45.9%. The dropout decreases the inference error up to 1.6% within the verified range. It is designed using a 65-nm 1P8M Logic CMOS, and has an area of

16 mm^2. It runs at 1.2 V. The DDLC and DIC run at 200 MHz, and the DDLC has a peak performance of 319 GOPS. The full efficiency is 1.80 TOPS/W and 36.5 GOPS/mm^2.

- ADAS SoC with RNN-FIS engine
This device is focused on advanced driving-assistance systems (ADAS) [240]. An intention-prediction processor has a four-layer RNN unit. The RNN unit has a matrix-processing unit, which can achieve an 8-bit 32-way SIMD operation, a 16-bit 16-way SIMD operation, and a 32-bit 8-way SIMD operation. It predicts an object within 1.24 ms, and online learning achieves less than a 5% error for 20 epochs. It was designed for a 65-nm 1P8M Logic CMOS, where driving and parking require 502 GOPS (one IPP requiring 116 GOPS) at 330 mW and 1.80 GOPS (one IPP requiring 0.944 GOPS) at 0.984 mW, respectively.

- Deep CNN processor for IoE
This processor for a CNN has a neuron processing engine (NPE) optimized for CNN processing, a dual-range MAC (DRMAC) used for low-power convolution, on-chip memory, and kernel compression [327]. Several CNN cores are connected through a shared memory bus, where each CNN core consists of two NPEs, two image buffers, two output buffers, and two kernel buffers. NPE has 32 DRMAC blocks, 32 ReLU blocks, and 8 Max Pool blocks. Each DRAMAC can perform a different convolution in parallel. The 8 DRMACs share one kernel and provide 8 outputs to reduce redundant memory accesses. DRMAC is 24-bit truncated fixed-point arithmetic, and can also perform a 16-bit operation. This design reduces the power consumption by 56% compared with a common MAC operation.
In addition, it reduces the off-chip memory access with a PCA. A PCA can be conducted using an MAC and is therefore executed on a DRMAC. This approach decreases the accuracy of the inference by 0.68%; however, the memory accesses for a kernel can be reduced by a maximum of 92%. The maximum kernel size is 15 × 15. The device is designed using a 65-nm 1P8M Logic CMOS, and has a size of 16 mm^2. When it runs at 125 MHz under 1.2 V, it results in 64 GOPS and 45 mW of power consumption.

- DNPU
A DNPU is a processor implemented for a CNN and an RNN on the same chip [325]. A CNN processor consists of four clusters, and a cluster has four PE groups. Each group has 12 PEs, and an adder-tree connects between them. A reconfigurable multiplier achieves a partial product on an LUT, and the results are fed to four 4-bit multipliers and two 8-bit multipliers to obtain the final 16-bit multiplication result. In addition to the multiplication, a new dynamic fixed-point arithmetic (as described in Appendix A) is supported, which outperforms a traditional dynamic fixed-point operation unit to obtain a higher accuracy. An RNN processor has a multiplier based on a quantizing table. It is fabricated using a 65-nm semi-

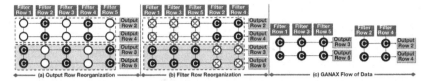

FIGURE 7.23 Data structure reorganization for transposed convolution [377].

conductor process, and has an area of 16 mm^2. It runs at 200 MHz within the range of 0.765–1.1 V. At 0.765 and 1.1 V, 34 and 279 mV of power is consumed, respectively.

- Convolutional-neural-network face-recognition processor
  A face recognition processor [121] has a 4 × 4 PE array configuration, and each PE has an RF and local memory. A PE has 4 units performing operations with 4 units of 16 16-bit MACs on each. Neighbor PEs are connected through an RF. It has a mask register, and thus a conditional MAC operation is possible. It is fabricated using a 65-nm semiconductor process, and has an area of 4 × 4 mm^2. It operates within the range of 5–100 MHz under 0.46–0.8 V. It also consumes 211 mW of power at 100 MHz under a 0.8-V driving voltage.

- AI processor for micro-robots
  This processor is focused on autonomous navigation for micro-robots [222], and consists of several 8-thread tree-search processors and a reinforce learning accelerator (RLA) for real-time decisions. An RLA applies a path planning and its learning is composed using a 6-pipeline stage RISC controller, map data memory, and a PE array with a 4 × 4 formation. It achieves 16 positions in parallel for a heuristic cost function. It is implemented using a 64-nm 1P8M triple-well CMOS, and has an area of 16 mm^2. At 7 MHz under 0.55 V and at 245 MHz under 1.2 V, it consumes 1.1 mW (7.27 mW in RLA) and 151 mW (56 uW) of power, respectively.

- Georgia Institute of Technology

  - GANAX
    GANAX focuses on zero-skipping obtained by zero-insertion for a transposed convolution [377]. Fig. 7.23 shows a reorganization of the data structure of GANAX, where the circle with "C" indicates a node of the calculation; otherwise, a node does not need to be calculated because of the multiplication by zero.
    The data restructuring starts from a reorganization of outputs, reorganization of inputs, and finally grouping the calculation. For the reorganization, GANAX needs an address generation unit with a strided memory access. Fig. 7.24 shows the top-level architecture. The processing node has a decoupled microarchitecture, which aims to decouple between the datapath for the calculation and the datapath for address generation. The decoupling means to have a controller on each decoupled unit. Between the datap-

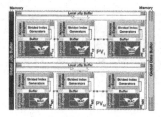 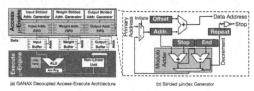

(a) GANAX Architecture.   (b) Decoupled PE Architecture of GANAX.

FIGURE 7.24 GANAX architecture [377].

aths, there are buffers from the address generation to the calculation unit. The strided memory address generation requires a multi-level strided address generation for a higher rank sparse tensor. This constraint limits the throughput to generate an address. To avoid the need for a complex strided calculation, a simple MAC unit is applied to calculate a timeline that exclusively calculates the indexes for a multi-level nested loop.

A software simulator was developed based on Eyeriss v1, and the performance was evaluated. The execution time was shown to be approximately half that of Eyeriss v1, and it seems that the transpose convolution in the benchmarks take a dilate factor of 2 and the linear execution on the timeline using the MAC unit. Thus, compared to Eyeriss v1, the fully active PE on GANAX achieves twice the utilization.

- SnaPEA

SnaPEA proposes a speculative pre-activation calculation for the ReLU activation function [105]. ReLU generates a zero when the pre-activation is a negative value. Therefore, as a baseline idea, two sets of weights are grouped, i.e., negatives and positives, and the dot-product calculation is started from the positive group. When the accumulation reaches zero or a negative value, the ReLU activation function can output a zero, and thus the calculation can be reduced to the number of positive weights at most.

The project introduces a threshold to speculatively terminate the dot-product calculation. When the accumulation reaches the threshold or less than a zero value, the calculation is terminated. Thus, the threshold for the speculative calculation determines the loss of the inferenced accuracy. When a relatively lower inference accuracy is acceptable for the user, the dot-product calculation can have a shorter execution time by a larger threshold.

A simulator based on Eyeriss v1 was developed and the performance evaluated. It achieves approximately twice the speedup and energy-efficiency on benchmarks. It was shown that small positive values in the activation generally have a slight effect on the final classification accuracy through the max-pooling filtering of small values. By controlling the decrease in the inference accuracy with an adjustment of the threshold adjustment,

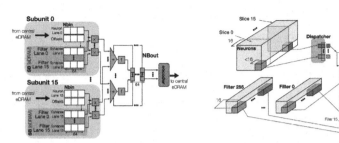

(a) Cnvlutin Core Architecture.   (b) Processing Order and Work-Assignment.

FIGURE 7.25 Cnvlutin architecture [109].

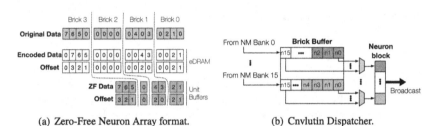

(a) Zero-Free Neuron Array format.   (b) Cnvlutin Dispatcher.

FIGURE 7.26 Cnvlutin ZFNAf and dispatch architectures [109].

a speculative calculation with a 3% loss in accuracy enhances the speedup by more than 50%.

- University of Toronto

  - Cnvlutin

    A zero-skipping operation method was proposed [109]. The analysis showed that 44% of the operations on average involve a zero value for the operand. Therefore, the authors focused on an improved execution performance by removing any unnecessary operations dynamically. They use zero-skipping with an offset addressing RAM with different parameters.

    They targeted a CNN as a potential application and used DaDianNao as a baseline architecture. The lane of an SIMD on a DaDianNao is decomposed, and the data structure and its input format are changed to realize a zero-skipping operation method, as shown in Fig. 7.25(a). Each lane is divided into two parts, a back-end and a front end, to flexibly access the data. The encoder in the last stage encodes the activations (output map) to achieve an offset. As shown in Fig. 7.25(b), an input map is re-arranged by a dispatcher to interleave vertically.

    The data structure of the activation on the proposed Zero-Free Neuron Array format (ZFNAf) is managed by unit bundling multiple continuous vectors, called a brick, as shown in Fig. 7.26(a). A brick is composed of a 2-element column, a vector column, and indexes corresponding to each vector. The index is an address offset for the weight buffer of the kernel,

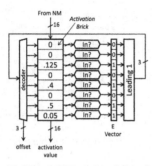

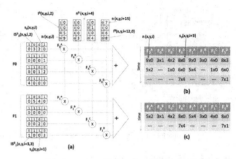

(a) Cnvlutin2 Dispatching Method.   (b) Operation Example of Cnvlutin2.

FIGURE 7.27 Dispatcher and operation example of Cnvlutin2 [213].

and is used for a read out of the necessary weight corresponding to the vector as two operand data. If the vector is zero, the vector is removed in its brick; there are only non-zero weights, and the necessary weight with an offset from the index is read. In addition, similar to a dispatcher used in a traditional processor for issuing an instruction, a similar method is used for selecting the brick, as shown in Fig. 7.26(b).

The authors compared the performance with DaDianNao on a cycle accurate simulator, which showed a 37% improvement in the execution performance. If designed using a 65-nm device, it achieves a 4.49% increase in area and 7% increase in power consumption.

- Cnvlutin2

Cnvlutin has an offset memory, which represents a 25% overhead for 16-bit values and bricks of 16 elements [213]. Cnvlutin2 focuses on such a footprint reduction and performance improvement using a new offsetting method.

This method aims to modify the dispatcher, as shown in Fig. 7.27(a). It stores data in the FIFO rule, and all elements in the FOFO generate a non-zero flag. A series of non-zero flags are fed into a number-leading zero unit, which generates an offset addressing the first non-zero data.

In addition, a filter also has an offset indicating address of a non-zero parameter. Thus, by comparing the offset between the activation and parameter, it reduces the number of cycles needed to perform a multiplication having zeros in the parameters, as shown in Fig. 7.27(b), (c) for the example provided in Fig. 7.27(b), (a).

- Stripes

Stripes is accelerator for conducting a matrix operation with a bit-serial operation [108]. The primary claim is that every layer has its own best numerical precision, and thus the numerical precision should be changed for every layer and neural network.

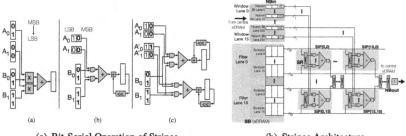

(a) Bit-Serial Operation of Stripes.   (b) Stripes Architecture.

FIGURE 7.28 Bit-serial operation and architecture of stripes [108].

The approach here is to make a bit-serial operation to report the variable operand width. The merit of using a bit-serial operation is a lack of dependency on this width; for example, a common design involves setting the maximum width of the operand for all datapaths, and such a concern is relaxed. The bit-serial is simple applying an AND logic gate and accumulation with a shift for the -position arrangement, as shown in Fig. 7.28(a), (c). In addition, under the premise of creating such a bit-serial operation for a particular operand, a speed up is achieved by the original bit width, as is an optimization of the data precision.

The authors claim the possibility of trading between inference accuracy and execution performance. This is based on the DaDianNao architecture for a consideration and evaluation of an architecture, as shown in Fig. 7.28(b), similar to that of Cnvlutin. Compared to DaDianNao, a 2.24-times greater execution performance is achieved on average with a 32% increase in area.

- ShapeShifter
ShapeShifter [237] focuses on removing the data word bit-field, and a portion of zeros for all data. This idea aggressively reduces the traffic and bandwidth requirements at the external memory access, generating a long latency and high energy consumption.

The primary idea to remove the zero-bit field is to group the data words, and remove the common zero bit-field, as shown in Fig. 7.29(a). This idea is independent from a numerical representation of a data word. The group with the bit-field removed has its own information to keep an all-zero data word in which 1-bit indicates a zero-value data word, and information of the non-removed bit-field width with a value of plus 1 is the bit-field width. Therefore, all-zero data words are also removed from the group.

This technique needs a decoder to store the compressed data into external memory and a decoder to decompress the group into a set of original data words, as shown in Fig. 7.29(b). Before the calculation, the compressed group of data words is decoded into a set of original data words. Thus, this baseline

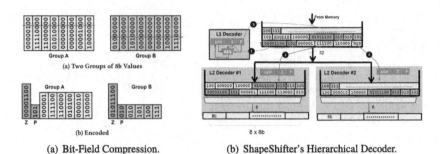

(a) Bit-Field Compression.   (b) ShapeShifter's Hierarchical Decoder.

FIGURE 7.29 ShapeShifter architecture [237].

technique contributes to zero-skipping for an external memory access and an external memory footprint reduction.

ShapeShifter is a designed extension of the Stripes architecture used to enhance the execution time, which the developers call SStripes. SStripes enhances the performance by 61% on average over Stripes with a DDR4-3200 memory configuration.

- Massachusetts Institute of Technology (MIT)

  - Eyeriss

    The focus here is to improve data reuse to maintain a smaller impact of data movement generating the major energy consumption. The authors considered several approaches to generate a reuse caused by the stationarity of the data, i.e., weight stationary (WS), output stationary (OS), and no local reuse (NLR).

    WS maintains parameters in local storage in every PE, and the parameters are read from the storage and do not move to other PEs. The OS maintains the accumulation in the local storage in every PE, and the accumulated value does not move to other PEs. The NLR does not maintain data in local storage, but the data moves across PEs.

    The compiler treats a one-dimension convolution and maps it onto the PE in the virtual space of the PE array. The compiler groups them together as a logical PE set, for example, a two-dimensional convolution can take such a set. The physical mapping takes several steps. First, it preserves the intra-set convolutional reuse and psum accumulation at the array level (inter-PE communication) [130]. Second, the same filter weights can be shared across sets (filter reuse), the same ifmap pixels can be shared across sets (ifmap reuse), and the partial sums across each set can be accumulated together [130]. The folding of multiple logical PEs from the same position of different sets onto a single physical PE exploits input data reuse and partial sum accumulation at the RF level [130]. The authors proposed a row stationary method in which a row of data in a multiple-dimension dataset is stationary in local storage. This is an accelerator for image recognition [130].

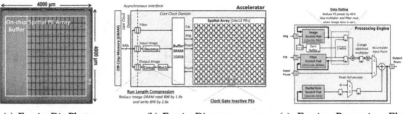

(a) Eyeriss Die Photo. (b) Eyeriss Diagram. (c) Eyeriss Processing Element.

FIGURE 7.30 Eyeriss [130].

An Eyeriss chip consists of a 108 KB buffer for temporal data and parameters called a global buffer, a systolic array datapath (processing engine), ReLU, and run-length compression/decompression unit as shown in Fig. 7.30(b). Except for the kernel used for convolution, the data are compressed when transferred to external memory and decompressed when transferred from external memory. Through a compression and decompression, the bandwidth for the image loading and storage are improved 1.9- and 2.6-fold, respectively. The processing engine has a 3-stage pipelined 16-bit fixed-point arithmetic datapath applied to one kernel row, as shown in Fig. 7.30(c).

The processing engine has an RF to hold the image data, an RF for a partial sum, and a memory block for the kernel, allowing the recycling of data in the systolic array. A dataflow is scheduled on a four-level external memory, buffer, systolic array, and processing engine for reuse of the data to decrease the energy consumption caused by a data movement [131].

The execution of AlexNet at 200 MHz under 1 V results in a 34.7 fps throughput and 278 mW of power consumption. Therefore, it achieves a peak throughput of 67.2 GOPS, and thus a power efficiency of 241.7 GOPS/W.

- Eyeriss v2
  Eyeriss v2 focuses on a reduction of the idling of PEs caused by inefficient mapping onto Eyeriss v1. The authors proposed a flexible interconnection network to provide data to every PE, as shown in Fig. 7.31(a), the upper group of which is the source cluster of the PEs, the middle group is the router cluster, and the bottom group is the destination PE cluster. The interconnection network supports broadcast, unicast, grouped multicast, and interleaved multicast to deliver data to the appropriate PE(s).
  Upon scaling to 16,384 PEs, the energy consumption is reduced to 70%–90% on three benchmark DNN models, and achieves an increase in speed to 967-times that of Eyeriss v1.

- Katholieke Universiteit Leuven: ENVISION
  ENVISION [270] executes with an SIMD operation on a 16 × 16 two-dimensional array with a 16-bit operand. The numerical representation of the

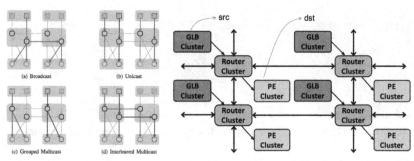

(a) Hierarchical Network in Eyeriss v2.   (b) Eyeriss v2 Configuration.

FIGURE 7.31 Eyeriss v2 architecture [132].

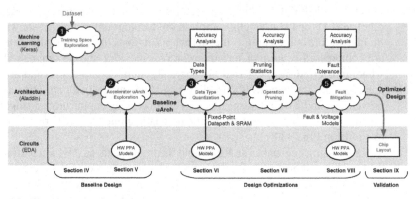

FIGURE 7.32 Design flow on Minerva [303].

16-bit operand is unknown. An element in the array consists of an MAC unit and takes a 6-stage pipeline configuration. It supports a sparse matrix operation with a guard flag memory, which disables the multiplication and memory access when the flag indicates zero. The outside of the array has a Huffman encoder to compress and decompress the data. This is fabricated using a 28-nm FDSOI semiconductor process, and achieves an area of 1.87 mm^2. It supports 0.65 to 1.1 V and consumes 6.5 mW of power on average when operating at 200 MHz.

- Harvard University

  - Minerva

    In this case, the authors researched a co-design environment including an algorithm, architecture, and logic circuit [303]. An auto-generation of the RTL code for the accelerator requires five stages. See Fig. 7.32.

    The first stage is a learning space exploration for a user-designed neural network model. It generates a baseline neural network topology and its trained parameters. The second stage is a selection of better parameters and a better model from thousands of learned models, thoroughly exploring the accelerator design space. The third stage is a quantization, which increases the suppression of the power consumption by 1.5-fold based on the task. The dynamic range of all DNN signals is analyzed and the slack is reduced in terms of data type precision [303]. The fourth step is a pruning by checking whether the parameter value is within the neighborhood of zero, and by checking the activity of the activation function, this step suppresses the power consumption by 2-fold. The last step is a failure relaxation for SRAM, which suppresses the power consumption by 2.7-fold. Thus, as the final result, an 8-fold decrease in the power consumption is expected.

Keras can be used for coding a neural network model. At stage 2, to exhaustively explore this space, we rely on Aladdin, a cycle-accurate design analysis tool for accelerators [303]. To achieve accurate results, Aladdin requires a detailed PPA hardware characterization to be fed into its models, as represented by the arrows from the circuit to architecture levels [303]. Minerva analyzes the SRAM supply voltage scaling to achieve a lower power consumption without any faults.

- Sparse deep-neural network engine

  A sparse deep-neural network engine was implemented on SoC [366]. This operation has a 5-stage pipeline configuration, and the 8 MAC units in the operational unit operate in parallel. The MAC unit performs 8-bit or 16-bit fixed-point arithmetic and has several rounding modes. It supports a zero-skipping operation to achieve an efficient pipelined execution, and supports skipping the edge-cutting. It is fabricated using a 28-nm TSMC semiconductor process, and runs at 667 MHz under 0.9 V; in addition, it runs at 1.2 GHz when enabling a razor flip-flop, and consumes 63.5 mW of power.

- Stanford University

  - EIE

    In this case, focus is on the sparse tensor and weight-sharing using a deep compression. An interleaved CSC sparse representation is applied.

    This is an accelerator for image recognition [183] implemented using model compression methods and a parameter compression [184]. Deep compression is used to remove unnecessary connections by pruning and unnecessary parameters by weight-sharing, and compress the parameters through Huffman coding. Quantization ranges from 2- to 8-bit in the case of VGG-16 when pruned by 96%. A combination of pruning, quantization, weight-sharing, and Huffman coding compresses the parameters to 1/35 the original size.

    An offset (index) is used to address non-zero data, and broadcast to all PEs to share the index and thereby address the appropriate operand of the parameters. Activations enter into FIFO, which are checked to determine whether non-zero data are present. The non-zero detection uses a number-leading zero, similar to that of Cnvlutin2 [213]. The broadcasted data are

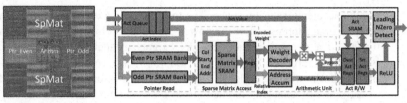

(a) EIE Chip Layout
(45nm process).

(b) Processing Element.

FIGURE 7.33 Efficient inference engine (EIE) [183].

stored in the activation queue in the PE. The index on the head entry in the activation queue shown in Fig. 7.33(b) is used as a memory address for memory storing pointers, and a read pointer is used for reading the encoded weight from the matrix memory. The number-leading zero is applied at the last stage of the PE.

The index of the activation is also used to address the appropriate weight when encoded using an interleaved CSC. The encoded weights are read from a sparse matrix SRAM and decoded before the operation with an activation having a non-zero value. A CSC encoding index is accumulated to address the appropriate position of the output.

The PE consists of a central control unit (CCU) for complete control, leading non-zero detection unit, and on-chip memory. The arithmetic unit performs a 16-bit fixed-point MAC operation decompression from a 4-bit encoded weight through an LUT. The MAC result is stored into an RF after its activation, and a maximum of 4K activations are stored in it. It is synthesized using a 45-nm TSMC GP standard VT library. It takes a 1.15-ns critical path (corresponding to 869 MHz), and has an area of 0.638024 mm^2. It consumes 9.157 mW of power with a 1.6 GOPS throughput. Thus, the EIE achieves a power efficiency of 174.7 GOPS/W.

- TETRIS

  Focus here is on the scalability of the accelerator architecture, which involves a huge number of memory accesses, as shown in Fig. 7.34(a) (at 500 MHz under an LPDDR3-1600 configuration). The authors considered stacking hyper memory cube (HMC) DRAM memory chips consisting of a PE array with software support [183].

  HMC is an 8-chip stacked cube. By using stacked memory (called 3D memory), it can integrate SRAM memory, buffer memory, and a PE array on a chip, and can achieve a higher performance. In addition, the authors proposed embedding an MAC unit into the memory chip for an efficient operation.

  Moreover, they also consider dataflow scheduling. In addition, an ifmap (input-memory), ofmap (output memory), and filter (kernel memory) are included, which realizes an efficient scheduling by bypassing different

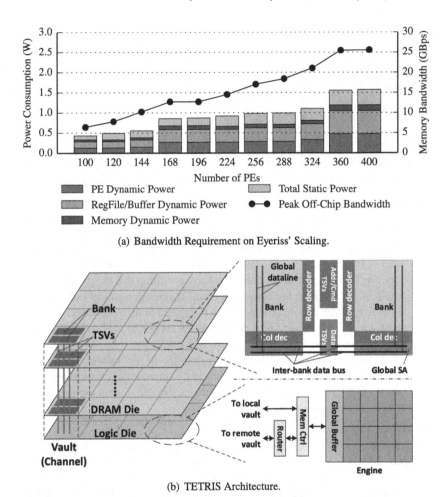

(a) Bandwidth Requirement on Eyeriss' Scaling.

(b) TETRIS Architecture.

FIGURE 7.34 Bandwidth requirement and TETRIS architecture [168].

memory to the RF, and not only inputs from ifmap to the RF. In addition, they also considered a partition method for the batch size, image size, input size, and output size to fit into the DRAM banks.

They indicated that the partition takes the following approach [183]. A batch partitioning scheme is less attractive for real-time latency-sensitive applications because it does not improve the latency for inference on each image. With Fmap (image) partitioning, the filters need to be replicated across all vaults. For the output partitioning, because all ifmaps contribute to all ofmaps, all ifmaps must be sent to all vaults, which requires remote vault accesses. The input partitioning applies accesses to ofmaps to generate both read and write traffic, and is therefore more critical than the ifmap access.

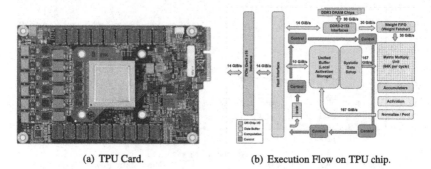

(a) TPU Card.   (b) Execution Flow on TPU chip.

FIGURE 7.35   Tensor processing unit (TPU) version 1 [211].

The authors proposed a scheduling method consisting of the following two ideas [183]. First, a greedy algorithm is used that explores the partitioning options for layer i without a back-tracing, assuming that the partitioning of the first i-1 layers in the optimal scheme are independent of those for the later layers. Second, bypass ordering is applied to the partitioned layers in each vault. This allows us to determine the ADRAM analytically without a time-consuming exhaustive search.

The system is evaluated under the assumption of a 65-nm semiconductor process at 500 MHz on a simulator, and improves the execution performance by 4.1-fold and the energy efficiency by 1.5-fold compared with a common two-dimensional implementation.

- STMicroelectronics
  In this case, an SoC composed using a configurable framework was developed for a CNN [153]. Eight convolutional accelerators (CAs) apply the convolution. Each CA has 36 16-bit fixed-point MAC units, and all results are summed by an adder-tree. This is fabricated using a 28-nm semiconductor process and has an area of 6.2×5.5 mm^2. It operates within a range of 200 MHz to 1.17 GHz. At 0.575 V, it consumes 41 mW of power on the AlexNet model.

- Google

  - Tensor processing unit
    Google revealed a TPU executing offloaded tasks from the TensorFlow API [211], and demonstrated its use for AlphaGo [326]. The system with installed TPUs has already been running for more than 1 year. It uses quantization, i.e., a numerical representation at 8-bits through a quantization of the operands of the multiplication [364]. See Fig. 7.35.

    It has a simple instruction sequence in which the host server sends a TPU instruction. It applies a co-processor but does not have cache memory, a branch prediction unit, out-of-order execution, or parallel execution used in traditional microprocessors [212]. It performs matrix operations such as a batch execution receiving instructions through the PCIe. The PE seems to have an MAD unit having an 8-bit multiplier, and multiple PEs compose a systolic array. After the matrix unit, a total of 4 MB of 32-bit accumulators are present, and seem to be accumulated for a large-scale matrix operation, which mainly consists of multiple 256×256 blocks of data. In addition, the initial value of an accumulator can be a bias value. It outputs 256 intermediate element results every clock cycle, and the PE also has a 16-bit operation mode, with a decrease in throughput of 1/4. The TPU-1 is specialized for a dense matrix operation.

It has a $96 \text{ K} \times 256 \times 8 \text{ b} = 24 \text{ MB}$ general-purpose buffer called a Unified Buffer, which performs with a double buffering to hide the latency of 256 cycles by overlapping a latency for the buffering and a latency for a matrix operation. The architecture of the instruction set is likely a complex instruction-set computer (CISC), and has a 12-byte length. Although it requires a four-stage pipeline, one stage can take multiple cycles, which differs from traditional pipelined processors in which every stage is executed in a single cycle. It does not have clean pipeline overlap diagrams, because the CISC instructions of the TPU can occupy a station for thousands of clock cycles, unlike a traditional RISC pipeline with a single clock cycle per stage [211]. Decoding the received instruction, the DMA transfers it from the system memory through the PCIe and stores it into DDR3 external memory when the parameters are necessary. The parameters are stored in a weight FIFO before the operation. At the same time, systolic array inputs from the operand data in a unified buffer using the synchronized timing of the systolic operation to the matrix unit through a systolic data setup unit.

The execution is 15-times higher, and the power efficiency is 30-times better than that of an NVIDIA K80 GPU. It runs at 92 TOPS with 40 W of power at its peak, and therefore the power efficiency is 2.3 TOPS/W.

- Edge TPU

  To design the edge TPU, the authors used the domain-specific language, Chisel. Chisel was chosen owing to its productivity for a small-scale team and its high parameterization. The peak throughput is 4 TOPS, and the power efficiency is 2 TOPS/W at 0.5 W. See Fig. 7.36.

- Intel

  Intel announced a strategy for an AI industry in November 2016 [68], including Lake Crest, which is a hardware strategy developed by the acquired Nervana System focusing on the learning process. In addition, Intel and Google announced flexible strategical collaboration providing a cloud infrastructure.

  - Nervana System: Nervana Engine

    Nervana System developed an accelerator integrating HBM having a 32 GiB size and 8 Tbps bandwidth through an interposer [77]. It is planned for release in 2017. The company was acquired by Intel in August 2016 [123].

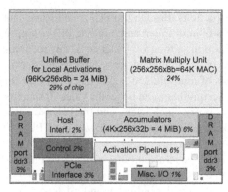

(a) TPU v1 Floor Plan.

(b) Edge TPU.

FIGURE 7.36 TPU-1 floor plan and edge-TPU [211][10].

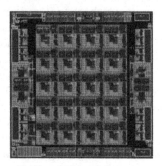

(a) Neural Network Processor Floorplan.

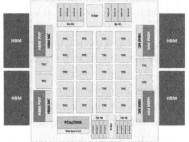

(b) Tensor Processing Cluster.

FIGURE 7.37 Spring crest [376].

Fig. 7.37(a) shows the floorplan. A 5×4 cluster array is used. One cluster has multiple local memories with a total capacity of 2.5 MB, and two matrix processing units (MPUs). The MPU has a 32×32 MAC array. Clusters are connected through a router.

The chip has $5 \times 4 \times 32 \times 32 \times 2 = 40960$ MACs and $5 \times 4 \times 2.5 = 50$ MB of total on-chip memory. The released model from Intel, Lake Crest, has 4×3 clusters, and achieves 40 TOPS with 210 W of power, achieving a power efficiency of 0.19 TOPS/W.

- Habana

The Gaudi processor [103] consists of eight tensor processing cores (TPCs), one general matrix multiply (GEMM) engine, and shared memory. The GEMM engine is shared with TPCs.

The TPC has local memory and does not have cache memory. TPC supports mixed-precision integer and floating-point operations of a 8-, 16-,

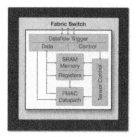

(a) Wafer Scale Engine (WSE).   (b) Scale of WSE.   (c) Processing Element, Sparse Linear Algebra (SLA).

FIGURE 7.38 Cerebras wafer scale engine and its processing element [163].

and 32-bit SIMD vector for Bfloat16. It is manufactured using a 16-nm TSMC process.

- Cerebras: wafer scale engine
  Cerebras released a wafer-scale machine learning accelerator [163] having an area of 46,255 mm^2, as shown in Fig. 7.38(a). It has a total on-chip memory of 18 GB. The core-to-core bandwidth is 1000 petabits per second, and an SRAM-to-core bandwidth is 9 petabytes per second. To achieve a defect tolerance, an interconnect resource is made with redundancy because a wafer-scale cannot avoid a defect failure. It operates at 0.8 V.

  Fig. 7.38(c) shows WSE's PE, called sparse linear algebra. It has an extremely simple configuration, a fused MAC, and a data-driven execution, the reservation station of which is ready to execute the instructions.

- Graphcore: intelligence processing unit
  The intelligence processing unit (IPU) has 1216 PEs and a 300 MB on-chip memory, with a 45 TB/s memory bandwidth [98]. At the center, an all-to-all exchange logic is horizontally placed.

  The PE has a mixed-precision of 16- and 32-bits and appears to apply a half-precision multiplication and single-precision addition as the floating-point arithmetic.

  IPU supports TensorFlow XLA. It also supports a low-level library called Poplar. An 8-card configuration achieves a rate of 16,000 images/s for ResNet50 training.

  It requires 75 W for logical applications and 45 W for the RAM, for a total power consumption of 120 W. It appears to achieve 4 Peta FLOPS. Thus, it achieves a power efficiency of 34.1 TFLOPS/W.

- Groq: tensor streaming processor
  Groq's tensor streaming processor (TSP) achieves a total of 1 Peta operations per cycle (1000 TOPS) at a 1.25-GHz operation [178]. Fig. 7.39(a) shows the TSP die photo. This layout has a row-based superlane placement, as shown in Fig. 7.39(b).

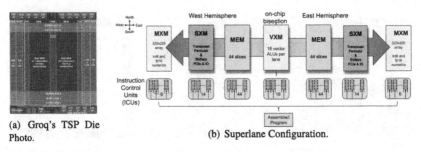

(a) Groq's TSP Die
Photo.

(b) Superlane Configuration.

FIGURE 7.39 Groq's tensor streaming processor (TSP) [178].

The instruction is just like a VLIW ISA and flows from the top to the bottom of the die layout. After a superlane fetch instruction is received, it executes the instruction on every module. A matrix unit, a switch unit, a memory unit, and a vector unit are applied. These units are mirrored horizontally along the superlane. One superlane consists of 16 lanes and a 512-Byte interconnection between units. The switch unit operates a transpose of the matrix, which is sometimes necessary for a matrix operation in the tensor. Therefore, after reading data from the memory unit, the data are fed into the switch unit, shuffled, and sent out to the matrix unit. The received VLIW instruction is sent to the borrow superlane, which is similar to the concept of an "instruction systolic array." The architecture is scalable, with a row-based replication of the superlane, and the 21st superlane is a redundant lane for defect tolerance. In total, the die includes 204,800 MACs, and thus achieves 409,600 operations per cycle. It operates at 1 GHz, and thus achieves 409.6 TOPS on the matrix units. A memory unit has 5.5 MB and is subdivided to 44 banks (each bank has 128 KB). The initial board of the system does not have external memory because of the abandonment of on-chip memory. The matrix unit supports 8-, 16-, and 32-bit integers for multiplication, and half- and single-precision floating-point numerical representations. In addition, it has 32-bit integer adders to accumulate the multiplication results.

The first TSP contains 26.8 billion transistors on a 725 mm^2 die using a 14-nm process and consumes 300 W of power. Inference for ResNet-50 runs at 20,400 inferences per second (IPS) with a latency of 0.04 ms.

- Tesla Motors: fully self driving

  Fig. 7.40 shows a fully self-driving chip. The two block at the left-bottom in the die photo of Fig. 7.40(a) are the deep learning accelerator. Each accelerator has a total on-chip memory of 32 MB, and a total of 9216 MACs composing a two-dimensional array. On the right side of the die, 6 ARM cores are placed [198]. The GPU is on the top side. Figs. 7.40(a) and 7.40(b) are vertically inversed.

  Activations are aligned before the 96 × 96 MAC array, and after the array, the post-activation is fed into the activation unit or bypassed to the write buffer, as shown in Fig. 7.40(b). The activation is calculated using a programmable

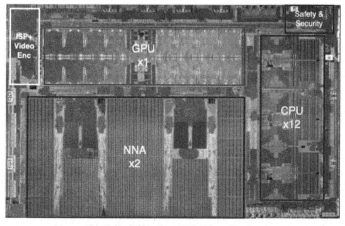

(a) Fully Self Driving (FSD) Die Photo.

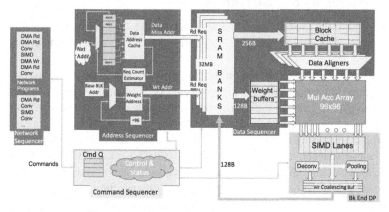

(b) Diagram of Neural Network Accelerator (NNA).

FIGURE 7.40 Tesla's fully self driving chip [198].

SIMD unit. It has a 260 mm^2 die area applying a 14-nm Samsung processor. It achieves 36.86 TOPS under 36 W of power at a clock frequency of 1 GHz. Thus, the PE has two MAC units, and achieves a power efficiency of 1 TOPS/W.

7.3 Quantum computing

Quantum machine learning using an annealing method as also been researched. Quantum computing is based on quantum theory, and is a paradigm applying a superposition to parallel processing. Superpositioning is used for its computing power, which means there are many numerical representations in a unit, although traditional digital computing uses a binary numerical representation of

1s or zeros. The unit of information based on a superposition is called a quantum bit (qubit).

There are two methods to realize a quantum computing machine, one method is a quantum gating method, and the other is a quantum annealing method. The quantum gating method is performed based on a quantum operator corresponding to a logical operation, and a gate based on a unitary matrix is implemented with a quantum gate. The quantum annealing method is a common approach to find the global minima, thus this method can be used to find the minimum value of any objective function from any set of candidates with a quantum fluctuation. It can be used for updating the parameters on machine learning, shortening the time to find the global minima for each parameter. The quantum learning method is ongoing, and studies have advanced both the quantum gating and quantum annealing.

7.4 Summary of case studies

Tables 7.1 and 7.2 summarize the hardware studies and products used for machine learning. Table 7.3, Table 7.4, and Table 7.5 show the implementation results.

Most studies have focused on the energy-efficiency in terms of energy consumption rather than only on the execution performance. A comparison with prior studies in terms of the energy efficiency has been made. Machine learning models, represented as "ML Model," in the first column of Table 7.3, are neuromorphic computing and DNNs labeled as Spiking Neural Network (SNN) and DNN, respectively. In the fourth column in Table 7.3, for quantization, Tsinghua University's "DP" indicates a Dynamic Precision. Intel's Xeon Phi on Knights Corner generation has 61 cores with a ring interconnection network, and it was reported that it can be optimized with OpenMP and MKL to achieve a 302-fold greater execution performance compared with a single-core execution with a non-optimized code for four-layer neural network mode [207]. NVIDIA's GTX 1080 (with a Pascal architecture) has at least a ten-fold higher execution performance than that of Intel's Xeon E5-2630 v3 at 2.4 GHz (with 16b cores) [323].

Fig. 7.41(a) shows a taxonomy of the implementation approach on most machine learning hardware. Fig. 7.41(b) shows the classification of digital or analog circuits, as well as the classification of temporal- or spatial-based computing for implementing a single soma. Fig. 7.41(c) shows a similar taxonomy, as shown in Fig. 3.8, as multiple implementations of the core unit.

7.4.1 Case study for neuromorphic computing

TrueNorth developed by IBM and Cornel University is a step ahead in terms of inference, and the chips for both inference and learning are at the same level. However, there are relatively fewer tape-out chips, and fewer physical verification than in the domain of neural network accelerators.

TABLE 7.1 Summary-I of SNN hardware implementation.

| | Interface | | | | Architecture — Compute Node | | Cluster Node | Processing Element Node | | | | | | |
| | | | | | | | | RAM Size | | | | | | |
Project or Institution Name	RAM [KB]	Decompression	Cluster Array Arrangement	# of Clusters [Units]	PE Array Arrangement	# of PEs in a Cluster [Units]	Instruction [Bytes]	Input [Bytes]	Weights [Bytes]	Output [Bytes]	Operand Precision	Zero Skipping	Pipeline Depth [Stages]	Act. Funct.
SpiNNaker TrueNorth	0	No	2D Mesh NoC	2048	Time-mux SIMD MAC (Xbar for Synapses)	18 / 256	32768 / 0	32768(Common) / 512 (SRAM)	13120 (SRAM, Shared with PEs)	N/A	1-bit	No	2	SSJ, Leak, Threshold
Tsinghua University	0	No	N/A	6	Time-mux SIMD MAC (Xbar for Synapses)	N/A	0	N/A	N/A	N/A	N/A	No	N/A	N/A
Zhejiang University	0	No	N/A	N/A	Time-mux SIMD MAC (Xbar for Synapses)	8	0	N/A	N/A	N/A	N/A	No	N/A	N/A

TABLE 7.2 Summary-II of DNN hardware implementation.

Project or Institution Name	Interface		Architecture												
			Compute Node												
					Cluster Node										
							Processing Element Node								
							RAM Size								
	RAM [KB]	Decompression	Cluster Array Arrangement	# of Clusters [Units]	PE Array Arrangement	# of PEs in a Cluster [Units]	Instruction [Bytes]	Input [Bytes]	Weights [Bytes]	Output [Bytes]	Operand Precision	Zero Skipping	Pipeline Depth [Stages]	Act. Funct.
neuFlow	0	No	2D Mesh NoC	1	N/A	N/A	N/A	N/A	N/A	N/A	N/A	No	N/A	N/A
Peking University	0	No	N/A	1	Adder-Tree	1	0	N/A	N/A	N/A	32bit float	No	N/A	N/A
University of Pittsburgh	0	No	N/A	1	Multi-thread	N/A	N/A	N/A	N/A	N/A	N/A	No	N/A	N/A
Tsinghua University	0	No	N/A	1	Adder-Tree	N/A	N/A	N/A	N/A	N/A	Dynamic	No	N/A	N/A
Microsoft Research	0	No	N/A	N/A	Systolic Array	N/A	0	0	0	0	32bit float	No	2	N/A
DianNao	0	No	SIMD	1	Adder-Tree	16	8192	2048 (Shared with PEs)	32768 (Shared with PEs)	2048 (Shared with PEs)	16bit fixed point	No	8	PLFA
DaDianNao	0	No	MIMD	16	Adder-Tree	16	N/A	N/A	N/A	2097152 (524288 × 4 eDRAMs)	16bit fixed point(inf) 32bit fixed point(train)	No	N/A	N/A
PuDianNao	0	No	SIMD	16	Adder-Tree	1	N/A	16384 (Shared)	8192 (Shared)	8192 (Shared)	16bit fixed point	No	6 (MLU)	Taylor Expansion
ShiDianNao	0	No	N/A	16	Systolic Array	64	32768 (Shared with PEs)	65536 (Shared with PEs)	131072 (Shared with PEs)	65536 (Shared with PEs)	16bit fixed	No	1	PLFA
Cambricon-ACC	0	No	N/A	N/A	Adder-Tree	N/A	N/A	N/A	N/A	N/A	16bit fixed	No	N/A	N/A
Cambricon-X	0	No	N/A	N/A	Adder-Tree	N/A	N/A	N/A	N/A	N/A	16bit fixed	No	N/A	N/A

TABLE 7.3 Summary-III of DNN hardware implementation.

Project or Institution Name	Interface		Architecture											
					Compute Node		Cluster Node							
							Processing Element Node							
							RAM Size							
	RAM	Decomp-ression	Cluster Array Arrangement	# of Clusters	PE Array Arrangement	# of PEs in a Cluster	Instruction	Input	Weights	Output	Operand Precision	Zero Skipping	Pipeline Depth	Act. Funct.
	[KB]			[Units]		[Units]	[Bytes]	[Bytes]	[Bytes]	[Bytes]			[Stages]	
K-Brain	0	No	2D Mesh NoC	4	SIMD, Systolic Array	4	N/A	N/A	N/A	N/A	N/A	No	4	N/A
UI/UX Proc.	N/A	No	N/A	N/A	NoC	DDLC×1 DIC×3	N/A	N/A	N/A	N/A	N/A	No	N/A	N/A
ADAS SoC											256bit/Way SIMD			
Deep CNN	N/A	No	Shared Mem Bus	N/A	MAC	32	N/A	N/A	N/A	N/A	N/A	No	N/A	ReLU
Cnvlutin	4096	No	SIMD	16	Adder-Tree	16	N/A	N/A	131072	N/A	16bit fixed point	Mult and Acc	N/A	N/A
Eyeriss	108	Run Length	N/A	1	Systolic Array	168	N/A	24(12-entry RF)	510(255-entry SRAM)	48(24-entry RF)	16bit fixed point	Mult and RAM Read	3	ReLU
EIE	N/A	Huffman Coding	N/A	1	MAC	1	N/A	8 Depth FIFO	131072 (including index data)	128×2 (64-entry RF×2), 32768 (Pointer RAM)	16bit fixed point	Mult	4	ReLU

TABLE 7.4 Summary-IV of machine learning hardware implementation.

Project or Institution Name	Compression			Fab or FPGA Vendor	Design		Design Result					Training Supported	Performance Evaluation		Network Model used for Evaluation	Description
	Model	Parameter			Library or Device	Process [nm]	Area		Clock Frequency [MHz]	Supply Voltage [V]	Power Consumption [W]		GOPS	Through-put		
		Weight Sharing	Operand Quantiz-ing				# of Gates [M Gates]	Area [mm²]								
SpiNNaker	N/A	N/A	N/A	UMC	N/A	130	N/A	N/A	N/A	N/A	N/A	N/A	N/A	N/A		
TrueNorth	No	No	No	Samsung	LPP	28 CMOS	5400	4.3	N/A	0.75	0.065	No	N/A	N/A		
Tsinghua University	No	No	No	N/A	N/A	120	N/A	N/A	N/A	N/A	N/A	N/A	N/A	N/A		
Zhejiang University	No	No	No	N/A	N/A	180	N/A	25	70	1.8	58.8	N/A	N/A	N/A		
neuFlow	No	No	No	Xilinx	Virtex6 LX760				200		10	N/A	N/A	N/A		
Peking University	No	No	No	Xilinx	Virtex7 VC707				100		18.61	No	61.62	N/A		Matrix Mult
University of Pittsburgh	No	No	No	Xilinx	Virtex6 LX760				150		25	N/A	2.4 / 9.6	N/A		Hidden Layer / Output Layer
Tsinghua University	Pruning	No	DP	Xilinx	Zynq 706				150		9.63	N/A	136.97	N/A	VCG16-SVD	
Microsoft Research	No	No	No	Altera	Stratix-V D5				N/A		25	N/A	N/A	N/A	CIFAR-10	
											25				ImageNet 1K	
															Imagenet 22K	
					Arria-10 GX1150						25				ImageNet 1K	
									N/A		265					
DianNao	No	No	No	TSMC	N/A	65	N/A	3	980	N/A	0.485	No	N/A	N/A		
DaDianNao	No	No	No	ST Tech.	LP	28	N/A	67.7	606	0.9	15.97	Yes	N/A	N/A		
PuDianNao	No	No	No	TSMC	GP	65	N/A	3.51	1000	N/A	0.596	Yes	1056	N/A	Various	
ShiDianNao	No	No	No	TSMC	N/A	65	N/A	4.86	1000	N/A	0.3201	N/A	N/A	N/A		
Cambricon-ACC	No	No	No	TSMC	GP std VT lib	65	N/A	56.24	N/A	N/A	1.6956	Yes	N/A	N/A	General-Purpose	
Cambricon-X	No	No	No	TSMC	GP std VT lib	65	N/A	6.38	N/A	N/A	0.954	Yes	N/A	N/A	General-Purpose	

TABLE 7.5 Summary-V of machine learning hardware implementation.

Project or Institution Name	Compression Parameter			Fab or FPGA Vendor	Design		Design Result					Training Supported	Performance Evaluation		Network Model used for Evaluation	Description
	Model	Weight Sharing	Operand Quantizing		Library or Device	Process [nm]	Area		Clock Frequency [MHz]	Supply Voltage [V]	Power Consumption [W]		GOPS	Through-put		
							# of Gates [M Gates]	Area [mm²]								
K-Brain	No	No	No	N/A	1P8M CMOS	65	3750	10	200	1.2	0.2131	Yes	3283	11.8 Gbps		Training
												No	82.1			Inference
UI/UX Proc.	Dropout	No	No	N/A	1P8M CMOS	65	N/A	16	200	1.2	N/A	Yes	319	N/A		DDLC
ADAS SoC	No	No	No	N/A	1P8M CMOS	65	N/A	N/A		N/A	0.33	Yes	116	N/A		Driving (IPS)
					CMOS						0.000984		0.944			
											0.000984		0.944			Parking (IPS)
Deep CNN	PCA	No	No	N/A	1P8M CMOS	65	N/A	16	125	1.2	0.045	N/A	64	N/A		
Cnvlutin	Dynamic Neuron Pruning	No	No	TSMC	N/A	65	N/A	3.13	N/A	N/A	0.45105	No	N/A	N/A	Alex, GoogleNet	with Zero-Skipping
															NN, VGG19, CNNM, CNNS	with Zero-Skipping and Pruning
Eyeriss	No	No	No	TSMC	LP 1P9M	65	1852	12.25	200	1	0.278	No	N/A	34.7	Alex	FPS
EIE	Pruning	Yes	Yes	TSMC	GP Std VT Lib	45	N/A	0.64	800	N/A	0.009157	No	1.6	N/A	Alex	1-PE Config.
								40.8			0.59		N/A	18.8 KFPS	Alex	64-PE Config.

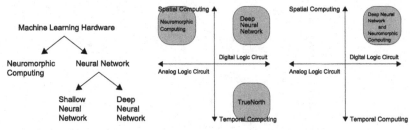

(a) Taxonomy of Machine Learning   (b) Taxonomy of Core Block.   (c) Taxonomy of Core Array.
Hardware.

FIGURE 7.41   Taxonomy of machine learning hardware.

It requires collaboration with neuroscience to reveal its functionality, and has a higher wall. It consumes approximately 50 mW of power, and therefore has several orders of magnitude better energy-efficiency than CPUs and GPUs. Each spike is a unit pulse, and an AER composed with a timing information is used for transferring to the destination node. Thus, it has good scalability with a traditional NoC.

Digital logic circuit implementation has difficulty in improving the throughput because of its time-multiplexed MAC operations. By contrast, an analog logic circuit implementation requires a DAC, an ADC, and amplifiers to interface with a part of the digital logic circuit, and therefore, it is difficult to improve the implementation density. Moreover, when implementing the learning functionality based on the STDP, a traditional memory cell array based configuration is difficult to achieve, making it also difficult to avoid a decrease in the implementation density.

7.4.2   Case study for deep neural network

The Chinese Academy of Sciences (CAS) has been one step ahead of other researches in terms of their results. However, other groups are close to catching up with the CAS research team.

For ASIC implementation, the die area remains at 50 mm^2, even when using only a semiconductor process such as a 65-nm device. In addition, a relatively lower clock frequency is considered, and thus it has overtaken the GPU in terms of energy-efficiency. A higher execution response with a lower clock frequency implies that a smaller number of execution clock cycles is required. For example, the number of accesses to external memory and its transferring data size have had major impacts on both the execution performance and the energy consumption. In addition, a small chip area and lower clock frequency have contributed to the higher energy efficiency.

In the case of ASIC implementation, there are two approaches, one is an application-specialized accelerator as demonstrated in studies conducted at KAIST, and the other is a domain-specific accelerator, as demonstrated in studies at CAS. For and FPGA implementation, a design fit to an FPGA architecture is required, and studies have focused on a framework for an FPGA-optimized design method and design space exploration, rather than an improvement in the execution performance.

Most PE designs use a 16-bit fixed-point arithmetic unit, and an adder-tree method. To shorten the wire delay and simplify the logic circuit, a clustering approach has been considered for bundling multiple PEs into a single cluster, applying a hierarchical structure. Between the hierarchy layers, a memory unit is applied to allow an interface for the reuse of data, or an NoC is used between clusters.

The parameters, activations, and output data have their own specific memory unit to cover a delay variation caused by different operations. Model optimization, model compression, parameter compression, data encoding, data flow optimization, zero-skipping, and approximation, as shown in Chapter 3, have been considered in recent studies.

A major problem is the memory capacity for the parameters, making it is difficult to carry all data onto the chip; therefore, access to external memory having a longer access latency and larger energy consumption is required. This problem remains a major research point. Recently, die-stacking DRAM chips on an accelerator chip have been considered to obtain a higher memory access bandwidth.

7.4.3 Comparison between neuromorphic computing and deep neural network hardware

An architecture was explored to allow a new storage element to be used in both neuromorphic computing and DNNs. Such a storage element is not yet common, and therefore, the main effort has been on validation based on a simulation of the set hardware parameters.

In [155], the authors compared between neuromorphic computing and a DNN in terms of the real hardware implementation. They claimed the following three points:

1. An SNN has a much lower accuracy than a DNN for the same recognition task.
2. DNN hardware is relatively simpler than SNN hardware under an embedded system level design constraint.
3. An SNN (STDP) has a narrower range of applications.

Chapter 8

Keys to hardware implementation

Chapter prior discusses see what is the deep learning tasks and see the points for developing a machine learning hardware. First, we discuss the market of machine learning hardware based on a market prediction related to such learning. Next, we consider the cases of FPGA and ASIC implementations required to design a hardware architecture to recover the nonrecurring engineering (NRE) and fabrication costs. Finally, we consider a basic strategy for an architecture development based on these results.

8.1 Market growth predictions

8.1.1 IoT market

Fig. 8.1 shows the predicted number of IoT installations and the market growth [53]. We can expect an aggressive market growth by 2020. The number of consumer installations and the scale of the market growth are greater than the total number of cross-industry and vertical-specific items.

8.1.2 Robotics market

Fig. 8.2 shows the shipment and market growth predictions [55][161]. We can expect a market growth in Asia. Autonomous robotics will the market drive

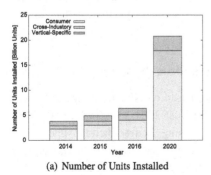

(a) Number of Units Installed

(b) Market Volume

FIGURE 8.1 Forecast on IoT.

Thinking Machines. https://doi.org/10.1016/B978-0-12-818279-6.00018-9

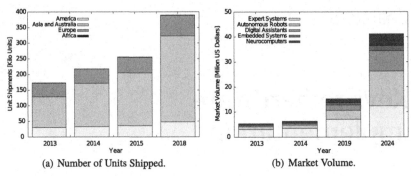

(a) Number of Units Shipped.   (b) Market Volume.

FIGURE 8.2 Forecast on robotics.

in the near future. After this phase, digital assistants and neuro-computers are anticipated to be involved in increasing the machine learning based software market [67][50].

8.1.3   Big data and machine learning markets

A report [66] predicted that the machine learning related market will grow to 1.7 billion US dollars by the year 2022. Hardware is anticipated to achieve aggressive growth between 2016 and 2022.

As described in Chapter 1, IoT and big data are equivalent to sampling the information of interest by the user as the entrance point, and reasoning and planning developed by a large amount of data based on an inference of the interest by the user as the exit point, respectively.

As another alternative, big data can be a general term for such a system, and robotics is a typical application.

The data analytics market based on IoT and robotics is anticipated to see a rapid market growth by 2020, as shown in Fig. 8.3. A special service is a primary market in the current big data era; however, computers and the cloud are driving the big-data related hardware market.

8.1.4   Artificial intelligence market in drug discovery

Fig. 8.4 shows the drug discovery market based on AI. The compound annual growth rate (CAGR) will reach 40% by the year 2024, as shown in Fig. 8.4(a). The cost for discovery is continuously increasing, as described in Appendix E.

Artificial intelligence based discovery contributes to reduced risk and cost. Fig. 8.4(b) shows the drug discovery market by region. It seems that the APAC region will become a larger market because India is a larger player within it.

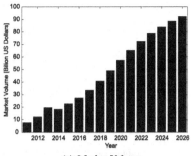

(a) Market Volume.

(b) Market Volume by Sub-type.

FIGURE 8.3 Forecast on big data.

(a) CAGR of Drug Discovery based on Artificial Intelligence.

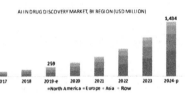

(b) Drug Discovery Market by Region.

FIGURE 8.4 Forecast on AI based drug discovery [94].

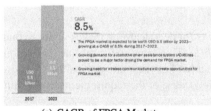

(a) CAGR of FPGA Market.

(b) FPGA Market Volume by Region.

FIGURE 8.5 Forecast on FPGA market [96].

8.1.5 FPGA market

The FPGA market will continue to increase, as shown in Fig. 8.5; however, its effect on the domain of deep learning remains relatively slight.

The FPGA market volume will also increase, as shown in Fig. 8.5. APAC will become a larger market owing to the need for a communication infrastructure in India and Indonesia.

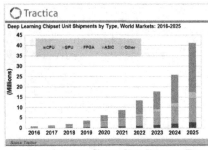

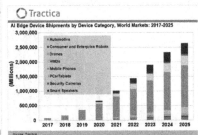

(a) Deep Learning Chipset Unit Shipment Forecast.

(b) Deep Learning based Edge Device Shipment Forecast.

FIGURE 8.6 Forecast on deep learning chip market [85][91].

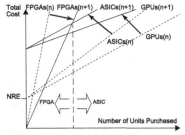

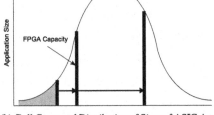

(a) Relationship between Total Cost and Number of Units Purchased.

(b) Bell Curve and Distribution of Sizes of ASIC Applications.

FIGURE 8.7 Cost functions and bell curve [355].

8.1.6 Deep learning chip market

The ASIC domain in chip unit shipments for deep learning makes up more than half of the market, as shown in Fig. 8.6(a). This trend will continue throughout the first half this decade. The FPGA market has the same rate as the CPU domain, with little opportunity for growth because of the requirements of domain-specific computing for high efficiency.

8.2 Tradeoff between design and cost

Fig. 8.7(a) shows the relationship between chip shipment and total cost on a user logic circuit design or an FPGA and ASIC [355]. Semiconductor process nodes n and $n + 1$ are shown as dashed and normal lines, respectively.

ASIC requires nonrecurring engineering (NRE) costs, including design tools and photo-masks, as well as fabrication costs. These costs are increased when using a more advanced semiconductor process. By contrast, an FPGA has relatively much lower NRE costs.

However, as shown in Table 2.1, ASICs have a lower cost per transistor than FPGAs, and the rate of growth in shipment costs across the age of the

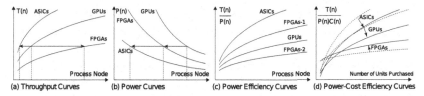

FIGURE 8.8 Throughput, power, and efficiency functions.

semiconductor process has turned out to be low through an improvement in semiconductor technologies (e.g., the slope of the line is lowered by introducing a newer semiconductor process, as shown in Fig. 8.7(a)). The cross point of the lines of the FPGA and ASIC on the same process node is a break-even point, and FPGAs are cost effective on the left side of the point, and ASICs are cost effective on the right side of the point.

Therefore, FPGAs are suitable as a mass variant and smaller production; by contrast, ASICs are suitable for a smaller variant and mass production. The NRE and fabrication costs on ASICs make segmentation possible in the market between ASICs and FPGAs. However, markets have demanded a variety of low volume production, and FPGAs have taken a share of the market since the late 1990s.

Fig. 8.7(b) shows a bell-curve, which is a histogram of the application market size required for ASIC implementation [355]. The three vertical bars show the capacity when the user implements a system with FPGAs. The gray area of the left side of the bar shows the market size in which the ASICs can be replaced with FPGAs when using process node n.

After the initial development of FPGAs, the first left-side and second-side bar in Fig. 8.7(b) show the growth rate. The growth has rapidly increased, and therefore, FPGA vendors have been challenged to add large numbers of memory blocks and DSP blocks on a chip. This extension has made it possible to implement a large-scale user logic circuit, and aggressively apply a newer semiconductor process for the integration fitting the mass-market based on the peak point of Fig. 8.7(b).

After the peak, small markets with replaceable FPGAs were present, and FPGA vendors were challenged to aggressively create a series of low-cost and high-performance devices for each market. As described in Appendix A, binary represented parameters and activations are the current trends on an FPGA for DNN applications, and thus there is the possibility to develop various binary neural network models, and FPGA vendors found such new markets.

Fig. 8.8 shows the throughput ($T(n)$), power-consumption ($P(n)$), power-efficiency ($T(n)/P(n)$), and effective efficiency ($T(n)/(P(n)C(n))$) for shipments when considering the cost $C(n)$. Let us consider an implementation trade-off between FPGAs and ASICs based on a neural network model development on a GPU.

Compared to GPU, ASIC and FPGA implementations have the possibility of higher and lower throughputs, respectively. This fact has indicated that ASICs can use older semiconductor processes efficiently by achieving the throughput of a GPU. However, FPGAs need to use newer semiconductor processes. GPUs also always use newer semiconductor processes, and thus FPGAs need to claim other benefits and take an alternative strategy. For example, FPGAs have sufficient flexibility to implement user logic circuits, and FPGA-based approaches need to actively use such positive characteristics. Moreover, as described in Appendix A, binary parameters and activations on a binary neural network have been well researched, thus there is the possibility that a 1-bit node of CLB can implement such a network model well. To utilize the reconfigurability of the FPGA, the establishment of a framework that can be applied to any neural network based on a binary approach, rather than applying a particular neural network model, will introduce a strong advantage.

However, regarding the implementation of ASICs, we can achieve a risk aversion by suppressing the entire cost by using an older semiconductor process. Both ASICs and FPGAs can suppress the power consumption ($P(n)$) more than GPUs. In FPGAs, the power efficiency ($T(n)/P(n)$) can be lower than that of a GPU if a user logic circuit has an inefficient throughput or performance (FPGA-2 curve in Fig. 8.8(c)). Thus, it is necessary to optimize the user logic circuit fitting the FPGA device architecture as much as possible, and the advantages of the time-to-market achieved by FPGAs cannot be obtained well.

As shown in the ASIC implementation examples for DNNs, the results show a lower power consumption and a higher throughput, thus resulting in a higher power efficiency on older semiconductor processes, such as a 65-nm process, than that of a GPU. GPUs have a chip area of 300–800 mm^2, however, whereas ASICs have a chip area of only 50 mm^2 or less, and thus ASICs can reduce the fabrication cost even when using the same semiconductor process if the same production volume is assumed. GPUs and ASICs both tend to reduce the effective efficiency ($T(n)/(P(n)C(n))$) by increasing the NRE and fabrication costs, and large production and shipment amounts are necessary (as shown in Fig. 8.8 (d)).

Thus, to improve the chip shipment, we need to design an architecture that can be applied to diverse markets, rather than to design a particular network model-specific architecture. In addition, the ASIC implementation can be combined with an older semiconductor process to reduce the total costs.

8.3 Hardware implementation strategies

This section considers a possible strategy toward the design of a DNN hardware based on the understanding described in the previous all chapters.

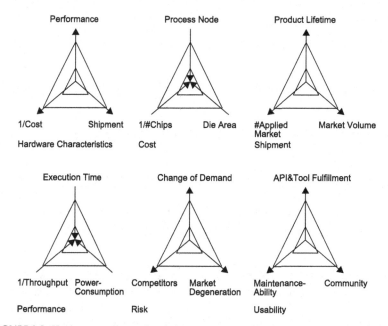

Performance

1/Cost — Shipment

Hardware Characteristics

Process Node

1/#Chips — Die Area

Cost

Product Lifetime

#Applied Market — Market Volume

Shipment

Execution Time

1/Throughput — Power-Consumption

Performance

Change of Demand

Competitors — Market Degeneration

Risk

API&Tool Fulfillment

Maintenance-Ability — Community

Usability

FIGURE 8.9 Hardware requirement break down.

8.3.1 Requirements of strategy planning

8.3.1.1 Constructing strategy planning

Machine learning has a role of recognition and/or prediction of the correlations among information having a major factor in information processing. It aims to improve the efficiency for users based on information obtained from the IoT and robot sensors, as described in Chapter 1.

Thus, we can predict a shorter turnaround time (TAT) required for such users to achieve a rapid decision to tackle competitors. Therefore, the major interest of network model developers is the time-to-market, which occurs mainly in the decision process (which we call time-to-authorization).

In addition, neural network model architects are interested in shortening the training time required to verify a code, validate training, and thus its execution performance. The design and implementation of machine learning specific hardware can be a differentiation factor for not only users and architects benefiting from time, but also system owners benefiting from the energy consumption and thermal control, which are major operating costs.

Before considering the strategy, let us look into detail into the hardware requirements, as shown in Fig. 8.9. The hardware characteristics are defined based on the performance factor, cost factor, and market shipment factor, namely, the differentiation factor, cost factor, and profit factor, respectively.

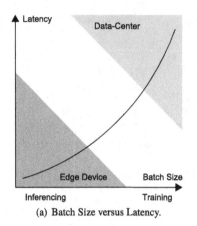
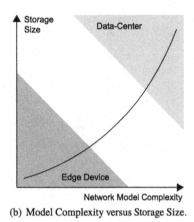

(a) Batch Size versus Latency.   (b) Model Complexity versus Storage Size.

FIGURE 8.10   Basic requirements to construct hardware architecture.

For the fabrication, the cost is most important factor to competition, which decreases profits, and influences the die area and the number of fabricated chips for a certain period. Market shipment is an important factor that directly determines the gross profit. In terms of the replacement duration of a product, we can gain more shipment volume per product if the lifetime is longer. The volume of a shipment per market, and the number of markets for one product, determine the full product price, and thus it returns to gross profit.

To obtain more users, from a hardware perspective, the product should have the highest power-efficiency as determined by the execution time (or TOPS value), or throughput, and power consumption. Before deploying a product, we should predict the risk on the market, which primary consists of a change in market trends (demands), market degeneration, and competitors. To avoid risk caused by a market degeneration, we need to apply the product to multiple market regions and or markets.

Users or owners must decide whether to buy our product. They may also be concerned whether the product is the most useful, and may not regard only the cost-performance requirements.

Fig. 8.10 shows the initial planning of the target segment on the market. For machine learning hardware, one point is the batch size versus latency requirement. Training and inferencing take a larger batch and a smaller batch, respectively. Every application segment has a different complexity for a neural network model, which relates to the storage requirement. As indicated, a sufficient on-chip memory size has a key role in the energy efficiency. For this reason, a target positioning such as the edge device and data-center is selected.

8.3.1.2   Strategy planning

In [292], the authors describe a positioning strategy, which can be categorized into three types: variety-, needs-, and access-based positioning.

FIGURE 8.11 Strategy planning.

Variety-based positioning aims to select particular products and/or services from many products and/or services. This positioning is economically justified if a product and/or service is the most superior in a particular industry.

Needs-based positioning aims to apply products and/or services to almost all needs of the particular customers. This positioning is justified if there is a need for various customer groups and/or if a combination of appropriate actions to apply products and/or services to the group is possible.

Access-base positioning aims to segment the customers with a difference in their access method to the products and or services. This positioning is determined based on the location and scale, or an aspect requiring a different action system from an ordinary action to effectively approach the customers.

Note that deep learning is not only about the industry, it is also a method to solve customer's issues or problems, as an application infrastructure. Therefore, we should define our targeting industries, customers, and location using a specific scale before developing a grand design. Industries include web-analytics, drug-discovery, autonomous-mobility, and older industries. Customers include governments, businesses, schools, and individuals, or are categorized into profit- and non-profit organizations. Location and scale include countries, prefectures, cities, and homes.

In terms of a datacenter, the customer is a particular service provider requiring a higher performance, applied to various industries, and lower-cost location(s) in terms of costs of the power consumption and thermal dissipation. For IoT, customers include various service providers requiring lower power consumption, applied to various industries, and various locations, not only on earth but also in space.

Let us apply the positioning of a strategy from a more general perspective, as shown in Fig. 8.11. The figure shows a radar chart, where every axis has a scale factor. When a larger scale is targeted, the hardware should have more flexibility and thus programmability.

A strategy is made based on the customers, industry, location(s), and scale. These determine the capable constraints of the die area, response time, and throughput. As the hardware characteristics indicate, machine learning hardware vendors can set up three basic strategies to compete with GPU vendors.

1. Performance competition
   They can aggressively use an advanced semiconductor process, and aggressively and directly compete with GPUs in terms of the execution performance.
2. Cost competition
   They can aggressively use an older semiconductor process, and aggressively claim a price-performance balance and differentiation from GPUs based on price.
3. Targeting alternative market
   They can find alternative markets that are difficult for GPUs, such as mobile and embedded devices.

By preliminarily designing a DSA, and by preparing an eco-system that provides optimization automatically based on its specific development tools, FPGAs can be a choice for owners.

Such tools have been researched for an automatic neural network hardware design [254][320]. In addition, FPGAs can use their reconfigurability, and apply it to both the inference and training of user logic circuit, and a simple switching between both at run-time is possible. Thus, FPGAs have an advantage in terms of implementation at different levels of precision for the inference and training (see Appendix A).

Regarding the ASIC implementation, by designing a programmable logic using a DSA, and by preparing its framework tool chain, ASIC RTL can be optimized to the user on demand, allowing the NRE cost to be shared among market players, thereby suppressing the total cost for the vendor.

8.3.2 Basic strategies

Machine learning hardware research is an extremely hot topic in research on computer architectures and products. It is clear that hardware that can solve such issues and/or problems, for users and owners easily.

8.3.2.1 Performance, usability, and risk control

Particular neural network model-specific accelerators have been well researched, with a focus on high-energy efficiency based on a performance with a high order of magnitude compared to traditional products. In addition to energy efficiency, three other aspects for users, architects, and owners exist.

1. High-performance execution
   It is a major portion of the time, as described in Chapter 5, which is a major factor delaying service for the developed model. However, various inference propositions to improve the throughput, latency, and energy efficiency have been studied. However, training is still dominated by GPUs. Regarding the architecture of the neural network models, the training process is major time-consuming aspect, as described in Chapter 5. Training requires large

amounts of temporal data from tensors and vectors as compared to inference (see Appendix A). Training requires a more efficient data flow and larger data amounts than inference machines are capable of handling.

2. Programmable hardware not hardwired hardware

Neural network model architects might aggressively attempt to develop and test different neural network models and thus specific hardware, particularly accelerators, cannot be responsible for their demand, and programmability has to be considered for a design. We do not require a superfluous reconfigurability for FPGAs or a superfluous programmability for microprocessors, but we do need such a fitting based on the characteristics of the neural network models. In addition, neural network hardware vendors must deal with the users, owners, and system integrators.

3. Independence from implementation

A computational model, its architecture, and the compiler infrastructure are preferable as a complete framework independent from ASICs and FPGAs, and as a tool generating a user-specific system as a soft IP. A tool user can choose an ASIC or FPGA implementation on demand. This approach reduces the risk of chip fabrication, and isolates the fabrication from the design flow. In addition, it is sufficient to provide an optimized IP to customers with their requested constraints for the FPGAs if the FPGA configures only a particular network model.

High-performance training has been researched, as described in Chapter 6, based on a binary gradient descent method and sparse tensors.

8.3.2.2 Compatibility from traditional systems

Although we tend to focus on hardware architectures, we should also focus on the needs of users, owners, and system integrators.

1. Development process

A machine learning subsystem having a different development process compared to a traditional process temporally decreases the productivity. We need to support a tool chain that supports a traditional development process. Machine learning hardware vendors should embed their specific development process into a traditional approach at least, and should hide the specific development process from users if possible.

2. Modeling tool

In the case of a special develop environment, users need time to understand the environment. This is a disadvantage, and the vendor will lose chance to be applied by owners if this time is longer than that of the competitors. A machine learning system that can use a traditional development environment and reduce the time for prototyping is expected.

3. Modeled code

Various platforms (systems) are evaluated using the same neural network model as a benchmark, and the owner may choose one product from the candidates. A neural network model code should have compatibility with most platforms. It is difficult to be taken by the user and owner if the code compatibility is not supported. For example, a platform supporting only a special language is clearly not acceptable by most and users, and will have difficulty being selected as one by the owners.

8.3.2.3 Integration into traditional system

Because most research and development are focused on accelerator hardware, a system architecture has not been a focus when considering its running environment. To be selected by various owners, we should hear the hardware requirements from users and owners, and for the neural network model design the compatibility described above. This is expected to be integrated into a traditional system for an easier operation.

1. Offloading method
   Users apply Python script language with deep learning frameworks running on Python's VM. By preparing a VM supporting machine learning hardware, a virtual instruction and API function should be directly run on the hardware when a supported instruction and/or function is detected. In general, a machine learning system needs an off-loading mechanism.
2. Single memory address space
   Offloading major task(s) of a neural network, data must be transferred between the accelerator subsystem and host system as seen in the GPU subsystem. This introduces optimization efforts for the code that are not inherently necessary. This is a major cold-start overhead to the execution. To remove the overhead, one approach is a uniform memory space between the host and accelerator. This solution requires support by the operating software.
3. Code morphing
   By preparing an intermediated representation between the virtual instructions and/or API functions and machine learning hardware, isolation occurs between a virtual instruction and/or an API function and the executing hardware; thus, a VM and machine learning hardware can be flexibly updated or modified at the same time. This trend can be seen in the intermediate instruction (IR) support, such as ONNX, described in Chapter 5. Instruction fusion and de-fusion methods used in traditional microprocessors, including code morphing software (CMS) [149] can be applied to a machine learning system to optimize the execution and can be adopted to the execution during run-time.

NVIDIA's GPUs and their eco-system are the de-facto standard for the neural network modeling community, and their development environment is also common. Studies have differentiated their energy-efficiency, a metric of which is the running costs, and such devices are appealing with an advantage of greater efficiency. Along with energy-efficiency on the hardware, the issues and problems incurred by users, architects, owners, and system integrators can be the seeds of an architecture design and its claim of differentiation.

8.3.3 Alternative factors

Google has issued a press-release on the TPU, and NVIDIA has developed and studied neural network accelerators, and we can also consider NVDLA and its patents. At NVIDIA, Professor Dally at Stanford University and his students have studied such an architecture. Therefore, NVIDIA can be a threat to start-up companies. AMD has also caught up with NVIDIA by supporting similar lower-level libraries.

8.4 Summary of hardware design requirements

We should design an architecture that has a data-movement oriented computation model if data movement is a major issue in terms of delay and energy consumption. Traditional systems have a premise in that all operand data are ready to be executed. Before an execution, load operand data by a memory access are required, resulting in a memory hierarchy. A memory hierarchy is the major reason for a delay and capacity limitation, and creates a bottleneck in the system. This can also be seen in a machine learning hardware system. A memory hierarchy consumes a larger area on a chip, and half die are used in microprocessors because the cache memory does not take exclusive storage of the data, resulting in a lower utilization of the die area.

Online learning does not require much storage. Currently large amounts of data are needed for a training system; however, transfer learning [309], which reuses the trained parameters in a different domain, has a high probability of achieving a breakthrough. In addition, a system needing a relatively small amount of training data can be a significant aspect if online learning, and not only pruning, is applied as a major approach.

Chapter 9

Conclusion

In this book, we looked into the details of machine learning hardware for not only hardware architectures and acceleration methods but also how machine learning tasks are run on platforms with baseline characteristics. The results show that external memory access is the first priority for both the execution performance and energy consumption, and thus the importance of energy-efficiency for both inference and training was introduced.

One approach to boosting the energy-efficiency is to skip the number of external memory accesses and execution clock cycles, and thus creating a sparse tensor during training is a popular approach, similar to pruning. This method can also be applied to the training task itself if a dynamic zero-skipping technique is developed and applied.

An FPGA, which has unique reconfigurability characteristics, lies between GPU and ASIC implementations in terms of energy-efficiency. Rather than compete in terms of energy-efficiency, focus should be given to other competitive points utilizing a reconfigurability. This includes a different optimization of neural network tasks in terms of both inference and training, and requires a hardware patch to update the task logic circuit.

ASIC has the highest energy efficiency with an optimization for targeting machine learning task(s). However, this approach has a higher NRE cost and requires a high volume production area, unlike an FPGA, which can be applied to such a small market. Thus, from a cost-performance perspective, the ASIC approach must have high flexibility and programmability to be applied to various neural networking tasks. This can be seen in GPUs, which have a domain-specific architecture for graphics processing, and similarly, a neural network domain-specific architecture should be designed.

FPGA and ASIC implementations should face the issues and problems of users and owners, such as the training performance, compatibility with other architectures, ease of porting from prototype to product, and a lower-energy consumption for both of inference and training.

Thinking Machines. https://doi.org/10.1016/B978-0-12-818279-6.00019-0

Appendix A

Basics of deep learning

Appendix A describes the basic elements of neural network models using a feedforward neural network model consisting of L layers. The first section introduces an equation for each neuron, called a unit. As described in the second section, the introduced equation model leads to a basic hardware model that can be implemented as real hardware. Third, the equations are represented as matrix operations, and the data layout, called a shape, is described. In addition, an initialization of the parameters is described. Moreover, the learning sequence using a matrix operation is introduced. Finally, some issues in the design of a DNN model are provided.

A.1 Equation model

This section considers modeling the feedforward neural network with an equation. Fig. A.1 shows an example of a feedforward neural network consisting of seven layers. Neuron i is connected to the synapse of neuron j. The neuron outputs a spike upon firing, which is represented by an activation function. Connection on a synapse between neurons i and j is represented by the connection intensity as a weight.

The output z_i of neuron i can be represented as a weighted edge with coefficient $w_{j,i}$. The weighted value is input into the activation function of neuron j. Neuron j is input from all synapses including neuron i and weighted, creating a pre-activation of the current. This is a summation of all weighted values. The

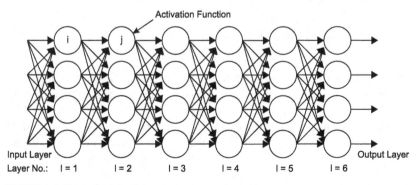

FIGURE A.1 Example of feedforward neural network model.

TABLE A.1 Activation functions for hidden layer [279].

Activation Function	$f(u)$	$f'(u)$
Hyperbolic Tangent	$f(u) = \tanh(u)$	$f'(u) = 1 - f^2(u)$
Sigmoid	$f(u) = 1/(1 + e^{-u})$	$f'(u) = f(u)(1 - f(u))$
Rectified Linear Unit	$f(u) = max(u, 0)$	$f'(u) = (u > 0) \; ? \; 1 : 0$

pre-activation is fed into an activation function, which generates a non-linear output.

A feedforward neural network is composed using a layer structure, where one layer consists of multiple neurons, and a weighted connection between layers is considered. The weight and bias are generally called an activation, and a set of parameters on the l-layer is called a parameter space for the l-layer.

A.1.1 Feedforward neural network model

Weight $w_{j,i}^{(l)}$ on a synapse on neuron j in the l-layer connected from neuron i in the $(l-1)$-layer is multiplied by input $x_i^{(l)}$ on the synapse of neuron i, and a pre-activation $u_j^{(l)}$ for neuron j can be represented as follows: [279].

$$u_j^{(l)} = \sum_i w_{j,i}^{(l)} x_i^{(l)} + b_j^{(l)} \qquad (A.1)$$

where $b_j^{(l)}$ is the bias. Output $z_j^{(l)}$ on neuron j is the output of the activation function $f_j^{(l)}(*)$, and can be represented as follows [279].

$$z_j^{(l)} = f_j^{(l)}(u_j^{(l)}) \qquad (A.2)$$

Here, $z_j^{(l)}$ is input $x_j^{(l+1)}$ on neuron k in the next $(l+1)$-layer. The activation function is described in next section.

A.1.2 Activation functions

A.1.2.1 Concept of activation function

Table A.1 shows typical activation functions. An activation function $f(u)$ must be derivative, as well as a non-linear monotone increasing or decreasing function.

An activation function involves a gradient vanishing problem. The gradient vanishing problem can be explained with an example using $\tanh(*)$ as the activation function. The activation function tends to be saturated to -1 or $+1$ on the output side layers. Thus, most update values for the gradient, as shown in Eq. (A.24), are zeros [253] because $f'(u)$ can be zero on the input side layers if an appropriate initialization is not applied. There is a possibility that we will be unable to obtain the local minima owing to a lower converging speed on the input side layers.

A.1.2.2 Rectified linear unit

A rectified linear unit (ReLU) function [172] outputs a pre-activation value when its value is greater than zero, and otherwise outputs zero. Thus, its derivative outputs a value of 1 if the pre-activation is greater than zero; otherwise, it outputs a zero. ReLU does not create a gradient vanishing because a neuron on the output side layer can create a back propagation using $\delta_j^{(l)}$; therefore, the input side layers obtain a sufficient update. However, a zero is output when the pre-activation is less than or equal to zero, indicating that the gradient is also zero, and thus learning is occasionally slower.

A Leaky ReLU function (LReLU) [253] aims to solve this problem with a modification of the ReLU function as follows.

$$f(u) = \begin{cases} u & (u > 0) \\ 0.01u & (\text{otherwise}) \end{cases} \tag{A.3}$$

An LReLU function outputs a small value when the pre-activation is less than zero, and avoids a zero gradient. Thus, it creates a chance to sufficiently back propagate to the input side layers.

In addition, a coefficient (slope) of "0.01" for $u \le 0$ can be parameterized as follows.

$$f(u) = \begin{cases} u & (u > 0) \\ p \times u & (\text{otherwise}) \end{cases} \tag{A.4}$$

This activation function is called a parametric ReLU (PReLU) function [191].

A.1.3 Output layer

A Sigmoid can be used for a binary classification, such as yes or no, or true or false, because an absolute large value can be zero or 1 based on the function. A derivative of the softmax function assumes that the loss function (explained in the next section) is a cross-entropy (where t_k is an entropy coefficient). See Table A.2.

A.1.4 Learning and back propagation

A.1.4.1 Loss and cost functions

Learning aims to close the gap between an output and label, and a function to evaluate the error is called an error or loss function. A loss is the geometric

TABLE A.2 Output layer functions [279].

Activation Function	$f(u)$	$f'(u)$	Use Case
Sigmoid	$f(u) = 1/(1 + e^{-u})$	$f'(u) = f(u)(1 - f(u))$	Binary Classification
Softmax	$f(u_k) = \frac{e^{u_k}}{\sum_{j=1}^{K} e^{u_j}}$	$f'(u_k) = f(u_k) - t_k$	Multiple Classifications

distance represented by the norm as follows:

$$E(x, y) = \left(\sum_i |x_i - y_i|^l\right)^{\frac{1}{l}} \tag{A.5}$$

A squared $l = 2$ norm is generally used because of its ease of use with a derivative of the norm and its calculation. The cost function has a regularization term to evaluate the cost and adjust the updating amount of the parameters. In the case of a multi-classification having N classes, it uses a cross-entropy, which is represented as follows.

$$E(y, \hat{y}) = -\frac{1}{N} \sum_{n=1}^{N} [y_n \log \hat{y}_n + (1 - y_n) \log(1 - \hat{y}_n)] \tag{A.6}$$

where $\hat{y}_n$ is a logistic regression function. The cross-entropy is generally combined with the softmax function in the last layer.

A.1.4.2 Back propagation

We want to update the parameters in the hidden layers with an error value of E. The error E can be changed through a fluctuation of the parameters during training. We then also want to obtain the update required for every weight and bias. Therefore, we need a derivative of the loss or error with weights and biases, as indicated by $\frac{\partial E}{\partial w}$ and $\frac{\partial E}{\partial b}$, respectively.

Before describing the back propagation process, we need to understand the *chain rule* used for the calculation of the derivative. Here, $\frac{\partial y}{\partial x}$ can be rewritten as follows:

$$\frac{\partial y}{\partial x} = \frac{\partial y}{\partial z} \frac{\partial z}{\partial x} \tag{A.7}$$

This rule is used for every derivative. Consider Fig. A.2, which shows a node of a feed-forward neural network [162]. We want a derivative of the loss value L on every node to calculate how much the node value, such as $\partial L/\partial x$, should be changed. Let us assume that one input is an activation, and the other input is a weight. These are multiplied and summed with other products.

The addition can be represented as follows.

$$z = x + y \tag{A.8}$$

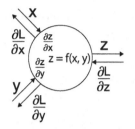

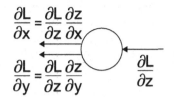

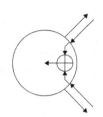

(a) Back Propagation with Partial Differences.

(b) Back Propagation with Chain Rule.

(c) Fan-out Treated as Addition to Back Propagation.

FIGURE A.2 Back propagation on operator [162].

The derivatives are thus the following:

$$\frac{\partial z}{\partial x} = \frac{\partial x}{\partial x} + \frac{\partial y}{\partial x} = 1 \qquad (A.9)$$

$$\frac{\partial z}{\partial y} = \frac{\partial x}{\partial y} + \frac{\partial y}{\partial y} = 1 \qquad (A.10)$$

Therefore, derivative $\partial L/\partial x$ is as follows:

$$\frac{\partial L}{\partial x} = \frac{\partial L}{\partial z}\frac{\partial z}{\partial x} = \frac{\partial L}{\partial z} \times 1 = \frac{\partial L}{\partial z} \qquad (A.11)$$

Here, $\partial L/\partial y$ is also the same. Thus, the derivative of the addition operator is applied as a distribution for the back propagation.

In the case of subtraction, the derivatives are as follows.

$$\frac{\partial z}{\partial x} = \frac{\partial x}{\partial x} - \frac{\partial y}{\partial x} = 1 \qquad (A.12)$$

$$\frac{\partial z}{\partial y} = \frac{\partial x}{\partial y} - \frac{\partial y}{\partial y} = -1 \qquad (A.13)$$

In the case of multiplication, the equation introduces the following derivatives:

$$\frac{\partial z}{\partial x} = \frac{\partial (x \times y)}{\partial x} = y\frac{\partial x}{\partial x} = y \qquad (A.14)$$

$$\frac{\partial z}{\partial y} = \frac{\partial (x \times y)}{\partial y} = x\frac{\partial y}{\partial y} = x \qquad (A.15)$$

Therefore, the derivative for the back propagation can be as follows:

$$\frac{\partial L}{\partial x} = \frac{\partial L}{\partial z}\frac{\partial z}{\partial x} = y\frac{\partial L}{\partial z} \qquad (A.16)$$

Here, $\frac{\partial L}{\partial y}$ is also obtained in the same way as $x\frac{\partial L}{\partial z}$. Thus, a multiplication node conducts an exchange of inputs. Regarding a fan-out from a node, multiple back propagations are derived from the following nodes, and can be a sum of the derivatives, as shown in Fig. A.2(c).

In the case of division, the derivatives are as follows.

$$\frac{\partial z}{\partial x} = \frac{\partial x}{\partial x} - \frac{\partial y^{-1}}{\partial x} = 1 \tag{A.17}$$

$$\frac{\partial z}{\partial y} = \frac{\partial x}{\partial y} - \frac{\partial y^{-1}}{\partial y} = y^{-2} \tag{A.18}$$

Our objective in using the loss function is to calculate the amount of parameter updating in the hidden layers. We then use the derivative, i.e., the amount of changes to the parameters by the forward propagation, which can be measured by the loss (or error, and/or an objective) function. The derivatives are represented as $\frac{\partial L}{\partial w^{(l)}}$ and $\frac{\partial L}{\partial b^{(l)}}$ for the weight and bias at the l-layer, respectively. By the chain rule, we can rewrite such an equation as follows:

$$\frac{\partial L}{\partial w^{(l)}} = \frac{\partial L}{\partial u^{(l)}} \frac{\partial u^{(l)}}{\partial w^{(l)}} \tag{A.19}$$

Bias can also be represented in the same way, where $u^{(l)}$ is the pre-activation at the l-layer, as shown in Eq. (A.1). Note that a pre-activation u at the l-th layer is $u^{(l)} = w^{(l)} z^{(l-1)} + b^{(l)}$. Therefore, we can calculate its derivative as follows:

$$\frac{\partial u^{(l)}}{\partial w^{(l)}} = z^{(l-1)} \tag{A.20}$$

and

$$\frac{\partial u^{(l)}}{\partial b^{(l)}} = 1 \tag{A.21}$$

Regarding the other term, $\frac{\partial L}{\partial u^{(l)}}$, we can also apply the chain rule as follows:

$$\delta^{(l)} = \sum \frac{\partial L}{\partial u^{(l)}} \tag{A.22}$$

$$= \sum \frac{\partial L}{\partial u^{(l+1)}} \frac{\partial u^{(l+1)}}{\partial u^{(l)}}$$

$$= \sum \delta^{(l+1)} \frac{\partial u_{(l+1)}}{\partial z^{(l)}} \frac{\partial z^{(l)}}{\partial u^{(l)}}$$

$$= \sum \delta^{(l+1)} w^{(l+1)} f'^{(l)}(u^{(l)})$$

$$= f'^{(l)}(u^{(l)}) \sum \delta^{(l+1)} w^{(l+1)}$$

The update of the weight $w_{j,i}^{(l)}$ on the connection from neuron i in the $(l-1)$-layer to neuron j in the l-layer is represented as follows [279].

$$w_{j,i}^{(l)} \longleftarrow w_{j,i}^{(l)} - \epsilon_j^{(l)} \frac{\partial L}{\partial w_{j,i}^{(l)}} \qquad (A.23)$$

where $\epsilon_j^{(l)}$ is a coefficient for the learning of neuron j in the l-layer, and is called the learning rate. The output layer, i.e., the last layer, consists of n neurons. Here, E_n is called an error function, and L_n is denoted as a loss function, showing a difference between the expected value d_n obtained from the label and the output $z_n^{(L)}$. There are various representations for the error function, and an average square error is one example. An error on the last layer, the L-layer, can be represented as $\delta^L = E_n$. Bias is also represented through a similar approach.

By converging δ^L to a small value, learning aims to update the parameters by closing the gap between the expected value and the output value. A set of input elements is called the input vector, and the output vector on a hidden layer can be called an activation. Learning with one expected value and one output to update the parameters is called online learning. Learning with a set of expected values and a set of outputs to update the parameters by the sets is called batch learning. Because batch learning requires a huge amount of data for the sets as well as a significant amount of intermediate data, a batch can be chunked and can learn using the unit of the chunked batch, which is called a mini-batch, i.e., mini-batch learning.

By using δ^L to update the parameters in the hidden layers, and propagating the updated calculation from the output layer $(l = L)$ to the input layer $(l = 1)$, a back propagation appears. The derivative based on changing the value of weight is previously obtained as follows:

$$\frac{\partial L}{\partial w_{j,i}^{(l)}} = \delta_j^{(l)} z_i^{(l-1)} \qquad (A.24)$$

where $\delta_j^{(l)}$ is the determined gradient descent amount for the weight, which can be obtained through the following equation [279]:

$$\delta_j^{(l)} = f_j'^{(l)}(u_j^{(l)}) \sum_k \delta_k^{(l+1)} w_{k,j}^{(l+1)} \qquad (A.25)$$

where $f_j'^{(l)}(*)$ is a derivative for the activation function $f_j^{(l)}(*)$ on neuron j in the l-layer. The calculation of $\delta_j^{(l)}$ on the l-layer, and propagating the value to the $(l-1)$-layer, is a so-called back propagation method applied to update the parameters in the hidden layers.

The derivative for the bias is similar to the case of a weight, but it does not have a source node, similar to a constant offset.

$$\frac{\partial L}{\partial b^{(l)}} = \delta^{(l)} \tag{A.26}$$

$$\delta^{(l)} = \delta^{(l+1)} \tag{A.27}$$

Bias can be updated using the gradient of the bias as follows.

$$b^{(l)} \longleftarrow b^{(l)} - \epsilon^{(l)} \frac{\partial L}{\partial b^{(l)}} \tag{A.28}$$

A.1.5 Parameter initialization

Initialization of the parameters requires a random setting. If the parameters have the same value, contiguous fully connected layers have the same value and thus have a uniform state across all neurons within the layers, and it is meaningless to have multiple parameters. Thus, each parameter should have different numbers at least.

A common initialization method is to use a uniform distribution for each parameter initialization, called Xavier's initialization [171], which is a method to take a standard deviation having $1/\sqrt{n}$, where n is the number of neurons in the preceding layer. For an ReLU, He's initialization method is used [191]. He's initialization uses a Gaussian distribution with a standard deviation of $2/\sqrt{n}$.

A.2 Matrix operation for deep learning

This section introduces a matrix representation for the described equation explained in the previous sections in this chapter. In addition, we consider the matrix and vector data layouts (shape of the tensor).

A.2.1 Matrix representation and its layout

Pre-activation $U^{(l)}$ at the l-layer can be represented by an affine transformation with the matrix equation using the weight matrix $W^{(l)}$, input activation $Z^{(l-1)}$, and bias vector $B^{(l)}$, as follows.

$$U^{(l)} = W^{(l)} Z^{(l-1)} + B^{(l)} \tag{A.29}$$

By including the bias vector $B^{(l)}$ into the weight matrix $W^{(l)}$ as a $J \times (I+1)$ matrix of the parameters, and adding a constant of 1 into $Z^{(l-1)}$ as $(I+1)$, Eq. (A.29) can be represented as $U^{(l)} = W^{(l)} Z^{(l-1)}$.

The output $Z^{(l)}$ at the l-layer is a set of outputs from the activation functions, and forms a vector, which can be represented as follows:

$$Z^{(l)} = f(U^{(l)}) \tag{A.30}$$

In the case of mini-batch learning, a matrix $\Delta^{(l)}$ has elements of $\delta_j^{(l)}$ of neuron j in the l-layer, which has a shape of $J \times N$, where J and N are the number

TABLE A.3 Array and layout for feedforward propagation.

Array	$Z^{(l-1)}$	$W^{(l)}$	$B^{(l)}$	$f^{(l)}(U^{(l)})$	$Z^{(l)}$
I/O	IN	IN	IN	OUT	OUT
Layout	$I \times N$	$J \times I$	$J \times 1$	$J \times N$	$J \times N$

TABLE A.4 Array and layout for back propagation.

Array	$W^{(l+1)}$	$\Delta^{(l+1)}$	$f'^{(l)}(U^{(l)})$	$\Delta^{(l)}$	$\partial W^{(l)}$	$\partial B^{(l)}$	$Z^{(l-1)}$
I/O	IN	IN	IN	OUT	TEMP	TEMP	IN
Layout	$K \times J$	$K \times N$	$J \times N$	$J \times N$	$J \times I$	$J \times 1$	$I \times N$

of neurons in the l-layer and the mini-batch size, respectively, and can be represented as follows [279].

$$\Delta^{(l)} = f'^{(l)}(U^{(l)}) \odot (W^{(l+1)\top} \Delta^{(l+1)}) \tag{A.31}$$

Operator $\odot$ is an element-wise multiplication called a Hadamard product. We then obtain the update amounts $\partial W^{(l)}$ and $\partial B^{(l)}$ through the following calculations [279].

$$\partial W^{(l)} = \frac{1}{N}(\Delta^{(l)} Z^{(l-1)\top}) \tag{A.32}$$

$$\partial B^{(l)} = \frac{1}{N}(\Delta^{(l)} 1^{\top}) \tag{A.33}$$

Therefore, a calculation needs a transposition of the tensor represented by "$\top$" in the equations.

Tables A.3 and A.4 show the data layouts (shapes) needed for inference and training with mini-batch size N, respectively.

A.2.2   Matrix operation sequence for learning

The sequence below shows the learning process for a feedforward neural network model with a mini-batch learning method. The mini-batch learning repeats the sequence from $l = L$ to $l = 1$.

1. Initialize $W^{(l)}$ and $B^{(l)}$
2. If $l = L$, then calculate $\Delta^{(L)}$ (mean squared error, for example)
3. If $l \neq L$, then calculate $\Delta^{(l)}$ (matrix multiplication and Hadamard product)
4. Calculate $\partial W^{(l)}$ and $\partial B^{(l)}$ (matrix multiplication)
5. Update the parameters using $\partial W^{(l)}$ and $\partial B^{(l)}$ (matrix subtraction)
6. Back to item-3

The learning sequence is extremely simple for feedforward neural networks. When the parameters exceed the matrix operation size on the hardware, a subdivision of the matrices and vectors, and the creation of sub-sequences, are necessary. This involves various temporal data, as shown in Tables A.3 and A.4. Inference and training use five and seven datasets, respectively. The hardware design needs to transfer these datasets efficiently between the arithmetic unit and external memory.

A.2.3   Learning optimization

Learning optimization has been aggressively studied. This section briefly describes the major approaches.

A.2.4   Bias-variance problem

We should evaluate the inference error rate upon the training and cross-validation to optimize the dimensions (a rank) for the activations. We can do so using a graph plotting, the x-axis of which is for the rank, and by plotting the errors. By checking the gap between the error curves, we can consider what state it is in.

When there is a large difference between the error in the training and the error in the cross-validation, a superfluous bias effect and an underfitting occur. When the training error is lower, but the cross-validation has a higher error, an overfitting occurs. This is called a bias-variance problem [277].

The learning curve used here is assumed to plot the error rate with the training data size on the x-axis. A gap between the curve of the training and a curve of the cross-validation occurs. For the learning curve during training, we will obtain a larger error rate when we try to increase the training data size owing to a lower compatibility between the parameter and input vector. We can see a generalization in the performance of the learning curve on the cross-validation; in addition, a smaller training data size introduces a larger error rate, and the error rate is decreased by increasing the training data size owing to a higher compatibility between the parameters and input data. Thus, the learning curve of the cross-validation is plotted at a higher position than the learning curve of the training. Therefore, we can evaluate the state and control the bias-variance problem.

The learning curves of the training and cross-validation show a higher bias with a smaller gap between curves for a smaller training data size. When a higher variance has a lower generalization performance, it shows a large gap between curves when a larger training data size is applied. This is an overfitting. In this state, the two curves have larger gap, and therefore, we are still able to obtain a lower learning curve on the cross-validation by increasing the number of training data (continuing the training). A neural network having a larger number of parameters, or a larger number of neurons in the hidden layers, larger number of hidden layers, or both, tends to be in a state of overfitting, and thus we can control this by adding a regularization term to the cost function.

A.2.4.1 Regularization

By adding a regularization term to the error function, the bias-validation problem can be controlled.

If the regularization coefficient has too large a value when the bias effect is large, an underfitting may constrain the parameters. In this case, we should try to decrease the regularization coefficient, or increase the number of parameters, to check whether the error rate can be lower at the cross-validation.

When the variance is too large, a weak regularization term and a small constraint for each parameter are obtained; thus, overfitting occurs. In this case, we should try to increase the regularization coefficient or decrease the number of parameters, and a regularization coefficient having the smallest error rate on the cross-validation is an appropriate value.

When optimizing the number of parameters, changes in the value of the regularization coefficient, and finding the number of parameters that gives the smallest value of an error function, are achieved by changing the regularization coefficient. Next, the number of parameters having the smallest error rate on the cross-validation is appropriate. In addition, we can evaluate the generalization by checking the error rate on the test set.

A weight decay is a common example of regularization. A weight decay adds L2 regularization $\frac{\lambda}{2}\|w\|^2$ to the cost (loss) function.

A.2.4.2 Momentum

By introducing an inertia in updating the parameter, the training avoids random tasks of the SGD, which is an inefficient updating.

$$\lambda_t \longleftarrow \alpha\lambda_{t-1} - \epsilon\frac{\partial L}{\partial W} \tag{A.34}$$

When updating, the weight is $w \longleftarrow w + \lambda_t$.

A.2.4.3 Adam

Adam is an algorithm for a first-order gradient-based optimization of the stochastic objective functions, based on adaptive estimates of the lower-order moments [223]. The method computes individual adaptive learning rates for different parameters from estimates of the first and second moments of the gradients [223]. Adam is based on a combination of ideas of Momentum and AdaGrad. In addition, Adam correlates a skew of the parameters by β.

$$m_t \longleftarrow \beta_1 m_{t-1} - (1 - \beta_1)\frac{\partial L}{\partial W} \tag{A.35}$$

$$v_t \longleftarrow \beta_2 v_{t-1} - (1 - \beta_2)\frac{\partial L^2}{\partial W^2} \tag{A.36}$$

Then, weight w is updated as follows.

$$w \longleftarrow w - \epsilon \left(\sqrt{\frac{v_t}{1 - \beta_2^t}} + \gamma \right)^{-1} \frac{m_t}{1 - \beta_1^t} \qquad (A.37)$$

where γ is a coefficient used to avoid a zero-divide.

Appendix B

Modeling of deep learning hardware

Appendix B describes an example of machine learning hardware developed based on prior studies. First, the basic concept of a parameter space is described. Next, the entire data-flow approach is provided. Finally, the processing element architecture is introduced.

B.1 Concept of deep learning hardware

B.1.1 Relationship between parameter space and propagation

Fig. B.1 shows the relationship between the interface and operations. It represents an operation needed for inference (forward propagation) and training (back propagation), composed using $J \times I$ parameters and J activation functions.

I neurons for a $(l-1)$-layer are shown at the bottom of Fig. B.1, $J \times I$ weights are shown in the center box, $J \times 1$ biases are placed on the left side, and $J \times 1$ activation functions are located on the right side. Fig. B.1(a) shows the path for forward propagation on the l-layer, and Fig. B.1(b) shows the path for back propagation. Here, $\delta_i^{(l-1)}$ for back propagation is represented as "partial delta" in Fig. B.1(b), which is also shown in Eq. (A.25).

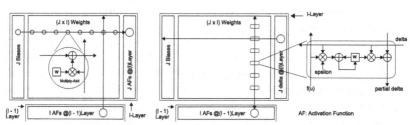

(a) Operations for Forward Propagation.

(b) Operations for Back Propagation.

FIGURE B.1 Parameter space and operations.

B.1.2 Basic deep learning hardware

Using the design shown in Fig. B.1, a feedforward neural network can be implemented.[1] Thus, by preparing an arithmetic unit for weights having up to three MAD logic circuits, we can implement a deep learning hardware having both inference and training capabilities. We can lay out these four units with a cyclic connection between neighbors, and the data path can be executed with a spiral data flow for the network. Not only online learning but also mini-batch learning can take this data path. When the parameter space exceeds the designed data path, a mechanism to sequence a subset of the parameter space is needed, and adding an error function to the hardware can be a realistic approach.

As presented here, machine learning hardware, particularly deep learning hardware, can be designed using a simple logic circuit, which requires efficient data streaming for the parameters.

B.2 Data-flow on deep learning hardware

The proposed baseline architecture can be treated as a swing data-flow architecture, as shown in Fig. B.2. In the first phase, the activation flows from bottom to top, and a partial product is generated, flowing from left to right of the parameter space, and finally reaching the activation buffer. During the second phase, the activation flows from right to left, and a partial product is generated from top to bottom of the parameter space and is finally stored in the activation buffer at the bottom.

Fig. B.2(c) shows a wave front of the pipeline for online forwarding. The input of the biases and activations make a wave front of a partial product, and the parameters "after" the wave front are set into every processing element. For a batch, a mini-batch having the maximum size of the parameter space is considered, as shown in Fig. B.2(d). Training can have such the mini-batch and flows inference first, and updating parameters on next and stores back the parameters to parameter memory.

B.3 Machine learning hardware architecture

Fig. B.3(a) shows the processing element (PE) architecture, which is replicated in the parameter space. PE supports both inference and training on the swinging data flow. Regarding the training, it takes two phases; the first is to update the weight, and the next is to calculate the partial delta. The first training phase assumes that the ReLU is used, and the learning rate is propagated on the derivative value path. Paths on the upper horizontal and right vertical sides are bidirectional, and tri-state transistors are used.

The set of PE arrays and buffers operates on a swinging flow. In addition, the flow can have a ring topology. Fig. B.3 shows the ring architecture in which data

---

[1] This requires a pipeline register and control of a sparse connection in a real implementation.

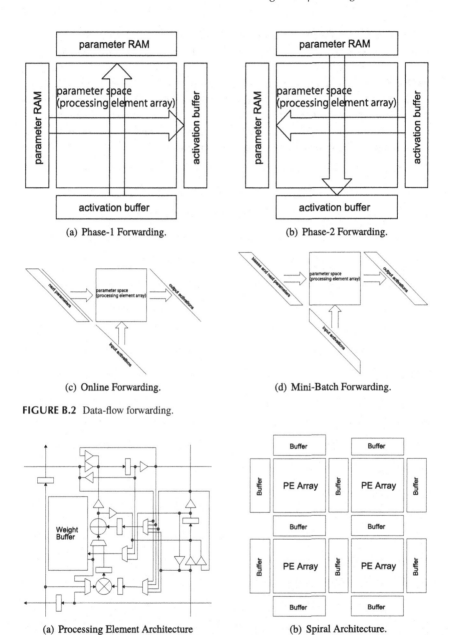

(a) Phase-1 Forwarding.

(b) Phase-2 Forwarding.

(c) Online Forwarding.

(d) Mini-Batch Forwarding.

FIGURE B.2 Data-flow forwarding.

(a) Processing Element Architecture

(b) Spiral Architecture.

FIGURE B.3 Processing element and spiral architecture.

flows in a spiral direction. An operation larger than the parameter space can be applied on the data path by repeating the output of the same set of activations, which forms a vector, and the data path changes the weights. The PE array and two buffers can form one tile, which operates as a task-level pipeline. One tile and/or a part of a tile array can be arranged into a set of independent spiral hardware architectures, and each can work in parallel. With this architecture, the batch size can be proportional to the number of tiles in the ring topology.

This is an extremely simple hardware architecture. When developing this architecture, a design scheduler and controller are needed, along with an interface to the external world. Although this is a specialized matrix operation, such an operation is sufficient to perform deep learning tasks.

Appendix C

Advanced network models

This appendix introduces variants of CNN, RNN, and AE, which the network models presented here are based on, through the combination of several techniques and/or models. Let us check the current architectural trend of network models, which will be helpful for network model development. In addition, a technique for using a residual is introduced.

C.1 CNN variants

C.1.1 Convolution architecture

C.1.1.1 Linear convolution

A filter is called a kernel in the deep learning domain. Each node of a kernel performs an MAD operation with the input of an activation. Here, "b" and "w" are a bias and weight, respectively. Activations labeled as "x" are shifted from right to left on the timeline.

A stride determines the amount of shift of the activations. When the stride factor is 1, the shift can be configured using FIFO. Then, multiplication is applied concurrently with the sending of the partial product to the left entry. When the stride is more than 1, the data path cannot use FIFO, and requires multiple unicasting to implement the stride distance. See Fig. C.1.

To support a case in which the kernel size exceeds the capacity of FIFO, the convolution needs a windowing stride method. A windowing stride method is applied to make a window correspond to the kernel size, and the activations are moved with the stride distance emulated by multiple unicasting. If the window

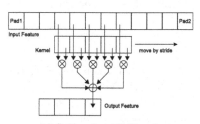

(a) Stride = 1 and Delite = 1.

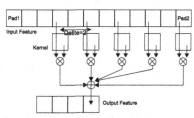

(b) Stride = 1 and Delite = 2.

FIGURE C.1 One-dimensional convolution.

includes three entries, the window moves from left to right by the stride distance. A stride factor of 1 requires four steps to move the window in this example.

The output size O in one-dimension is calculated through the following equation:

$$O = \frac{A - (K + (K - 1)(D - 1)) + P_1 + P_2}{S} + 1 \qquad (C.1)$$

where A, K, D, P_1, P_2, and S are the activation size, kernel size, dilation size, padding size on one side, padding size on the other side, and stride, respectively. Each variable is a positive integer. Dividing by S does not produce a remainder. If the convolution produces a remainder, then the variable(s) has a failed size. In addition, the kernel size K must be an odd number because the center of the kernel is needed.

C.1.1.2 Higher rank convolution

All multiplied values in the kernel window must be summed. Let us assume that the element of the kernel is in a 2D window, with one weight in one position of the window. A 2D convolution with a 3×3 kernel can be mapped onto a 2D activation called an input feature map. An element of the window performs an MAD operation. The window must move in horizontal-first or vertical-first order with the stride. The output, called the output feature map size O_D for D-dimension, can be represented as follows.

$$O_D = \prod_{d=1}^{D} O_d \qquad (C.2)$$

C.1.1.3 Linear transposed convolution

A transposed convolution is a type of reverse convolution, and the output of the convolution is equivalent to the input of the transposed convolution. The output size O in one-dimension is calculated through the following equation.

$$O = (A - 1) \times S + (K + (K - 1)(D - 1)) - (P_1 + P_2) \qquad (C.3)$$

The transposed convolution must have an even kernel size K. A typical kernel size K is even. Similar to a traditional convolution, we obtain the entire shape (size) of the output, O_D.

C.1.1.4 Channels

In the case of an image frame, there are three frames, red, green, and blue. This group having the same tensor shape is called a channel. The convolution inputs an activation tensor, called an input feature map, having a channel size $C^{(l-1)}$. One convolution generating one element is applied for the channel size $C^{(l-1)}$, and the results are summed. An output feature map having a channel size $C^{(l)}$ is output.

C.1.1.5 Complexity

Calculation for one convolution takes $\prod_{d=1}^{D} K_d$ elements, and therefore it takes $\prod_{d=1}^{D} K_d$ MACs. Let us represent the channel size as C. Then, the computational complexity on the l-layer of the D-dimensional convolution is as follows.

$$Cmp^{(l)} = C^{(l-1)} \times C^{(l)} \times \prod_{d=1}^{D} O_d^{(l)} \times K_d^{(l)} \tag{C.4}$$

The memory access complexity of cache memory depends on a dilate factor D, in which an increase in D decreases the chance to load from the cache line, namely, it reduces the amount of accessible data words by $O(1/D)$. Thus, it increases the number of memory accesses by D times (increasing the cache miss rate by D times) for activation. In addition, the complexity also depends on the stride factor S, in which an increase in S also increases the number of memory accesses S times for activation. Both the dilate factor and stride factor affect only the first-order dimension mapped contiguously onto a memory space. The load complexity can then be represented as follows:

$$Ld^{(l)} = C^{(l-1)} \times (A_1^{(l)} \times D_1^{(l)} \times S_1^{(l)} + \prod_{d=2}^{D} A_d^{(l)}) + C^{(l)} \times \prod_{d=1}^{D} K_d^{(l)} \tag{C.5}$$

The output feature map should be stored back to memory. The storage complexity can be represented as follows:

$$St^{(l)} = C^{(l)} \times \prod_{d=1}^{D} O_d^{(l)} \tag{C.6}$$

The total complexity can be obtained by a sum of three equations. In addition, the output feature map size $O_d, d \in D$ can be represented in order.

$$O_d^{(l)} \approx \frac{A_d^{(l)} - K_d^{(l)} D_d^{(l)}}{S_d^{(l)}} \tag{C.7}$$

Thus, the computational complexity can be reduced by large factors of the dilation and stride. However, the load complexity can be increased by these factors as well. In addition, the channel size on the layer, $C^{(l)}$, increases all complexities.

C.1.2 Back propagation for convolution

C.1.2.1 Back propagation for linear convolution

Our objective for the back propagation is to obtain a derivative for updating the kernel, and to obtain a gradient to back propagate. First, we consider the calculation for the derivative. We can observe a pre-activation of the forward propagation in a linear convolution as follows.

$$u_j = \sum_{n=0}^{K-1} k_n map_{D \times n + S \times j + P_1} \tag{C.8}$$

where map is an input map, which includes the input feature map A and padding P_1 and P_2. The subscript n is within the range of $0 \leq n < K$. Let us set the input feature map, a_i, as W, where the subscript is within the range of $0 \leq i < A$. In addition, the output feature map o_j ranges within $0 \leq j < O_D$. Moreover, the subscript of a_i can be rewritten as follows.

$$n = (i - j \times S)/D \tag{C.9}$$

Then, n is an integer index, and thus should have the following rule.

$$(i - j \times S) \mod D = 0 \tag{C.10}$$

The input map map consists of an input feature map A and padding(s) P as follows:

$$map_m = \begin{cases} p \ (m < P_1) \\ a_{m-P_1} \ (P_1 \leq m < A + P_1), \ ((m + P_1) \mod D = 0) \\ p \ (P_1 \leq m < A + P_1), \ ((i + P_1) \mod D \neq 0) \\ p \ (A + P_1 \leq m < A + P_1 + P_2) \end{cases} \tag{C.11}$$

where p is the padding value of a constant. The subscript m has a relationship with subscript i, indicating an element of the input feature map as follows.

$$i = m - P_1 \tag{C.12}$$

A derivative can be represented by a chain-rule in the following manner:

$$\frac{\partial L}{\partial k_n^{(l)}} = \sum \frac{\partial L}{\partial u_j^{(l)}} \frac{\partial u_j^{(l)}}{\partial k_n^{(l)}} \tag{C.13}$$

$$= \sum \frac{\partial L}{\partial u_j^{(l)}} a_{(j \times S + D \times n)}^{(l)}$$

Similar to Eq. (A.25), we obtain $\delta^{(l)}$ for the l-th layer of the convolution.

$$\delta_j^{(l)} = \sum \frac{\partial L}{\partial u_j^{(l)}} \tag{C.14}$$

$$= \sum \frac{\partial L}{\partial u_h^{(l+1)}} \frac{\partial u_h^{(l+1)}}{\partial u_j^{(l)}}$$

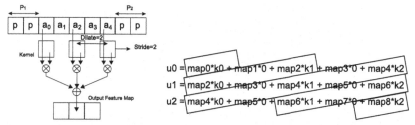

(a) Example of Convolution: Stride = 2 and Delite = 2.   (b) Gradient Calculation Example.

FIGURE C.2 Derivative calculation for linear convolution.

$$= \sum \frac{\partial L}{\partial u_h^{(l+1)}} \frac{\partial u_h^{(l+1)}}{\partial z_j^{(l)}} \frac{\partial z_j^{(l)}}{\partial u_j^{(l)}}$$

$$= f_j'(u_j^{(l)}) \sum_h \delta_h^{(l+1)} w_{h,j}^{(l+1)}$$

The kernel size K is obtained by a conversion of Eq. (C.1).

$$K = \frac{(A + P_1 + P_2) - (O_D - 1)S - 1}{D} + 1 \qquad (C.15)$$

Next, let us consider the gradient calculation for the input feature map to back propagate. To consider the details of the calculation, let us use the example shown in Fig. C.2(a). The stride and dilation factors are both 2. The pre-activation elements are represented as follows.

$$u_0 = map_0 k_0 + map_2 k_1 + map_4 k_2 \qquad (C.16)$$
$$u_1 = map_2 k_0 + map_4 k_1 + map_6 k_2$$
$$u_2 = map_4 k_0 + map_6 k_1 + map_8 k_2$$

Every gradient can be represented by a chain-rule as follows.

$$\frac{\partial L}{\partial map_m} = \sum_p^{O_D - 1} \frac{\partial L}{\partial u_p} \frac{\partial u_p}{\partial map_m} \qquad (C.17)$$

The derivative $\partial L / \partial u_p$ is δ. We need to carefully observe the pattern in the gradient calculation for formalization.

Fig. C.2(b) shows a sum of non-zero positions to obtain a derivative of $\partial u_p / \partial a_i$. This implies a possibility of using a convolutional operation to calculate the gradient. Let us consider the use of a convolutional operation for the gradient calculation. Fig. C.2(b) shows that stride factor S and dilation factor D for a forward convolution are exchanged in the gradient calculation.

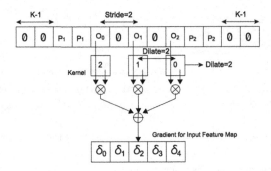

FIGURE C.3   Gradient calculation for linear convolution.

Note that we must calculate five gradients of the input feature map for the example, and there is no need for padding. In addition, Fig. C.2(b) shows the need for padding including the kernel size, $P' = K - 1$, as indicated by $m = 0$ and $m = 8$, in addition to padding P_1 and P_2. Moreover, this also implies that the filter for the gradient calculation is the same as the kernel in the forward convolution.

Let us check the subscript in the derivative. For example, a gradient of $m = 4$ has the following derivative:

$$\frac{\partial L}{\partial map_4} = \delta_0 k_2 + \delta_1 k_1 + \delta_2 k_0 \tag{C.18}$$

Thus, the filter for the gradient calculation has a flipped order. Therefore, we obtain the gradient calculation with a convolutional operation, as shown in Fig. C.3.

We can summarize the rule of the derivative and the gradient calculations for a linear convolution as follows.

1. For a derivative, an update of the amount for the kernel is obtained through Eq. (C.14), which consists of a multiplication of the input feature map element and δ.
2. For the gradient, its calculation can be achieved through a convolutional operation.
3. For a convolutional operation on a gradient calculation, an inverse order of kernel is applied, and the stride and dilation are exchanged.

C.1.2.2   Back propagation for high-rank convolution

In the case of a convolution having a higher rank, such as with two dimensions or more, the same rule is applied. For every dimension, the kernel order is the inverse for a gradient calculation.

For a convolution with channels, the sum of the derivatives of every channel based on the chain-rule should be applied because the output feature map element has the sum of the pre-activations.

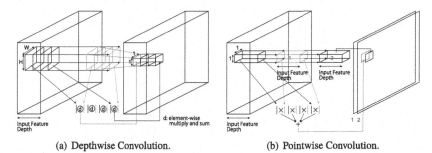

(a) Depthwise Convolution.   (b) Pointwise Convolution.

FIGURE C.4 Lightweight convolutions.

C.1.3   Convolution variants

C.1.3.1   Lightweight convolution

As described in Section 4.6, the convolution consists of a significant number of MAD operations. Therefore, studies have been conducted to reduce the workload by changing the kernel size and convolution unit, such as using a depth-wise convolution and pointwise convolution, as shown in Fig. C.4.

- Depth-wise convolution
  Fig. C.4(a) shows a depth-wise two-dimension convolution. The input feature map is on the far left side and has a depth equal to the number of channels. Whereas a single kernel in an ordinary 2D convolution applies numerous convolutions equivalent to the depth of the input feature map, and takes the sum of the results, a depth-wise convolution does not apply such depth-wise additions. Thus, a depth-wise convolution requires a number of kernels equal to the depth of the input feature map, and outputs the same number of channels as the output feature map. This approach has a constraint of $C^{(l-1)} = C^{(l)}$ on the original convolution before applying this approach, and thus $C^{(l-1)} = 1$.

$$Cmp^{(l)} = C^{(l)} \times \prod_{d=1}^{D} O_d^{(l)} \times K_d^{(l)} \tag{C.19}$$

$$Ld^{(l)} = A_1^{(l)} \times D_1^{(l)} \times S_1^{(l)} + \prod_{d=2}^{D} A_d^{(l)} + C^{(l)} \times \prod_{d=1}^{D} K_d^{(l)} \tag{C.20}$$

$$St^{(l)} = C^{(l)} \times \prod_{d=1}^{D} O_d^{(l)} \tag{C.21}$$

- Pointwise convolution
  Fig. C.4(b) shows a pointwise two-dimensional convolution. As the name indicates, it has 1×1 kernels. Thus, it has a depth direction dot product between the input feature map and the kernel with depth. Similar to a traditional

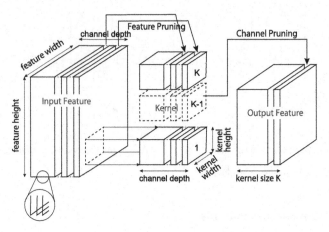

FIGURE C.5 Summary of pruning the convolution.

convolution, it can have multiple channels.

$$Cmp^{(l)} = C^{(l-1)} \times C^{(l)} \times \prod_{d=1}^{D} O_d^{(l)} \tag{C.22}$$

$$Ld^{(l)} = C^{(l-1)} \times (A_1^{(l)} \times D_1^{(l)} \times S_1^{(l)} + \prod_{d=2}^{D} A_d^{(l)}) + C^{(l-1)} \times C^{(l)} \tag{C.23}$$

$$St^{(l)} = C^{(l)} \times \prod_{d=1}^{D} O_d^{(l)} \tag{C.24}$$

$$O_d^{(l)} \approx \frac{A_d^{(l)} - D_d^{(l)}}{S_d^{(l)}} \tag{C.25}$$

C.1.3.2   Pruning the convolution

Fig. C.5 shows a summary of pruning the convolution. There are two types of pruning: feature pruning and channel pruning.

- Feature pruning
  Feature pruning is the pruning of channel(s) in the input feature map. The pruning makes unnecessary depth(s) of kernel in every channels corresponding position to the pruned input feature map's channel(s) which operates the convolution with the kernel. The channel size for the input feature map can be rewritten based on the pruning rate as follows.

$$\hat{C}^{(l-1)} \approx \alpha_f C^{(l-1)} \tag{C.26}$$

- Channel pruning

  Channel pruning is applied to prune the kernel(s). The pruning makes unnecessary output feature map's channel(s) in every channels corresponding position to the pruned kernel(s) which should be operated with the kernel(s). Thus, the channel pruning introduces feature pruning on the next layer. The channel size for the output feature map can be rewritten based on the pruning rate as follows.

$$\hat{C}^{(l)} \approx \alpha_c C^{(l)} \tag{C.27}$$

C.1.4 Deep convolutional generative adversarial networks

A CNN is popularly used as a supervised model by applying a generative adversarial network (GAN), and can function as an unsupervised model. This model is called a deep convolutional generative adversarial network (DCGAN) [295].

In general, a neural network model outputs an inference from the input information, and a DCGAN consists of a generator model and a discriminator model. A generator model generates the demanded information, and a discriminator model generates a probability that the generated information will be near the information used for training, as a detection of authenticity. The output of a generator can be used for the creation of a training dataset.

A DCGAN has tips to improve its functionalities, as follows: [295]

1. replacing the pooling layer with a convolution layer at the discriminator model;
2. replacing the convolutional layer with a factorial convolutional layer;
3. applying a batch normalization to a generative model and a discriminative model;
4. removing the fully connected layers;
5. applying an ReLU activation function to the hidden layers in a generative model, and applying tanh to the output layer; and
6. applying a leaky ReLU activation function to all layers in the discriminative model (see Appendix A).

By using Adam instead of the momentum for an optimization of the updating parameters, the generative model can be stabilized. Instability is a well-known weak point of a GAN.

C.2 RNN variants

C.2.1 RNN architecture

A series of data words also have certain features, such as voice, text, or stock prices. These sequential data can be treated by an RNN, which memorizes some of the past features.

An RNN does not have a constraint of the input data word length but has a constraint on the memory duration. An RNN has a recurrent connection(s) that

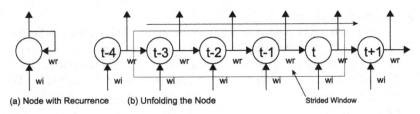

FIGURE C.6 Recurrent node with unfolding.

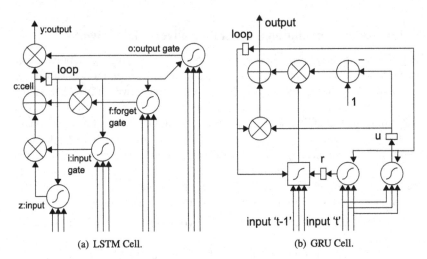

(a) LSTM Cell.　　　　　　　(b) GRU Cell.

FIGURE C.7 LSTM and GRU cells.

inputs the activation(s). A back propagation in a recurrent structure has yet to be solved because we use a chain rule to make the derivatives. Instead, it takes an unfolding which unfolds timeline behavior of unit to space, as shown in Fig. C.6. This method is called back-propagation through time (BPTT).

Multiple multiplications by weight having an absolute value of less than 1 makes a vanishing.

C.2.2　LSTM and GRU cells

C.2.2.1　Long-short term memory

Long-short term memory (LSTM) approaches to the vanishing problem to keep feature longer time. Fig. C.7(a) shows the unit of the neuron, called a cell, which consists of several sigmoidal functions. An LSTM cell has three types of gate: input, forgetting, and output. A small square box represents a delay. A memory loop-back is fed into the input and the input gate sigmoidal, σ.

$$\bar{z}^t = W_z x^t + R_z y^{t-1} + b_z \tag{C.28}$$

$$z^t = g(\bar{z}^t)$$
$$\bar{i}^t = W_i x^t + R_i y^{t-1} + b_i$$
$$i^t = \sigma(\bar{i}^t)$$
$$\bar{f}^t = W_f x^t + R_f y^{t-1} + b_f$$
$$f^t = \sigma(\bar{i}^t)$$
$$c^t = z^t \odot i^t + c^{t-1} \odot f^t$$
$$\bar{o}^t = W_o x^t + R_o y^{t-1} + p_o \odot c^t + b_o$$
$$o^t = \sigma(\bar{o}^t)$$
$$y^t = h(c^t) \odot o^t$$

For the back propagation, every δ in the LSTM is as follows.

$$\delta y^t = \Delta^t + R_z^\top \delta z^{t+1} + R_i^\top \delta i^{t+1} + R_f^\top \delta f^{t+1} + R_o^\top \delta o^{t+1} \qquad \text{(C.29)}$$
$$\delta \bar{o}^t = \delta y^t \odot h(c^t) \odot \sigma'(o^t)$$
$$\delta c^t = \delta y^t \odot o^t \odot h'(c^t) + p_o \odot \delta \bar{o}^t + p_i \odot \delta \bar{i}^{t+1} + p_f \odot \delta \bar{f}^{t+1} +$$
$$\qquad \delta c^{t+1} \odot f^{t+1}$$
$$\delta \bar{f}^t = \delta c^t \odot c^{t-1} \odot \sigma'(f^t)$$
$$\delta \bar{i}^t = \delta c^t \odot z^t \odot \sigma'(\bar{i}^t)$$
$$\delta \bar{z}^t = \delta c^t \odot i^t \odot g'(z^t)$$

where Δ^t is the vector of deltas passed down from the layer above. The gradients are as follows.

$$\delta W_* = \sum_{t=o}^{T} \langle \delta *^t, x^t \rangle \qquad \text{(C.30)}$$

$$\delta R_* = \sum_{t=0}^{T-1} \langle \delta *^{t+1}, y^t \rangle$$

$$\delta b_* = \sum_{t=0}^{T} \delta *^t$$

$$\delta p_i = \sum_{t=0}^{T-1} c^t \odot \delta \bar{i}^{t+1}$$

$$\delta p_f = \sum_{t=0}^{T-1} c^t \odot \delta \bar{f}^{t+1}$$

$$\delta p_o = \sum_{t=0}^{T} c^t \odot \delta \bar{o}^t$$

where $*$ can be any of $\{\bar{z}, \bar{i}, \bar{f}, \text{ or } \bar{o}\}$, and $\langle *_1, *_2 \rangle$ denotes the outer product of two vectors.

C.2.2.2 Gated recurrent unit

A simplified RNN cell can be represented by a relatively smaller number of gates, as shown in Fig. C.7(b). Note that there are two time-domains of the output loop. The u and r gates have the same form as Eq. (C.28) but also a non-delayed feedback loop ($h^{(t)}$). The u gate is used for selecting either the prior output or the prior input, similar to a multiplexing using u.

C.2.3 Highway networks

A highway network [337] is a challenge in terms of easily developing a deeper network model, and a network model easily obtains a training effect. Each layer can be written as an affine transformation by vector $\mathbf{x}$ and weight $\mathbf{W_H}$ as follows:

$$\mathbf{y} = \begin{cases} \mathbf{x} & \text{if } \mathbf{T}(\mathbf{x}, \mathbf{W_T}) = 0 \\ \mathbf{H}(\mathbf{x}, \mathbf{W_H}) & \text{if } \mathbf{T}(\mathbf{x}, \mathbf{W_T}) = 1 \end{cases} \tag{C.31}$$

Here, $\mathbf{T}(\mathbf{x}, \mathbf{W_T}) = sigmoid(\mathbf{W_T}^\top \mathbf{x} + \mathbf{b_T})$ is the affine transformation. By defining the transformation as a zero or unit vector, the layer output can be defined. The gradient can then be as follows:

$$\frac{d\mathbf{y}}{d\mathbf{x}} = \begin{cases} \mathbf{I} & \text{if } \mathbf{T}(\mathbf{x}, \mathbf{W_T}) = 0 \\ \mathbf{H}'(\mathbf{x}, \mathbf{W_H}) & \text{if } \mathbf{T}(\mathbf{x}, \mathbf{W_T}) = 1 \end{cases} \tag{C.32}$$

where $\mathbf{I}$ is the unit vector.

C.3 Autoencoder variants

C.3.1 Stacked denoising autoencoders

A denoising AE is a network model that makes a highly accurate output possible even if the input data x are deficient [359]. Producing input data x from deficient input data $\tilde{x}$, the model obtains the reconstructed z from the input data $\tilde{x}$ by inputting x into the encoder of the AE. Using a loss function constructed from the input data x and z, the model obtains the parameter set that is close to the input data x from the deficient input data $\tilde{x}$ by training to small reconstruction error.

A stacked denoising AE is a network model proposed for making possible the use of training data including deficient data $\tilde{x}$ [359]. At the l-layer, the encoder is obtained using a denoising AE, which is used for training of the $l + 1$-layer by stacking the layers obtained at the $l - 1$-layer construction. For each denoising training, input data $\tilde{x}$ are used only for the first time.

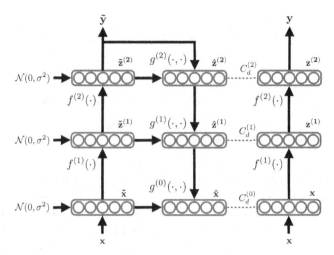

FIGURE C.8 Ladder network model [300].

The parameter from each encoder can be used for a layer generating data without a deficiency. A denoising AE coder and a network model obtained by repeatedly stacking the layers can be used for generating labeled training data in some network models such as an SVM and logistic regression.

C.3.2 Ladder networks

A ladder network model was proposed as an unsupervised model [358], and was extended to a model that can efficiently learn with a relatively large amount of unlabeled training data and fewer labeled training data [300]. See Fig. C.8.

It prepares an AE, which composes a neural network model (defined as $Encoder_{clear}$), to update the parameters. The encoder shares the parameters and $Encoder_{clear}$ and updates the parameters with interference between the AE and $Encoder_{clear}$. The AE topology is composed of L layers Upper layers having a high context are derived from a detailed representation at the bottom layers through the use of a combinatorial function with a reconstructed value $\hat{z}^{(L-l)}$ at the $L - l$-layer on the decoder combining the input $\tilde{z}^{(l)}$ at the l-layer on the encoder and the input $u^{(l+1)}$ at the $L - l$-layer. The encoder path that inputs $\tilde{z}^{(l)}$ into a combinatorial function on the decoder is called a lateral connection. When outputting $\tilde{y}$ on an encoder with noise, from input $\tilde{x}$ to the AE, cross entropy CE is obtained.

Moreover, we obtain the cost at the l-layer from the input $z^{(l)}$ to the activation function of $Encoder_{clear}$ and the reconstruction $\hat{z}^{(L-l)}$ on the decoder of the AE. Learning is achieved with a cost function, which is the sum of CE and RC. Here, $\tilde{z}^{(l)}$ and $\hat{z}^{(L-l)}$ add Gaussian noise and normalization. Large and small ratios of labeled training data in the dataset have a value of $u^{(l+1)}$ and $\tilde{z}^{(l)}$, respectively [291].

Using this combinatorial function, a significant amount of Gaussian noise occurs when there are numerous labeled training samples and the cost function is affected by CE; in addition, a large number of lateral connections occur when there are few labeled training samples and the cost function is affected by RC. Therefore, a ladder network has strong robustness even if the number of labeled training samples is changed, namely, if the environment has changed.

C.3.3 Variational autoencoders

C.3.3.1 Concept of variational autoencoders

VAE is one model of generative versus discriminative modelings for the problem similar to GAN model does. A generative model generates information having learned feature(s). A discriminative model maps the information to the label(s), which means it discriminates between generated information and information that occurs in the real world. A VAE is a variant of an AE, a generative model is a decoder, and a discriminative model is an encoder, but has latent variable(s)[1] between them.

An encoder (recognition) model is a function of the input variables, which uses one set of parameters to model the relation between the input and latent variables [225]. By contrast, a decoder model has an output function equivalent to the input of the encoder, which uses a set of parameters to model the relation between the latent-variables and the output. In [225], the authors describe the generative modeling in a VAE as an implicit form of regularization; by forcing the representation to be meaningful for data generation, we bias the inverse of the process, which maps from the input to the representation, and into a certain mold.

C.3.3.2 Modeling of variational autoencoders

Let us assume that the input vector D having N-dimensions is independently and identically distributed. Then, the probability of input element x given parameters θ is factorized as a product of the individual element probabilities [225]. The probabilities can be represented by a log-probability assigned to the input as follows.

$$\log p_\theta(D) = \sum_{x \in D} \log p_\theta(x), \tag{C.33}$$

where the log-probability $\log p_\theta(x)$ is translated as follows: [225].

$$\log p_\theta(x) = E_{q_\phi(z|x)}[\log p_\theta(x)] \tag{C.34}$$
$$= E_{q_\phi(z|x)}[\log \frac{p_\theta(x, z)}{p_\theta(z|x)}]$$

---

[1] Latent variables cannot be observed themselves as observable variables but are variables inferred from other observable variable(s).

$$= E_{q_\phi(z|x)}[\log \frac{p_\theta(x,z)}{q_\phi(z|x)}] + E_{q_\phi(z|x)}[\log \frac{q_\phi(z|x)}{p_\theta(z|x)}]$$

where z is a latent variable. The second term is the Kullback-Leibler (KL) divergence between $q_\phi(z|x)$ and $p_\theta(z|x)$, which is non-negative [225]. The smaller gap in terms of the KL divergence for distribution $p_\theta(z|x)$ is approximated by the better $q_\phi(z|x)$. The first term is called an evidence lower bound (ELBO), which determines the boundary of the value because the KL divergence has a non-negative value. The encoder q and decoder p can be represented as a parametric inference model $q_\phi(z|x)$ having variational parameters ϕ as a directed graph, and is thus as follows [225].

$$q_\phi(z|x) \approx p_\theta(z|x) \tag{C.35}$$

The prior distribution $p_\theta(z)$ gives a mapping between them.

C.4 Residual networks

C.4.1 Concept of residual networks

Training on a deeper neural network model is difficult because it is easier to saturate the accuracy on a such a model, which is unrelated to an overfitting. In [190], this is called a degradation problem.

A residual network (ResNet) is a network model that uses a residual function referencing the input and output vectors, which makes it easy to develop a deeper network model [190]. A deeper network model easily incurs a gradient vanishing, and a normalization layer is generally used in a CNN. Rather than using shallow networks to develop a deeper network model, ResNet solves the gradient vanishing problem by applying a residual of the preceding layer output. It assumes that a layer $H(x)$ has a degradation of $F(x) := H(x) - x$ as residual x. By adding the residual, x, as $H(x) := F(x) + x$, the layer can be compensated. The main goal of such a skipped connection is to enable the information to flow through many layers without attenuation [379].

C.4.2 Effect of residual network

The authors in [280] concluded that it is difficult to make a deeper network. There are three singularities that incur such difficulty, namely, linear dependence singularities, elimination singularities, and overlap singularities.

Linear dependence singularities are made only in linear networks. Elimination and overlap singularities are created in non-linear networks. These singularities are all related to the non-identifiability of the model. The elimination and overlap singularities cause a degeneration or higher-order saddles.

Elimination singularities arise when a hidden unit is effectively killed when its incoming (or outgoing) weights become zero. This makes the outgoing (or incoming) connections of the unit non-identifiable. Overlap singularities are caused by the permutation symmetry of the hidden units at a given layer, and arise when two units become identical when their incoming weights become identical. Skip connections between adjacent layers break the elimination singularities by ensuring that the units are active for at least some inputs, even when their adjustable incoming or outgoing connections become zero. They remove the overlapping singularities by breaking the permutation symmetry of the hidden units at a given layer. Thus, even when the adjustable incoming weights of two units become identical, the units do not collapse into each other because their distinct skip connections still disambiguate them. They also eliminate the linear dependence singularities by adding linearly independent inputs to the units.

To understand the optimization landscape of ResNet, the authors in [185] proved that linear residual networks have no critical points other than the global minimum. Furthermore, the authors of [117] demonstrated that as the depth increases, the gradients of plain networks resemble white noise and become less correlated. This phenomenon, which is referred to as a shattered gradient problem, makes training more difficult. It is thus demonstrated that residual networks reduce the shattering compared to plain networks, leading to numerical stability and easier optimization. Another effect is the norm preservation of the error gradient because it propagates in the backward path [379]. As the network becomes deeper, its building blocks become more norm-preserving.

C.5 Graph neural networks

A graph represents the relationship among nodes with edges connecting them. The representation of the relationship can be applied to the analytics, which can be represented as a graph. A neural network for a graph problem is also now considered.

C.5.1 Concept of graph neural networks

Consider [374], which discusses the basic property of neural networks for a graph, the so-called graph neural networks (GNNs). Graph G consists of a set of nodes $v \in V$ and set of edges $e \in E$, $G = (V, E)$. Edge e can be represented by a combination of two nodes $v = \{e_i, e_j\}$, and the position in between the braces $\{\}$ can make an order, and thus a directed edge $\vec{v}$ is possible.

Graph G has a node feature X_v for $v \in V$. Every node v can have a representation feature h_v whose context is defined by a neural network model architect. There are two major tasks for a GNN, a similarity test between graphs and a graph-classification.

A GNN infers that the prediction or classification based on the representation feature vector h_v, which is on every node v, is propagated on the graph G.

The major unique layers in a GNN are the aggregation A, combine C, and readout R. Aggregation aims at a sampling of feature vectors $u \in \chi(v)$ on node

v, where χ provides connected node(s) representation feature vectors u, and a feature extraction is applied with parameter(s) W trained before the inference. This is similar to that applied to a layer on a feedforward neural network, convolutional neural network, or other network type.

Some types of major unique layers have been studied; for example, let us look at a template of the layers. Aggregation A is as follows.

$$a_v^{(k)} = A^{(k)}(\{h_u^{(k-1)} : u \in \chi(v)\}) \tag{C.36}$$

Here, we discuss a deep neural network where the layers are stacked, and the superscript k indicates the k-th layer. One aggregation example is represented as follows:

$$a_v^{(k)} = MAX(\{ReLU(W \cdot h_u^{(k-1)}), \forall u \in \chi(v)\}) \tag{C.37}$$

The aggregation, $A = MAX$, is a rank function, which indicates unique features after obtaining the post-activation(s) through an ReLU function. In this case, aggregation MAX identifies the unique activation(s).

Another aggregation $MEAN$ thins every node group by a number of features obtained by MAX. After the $MEAN$ aggregation, the number of extracted nodes in every group is obtained by the number of nodes before the aggregation divided by the number of features through MAX. Aggregation SUM does the following:

One combine C can also be represented by its template as follows.

$$h_v^{(k)} = C^{(k)}(h_u^{(k-1)}, a_v^{(k)}) \tag{C.38}$$

Thus, the representation feature vector is equivalent to a feature map in a convolutional neural network. One combination example is represented as follows.

$$C^{(k)}(*) = W \cdot \left[h_u^{(k-1)}, a_v^{(k)} \right] \tag{C.39}$$

where bracket [] is a concatenation. The parameters are equivalent to a kernel in a convolutional neural network.

A readout aggregation aims to fetch the needed representation feature $h^{(K)} = h_G$ at the last layer K for graph G. The template of R is represented as follows.

$$h_G = R(\{h_v^{(K)} | v \in G\}) \tag{C.40}$$

By stacking A, C, and finally R, we obtain a GNN model which infers the input of node feature X_v.

Appendix D

National research and trends and investment

This appendix introduces projects on AI being conducted in China, the USA, Europe, and Japan. Details were described in the document [23], and therefore, such projects are briefly introduced here.

D.1 China

China releases a five-year plan every five years and is currently on its 13th five-year plan (2016 to 2020). With this plan, China aims to become a top science and technology country.

China has already started the development of in-house computer systems for high-performance computing, and is aggressively investing in companies developing semiconductor technologies. They started with investments in DRAM, and the Tsinghua Unigroup has aggressively invested sums approaching those of Taiwanese and American companies [52][145][144][188]. They might catch up with these countries in terms of semiconductor technology, mainly in the design fabrication of memory chips (DRAM and NAND flash memories), after which they will develop, fabricate, and ship their own technologies for various architectures and fabrications.[1]

Currently, advanced AI researches are mainly being conducted by Chinese universities, which will be able to ship their first machine learning computer products globally owing to their aggressive investments.

D.1.1 Next generation AI development plan

The government released its next-generation AI development plan [84]. China has targeted an advancement in fundamental AI theory development, and aims to enhance a portion of its technology and application by 2025. Enhancing all theories, technologies, and applied technology domains of AI, China has a final target to be a primary AI innovation center globally by year 2030.

This aim consists of six missions: The development of an open and cooperative AI science technology innovation system; the creation of a high-end and highly efficient smart economy; the realization of a safe and convenient smart social society; an enhanced unification between AI industry and military; the

---

[1] China is also investing in Africa, the last frontier for the semiconductor product market.

development of a ubiquitous, safe, and highly efficient smart infrastructure; and the development of a future vision for the major next-generation AI science and technology industries. The country has also developed a short-term plan, i.e., 3-year action plan for next-generation AI industry investment. This includes neural network chip targeting 128 TOPS (with a 16-bit floating-point) and 1 TFLOPS/W for cloud chips by 2020. Cambricon, a start-up company collaborating with CAS, as described in Chapter 7, has received government investments.

D.2 USA

"The America COMPETES Act" was enacted in August 2007. The law aims at aggressively investing in research on innovation and human resource education. This law has led to investments in AI technologies. In March 2012, the "Big Data Research and Development Initiative" was released, which invested 200 million dollars into big data research.

D.2.1 SyNAPSE program

The Defense Advanced Research Projects Agency (DARPA) started a program called Systems of Neuromorphic Adaptive Plastic Scalable Electronics (SyNAPSE) [42], for achieving a scalable device at the biology-level for use in an electronic neuromorphic machine. This program has focused on new types of computational models based on computations having a function at the mammalian brain level, for example, they created a challenge to develop intelligent robotics. This program started in 2008, with a budget of 102.6 million dollars as of January 2013. The project had a plan to end by 2016, and IBM TrueNorth was the end result [261].

D.2.2 UPSIDE program

Instead of electronics engineering based on a complementary metal-oxide-semiconductor (CMOS), DARPA started a program called Unconventional Processing of Signals for Intelligent Data Exploitation (UPSIDE), which is a challenge to develop signal processing using a device array based on physics [104]. The program challenges the development of a model of a self-organizing array, which does not need the programming required by a conventional digital processor. As an interdisciplinary approach, the program consists of three stages: Task-1 is a program used to develop a computational model, and provides demonstrations and benchmarks with image processing applications. Task-2 is program used to demonstrate the inference module implemented with a mixed signal CMOS. Task-3 is program used to demonstrate a non-CMOS emerging nanoscale device. The Cortical processor project used in the UPSIDE program implements a mixed signal CMOS device based on physics, and challenges participants to achieve high-performance, low-power computation. The challenge in 2016 was to show a high inference performance for motion and anomaly detection without a large amount of training data.

D.2.3 MICrONS program

The Intelligence Advanced Research Projects Activity (IARPA) supports a research program called Machine Intelligence from Cortical Networks (MICrONS) through an interdisciplinary approach for understanding the cognition and computations in a mammalian brain [22]. The program applies reverse engineering of a brain algorithm to revolve machine learning. This is a 5-year program and consists of three phases: The first phase is to generalize and create a taxonomy. The second phase is to elucidate a universal cognition function. The third phase is to evaluate each project.

D.3 EU

The FP7 program has invested 50 million Euros into natural language processing such as language analytics tools and machine translation projects.

The Human Brain Project (HBP) is based on ICT research to promote and provide an infrastructure for neuroscience, computational science, and drug discovery [15]. During the ramp-up phase, six ICT platforms were developed and provided to users. Specific Grant Agreement One (SGA1) which has succeeded from the ramp-up phase, was a phase of integrating these platforms between April 2016 and April 2018. During this phase, a neuroscience workshop was supported for robotics and computational science using the brain, which facilitated research on the organization and theories of the brain to establish a brain model and simulation. The SpiNNaker project developed by Manchester University was applied to this project [220].

D.4 Japan

D.4.1 Ministry of Internal Affairs and Communications

The National Institute of Information and Communications Technology (NICT) studies brain science and develops AI technology based on big data. In April 2016, the Center for Information and Neural Networks (CiNet) began research and development primarily in the data utilization field under the fourth mid- and long-term schedules. CiNet focuses on control of a visuomotor, and conducts research into pain, as well as the integration of multi-sensory aspects, higher-order cognition, and decision-making; they have also studied language for higher-order brain function areas, such as in the field of social neuroscience. The Advanced Telecommunications Research Institute International (ATR) develops technologies applied to robotics based on knowledge about the brain.

D.4.2 MEXT

The Ministry of Education, Culture, Sports, Science and Technology (MEXT) started the Advanced Integrated Intelligence Platform Project (AIP) integrated with AI, big data, IoT, and cyber-security in 2016. AIP was established in April

2016 by RIKEN. AIP conducts research and development on basic AI technology, facilitates improvements in science, contributes to the societal implementation of the application area, and conducts training for data scientists and cyber security personnel. Among the growing challenges of the post-K computer era, a neural mechanism to implement thinking and its application to AI has been elucidated, and a large-scale neural circuit realizing thinking has been created by composing a large-scale hierarchical model fused with big data, aiming at its challenging application to AI.

D.4.3 METI

In May 2015, the National Institute of Advanced Industrial Science and Technology (AIST) established an AI research center to maintain basic technologies such as next-generation neurocomputers, data-intelligence integrated AI, research and development into the next framework, and modules facilitating fundamental technological utilization. They focus on two themes:

1. Based on an understanding of engineering and the mechanisms in a mammalian brain that create its intelligence, a computer that achieves a flexible information processing similar to the human brain has been realized, and research into neurocomputing using a neurocircuit and neurons conducting information processing in the brain has been conducted.
2. Research has been conducted into complex decision and action making, as well as the reasoning process, through an integration with training technology using patterns from big data, understanding technology for the meaning of text and knowledge collected from human society, and applying inference technology using such text and knowledge.

AIST established the AI Bridging Cloud Infrastructure (ABCI) in 2017 [58], which will be used for autonomous driving, a state of understanding for machinery, and support of medical diagnosis, and aims to share training data and a deep learning model development infrastructure among users, focusing on a fast-acting base construction against company-led deep learning in the United States [181].

D.4.4 Cabinet office

The Impulsing Paradigm Change through Disruptive Technologies (ImPACT) program aims to establish a world standard in brain information decoding technology that visualizes various thinking and feedback technology to maintain a user-demanded statement of the brain, as well as the development of a large-scale brain information infrastructure. It has an aim to provide common resources by 2020.

Appendix E

Machine learning and social

The impact of machine learning on society with industries and next-generation industries is considered. Next, social business and a shared economy are introduced. The coexistence of humans and machines, and the involvement between society and individuals, are considered. Finally, the relationship between machines and the nation state is discussed.

E.1 Industry

E.1.1 Past industries

The number of workers in original industries such as agriculture, dairy, forestry, and fishing industries are continuously decreasing based on the workload [73]. A declining birthrate problem [72] and an aging problem [57] have expedited a decrease in this area. See Fig. E.1. To reduce the workload, we can utilize big data and machine learning. By managing and controlling the growth and environment, we can rapidly prepare a counterplan for the near future with a prediction placed on a timeline. In addition, we can periodically manage its state, we can automatically improve the environment. Such industries are heavily dependent on weather, weather prediction and the ability to under different weather conditions are necessary. Moreover, not only products but also machine learning can be applied to reduce the workload on workers to achieve better efficiency, safety, and serviceability for the environment.

A complex system such as a plant monitored IoT can support a predictive maintenance. It can also be applied to an infrastructure network such as electricity, gas, water, and communication, as well as transportation system traffic management. Singapore has already used machine learning for a traffic management for transportation systems [69]. In business, a system that gathers the correlation between the weather information and amount of sales in each shop was developed in previous decades [324]. In addition, a line of flow analysis in a shop is applied to improve the layout [217]. Using machine learning, such a traditional system must compete with new systems using machine learning, and therefore, this trend introduces lower prices for a wall of installation. Machine learning is also applied to logistics [170]. A report predicted that autonomous driving technology for transportation will consume more than 30% of the total machine learning market [23]. Futures and stock transactions, which require very fast trading, are also applying machine learning [235].

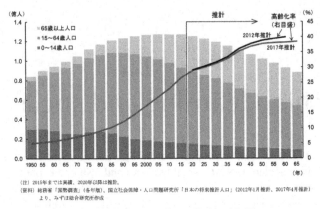

(a) **Population Forecast (Aging Problem) in Japan.**

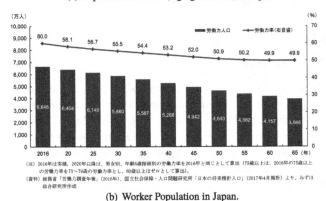

(b) **Worker Population in Japan.**

FIGURE E.1 Populations in Japan [200].

Regarding the machinery, electricity, and electronics industries, an evaluation of the yield, which is an index of production failure, is needed. To improve the production process for an improved yield, we can apply machine learning, including quantitative sampling, and correlation among factors, and thus a quantitative adjustment counterplan. Regarding news reports and information from the media, machine learning can evaluate the correlation between information and media consumption, and the media can make decisions in terms of priority for news releases. In addition, the likelihood of information can be evaluated using a machine learning based system. A new type of vending machine was introduced in Japan, which predicts the buyer's preferences and displays a recommendation; the inference and resulting information are collected to create big data for near future sales [227]. In addition, such big data itself can be a product. Web advertisements also use machine learning for predicting user preferences and for displaying recommended advertisements [127].

The cost of the processing and production used in each industry; optimizing the materials, products, and information; and transportation will decrease, thus introducing lower prices or promoting the room for greater high-added value. Therefore, a business strategy aiming at a highly added value must consider the gap between the added value and user demand, and thus matching them will be extremely important. Namely, machine learning can predict existing and well-known markets, and new markets reflected based on taste incur difficulty for machine learning. Time is required to learn the taste of users. In addition, the creation of a new market becomes more difficult.

E.1.2   Next industry

In the field of robotics, a robot can grasp an object randomly placed on a table [76], and technology is used to put an object into a cage, both requiring machine learning. Regarding Industry4.0, the production line has been dynamically changed by and adapted to customer needs, targeting a highly efficient production system from order to release, including stock management for materials and products [219]. To realize Industry4.0, factory automation robots have to autonomously work with each other and become adapted to changes in the production line. Therefore, machine learning for planning has been researched [216]. In addition, robotics used to assemble other robots has also been studied [176].

Management tasks are suitable for machine learning. In addition, machine learning can be applied to improve a factory environment, and to manage the state for workers and robots, such a system has been applied to fields such as education, medicine, and welfare. Moreover, anomaly detection based on machine learning can be applied to fraudulent accounting [116]. By applying machine learning to manage resources such as water, food, and materials, and to control transport and trading for financial purposes, we can consider applications of machine learning to construct a cycle between production and consumption, and to construct a recycling system, for suppressing the consumption of finite resources and their increasing prices based on an increasing the population.

Medical applications [230] for the detection of illness at an early stage [326], and a counterfactual estimate [209], are considered. Not only detection of cancer based on image recognition [157] and prediction, but also remote operation based on robotics, is already being used [70]. Operational data can be recoded and applied to general doctors to improve their techniques. By applying machine learning to the medical field, the role of doctors being reconsidered [106].

Machine learning is also applied to drug discovery [299]. When making new drugs, to find a better or the best combination of materials and predict their volume from extremely large numbers of combinational patterns, a traditional approach requires experience and intuition from engineering, and therefore requires more time and more costs for finding a better or the best version. Automation based on robotics is applied to find candidate compounds; however, virtual screening has been proposed, and machine learning has been applied to predict the inference among molecules. By suppressing the cost for discovery, which returns to the original price, it contributes to reducing the medical bills involved with a declining birthrate. A system based on autonomous experimentation and analysis rather than on software simulations has been studied and developed [381].

A plagiarism of reports and other documents is currently a serious problem [338][112][375]. A detection system for this issue has also been studied and developed [81]. The role of universities and colleges in this area being reconsidered. The boundary between research domains has created a new paradigm; however, such a partitioning between humanities and the sciences is illogical. If domains operate using the same algorithm, the algorithm can be applied to different domains to solve each problem. Interference between such domains should be overcome with an algorithm-driven approach. Machine learning can be applied to unify the problem in different domains.

E.1.3 Open-sourced software and hardware

If an object has a modular structure and can be designed as part of a system, then both the software and hardware can be standardized. Once the standardization is advanced, it achieves rapid growth through open sourcing, although the market share can be easily decreased by the slow decisions of traditional companies monopolizing their market. This is a trend of monopolization in the market, and a major decision regarding the price and specifications of the product for the market must be made. Thus, the trend can be viewed as an agitation for an expulsion of monopolizing companies.

Hardware production has a yield issue and variations in manufacturing, and the uniformity of a product cannot be guaranteed, which differs from the soft-copy nature of software. However, this means that the issue can be simply solved by reconciling the gap between modules and by starting from a simple domain having an explicit and sharable issue. For example, it is possible to start from a simple issue having a small gap, and creating a standard, followed by advancing into a domain requiring high production accuracy. We can choose both a software or hardware implementation for our solution based on a cost evaluation.

In the domain of machine learning, a specific company may monopolize datasets used for training. By contrast, a company can take advantage of open sourcing, and collaboration can be then aggressively applied; new trends can therefore be created using this conflict.

E.1.4 Social business and shared economy

There is a trend toward monetizing social problems through services, i.e., teaching how to fish rather than simply providing the fish. Companies having a business model based on luck or on products preferred by engineers when taking into account the fact that trends of services and products have become stagnant. In society, under the premise of consumption growth based on population growth, management ability is not a concern; however, a company may incur a serious problem during a phase of population decline and a slowdown of consumption.

One example is a sharing economy that makes sharable resources and services. A sharing economy is defined as an "intermediating service to lend idling assets held by individuals" [89]. Past services for sharing have been limited, such as shared riding in a taxi, renting a space, parking, and conference rooms. Recently, not only room or home rentals (living spaces), but also accommodation support services for them [59], as well as car sharing [64], parking sharing [61], and wear sharing [60], have become businesses.

From the perspective of a cost-effectiveness matching the requirement of each user, as shown in shared services, the types of such services have increased, and we currently have various choices. From a lent space to an object, the sharing economy has grown to include shared locations, transportation, resources, and workers (out-sourcing) [89]. However, a sharing economy system can work well only with a real-time database for registered users, not only recommendations but also matching among users through the introduction of machine learning as an optimization has become possible. Moreover, there is a viewpoint that a sharing economy is exploitive for both service providers and users [349].

E.2   Machine learning and us

Machine learning is a category similar to a cutting tool such as cutters, knifes, or scissors. There are various scissors optimized for various purposes, and similarly a machine learning model can be optimized for the specific purposes of the customer. Although such utilities have improved our lives, we should be cautious with their use.

E.2.1   Replaceable domain with machine learning

Some people worry about replacing workers with machine learning and/or robotics. They worry about a loss of employment opportunities. The domain for employee replacement has the following three properties:

1. It can be represented by mathematics (easy to model a neural network architecture)
2. A need for higher efficiency (reducing the deployment time and/or utilization of resources), and
3. Lowering the introduction wall (cost for introduction and for operations are lower than the cost of reduction by replacement)

Lawyers, medical doctors, traders, and so on are in a white collar domain having a higher replacement effectiveness. Fraudulent account detection is possible [116], and therefore domains mainly for procedural processing, such management, also have a chance of replacement. Simple management and low cost do not need replacement with machine learning, because automation can be applied for such processes. Providing an automation system combining notices, propositions, and planning with higher added value by machine learning can be one reason for using a machine learning system. Applying machine learning to the legal profession has also been considered, and a support system for legal documents [242] is already in use.

Various domains can be represented through mathematics with advancements in science revealing the issues and their complexities. Issues represented as mathematics can be solved through their calculations. Instead of calculations, we can use a neural network model as a solution to approximate computing. Robotics has also advanced from simple problems, allowing robots and workers to achieve a collaborative work environment, and thus, the replacement began from white collar to blue collar workers. For example, the assembly of smartphones requires workers; however, companies are now using factory automation robotics because salaries have increased [218].

As previously described, the introduction of machine learning for traditional markets is easy owing to advances in market research. Therefore, in domains independent from market constraints, and in new domains, machine learning itself has difficulty being a replacement. Machines do not get tired and work accurately on redundant processes with a defined sequence. They also do not have a personality, and do not become discontent. The first phase will be a support for people with large workloads.

E.2.2 Consolidation of industry

An employment contract is important after the beginning of a replacement with machines. For workers to be in a better position than robots, they require talent and ability. Paperwork based on information processing can reduce the processing time through automation. Office employees require the ability to notice and advise, and apply data analytics based on a plan generated through machine learning. Thus, an over speed for advanced replacement creates a higher requirement for employees, which might create friction between the employer and employees. Managers must have the ability to find areas requiring notices and advice and reflect such issues to management. Machine learning is a useful approach in this regard.

For a particular industry, the introduction of machine learning and big data analytics can result in a change in market share. Thus, there is possibility of industry consolidation to maintain such market share. The industry may be up in the air after consolidation. Thus, there is possibility that the methodology of the company and its employment may change. For example, organizing a team for a particular project and product development, the team members may decide to dismiss the team or continue to develop with them (for maintenance), and thus a "temporal" company can be organized for a particular purpose.

E.2.3   A simplified world

Current markets and transportation systems have a complex network. In particular, there are intermediaries between producers and consumers. Thus, there is company running a portal site as a marketplace for consumers by gathering producers. A higher-level portal can be used to gather more users, analyze trends in the marketplace, and provide a higher service fitting various individuals.

At that time, big data is generated by gathering personal trending information along with particular characteristics. A machine learning system is needed to analyze the data, and a short time-to-market and short response time are needed for users who require a better neural network model development; as a result, a better machine learning hardware is needed. Such a marketplace of a higher-level portal site is equivalent to a combination of curation (recommendation) and searching services.

For a unique item, a curation service cannot provide reliability assurance, and it becomes difficult to search for a user's preferred item from major and popular items, which incurs a problem of bias in the search and recommendation because the vendor will want to sell a profitable item to the user. This depends heavily on the information providers, and thus confidence among people has a key role. A mechanism providing reliability assurance is a system having the combination of a block chain and machine learning.

We recognize the complexity of transport between producers and consumers, and a P2P transport service based on block chain may be possible in the near future. Namely, software for direct transportation between them can be realized. Intermediates are no longer necessary.

E.3   Society and individuals

E.3.1   Introduction of programming into education

One method is a collaboration of solution providers and solution developers for a specific problem. However, a solution can be represented as an algorithm, and if a user has the skills to code an algorithm as a software program, the user can reduce the cost and time taken for documenting the specifications, and for the procedures.

Humanities also require programming, and have obtained engineering techniques; thus, users in this area can advance their domain, and return to society with new knowledge. For example, for a study of history, a database can be used, and history as information can be managed. Users will obtain new knowledge based on a correlation of events, visualizing the weather, earth sciences, geopolitics, or plagues, creating a new knowledge and finding faults through common sense, which can provide not only a highly accurate history, but can also find interference among such aspects, along with a visualization of the inference between social structures and human action.

Although traditional methods take a deductive approach, machine learning takes an inductive approach to reveal or solve the problem [264]. This seems to be at first glance an incompatible and conventional method; however, at the least, an inductive approach needs the required specifications defining the inductive task. After the specifications, the choice between taking a traditional programming-based approach or a statistics-based machine learning approach has importance. We can also take into account machine learning to determine the choice, and we should effectively decide based on the cost versus performance, time to deploying, and time to authorizing as well as the time to deployment and authorization.

E.3.2 Change in values

It is common knowledge that information on the Internet is free, and it is easy to use and spread. However, infringing on a copyright, disseminating false or fake information, and tampering with reports are serious problems. Therefore, Internet users need to have a higher literacy.

Although we might believe that we have application software to make a recommendation and curation sites to gather profitable information, these do not guarantee the quality of information such as its correctness. An unauthorized use of information of a non-medical basis has occurred [344]. Thus, a search service displaying whether information has a proper medical basis has been developed [83].

Recently, fake news has become a serious problem [307]; therefore, reporters must consider a mechanism to allow them to check whether news is factual, taking into account the confidence information of the providers, and we therefore acknowledge the importance of personal connections. Along with information, food sources have previously faced the same trends. Transparency of the producers to the consumers is necessary, and consumers will directly buy from producers if they have confidence in the products (foods). Producers can then set a price based on the quality of their products. There is a possibility that this trend in the food market can be applied to the information domain.

The importance of literacy regarding trade will increase for all products, including not only both tangible and intangible properties and products, but also information. This trend introduces the idea that confidence can be one of the keys to trading. Thus, we will require a system allowing a personal connection. In addition, advanced automation has created a problem of responsibility between the producer and consumer for direct trading, and thus an individual's decision and judgment will soon be tested more than now. Namely, taking into account machines for decision making and judgment, there is a possibility to be aware of unexpected damage or loss after an incident. This might be similar to a user's inexperience during the start-up phase of a service offering a new convenience (e.g., a combination of an EC card and a one-click system).

In addition to information such as history and records, personal careers can be managed by block chain. To make it unnecessary to hide personal, business, and or legal failures, we can make it commonly accepted that humans occasionally fail, and thus there is possibility of promoting a fault tolerance. However, an automation system has an issue of revealing information automatically, and therefore privacy will remain a serious issue. If we solve the privacy issue and entrust it to society rather than the nation, the privacy issue can become a business commodity. In addition, there is the possibility that a simple automation might be left to other matters, thereby making social problems no longer interesting. Thus, we need a mechanism providing an incentive to feel and experience interest in social problems rather than non-interest, or a mechanism having a rationality similar to a block chain that views a fair action as better than a cheating action (non-interesting in this case).

Humans have a limited and finite time on this planet. They want time for personal use, i.e., spending time with their family, and as a public individual. These are individual dependent, and there are various demands, in which each person wants their own time allocation. At present, personal time and time spent with family have higher priority, and we tend to neglect time in our relations with society (such as the local community and administrations). To allocate an individual's items having a higher priority, a higher efficiency over other items is needed, and thus all domains must be optimized to achieve efficiency. Therefore, items having a longer distance from personal items can be aggressively optimized with a higher efficiency.

To promote the use of information technology in administrative and social problems, we need a new user interface to apply information processing on a computer, and reduce manual sequences, namely, simplifying the account and avoiding alterations will be needed; thus, we can apply a machine learning system to such types of jobs needing an approximation. If we can treat items as digital information, developing a system to perform information processing based on requirement specifications will be sufficient.

In addition, we should work actively rather than passively. There are people who passively work and believe that working time is for earning money; one third of the time during the day is for sleeping, and the remaining third is for working. Thus, we can think of this time to be valuable for fun and enjoying our work. One method is to match between work responsibility and hobbies interest. Moreover, by promoting the flow of human resources, there is a possibility of entering various types of industries, although entering a university to find employment should be promoted.

E.3.3 Social support

Aging is the most serious problem in Japan [57], and the burden on younger people is increasing; they cannot support older people, and yet an increasing number of older people are being supported by a smaller number of young people. In Japan, we have observed a phenomenon in which middle-income has shifted to low-income, and the number of poor people has increased [346]. Disparity is widening for all ages, incomes, and employment. This problem has introduced a disparity in terms of medical and welfare support, and we need to rethink about our social infrastructure.

Foreseeing a decrease in the working population in the future, medical and welfare systems need to reduce their costs entirely. Not only medical facilities and a reduction of their running costs, but also automation and simplification for the procedures based on data analytics and machine learning, a mechanism for optimizing services to each person is required. As a mechanism standing by people, a portion of the medical and welfare costs including unnecessary medicines should be used for people needing services and support. Namely, rather than today's equality in medical and welfare (i.e., the same allocation of services to all people including those not needing the service), equity to those who do (thus, an optimized allocation of services to people who need them) is required.

By introducing a social business, we need to rethink about the role of non-profit organizations (NPOs) and non-governmental organizations (NGOs). NPOs aim to solve social problems [88]. NPOs also focus on non-profits, whereas NGOs cover the private sector areas that the government cannot [88]. NPOs and NGOs work to overcome social issues that cannot be solved by for-profit organizations such traditional companies and traditional government; however, there seems to be a bridge between groups and information technologies.

By contrast, when we consider a support mechanism for handicapped persons and neat persons, in terms of social participation support, a social business model might be effective because such businesses work to obtain profit from social problems and the profits can be allocated to the people. The aging problem is about to become a serious issue, and as a second life for current workers, NPOs, NGOs, and social businesses are useful. The population will be concentrated in urban areas, and this is creating a serious problem regarding the depopulation of rural areas [49], and making empty houses unmaintained. In rural areas, owing to aging and depopulation problems, electric commerce (EC) is being used for older persons without transportation, and for restructuring the rural to medical and welfare centered social; however, we cannot know the area after they have passed way. For example, drones have been considered to solve this problem.

E.3.4 Crime

The number of reported cases of criminal activities has decreased in the past 10 years, and all reported cases of serious crimes have declined. However, the number of reported cases for light crimes such as stalking has increased [56]. Communications fraud peaked in 2014, and money-laundering has been increasing. In addition, an aging population is now a serious problem [65]. One reason for the higher recidivism rate is a difficulty of rehabilitation. Aging and the recidivism rate have increased the detention costs. A reduction of the detention costs is needed to support such rehabilitation.

Criminals and crime preliminary groups can also use machine learning and big data analytics. Machine learning has a lower wall regarding its introduction not only for nations but also for criminal groups. We will need block chain to create a difficulty of falsification, and tracking and monitoring of property flow in a cashless society. Manual input by hand can introduce falsification; therefore, we must also improve the user interface.

E.4   Nation

E.4.1   Police and prosecutors

Monitoring using camera networks already installed in the city. Important facilities and places use it with face recognition technology [333]. It is used for not only traditional criminal investigations but also terrorisms. Therefore, national government also uses machine learning systems. Government organizations collect information from monitoring cameras and social networking services (SNSs) on a daily basis [228], and from the perspective of personal information protection edge-computing and/or fog-computing have been introduced to avoid collecting personal information on the cloud and/or servers.

E.4.2   Administrative, legislative, and judicial

Advanced improvements and optimization of administrative services have reduced the cost for such services, and as a result, has suppressed taxes or resulted in a decrease in tax payments involved in the population decrease. However, if a superfluous improvement and optimization are applied, then there will be the possibility of the monitoring and management of individuals by nations (or administrators).

It is easy to apply machine learning and big-data analytics to administrators and legislators requiring objective and logical consistency. Legislative and judicial tasks are information processes that inherently involve logic, and there is a possibility to apply machine learning to these areas from an engineering perspective. For example, the legislative branch consists of the constitution, and traditional laws cannot be adapted for the changing of society. By introducing an information processing system into such laws, obtaining a decision by a logical consistency from a machine learning system, a judge and jury can make a decision including the extenuating circumstances involved in the person's age based on objective information. In addition, engineering the law is possible. Management is a specialty for computing systems including machine learning, and therefore, it can be applied to workers of the administrative, legislative, and judicial branches. This means there is the possibility to use block chain, big-data analytics, and machine learning for words and deeds with traceability.

E.4.3 Military affairs

Applying machine learning to not only societal problems identified from crowds without identifying individuals, but also military use, is in progress [71]. Israel is the number one exporter of unmanned airplane in the world and created such an industry. Autonomous driving technologies can be applied and diverted to military, and they are already used in military facilities such as missiles.

Developed countries with advanced technologies have a relatively more difficulty to create a military incident compared with undeveloped countries. Internal strife occurs mainly in underdeveloped nations. Even if the military of developed nations intervenes through peace keeping operations (PKOs), an organization creating a problem, without advanced military forces, can construct a human shield using the locals to oppose the intervention. Therefore, the use of robots, which recognize soldiers and act against a military force only when close to them, has been suggested.

In addition, the non-profitable and non-government organization, International Committee for Robot Arms Control (ICRAC) studied the control of a burnup of military robotics and considered a national collaboration, in order to limit the use of military robots [44].

Moreover, the Defense Science and Technology Laboratory (DSTL) organized by the United Kingdom created a competition with a maximum reward of 40,000 pounds to consider technologies and their base ideas through a collection rather than to collect and hire human resources [90]. In Japan, scientists are apprehensive about not only introducing companies having advanced technologies into the military [51] but also diverting science and its technologies to the military through the government.

Bibliography

[1] 20 Newsgroups, http://qwone.com/%7Ejason/20Newsgroups/.
[2] A sound vocabulary and dataset, https://research.google.com/audioset/.
[3] Acoustic scene classification, http://www.cs.tut.fi/sgn/arg/dcase2016/task-acoustic-scene-classification.
[4] AVA Actions Dataset, https://research.google.com/ava/.
[5] AVSpeech, https://looking-to-listen.github.io/avspeech/explore.html.
[6] Build with Watson, https://www.ibm.com/watson/developercloud/.
[7] Common Voice, https://voice.mozilla.org/ja/datasets.
[8] Data Sets, https://www.technology.disneyanimation.com/collaboration-through-sharing.
[9] Deep Instinct, http://www.deepinstinct.com.
[10] Edge TPU, https://cloud.google.com/edge-tpu/.
[11] Fashion-MNIST, https://github.com/zalandoresearch/fashion-mnist/blob/master/README.md.
[12] Freesound 4 seconds, https://archive.org/details/freesound4s.
[13] Google-Landmarks: a New Dataset and Challenge for Landmark Recognition, https://storage.googleapis.com/openimages/web/index.html.
[14] Google Self-Driving Car Project, https://www.google.com/selfdrivingcar/.
[15] Human Brain Project, https://www.humanbrainproject.eu/en_GB/2016-overview.
[16] KITTI Vision Benchmark Suite, http://www.cvlibs.net/datasets/kitti/.
[17] Labeled Faces in the Wild, http://vis-www.cs.umass.edu/lfw/.
[18] Large-scale CelebFaces Attributes (CelebA) Dataset, http://mmlab.ie.cuhk.edu.hk/projects/CelebA.html.
[19] MegaFace and MF2: Million-Scale Face Recognition, http://megaface.cs.washington.edu.
[20] Moments in Time Dataset, http://moments.csail.mit.edu.
[21] MOTOBOT ver. 1, http://global.yamaha-motor.com/jp/showroom/event/2015tokyomotorshow/sp/exhibitionmodels/mgp/#_ga=1.111874052.1631556073.1470996719&r=s&r=s.
[22] Neuroscience Programs at IARPA, https://www.iarpa.gov/index.php/research-programs/neuroscience-programs-at-iarpa.
[23] Next-generation artificial intelligence promotion strategy, http://www.soumu.go.jp/main_content/000424360.pdf.
[24] Open Images Dataset V5 + Extensions, https://ai.googleblog.com/2018/03/google-landmarks-new-dataset-and.html, March.
[25] PCA Whitening, http://ufldl.stanford.edu/tutorial/unsupervised/PCAWhitening/.
[26] Princeton ModelNet, http://modelnet.cs.princeton.edu.
[27] PyTorch, https://github.com/pytorch/pytorch.
[28] Scene Parsing, http://apolloscape.auto/scene.html.
[29] Scene Parsing, https://bdd-data.berkeley.edu.
[30] ShapeNet, https://www.shapenet.org/about.
[31] SUN database, http://groups.csail.mit.edu/vision/SUN/.

[32] The CIFAR-10 dataset, http://www.cs.utoronto.ca/%7Ekriz/cifar.html.

[33] The MNIST Database, http://yann.lecun.com/exdb/mnist/.

[34] UCF101 - Action Recognition Data Set, https://www.crcv.ucf.edu/data/UCF101.php.

[35] Vivado Design Suite - HLx Edition, https://www.xilinx.com/products/design-tools/vivado.html.

[36] YouTube-8M Segments Dataset, https://research.google.com/youtube8m/.

[37] YouTube-BoundingBoxes Dataset, https://research.google.com/youtube-bb/.

[38] Mask-Programmable Logic Devices, June 1996.

[39] Using Programmable Logic for Gate Array Designs, https://www.altera.co.jp/content/dam/altera-www/global/ja_JP/pdfs/literature/an/archives/an051_01.pdf, January 1996, Application Note 51.

[40] Xilinx HardWire^{TM} FpgASIC Overview, June 1998.

[41] International Technology Roadmap for Semiconductors, November 2001.

[42] DARPA SyNAPSE Program, http://www.artificialbrains.com/darpa-synapse-program, 2008.

[43] Generating Functionally Equivalent FPGAs and ASICs with a Single Set of RTL and Synthesis/Timing Constraints, https://www.altera.com/content/dam/altera-www/global/en_US/pdfs/literature/wp/wp-01095-rtl-synthesis-timing.pdf, February 2009, WP-01095-1.2.

[44] International Committee for Robot Arms Control, http://icrac.net, 2009.

[45] NVIDIA's Next Generation CUDA Compute Architecture: Fermi, https://www.nvidia.com/content/PDF/fermi_white_papers/NVIDIA_Fermi_Compute_Architecture_Whitepaper.pdf, 2009, White Paper.

[46] IBM - Watson Defeats Humans in "Jeopardy!", https://www.cbsnews.com/news/ibm-watson-defeats-humans-in-jeopardy/, February 2011.

[47] https://www.intel.co.jp/content/www/jp/ja/history/history-intel-chips-timeline-poster.html.

[48] NVIDIA's Next Generation CUDA Compute Architecture: Kepler GK110, https://www.nvidia.com/content/PDF/kepler/NVIDIA-Kepler-GK110-Architecture-Whitepaper.pdf, 2012, White Paper.

[49] Population concentration and depopulation in the three major metropolitan areas, http://www.soumu.go.jp/johotsusintokei/whitepaper/ja/h24/html/nc112130.html, 2012.

[50] Big-Data Market Forecast by Sub-type, 2011-2017 (in $US billions), http://wikibon.org/w/images/c/c7/BigDataMarketForecastBySubType2013.png, 2013.

[51] Where to Go Japanese Technology? - Expanding "Military" Diversion -, http://www.nhk.or.jp/gendai/articles/3481/1.html, April 2014.

[52] China's Tsinghua HD talks with Micron for acquisition, http://jp.reuters.com/article/tsinghua-micron-chairman-idJPKCN0PX0JX20150723, July 2015.

[53] Gartner Says 6.4 Billion Connected "Things" Will Be in Use in 2016, Up 30 Percent From 2015, http://www.gartner.com/newsroom/id/3165317, November 2015.

[54] Intel Acquisition of Altera, https://newsroom.intel.com/press-kits/intel-acquisition-of-altera/, December 2015.

[55] World Robotics 2015 Industrial Robots, http://www.ifr.org/industrial-robots/statistics/, 2015.

[56] 2016 Police White Paper, https://www.npa.go.jp/hakusyo/h28/gaiyouban/gaiyouban.pdf, 2016.

[57] 2016 White Paper on Aging Society (whole version), http://www8.cao.go.jp/kourei/whitepaper/w-2016/html/zenbun/index.html, 2016.

[58] AI Bridging Cloud Infrastructure (ABCI), http://www.itri.aist.go.jp/events/sc2016/pdf/P06-ABCI.pdf, November 2016.

[59] Airbnb, http://sharing-economy-lab.jp/share-business-service, 2016.

[60] airCloset, https://www.air-closet.com, 2016.

[61] akippa, https://www.akippa.com, 2016.

[62] Arria 10 Core Fabric and General Purpose I/Os Handbook, https://www.altera.com/content/dam/altera-www/global/en_US/pdfs/literature/hb/arria-10/a10_handbook.pdf, June 2016, Arria 10 Handbook, Altera Corp.

[63] Build AI Powered Music Apps, http://niland.io, 2016.

[64] CaFoRe, http://cafore.jp, 2016.

[65] Current state of recidivism and countermeasures, http://www.moj.go.jp/housouken/housouken03_00086.html, 2016.

[66] Deep Learning Market worth 1,722.9 Million USD by 2022, http://www.marketsandmarkets.com/PressReleases/deep-learning.asp, November 2016.

[67] Forecast of Big Data market size, based on revenue, from 2011 to 2026 (in billion U.S. dollars), http://www.statista.com/statistics/254266/global-big-data-market-forecast/, 2016.

[68] Intel Artificial Intelligence: Unleashing the Next Wave, https://newsroom.intel.com/press-kits/intel-artificial-intelligence-unleashing-next-wave/, November 2016.

[69] Intelligent transport systems, https://www.lta.gov.sg/content/ltaweb/en/roads-and-motoring/managing-traffic-and-congestion/intelligent-transport-systems.html, 2016.

[70] Intuitive Surgical, Inc., http://www.intuitivesurgical.com/, 2016.

[71] Israel Endless-War, http://mainichi.jp/endlesswar/, August 2016.

[72] Japan's population trends, http://www.mhlw.go.jp/file/06-Seisakujouhou-12600000-Seisakutoukatsukan/suii2014.pdf, 2016.

[73] Labor force survey long-term time series data, http://www.stat.go.jp/data/roudou/longtime/03roudou.htm, 2016.

[74] Movidius + Intel = Vision for the Future of Autonomous Devices, http://www.movidius.com/news/ceo-post-september-2016, March 2016.

[75] Movidius and DJI Bring Vision-Based Autonomy to DJI Phantom 4, http://www.movidius.com/news/movidius-and-dji-bring-vision-based-autonomy-to-dji-phantom-4, March 2016.

[76] MUJIN PickWorker, http://mujin.co.jp/jp#products, 2016.

[77] Nervana Engine, http://www.nervanasys.com/technology/engine, 2016.

[78] NVIDIA's Next Generation CUDA Compute Architecture: Kepler GK110, http://www.nvidia.com/object/gpu-architecture.html#source=gss, 2016 (outdated).

[79] SENSY, http://sensy.jp, 2016.

[80] The Next Rembrandt, https://www.nextrembrandt.com, April 2016.

[81] U.S.-based venture develops a system to automatically determine whether papers are plagiarized or not, https://gakumado.mynavi.jp/gmd/articles/30456, January 2016.

[82] Vision Processing Unit, http://www.movidius.com/solutions/vision-processing-unit, 2016.

[83] Yahoo Search is now able to search for "breast cancer treatment guidelines for patients", http://promo.search.yahoo.co.jp/news/service/20161027131836.html, October 2016.

[84] 2017 Survey of Actual Conditions for Manufacturing Base Technology, https://www.meti.go.jp/meti_lib/report/H29FY/000403.pdf, 2017.

[85] Deep Learning Chipset Shipments to Reach 41.2 Million Units Annually by 2025, https://www.tractica.com/newsroom/press-releases/deep-learning-chipset-shipments-to-reach-41-2-million-units-annually-by-2025/, March 2017.

[86] File:TI TMS32020 DSP die.jpg, https://commons.wikimedia.org/wiki/File:TI_TMS32020_DSP_die.jpg, August 2017.

[87] IMAGENET Large Scale Visual Recognition Challenge (ILSVRC) 2017 Overview, http://image-net.org/challenges/talks_2017/ILSVRC2017_overview.pdf, 2017.

[88] Q & A about NPO: Basic knowledge of NPO, http://www.jnpoc.ne.jp/?page_id=134, September 2017.

[89] Sharing economy lab, https://www.airbnb.com, 2017.

[90] UK military lab launches £40,000 machine learning prize, http://www.wired.co.uk/article/dstl-mod-data-science-challenge-2017, April 2017.

[91] Artificial Intelligence Edge Device Shipments to Reach 2.6 Billion Units Annually by 2025, https://www.tractica.com/newsroom/press-releases/artificial-intelligence-edge-device-shipments-to-reach-2-6-billion-units-annually-by-2025/, September 2018.

[92] BDD100K: a Large-scale Diverse Driving Video Database, https://bair.berkeley.edu/blog/2018/05/30/bdd/, May 2018.

[93] BFLOAT16 - Hardware Numerics Definition, https://software.intel.com/sites/default/files/managed/40/8b/bf16-hardware-numerics-definition-white-paper.pdf, November 2018.

[94] Artificial Intelligence (AI) in Drug Discovery Market by Component (Software, Service), Technology (ML, DL), Application (Neurodegenerative Diseases, Immuno-Oncology, CVD), End User (Pharmaceutical & Biotechnology, CRO), Region - Global forecast to 2024, https://www.marketsandmarkets.com/Market-Reports/ai-in-drug-discovery-market-151193446.html, 2019.

[95] End to end deep learning compiler stack, 2019.

[96] FPGA Market by Technology (SRAM, Antifuse, Flash), Node Size (Less than 28 nm, 28-90 nm, More than 90 nm), Configuration (High-End FPGA, Mid-Range FPGA, Low-End FPGA), Vertical (Telecommunications, Automotive), and Geography - Global Forecast to 2023, https://www.marketsandmarkets.com/Market-Reports/fpga-market-194123367.html, December 2019.

[97] Halide - a language for fast, portable computation on images and tensors, 2019.

[98] Intelligence Processing Unit, https://www.graphcore.ai/products/ipu, 2019.

[99] Open neural network exchange format, 2019.

[100] An open source machine learning library for research and production, 2019.

[101] Shave v2.0 - microarchitectures - intel movidius, 2019.

[102] CEVA NeuPro-S, https://www.ceva-dsp.com/product/ceva-neupro/, October 2020.

[103] Gaudi ai training, October 2020.

[104] UPSIDE / Cortical Processor Study, http://rebootingcomputing.ieee.org/images/files/pdf/RCS4HammerstromThu515.pdf, Dan Hammerstrom.

[105] Vahideh Akhlaghi, Amir Yazdanbakhsh, Kambiz Samadi, Rajesh K. Gupta, Hadi Esmaeilzadeh, Snapea: Predictive early activation for reducing computation in deep convolutional neural networks, in: Proceedings of the 45th Annual International Symposium on Computer Architecture, ISCA '18, IEEE Press, 2018, pp. 662–673.

[106] Ako Kano, How much artificial intelligence can support doctors, http://techon.nikkeibp.co.jp/atcl/feature/15/327441/101400132/?ST=health&P=1, October 2016.

[107] F. Akopyan, J. Sawada, A. Cassidy, R. Alvarez-Icaza, J. Arthur, P. Merolla, N. Imam, Y. Nakamura, P. Datta, G. Nam, B. Taba, M. Beakes, B. Brezzo, J.B. Kuang, R. Manohar, W.P. Risk, B. Jackson, D.S. Modha, Truenorth: design and tool flow of a 65 mw 1 million neuron programmable neurosynaptic chip, IEEE Transactions on Computer-Aided Design of Integrated Circuits and Systems 34 (10) (Oct 2015) 1537–1557.

[108] Jorge Albericio, Patrick Judd, A. Delmás, S. Sharify, Andreas Moshovos, Bit-pragmatic deep neural network computing, CoRR, arXiv:1610.06920 [abs], 2016.

[109] Jorge Albericio, Patrick Judd, Tayler Hetherington, Tor Aamodt, Natalie Enright Jerger, Andreas Moshovos, Cnvlutin: ineffectual-neuron-free deep neural network computing, in: 2016 ACM/IEEE International Symposium on Computer Architecture (ISCA), June 2016.

[110] M. Alwani, H. Chen, M. Ferdman, P. Milder, Fused-layer cnn accelerators, in: 2016 49th Annual IEEE/ACM International Symposium on Microarchitecture (MICRO), Oct 2016, pp. 1–12.

[111] Marcin Andrychowicz, Misha Denil, Sergio Gomez, Matthew W. Hoffman, David Pfau, Tom Schaul, Nando de Freitas, Learning to learn by gradient descent by gradient descent, CoRR, arXiv:1606.04474 [abs], 2016.

[112] Rumiko Azuma, Noriko Katsutani, Attitude survey and analysis of college students' illegal copy, in: The 40th Annual Conference of JESiE, JESiE '15, 2015.

[113] Lei Jimmy Ba, Rich Caurana, Do deep nets really need to be deep?, CoRR, arXiv:1312.6184 [abs], 2013.

[114] Dzmitry Bahdanau, Kyunghyun Cho, Yoshua Bengio, Neural machine translation by jointly learning to align and translate, CoRR, arXiv:1409.0473 [abs], 2014.

[115] Brian Bailey, The impact of Moore's law ending, 2018.

[116] Chris Baker, Internal expense fraud is next on machine learning's list, https://techcrunch.com/2016/10/18/internal-expense-fraud-is-next-on-machine-learnings-list/, October 2016.

[117] David Balduzzi, Marcus Frean, Lennox Leary, J.P. Lewis, Kurt Wan-Duo Ma, Brian McWilliams, The shattered gradients problem: if resnets are the answer, then what is the question?, CoRR, arXiv:1702.08591 [abs], 2017.

[118] Kelly Bit, Bridgewater is said to start artificial-intelligence team, http://www.bloomberg. com/news/articles/2015-02-27/bridgewater-is-said-to-start-artificial-intelligence-team, February 2015.

[119] K.A. Boahen, Point-to-point connectivity between neuromorphic chips using address events, IEEE Transactions on Circuits and Systems. 2, Analog and Digital Signal Processing 47 (5) (May 2000) 416–434.

[120] M. Bohr, A 30 year retrospective on Dennard's MOSFET scaling paper, IEEE Solid-State Circuits Society Newsletter 12 (1) (Winter 2007) 11–13.

[121] Kyeongryeol Bong, Sungpill Choi, Changhyeon Kim, Sanghoon Kang, Youchang Kim, Hoi-Jun Yoo, A 0.62mW ultra-low-power convolutional-neural- network face-recognition processor and a CIS integrated with always-on Haar-like face detector, in: 2017 IEEE International Solid-State Circuits Conference (ISSCC), February 2017.

[122] S. Brown, R. Francis, J. Rose, Z. Vranesic, Field-Programmable Gate Arrays, Springer/Kluwer Academic Publishers, May 1992.

[123] Diane Bryant, The foundation of artificial intelligence, https://newsroom.intel.com/editorials/ foundation-of-artificial-intelligence/, August 2016.

[124] Doug Burger, James R. Goodman, Alain Kägi, Memory bandwidth limitations of future microprocessors, SIGARCH Computer Architecture News 24 (2) (May 1996) 78–89.

[125] Andrew Canis, Jongsok Choi, Mark Aldham, Victor Zhang, Ahmed Kammoona, Jason H. Anderson, Stephen Brown, Tomasz Czajkowski, LegUp: high-level synthesis for FPGA-based processor/accelerator systems, in: Proceedings of the 19th ACM/SIGDA International Symposium on Field Programmable Gate Arrays, FPGA '11, New York, NY, USA, ACM, 2011, pp. 33–36.

[126] Vincent Casser, Sören Pirk, Reza Mahjourian, Anelia Angelova, Depth prediction without the sensors: leveraging structure for unsupervised learning from monocular videos, CoRR, arXiv:1811.06152 [abs], 2018.

[127] Olivier Chapelle, Eren Manavoglu, Romer Rosales, Simple and scalable response prediction for display advertising, ACM Transactions on Intelligent Systems and Technology 5 (4) (Dec 2014) 61:1–61:34.

[128] Tianshi Chen, Zidong Du, Ninghui Sun, Jia Wang, Chengyong Wu, Yunji Chen, Olivier Temam, DianNao: a small-footprint high-throughput accelerator for ubiquitous machine-learning, in: Proceedings of the 19th International Conference on Architectural Support for Programming Languages and Operating Systems, ASPLOS '14, New York, NY, USA, ACM, 2014, pp. 269–284.

[129] Y. Chen, T. Luo, S. Liu, S. Zhang, L. He, J. Wang, L. Li, T. Chen, Z. Xu, N. Sun, O. Temam, DaDianNao: a machine-learning supercomputer, in: 2014 47th Annual IEEE/ACM International Symposium on Microarchitecture, Dec 2014, pp. 609–622.

[130] Y.H. Chen, T. Krishna, J. Emer, V. Sze, 14.5 Eyeriss: an energy-efficient reconfigurable accelerator for deep convolutional neural networks, in: 2016 IEEE International Solid-State Circuits Conference (ISSCC), Jan 2016, pp. 262–263.

[131] Yu-Hsin Chen, Joel Emer, Vivienne Sze, Eyeriss: a spatial architecture for energy-efficient dataflow for convolutional neural networks, in: 2016 ACM/IEEE International Symposium on Computer Architecture (ISCA), June 2016.

[132] Yu-Hsin Chen, Joel S. Emer, Vivienne Sze, Eyeriss v2: a flexible and high-performance accelerator for emerging deep neural networks, CoRR, arXiv:1807.07928 [abs], 2018.

[133] Sharan Chetlur, Cliff Woolley, Philippe Vandermersch, Jonathan Cohen, John Tran, Bryan Catanzaro, Evan Shelhamer, cuDNN: efficient primitives for deep learning, CoRR, arXiv: 1410.0759 [abs], 2014.

[134] Ping Chi, Shuangchen Li, Cong Xu, Tao Zhang, Jishen Zhao, Yongpan Liu, Yu Wang, Yuan Xie, Prime: a novel processing-in-memory architecture for neural network computation in reram-based main memory, in: 2016 ACM/IEEE International Symposium on Computer Architecture (ISCA), June 2016.

[135] Yoojin Choi, Mostafa El-Khamy, Jungwon Lee, Towards the limit of network quantization, CoRR, arXiv:1612.01543 [abs], 2016.

[136] P. Chow, Soon Ong Seo, J. Rose, K. Chung, G. Paez-Monzon, I. Rahardja, The design of a SRAM-based field-programmable gate array-Part II: circuit design and layout, IEEE Transactions on Very Large Scale Integration (VLSI) Systems 7 (3) (Sept 1999) 321–330.

[137] P. Chow, Soon Ong Seo, J. Rose, K. Chung, G. Paez-Monzon, I. Rahardja, The design of an SRAM-based field-programmable gate array. I. Architecture, IEEE Transactions on Very Large Scale Integration (VLSI) Systems 7 (2) (June 1999) 191–197.

[138] E. Chung, J. Fowers, K. Ovtcharov, M. Papamichael, A. Caulfield, T. Massengill, M. Liu, D. Lo, S. Alkalay, M. Haselman, M. Abeydeera, L. Adams, H. Angepat, C. Boehn, D. Chiou, O. Firestein, A. Forin, K.S. Gatlin, M. Ghandi, S. Heil, K. Holohan, A. El Husseini, T. Juhasz, K. Kagi, R.K. Kovvuri, S. Lanka, F. van Megen, D. Mukhortov, P. Patel, B. Perez, A. Rapsang, S. Reinhardt, B. Rouhani, A. Sapek, R. Seera, S. Shekar, B. Sridharan, G. Weisz, L. Woods, P. Yi Xiao, D. Zhang, R. Zhao, D. Burger, Serving dnns in real time at datacenter scale with project brainwave, IEEE MICRO 38 (2) (Mar 2018) 8–20.

[139] Corinna Cortes, Vladimir Vapnik, Support-vector networks, Machine Learning 20 (3) (Sep 1995) 273–297.

[140] M. Courbariaux, Y. Bengio, J.-P. David, Training deep neural networks with low precision multiplications, ArXiv e-prints, Dec 2014.

[141] Matthieu Courbariaux, Yoshua Bengio, BinaryNet: training deep neural networks with weights and activations constrained to +1 or −1, CoRR, arXiv:1602.02830 [abs], 2016.

[142] Matthieu Courbariaux, Yoshua Bengio, Jean-Pierre David, BinaryConnect: training deep neural networks with binary weights during propagations, CoRR, arXiv:1511.00363 [abs], 2015.

[143] Elliot J. Crowley, Gavin Gray, Amos J. Storkey, Moonshine: distilling with cheap convolutions, in: S. Bengio, H. Wallach, H. Larochelle, K. Grauman, N. Cesa-Bianchi, R. Garnett (Eds.), Advances in Neural Information Processing Systems, Vol. 31, Curran Associates, Inc., 2018, pp. 2888–2898.

[144] Tim Culpan, Jonathan Browning, China's Tsinghua buys western digital stake for $3.8 billion, https://www.bloomberg.com/news/articles/2015-12-11/tsinghua-unigroup-to-buy-1-7-billion-stake-in-siliconware, December 2015.

[145] Tim Culpan, Brian Womack, China's Tsinghua buys western digital stake for $3.8 billion, https://www.bloomberg.com/news/articles/2015-09-30/china-s-tsinghua-buys-western-digital-stake-for-3-8-billion, September 2015.

[146] W.J. Dally, B. Towles, Route packets, not wires: on-chip interconnection networks, in: Design Automation Conference, 2001. Proceedings, 2001, pp. 684–689.

[147] David Moloney, 1tops/w software programmable media processor, August 2011.

[148] M. Davies, N. Srinivasa, T. Lin, G. Chinya, Y. Cao, S.H. Choday, G. Dimou, P. Joshi, N. Imam, S. Jain, Y. Liao, C. Lin, A. Lines, R. Liu, D. Mathaikutty, S. McCoy, A. Paul, J. Tse, G. Venkataramanan, Y. Weng, A. Wild, Y. Yang, H. Wang, Loihi: a neuromorphic manycore processor with on-chip learning, IEEE MICRO 38 (1) (January 2018) 82–99.

[149] James C. Dehnert, Brian K. Grant, John P. Banning, Richard Johnson, Thomas Kistler, Alexander Klaiber, Jim Mattson, The transmeta code morphing™ software: using speculation, recovery, and adaptive retranslation to address real-life challenges, in: Proceedings of the International Symposium on Code Generation and Optimization: Feedback-Directed and Runtime Optimization, CGO '03, Washington, DC, USA, IEEE Computer Society, 2003, pp. 15–24.

[150] Mike Demler, Mythic multiplies in a flash - analog in-memory computing eliminates dram read/write cycles, August 2018, pp. 8–20.

[151] Li Deng, A tutorial survey of architectures, algorithms, and applications for deep learning, in: APSIPA Transactions on Signal and Information Processing, January 2014.

[152] Peter J. Denning, The working set model for program behavior, Communications of the ACM 26 (1) (Jan 1983) 43–48.

[153] Giuseppe Desoli, Nitin Chawla, Thomas Boesch, Surinder pal Singh, Elio Guidetti, Fabio De
       Ambroggi, Tommaso Majo, Paolo Zambotti, Manuj Ayodhyawasi, Harvinder Singh, Nalin
       Aggarwal, A 2.9TOPS/W deep convolutional neural network SoC in FD-SOI 28nm for in-
       telligent embedded systems, in: 2017 IEEE International Solid-State Circuits Conference
       (ISSCC), February 2017.

[154] L. Devroye, T. Wagner, Distribution-free performance bounds for potential function rules,
       IEEE Transactions on Information Theory 25 (5) (Sep. 1979) 601–604.

[155] Zidong Du, Daniel D. Ben-Dayan Rubin, Yunji Chen, Liqiang He, Tianshi Chen, Lei Zhang,
       Chengyong Wu, Olivier Temam, Neuromorphic accelerators: a comparison between neuro-
       science and machine-learning approaches, in: Proceedings of the 48th International Sympo-
       sium on Microarchitecture, MICRO-48, New York, NY, USA, ACM, 2015, pp. 494–507.

[156] Zidong Du, Robert Fasthuber, Tianshi Chen, Paolo Ienne, Ling Li, Tao Luo, Xiaobing Feng,
       Yunji Chen, Olivier Temam, ShiDianNao: shifting vision processing closer to the sensor, in:
       Proceedings of the 42Nd Annual International Symposium on Computer Architecture, ISCA
       '15, New York, NY, USA, ACM, 2015, pp. 92–104.

[157] enlitic. Deep learning technology can save lives by helping detect curable diseases early,
       http://www.enlitic.com/solutions.html.

[158] Hadi Esmaeilzadeh, Emily Blem, Renee St. Amant, Karthikeyan Sankaralingam, Doug
       Burger, Dark silicon and the end of multicore scaling, in: Proceedings of the 38th Annual
       International Symposium on Computer Architecture, ISCA '11, New York, NY, USA, ACM,
       2011, pp. 365–376.

[159] Steve K. Esser, Rathinakumar Appuswamy, Paul Merolla, John V. Arthur, Dharmendra S.
       Modha, Backpropagation for energy-efficient neuromorphic computing, in: C. Cortes, N.D.
       Lawrence, D.D. Lee, M. Sugiyama, R. Garnett (Eds.), Advances in Neural Information Pro-
       cessing Systems, Vol. 28, Curran Associates, Inc., 2015, pp. 1117–1125.

[160] C. Farabet, B. Martini, B. Corda, P. Akselrod, E. Culurciello, Y. LeCun, NeuFlow: a run-
       time reconfigurable dataflow processor for vision, in: CVPR 2011 Workshops, June 2011,
       pp. 109–116.

[161] Daniel Feggella, Valuing the artificial intelligence market, graphs and predictions for 2016
       and beyond, http://techemergence.com/valuing-the-artificial-intelligence-market-2016-and-
       beyond/, March 2016.

[162] Fei-Fei Li, Justin Johnson, Serena Yeung, Lecture 4: Backpropagation and neural networks,
       2017.

[163] Andrew Feldman, Cerebras wafer scale engine: Why we need big chips for deep learning,
       August 2019.

[164] Asja Fischer, Christian Igel, An Introduction to Restricted Boltzmann Machines, Springer
       Berlin Heidelberg, Berlin, Heidelberg, 2012, pp. 14–36.

[165] J. Fowers, K. Ovtcharov, M. Papamichael, T. Massengill, M. Liu, D. Lo, S. Alkalay, M.
       Haselman, L. Adams, M. Ghandi, S. Heil, P. Patel, A. Sapek, G. Weisz, L. Woods, S. Lanka,
       S.K. Reinhardt, A.M. Caulfield, E.S. Chung, D. Burger, A configurable cloud-scale dnn
       processor for real-time ai, in: 2018 ACM/IEEE 45th Annual International Symposium on
       Computer Architecture (ISCA), June 2018, pp. 1–14.

[166] Yao Fu, Ephrem Wu, Ashish Sirasao, Sedny Attia, Kamran Khan, Ralph Wittig, Deep
       learning with INT8 optimization on Xilinx devices, https://www.xilinx.com/support/
       documentation/white_papers/wp486-deep-learning-int8.pdf, November 2016.

[167] J. Fung, S. Mann, Using multiple graphics cards as a general purpose parallel computer:
       applications to computer vision, in: Proceedings of the 17th International Conference on
       Pattern Recognition, 2004. ICPR 2004, Vol. 1, Aug 2004, pp. 805–808.

[168] Mingyu Gao, Jing Pu, Xuan Yang, Mark Horowitz, Christos Kozyrakis, Tetris: scalable and
       efficient neural network acceleration with 3d memory, in: Proceedings of the Twenty-Second
       International Conference on Architectural Support for Programming Languages and Oper-
       ating Systems, ASPLOS '17, New York, NY, USA, Association for Computing Machinery,
       2017, pp. 751–764.

[169] H.L. Garner, The residue number system, IRE Transactions on Electronic Computers EC-8 (2) (June 1959) 140–147.

[170] Ben Gesing, Steve J. Peterson, Dirk Michelsen, Artificial intelligence in logistics, 2018.

[171] Xavier Glorot, Yoshua Bengio, Understanding the difficulty of training deep feedforward neural networks, in: Aistats, Vol. 9, 2010, pp. 249–256.

[172] Xavier Glorot, Antoine Bordes, Yoshua Bengio, Deep sparse rectifier neural networks, in: Aistats, Vol. 15, 2011, p. 275.

[173] M. Gokhale, B. Holmes, K. Iobst, Processing in memory: the Terasys massively parallel PIM array, Computer 28 (4) (Apr 1995) 23–31.

[174] Google, TensorFlow is an open source software library for machine intelligence, https://www.tensorflow.org.

[175] Micha Gorelick, Ian Ozsvald, High-Performance Python, O'Reilly Japan, 2015.

[176] Andrew Griffin, Robot 'mother' builds babies that can evolve on their own, http://www.independent.co.uk/life-style/gadgets-and-tech/news/robot-mother-builds-babies-that-can-evolve-on-their-own-10453196.html, August 2015.

[177] Suyog Gupta, Ankur Agrawal, Kailash Gopalakrishnan, Pritish Narayanan, Deep learning with limited numerical precision, CoRR, arXiv:1502.02551 [abs], 2015.

[178] D. Abts, J. Ross, J. Sparling, M. Wong-VanHaren, M. Baker, T. Hawkins, A. Bell, J. Thompson, T. Kahsai, G. Kimmell, J. Hwang, R. Leslie-Hurd, M. Bye, E.R. Creswick, M. Boyd, M. Venigalla, E. Laforge, J. Purdy, P. Kamath, D. Maheshwari, M. Beidler, G. Rosseel, O. Ahmad, G. Gagarin, R. Czekalski, A. Rane, S. Parmar, J. Werner, J. Sproch, A. Macias, B. Kurtz, Think fast: a tensor streaming processor (TSP) for accelerating deep learning workloads, in: 2020 ACM/IEEE 47th Annual International Symposium on Computer Architecture (ISCA), 2020, pp. 145–158.

[179] Philipp Gysel, Mohammad Motamedi, Soheil Ghiasi, Hardware-oriented approximation of convolutional neural networks, CoRR, arXiv:1604.03168 [abs], 2016.

[180] Tom R. Halfhill, Ceva sharpens computer vision, http://www.linleygroup.com/mpr/article.php?url=mpr/h/2015/11389/11389.pdf, April 2015, Microprocessor Report.

[181] Kentaro Hamada, AIST launches AI-specific supercomputer development. aiming for the world's best with deep learning, http://jp.reuters.com/article/sansoken-idJPKBN13K0TQ?pageNumber=2, November 2016.

[182] Song Han, Junlong Kang, Huizi Mao, Yiming Hu, Xin Li, Yubin Li, Dongliang Xie, Hong Luo, Song Yao, Yu Wang, Huazhong Yang, William J. Dally, ESE: efficient speech recognition engine with compressed LSTM on FPGA, CoRR, arXiv:1612.00694 [abs], 2016.

[183] Song Han, Xingyu Liu, Huizi Mao, Jing Pu, Ardavan Pedram, Mark A. Horowitz, William J. Dally, EIE: efficient inference engine on compressed deep neural network, CoRR, arXiv:1602.01528 [abs], 2016.

[184] Song Han, Huizi Mao, William J. Dally, Deep compression: compressing deep neural network with pruning, trained quantization and Huffman coding, CoRR, arXiv:1510.00149 [abs], 2015.

[185] Moritz Hardt, Tengyu Ma, Identity matters in deep learning, CoRR, arXiv:1611.04231 [abs], 2016.

[186] Reiner Hartenstein, Coarse grain reconfigurable architecture (embedded tutorial), in: Proceedings of the 2001 Asia and South Pacific Design Automation Conference, ASP-DAC '01, New York, NY, USA, ACM, 2001, pp. 564–570.

[187] Soheil Hashemi, Nicholas Anthony, Hokchhay Tann, R. Iris Bahar, Sherief Reda, Understanding the impact of precision quantization on the accuracy and energy of neural networks, CoRR, arXiv:1612.03940 [abs], 2016.

[188] Atsushi Hattori, The birth of China's largest memory maker - Tsinghua Unigroup consolidates XMC's memory manufacturing division, http://news.mynavi.jp/news/2016/07/29/213/, July 2016.

[189] Kaiming He, Georgia Gkioxari, Piotr Dollár, Ross B. Girshick, Mask R-CNN, CoRR, arXiv:1703.06870 [abs], 2017.

[190] Kaiming He, Xiangyu Zhang, Shaoqing Ren, Jian Sun, Deep residual learning for image recognition, CoRR, arXiv:1512.03385 [abs], 2015.

[191] Kaiming He, Xiangyu Zhang, Shaoqing Ren, Jian Sun, Delving deep into rectifiers: surpassing human-level performance on ImageNet classification, CoRR, arXiv:1502.01852 [abs], 2015.

[192] Nicole Hemsoth, Deep learning pioneer pushing GPU neural network limits, https://www.nextplatform.com/2015/05/11/deep-learning-pioneer-pushing-gpu-neural-network-limits/, May 2015.

[193] John L. Hennessy, David A. Patterson, Computer Architecture - a Quantitative Approach, 6th edition, Elsevier, 2019.

[194] Maurice Herlihy, J. Eliot B. Moss, Transactional memory: architectural support for lock-free data structures, SIGARCH Computer Architecture News 21 (2) (May 1993) 289–300.

[195] G.E. Hinton, Deep belief networks, Scholarpedia 4 (5) (2009) 5947, revision #91189.

[196] Geoffrey Hinton, Oriol Vinyals, Jeff Dean, Distilling the knowledge in a neural network, arXiv e-prints, arXiv:1503.02531, Mar 2015.

[197] Geoffrey E. Hinton, Alexander Krizhevsky, Ilya Sutskever, Nitish Srivastva, System and method for addressing overfitting in a neural network, https://patents.google.com/patent/US9406017B2/en, September 2019.

[198] E. Talpes, D.D. Sarma, G. Venkataramanan, P. Bannon, B. McGee, B. Floering, A. Jalote, C. Hsiong, S. Arora, A. Gorti, G.S. Sachdev, Compute solution for Tesla's full self-driving computer, IEEE MICRO 40 (2) (2020) 25–35.

[199] Richard C. Holt, Some deadlock properties of computer systems, ACM Computing Surveys 4 (3) (September 1972) 179–196.

[200] Nahoko Horie, Declining Birthrate and Aging Will Reduce Labor Force Population by 40, Research Report, 2017.

[201] Md. Zakir Hossain, Ferdous Sohel, Mohd Fairuz Shiratuddin, Hamid Laga, A comprehensive survey of deep learning for image captioning, CoRR, arXiv:1810.04020 [abs], 2018.

[202] Allen Huang, Raymond Wu, Deep learning for music, CoRR, arXiv:1606.04930 [abs], 2016.

[203] Itay Hubara, Matthieu Courbariaux, Daniel Soudry, Ran El-Yaniv, Yoshua Bengio, Quantized neural networks: training neural networks with low precision weights and activations, CoRR, arXiv:1609.07061 [abs], 2016.

[204] G. Indiveri, F. Corradi, N. Qiao, Neuromorphic architectures for spiking deep neural networks, in: 2015 IEEE International Electron Devices Meeting (IEDM), Dec 2015, pp. 4.2.1–4.2.4.

[205] Yu Ji, YouHui Zhang, ShuangChen Li, Ping Chi, CiHang Jiang, Peng Qu, Yuan Xie, Wen-Guang Chen, Neutrams: neural network transformation and co-design under neuromorphic hardware constraints, in: 2016 49th Annual IEEE/ACM International Symposium on Microarchitecture (MICRO), October 2016, pp. 1–13.

[206] Huaizu Jiang, Deqing Sun, Varun Jampani, Ming-Hsuan Yang, Erik G. Learned-Miller, Jan Kautz, Super slomo: high quality estimation of multiple intermediate frames for video interpolation, CoRR, arXiv:1712.00080 [abs], 2017.

[207] L. Jin, Z. Wang, R. Gu, C. Yuan, Y. Huang, Training large scale deep neural networks on the Intel Xeon Phi Many-Core coprocessor, in: 2014 IEEE International Parallel Distributed Processing Symposium Workshops, May 2014, pp. 1622–1630.

[208] JIS, JIS Z 8101-1: 1999, 1999.

[209] F.D. Johansson, U. Shalit, D. Sontag, Learning representations for counterfactual inference, ArXiv e-prints, May 2016.

[210] Esa Jokioinen, Remote & autonomous ships - the next steps, http://www.rolls-royce.com/~/media/Files/R/Rolls-Royce/documents/customers/marine/ship-intel/aawa-whitepaper-210616.pdf, 2016.

[211] Jouppi Norm, Google supercharges machine learning tasks with TPU custom chip, https://cloudplatform.googleblog.com/2016/05/Google-supercharges-machine-learning-tasks-with-custom-chip.html?m=1, May 2016.

[212] Norman P. Jouppi, Cliff Young, Nishant Patil, David Patterson, Gaurav Agrawal, Raminder Bajwa, Sarah Bates, Suresh Bhatia, Nan Boden, Al Borchers, Rick Boyle, Pierre luc Cantin, Clifford Chao, Chris Clark, Jeremy Coriell, Mike Daley, Matt Dau, Jeffrey Dean, Ben Gelb, Tara Vazir Ghaemmaghami, Rajendra Gottipati, William Gulland, Robert Hagmann, C. Richard Ho, Doug Hogberg, John Hu, Robert Hundt, Dan Hurt, Julian Ibarz, Aaron Jaffey, Alek Jaworski, Alexander Kaplan, Harshit Khaitan, Andy Koch, Naveen Kumar, Steve Lacy, James Laudon, James Law, Diemthu Le, Chris Leary, Zhuyuan Liu, Kyle Lucke, Alan Lundin, Gordon MacKean, Adriana Maggiore, Maire Mahony, Kieran Miller, Rahul Nagarajan, Ravi Narayanaswami, Ray Ni, Kathy Nix, Thomas Norrie, Mark Omernick, Narayana Penukonda, Andy Phelps, Jonathan Ross, Matt Ross, Amir Salek, Emad Samadiani, Chris Severn, Gregory Sizikov, Matthew Snelham, Jed Souter, Dan Steinberg, Andy Swing, Mercedes Tan, Gregory Thorson, Bo Tian, Horia Toma, Erick Tuttle, Vijay Vasudevan, Richard Walter, Walter Wang, Eric Wilcox, Doe Hyun Yoon, In-datacenter performance analysis of a tensor processing unit, in: 2017 ACM/IEEE 44th Annual International Symposium on Computer Architecture (ISCA), IEEE Computer Society, June 2017.

[213] Patrick Judd, Alberto Delmas Lascorz, Sayeh Sharify, Andreas Moshovos, Cnvlutin2: ineffectual-activation-and-weight-free deep neural network computing, CoRR, arXiv:1705.00125 [abs], 2017.

[214] Daisuke Kadowaki, Ryuji Sakata, Kesuke Hosaka, Yuji Hiramatsu, Data Analysis Techniques to Win Kaggle, Gijutsu-Hyohron Co., Ltd., 2019, pp. 271–304.

[215] Dhiraj D. Kalamkar, Dheevatsa Mudigere, Naveen Mellempudi, Dipankar Das, Kunal Banerjee, Sasikanth Avancha, Dharma Teja Vooturi, Nataraj Jammalamadaka, Jianyu Huang, Hector Yuen, Jiyan Yang, Jongsoo Park, Alexander Heinecke, Evangelos Georganas, Sudarshan Srinivasan, Abhisek Kundu, Misha Smelyanskiy, Bharat Kaul, Pradeep Dubey, A study of BFLOAT16 for deep learning training, CoRR, arXiv:1905.12322 [abs], 2019.

[216] Péter Karkus, David Hsu, Wee Sun Lee, Qmdp-net: deep learning for planning under partial observability, CoRR, arXiv:1703.06692 [abs], 2017.

[217] Yoshinobu Kato, Power of flow analysis that overturns the belief that there is no waste, http://itpro.nikkeibp.co.jp/atcl/watcher/14/334361/102700403/, November 2015.

[218] Toshimitsu Kawano, Foxconn manufacturing iPhone introduces 40,000 robots, accelerating replacement with humans, http://gigazine.net/news/20161007-foxconn-install-40000-robot/, 2016.

[219] Toshimitsu Kawano, What is Germany's fourth industrial revolution, "Industry 4.0"?, http://monoist.atmarkit.co.jp/mn/articles/1404/04/news014.html, 2016.

[220] M.M. Khan, D.R. Lester, L.A. Plana, A. Rast, X. Jin, E. Painkras, S.B. Furber, SpiNNaker: mapping neural networks onto a massively-parallel chip multiprocessor, in: 2008 IEEE International Joint Conference on Neural Networks (IEEE World Congress on Computational Intelligence), June 2008, pp. 2849–2856.

[221] Emmett Kilgariff, Henry Moreton, Nick Stam, Brandon Bell, NVIDIA Turing architecture in-depth, https://devblogs.nvidia.com/nvidia-turing-architecture-in-depth/, September 2018.

[222] Y. Kim, D. Shin, J. Lee, Y. Lee, H.J. Yoo, 14.3 A 0.55V 1.1mW artificial-intelligence processor with PVT compensation for micro robots, in: 2016 IEEE International Solid-State Circuits Conference (ISSCC), Jan 2016, pp. 258–259.

[223] Diederik P. Kingma, Jimmy Ba, Adam: a method for stochastic optimization, in: Yoshua Bengio, Yann LeCun (Eds.), 3rd International Conference on Learning Representations, ICLR 2015, Conference Track Proceedings, San Diego, CA, USA, May 7-9, 2015, 2015.

[224] Diederik P. Kingma, Danilo Jimenez Rezende, Shakir Mohamed, Max Welling, Semi-supervised learning with deep generative models, CoRR, arXiv:1406.5298 [abs], 2014.

[225] Diederik P. Kingma, Max Welling, An introduction to variational autoencoders, CoRR, arXiv:1906.02691 [abs], 2019.

[226] A.C. Klaiber, H.M. Levy, A comparison of message passing and shared memory architectures for data parallel programs, in: Proceedings of the 21st Annual International Symposium on

Computer Architecture, ISCA '94, Los Alamitos, CA, USA, IEEE Computer Society Press, 1994, pp. 94–105.

[227]   Kayo Kobayashi, Behind the scenes of product planning: vending machines that identify with sensors and display "recommended", http://www.nikkeibp.co.jp/article/column/20101221/255381/, December 2010.

[228]   Kate Kochetkova, The dark side of face recognition technology, https://blog.kaspersky.co.jp/bad-facial-recognition/12343/, September 2016.

[229]   Teuvo Kohonen, Self-Organized Map, Springer Japan, June 2005.

[230]   Igor Kononenko, Machine learning for medical diagnosis: history, state of the art and perspective, Artificial Intelligence in Medicine 23 (1) (Aug 2001) 89–109.

[231]   Alex Krizhevsky, Ilya Sutskever, Geoffrey E. Hinton, ImageNet classification with deep convolutional neural networks, in: F. Pereira, C.J.C. Burges, L. Bottou, K.Q. Weinberger (Eds.), Advances in Neural Information Processing Systems 25, Curran Associates, Inc., 2012, pp. 1097–1105.

[232]   Sun-Yuan Kung, On supercomputing with systolic/wavefront array processors, Proceedings of the IEEE 72 (7) (July 1984) 867–884.

[233]   I. Kuon, J. Rose, Measuring the gap between FPGAs and ASICs, IEEE Transactions on Computer-Aided Design of Integrated Circuits and Systems 26 (2) (Feb 2007) 203–215.

[234]   Duygu Kuzum, Rakesh G.D. Jeyasingh, Byoungil Lee, H.-S. Philip Wong, Nanoelectronic programmable synapses based on phase change materials for brain-inspired computing, Nano Letters 12 (5) (2012) 2179–2186.

[235]   Yasuo Kyobe, Innovate stock trading with AI trading Alpaca, http://bizzine.jp/article/detail/1738, July 2016.

[236]   Gustav Larsson, Michael Maire, Gregory Shakhnarovich, Fractalnet: ultra-deep neural networks without residuals, CoRR, arXiv:1605.07648 [abs], 2016.

[237]   Alberto Delmás Lascorz, Sayeh Sharify, Isak Edo, Dylan Malone Stuart, Omar Mohamed Awad, Patrick Judd, Mostafa Mahmoud, Milos Nikolic, Kevin Siu, Zissis Poulos, et al., Shapeshifter: enabling fine-grain data width adaptation in deep learning, in: Proceedings of the 52nd Annual IEEE/ACM International Symposium on Microarchitecture, MICRO '52, New York, NY, USA, Association for Computing Machinery, 2019, pp. 28–41.

[238]   C.L. Lawson, R.J. Hanson, D.R. Kincaid, F.T. Krogh, Basic linear algebra subprograms for Fortran usage, ACM Transactions on Mathematical Software 5 (3) (Sep 1979) 308–323.

[239]   Y. Lecun, L. Bottou, Y. Bengio, P. Haffner, Gradient-based learning applied to document recognition, Proceedings of the IEEE 86 (11) (Nov 1998) 2278–2324.

[240]   K.J. Lee, K. Bong, C. Kim, J. Jang, H. Kim, J. Lee, K.R. Lee, G. Kim, H.J. Yoo, 14.2 A 502GOPS and 0.984mW dual-mode ADAS SoC with RNN-FIS engine for intention prediction in automotive black-box system, in: 2016 IEEE International Solid-State Circuits Conference (ISSCC), Jan 2016, pp. 256–257.

[241]   Ruby B. Lee, Subword parallelism with max-2, IEEE MICRO 16 (4) (Aug 1996) 51–59.

[242]   LegalForce, Make all logal risk controllable.

[243]   S. Li, C. Wu, H. Li, B. Li, Y. Wang, Q. Qiu, FPGA acceleration of recurrent neural network based language model, in: Field-Programmable Custom Computing Machines (FCCM), 2015 IEEE 23rd Annual International Symposium on, May 2015, pp. 111–118.

[244]   E. Lindholm, J. Nickolls, S. Oberman, J. Montrym, NVIDIA Tesla: a unified graphics and computing architecture, IEEE MICRO 28 (2) (March 2008) 39–55.

[245]   Daofu Liu, Tianshi Chen, Shaoli Liu, Jinhong Zhou, Shengyuan Zhou, Olivier Teman, Xiaobing Feng, Xuehai Zhou, Yunji Chen, PuDianNao: a polyvalent machine learning accelerator, in: Proceedings of the Twentieth International Conference on Architectural Support for Programming Languages and Operating Systems, ASPLOS '15, New York, NY, USA, ACM, 2015, pp. 369–381.

[246]   Guilin Liu, Fitsum A. Reda, Kevin J. Shih, Ting-Chun Wang, Andrew Tao, Bryan Catanzaro, Image inpainting for irregular holes using partial convolutions, CoRR, arXiv:1804.07723 [abs], 2018.

[247] S. Liu, Z. Du, J. Tao, D. Han, T. Luo, Y. Xie, Y. Chen, T. Chen, Cambricon: an instruction set architecture for neural networks, in: 2016 ACM/IEEE 43rd Annual International Symposium on Computer Architecture (ISCA), June 2016, pp. 393–405.

[248] Wei Liu, Dragomir Anguelov, Dumitru Erhan, Christian Szegedy, Scott E. Reed, Cheng-Yang Fu, Alexander C. Berg, SSD: single shot multibox detector, CoRR, arXiv:1512.02325 [abs], 2015.

[249] W. Lu, G. Yan, J. Li, S. Gong, Y. Han, X. Li, Flexflow: a flexible dataflow accelerator architecture for convolutional neural networks, in: 2017 IEEE International Symposium on High Performance Computer Architecture (HPCA), Feb 2017, pp. 553–564.

[250] Bill Lubanovic, Introduction to Python3, O'Reilly Japan, 2015.

[251] Y. Lv, Y. Duan, W. Kang, Z. Li, F.Y. Wang, Traffic flow prediction with big data: a deep learning approach, IEEE Transactions on Intelligent Transportation Systems 16 (2) (April 2015) 865–873.

[252] Yufei Ma, Yu Cao, Sarma Vrudhula, Jae-sun Seo, Optimizing loop operation and dataflow in FPGA acceleration of deep convolutional neural networks, in: Proceedings of the 2017 ACM/SIGDA International Symposium on Field-Programmable Gate Arrays, FPGA '17, New York, NY, USA, ACM, 2017, pp. 45–54.

[253] Andrew L. Maas, Awni Y. Hannun, Andrew Y. Ng, Rectifier nonlinearities improve neural network acoustic models, in: ICML Workshop on Deep Learning for Audio, Speech, and Language Processing, ICML '13, 2013.

[254] D. Mahajan, J. Park, E. Amaro, H. Sharma, A. Yazdanbakhsh, J.K. Kim, H. Esmaeilzadeh, TABLA: a unified template-based framework for accelerating statistical machine learning, in: 2016 IEEE International Symposium on High Performance Computer Architecture (HPCA), March 2016, pp. 14–26.

[255] T. Makimoto, The hot decade of field programmable technologies, in: 2002 IEEE International Conference on Field-Programmable Technology, 2002. (FPT). Proceedings, Dec 2002, pp. 3–6.

[256] John Markoff, Computer wins on 'Jeopardy!': trivial, it's not, http://www.nytimes.com/2011/02/17/science/17jeopardy-watson.html?pagewanted=all&_r=0, February 2011.

[257] Henry Markram, Joachim Lübke, Michael Frotscher, Bert Sakmann, Regulation of synaptic efficacy by coincidence of postsynaptic APs and EPSPs, Science 275 (5297) (1997) 213–215.

[258] D. Matzke, Will physical scalability sabotage performance gains?, Computer 30 (9) (Sep 1997) 37–39.

[259] Warren S. McCulloch, Walter Pitts, A logical calculus of the ideas immanent in nervous activity, in: Neurocomputing: Foundations of Research, MIT Press, Cambridge, MA, USA, 1988, pp. 15–27.

[260] P. Merolla, J. Arthur, F. Akopyan, N. Imam, R. Manohar, D.S. Modha, A digital neurosynaptic core using embedded crossbar memory with 45pJ per spike in 45nm, in: 2011 IEEE Custom Integrated Circuits Conference (CICC), Sept 2011, pp. 1–4.

[261] Paul A. Merolla, John V. Arthur, Rodrigo Alvarez-Icaza, Andrew S. Cassidy, Jun Sawada, Filipp Akopyan, Bryan L. Jackson, Nabil Imam, Chen Guo, Yutaka Nakamura, Bernard Brezzo, Ivan Vo, Steven K. Esser, Rathinakumar Appuswamy, Brian Taba, Arnon Amir, Myron D. Flickner, William P. Risk, Rajit Manohar, Dharmendra S. Modha, A million spiking-neuron integrated circuit with a scalable communication network and interface, Science 345 (6197) (2014) 668–673.

[262] M. Mikaitis, D.R. Lester, D. Shang, S. Furber, G. Liu, J. Garside, S. Scholze, S. Höppner, A. Dixius, Approximate fixed-point elementary function accelerator for the spinnaker-2 neuromorphic chip, in: 2018 IEEE 25th Symposium on Computer Arithmetic (ARITH), June 2018, pp. 37–44.

[263] Nikola Milosevic, Equity forecast: predicting long term stock price movement using machine learning, CoRR, arXiv:1603.00751 [absx], 2016.

[264] Kazutaka Mishima, Machine learning that changes the world, who programs 1 trillion IoT devices, http://monoist.atmarkit.co.jp/mn/articles/1612/13/news049.html, December 2016.

[265] Asit K. Mishra, Eriko Nurvitadhi, Jeffrey J. Cook, Debbie Marr, WRPN: wide reduced-precision networks, CoRR, arXiv:1709.01134 [abs], 2017.

[266] Daisuke Miyashita, Edward H. Lee, Boris Murmann, Convolutional neural networks using logarithmic data representation, CoRR, arXiv:1603.01025 [abs], 2016.

[267] T. Miyato, A.M. Dai, I. Goodfellow, Virtual adversarial training for semi-supervised text classification, ArXiv e-prints, May 2016.

[268] D.I. Moldovan, On the design of algorithms for VLSI systolic arrays, Proceedings of the IEEE 71 (1) (Jan 1983) 113–120.

[269] J. Montrym, H. Moreton, The GeForce 6800, IEEE MICRO 25 (2) (March 2005) 41–51.

[270] Bert Moons, Roel Uytterhoeven, Wim Dehaene, Marian Verhelst, ENVISION: a 0.26-to-10TOPS/W subword-parallel dynamic-voltage-accuracy-frequency-scalable convolutional neural network processor in 28nm FDSOI, in: 2017 IEEE International Solid-State Circuits Conference (ISSCC), February 2017.

[271] G.E. Moore, Cramming more components onto integrated circuits, Proceedings of the IEEE 86 (1) (Jan 1998) 82–85.

[272] MPI, The Message Passing Interface (MPI) standard.

[273] Mu-hyun. Google's AL Program "AlphaGo" won Go World Champion, https://japan.cnet.com/article/35079262/, March 2016.

[274] Ann Steffora Mutschler, Debug tops verification tasks, 2018.

[275] H. Nakahara, T. Sasao, A deep convolutional neural network based on nested residue number system, in: 2015 25th International Conference on Field Programmable Logic and Applications (FPL), Sept 2015, pp. 1–6.

[276] Satoshi Nakamoto, Bitcoin: a peer-to-peer electronic cash system, https://bitcoin.org/bitcoin.pdf, December 2010.

[277] Andrew Ng, Machine learning, https://www.coursera.org/, September 2016.

[278] J. Nickolls, W.J. Dally, The GPU computing era, IEEE MICRO 30 (2) (March 2010) 56–69.

[279] Takayuki Okatani, Deep Learning, 1st edition, Machine Learning Professional Series, Kodansha Ltd., April 2015.

[280] A. Emin Orhan, Skip connections as effective symmetry-breaking, CoRR, arXiv:1701.09175 [abs], 2017.

[281] A. Ouadah, Pipeline defects risk assessment using machine learning and analytical hierarchy process, in: 2018 International Conference on Applied Smart Systems (ICASS), Nov 2018, pp. 1–6.

[282] Kalin Ovtcharov, Olatunji Ruwase, Joo-Young Kim, Jeremy Fowers, Karin Strauss, Eric Chung, Accelerating Deep Convolutional Neural Networks Using Specialized Hardware, February 2015.

[283] Kalin Ovtcharov, Olatunji Ruwase, Joo-Young Kim, Jeremy Fowers, Karin Strauss, Eric S. Chung, Toward accelerating deep learning at scale using specialized hardware in the data-center, in: Hot Chips: a Symposium on High Performance Chips (HC27), August 2015.

[284] Andrew Owens, Phillip Isola, Josh McDermott, Antonio Torralba, Edward H. Adelson, William T. Freeman, Visually indicated sounds, CoRR, arXiv:1512.08512 [abs], 2015.

[285] S. Palacharla, N.P. Jouppi, J.E. Smith, Complexity-effective superscalar processors, in: Computer Architecture, 1997. Conference Proceedings. The 24th Annual International Symposium on, June 1997, pp. 206–218.

[286] S. Park, K. Bong, D. Shin, J. Lee, S. Choi, H.J. Yoo, 4.6 A1.93TOPS/W scalable deep learning/inference processor with tetra-parallel MIMD architecture for big-data applications, in: 2015 IEEE International Solid-State Circuits Conference - (ISSCC) Digest of Technical Papers, Feb 2015, pp. 1–3.

[287] S. Park, S. Choi, J. Lee, M. Kim, J. Park, H.J. Yoo, 14.1 A 126.1mW real-time natural UI/UX processor with embedded deep-learning core for low-power smart glasses, in: 2016 IEEE International Solid-State Circuits Conference (ISSCC), Jan 2016, pp. 254–255.

[288] Taesung Park, Ming-Yu Liu, Ting-Chun Wang, Jun-Yan Zhu, Semantic image synthesis with spatially-adaptive normalization, CoRR, arXiv:1903.07291 [abs], 2019.

[289] M. Pease, R. Shostak, L. Lamport, Reaching agreement in the presence of faults, Journal of the ACM 27 (2) (Apr 1980) 228–234.

[290] M. Peemen, B. Mesman, H. Corporaal, Inter-tile reuse optimization applied to bandwidth constrained embedded accelerators, in: 2015 Design, Automation Test in Europe Conference Exhibition (DATE), March 2015, pp. 169–174.

[291] Mohammad Pezeshki, Linxi Fan, Philemon Brakel, Aaron C. Courville, Yoshua Bengio, Deconstructing the ladder network architecture, CoRR, arXiv:1511.06430 [abs], 2015.

[292] Michael E. Porter, What is strategy?, Harvard Business Review 74 (6) (1996).

[293] Jiantao Qiu, Jie Wang, Song Yao, Kaiyuan Guo, Boxun Li, Erjin Zhou, Jincheng Yu, Tianqi Tang, Ningyi Xu, Sen Song, Yu Wang, Huazhong Yang, Going deeper with embedded FPGA platform for convolutional neural network, in: Proceedings of the 2016 ACM/SIGDA International Symposium on Field-Programmable Gate Arrays, FPGA '16, New York, NY, USA, ACM, 2016, pp. 26–35.

[294] J.R. Quinlan, Simplifying decision trees, International Journal of Man-Machine Studies 27 (3) (Sep 1987) 221–234.

[295] Alec Radford, Luke Metz, Soumith Chintala, Unsupervised representation learning with deep convolutional generative adversarial networks, CoRR, arXiv:1511.06434 [abs], 2015.

[296] Md Aamir Raihan, Negar Goli, Tor M. Aamodt, Modeling deep learning accelerator enabled gpus, CoRR, arXiv:1811.08309 [abs], 2018.

[297] B. Rajendran, F. Alibart, Neuromorphic computing based on emerging memory technologies, IEEE Journal on Emerging and Selected Topics in Circuits and Systems 6 (2) (June 2016) 198–211.

[298] Ariel Ortiz Ramirez, An overview of intel's mmx technology, Linux Journal 1999 (61es) (May 1999).

[299] B. Ramsundar, S. Kearnes, P. Riley, D. Webster, D. Konerding, V. Pande, Massively multitask networks for drug discovery, ArXiv e-prints, Feb 2015.

[300] Antti Rasmus, Harri Valpola, Mikko Honkala, Mathias Berglund, Tapani Raiko, Semi-supervised learning with ladder network, CoRR, arXiv:1507.02672 [abs], 2015.

[301] M. Rastegari, V. Ordonez, J. Redmon, A. Farhadi, XNOR-Net: ImageNet classification using binary convolutional neural networks, ArXiv e-prints, Mar 2016.

[302] M.S. Razlighi, M. Imani, F. Koushanfar, T. Rosing, Looknn: neural network with no multiplication, in: Design, Automation Test in Europe Conference Exhibition (DATE), 2017, March 2017, pp. 1775–1780.

[303] B. Reagen, P. Whatmough, R. Adolf, S. Rama, H. Lee, S.K. Lee, J.M. Hernández-Lobato, G.Y. Wei, D. Brooks, Minerva: enabling low-power, highly-accurate deep neural network accelerators, in: 2016 ACM/IEEE 43rd Annual International Symposium on Computer Architecture (ISCA), June 2016, pp. 267–278.

[304] R. Reed, Pruning algorithms-a survey, IEEE Transactions on Neural Networks 4 (5) (Sep 1993) 740–747.

[305] Steffen Rendle, Christoph Freudenthaler, Zeno Gantner, Lars Schmidt-Thieme, BPR: Bayesian personalized ranking from implicit feedback, CoRR, arXiv:1205.2618 [abs], 2012.

[306] Reuters. Reuters corpus, http://about.reuters.com/researchandstandards/corpus/.

[307] Adi Robertson, How to fight lies, tricks, and chaos online, 2019.

[308] Chuck Rosenberg, Improving photo search: a step across the semantic gap, https://research.googleblog.com/2013/06/improving-photo-search-step-across.html, June 2013, Google Research Blog.

[309] Sebastian Ruder, Transfer learning - machine learning's next frontier, http://sebastianruder.com/transfer-learning/index.html, March 2017.

[310] D.E. Rumelhart, G.E. Hinton, R.J. Williams, Learning internal representations by error propagation, in: Parallel Distributed Processing: Explorations in the Microstructure of Cognition, Vol. 1, MIT Press, Cambridge, MA, USA, 1986, pp. 318–362.

[311] David E. Rumelhart, Geoffrey E. Hinton, Ronald J. Williams, Learning representations by back-propagating errors, Nature 323 (October 1986) 533–536.

[312] Alexander M. Rush, Sumit Chopra, Jason Weston, A neural attention model for abstractive sentence summarization, CoRR, arXiv:1509.00685 [abs], 2015.

[313] Ruslan Salakhutdinov, Andriy Mnih, Geoffrey Hinton, Restricted Boltzmann machines for collaborative filtering, in: Proceedings of the 24th International Conference on Machine Learning, ICML '07, New York, NY, USA, ACM, 2007, pp. 791–798.

[314] A.G. Salman, B. Kanigoro, Y. Heryadi, Weather forecasting using deep learning techniques, in: 2015 International Conference on Advanced Computer Science and Information Systems (ICACSIS), Oct 2015, pp. 281–285.

[315] A.L. Samuel, Some studies in machine learning using the game of checkers, IBM Journal of Research and Development 44 (1.2) (Jan 2000) 206–226.

[316] Choe Sang-Hun, Google's computer program beats Lee Se-dol in Go tournament, http://www.nytimes.com/2016/03/16/world/asia/korea-alphago-vs-lee-sedol-go.html, March 2016.

[317] A.W. Savich, M. Moussa, S. Areibi, The impact of arithmetic representation on implementing MLP-BP on FPGAs: a study, IEEE Transactions on Neural Networks 18 (1) (Jan 2007) 240–252.

[318] André Seznec, Stephen Felix, Venkata Krishnan, Yiannakis Sazeides, Design tradeoffs for the alpha EV8 conditional branch predictor, in: Proceedings of the 29th Annual International Symposium on Computer Architecture, ISCA '02, Washington, DC, USA, IEEE Computer Society, 2002, pp. 295–306.

[319] Ali Shafiee, Anirban Nag, Naveen Muralimanohar, Rajeev Balasubramonian, John Paul Strachan, Miao Hu, R. Stanley Williams, Vivek Srikumar, ISAAC: a convolutional neural network accelerator with in-situ analog arithmetic in crossbars, in: 2016 ACM/IEEE International Symposium on Computer Architecture (ISCA), June 2016.

[320] Hardik Sharma, Jongse Park, Divya Mahajan, Emmanuel Amaro, Joon Kyung Kim, Chenkai Shao, Asit Mishra, Hadi Esmaeilzadeh, From high-level deep neural models to FPGAs, in: 2016 Annual IEEE/ACM International Symposium on Microarchitecture (MICRO), March 2016.

[321] John Paul Shen, Mikko H. Lipasti, Modern Processor Design: Fundamentals of Superscalar Processors, beta edition, McGraw-Hill, 2003.

[322] Juncheng Shen, De Ma, Zonghua Gu, Ming Zhang, Xiaolei Zhu, Xiaoqiang Xu, Qi Xu, Yangjing Shen, Gang Pan, Darwin: a neuromorphic hardware co-processor based on Spiking Neural Networks, Science in China. Information Sciences 59 (2) (2016) 1–5.

[323] Shaohuai Shi, Qiang Wang, Pengfei Xu, Xiaowen Chu, Benchmarking state-of-the-art deep learning software tools, CoRR, arXiv:1608.07249 [abs], 2016.

[324] Tadatsugu Shimazu, Analyzing POS data is at the forefront of sales, http://business.nikkeibp.co.jp/article/topics/20080207/146641/?rt=nocnt, February 2008.

[325] Dongjoo Shin, Jinmook Lee, Jinsu Lee, Hoi-Jun Yoo, DNPU: an 8.1TOPS/W reconfigurable CNN-RNN processor for general-purpose deep neural networks, in: 2017 IEEE International Solid-State Circuits Conference (ISSCC), February 2017.

[326] David Silver, Aja Huang, Chris J. Maddison, Arthur Guez, Laurent Sifre, George van den Driessche, Julian Schrittwieser, Ioannis Antonoglou, Veda Panneershelvam, Marc Lanctot, Sander Dieleman, Dominik Grewe, John Nham, Nal Kalchbrenner, Ilya Sutskever, Timothy Lillicrap, Madeleine Leach, Koray Kavukcuoglu, Thore Graepel, Demis Hassabis, Mastering the game of Go with deep neural networks and tree search, Nature 529 (2016) 484–489, arXiv:1602.01528 [abs], 2016.

[327] J. Sim, J.S. Park, M. Kim, D. Bae, Y. Choi, L.S. Kim, 14.6 A 1.42TOPS/W deep convolutional neural network recognition processor for intelligent IoE systems, in: 2016 IEEE International Solid-State Circuits Conference (ISSCC), Jan 2016, pp. 264–265.

[328] D. Sima, The design space of register renaming techniques, IEEE MICRO 20 (5) (Sep 2000) 70–83.

[329] Jim Smith, Ravi Nair, Virtual Machines: Versatile Platforms for Systems and Processes, The Morgan Kaufmann Series in Computer Architecture and Design, Morgan Kaufmann Publishers Inc., 2005.

[330] G.S. Snider, Spike-timing-dependent learning in memristive nanodevices, in: 2008 IEEE International Symposium on Nanoscale Architectures, June 2008, pp. 85–92.

[331] J. Snoek, H. Larochelle, R.P. Adams, Practical Bayesian optimization of machine learning algorithms, ArXiv e-prints, Jun 2012.

[332] A. Sodani, R. Gramunt, J. Corbal, H.S. Kim, K. Vinod, S. Chinthamani, S. Hutsell, R. Agarwal, Y.C. Liu, Knights landing: second-generation Intel Xeon Phi product, IEEE MICRO 36 (2) (Mar 2016) 34–46.

[333] Olivia Solon, Advanced facial recognition technology used in criminal investigations in more than 20 countries, http://wired.jp/2014/07/23/neoface/, July 2014.

[334] J. Son Chung, A. Senior, O. Vinyals, A. Zisserman, Lip reading sentences in the wild, ArXiv e-prints, Nov 2016.

[335] Viji Srinivasan, David Brooks, Michael Gschwind, Pradip Bose, Victor Zyuban, Philip N. Strenski, Philip G. Emma, Optimizing pipelines for power and performance, in: Proceedings of the 35th Annual ACM/IEEE International Symposium on Microarchitecture, MICRO 35, Los Alamitos, CA, USA, IEEE Computer Society Press, 2002, pp. 333–344.

[336] Nitish Srivastava, Geoffrey Hinton, Alex Krizhevsky, Ilya Sutskever, Ruslan Salakhutdinov, Dropout: a simple way to prevent neural networks from overfitting, Journal of Machine Learning Research 15 (1) (Jan 2014) 1929–1958.

[337] Rupesh Kumar Srivastava, Klaus Greff, Jürgen Schmidhuber, Training very deep networks, CoRR, arXiv:1507.06228 [abs], 2015.

[338] Kazunari Sugimitsu, The current state of "co-he-he" problems in universities, countermeasures and their problems, http://gakkai.univcoop.or.jp/pcc/paper/2010/pdf/58.pdf, July 2016.

[339] Charlie Sugimoto, NVIDIA GPU Accelerates Deep Learning, May 2015.

[340] Baohua Sun, Daniel Liu, Leo Yu, Jay Li, Helen Liu, Wenhan Zhang, Terry Torng, Mram co-designed processing-in-memory cnn accelerator for mobile and iot applications, 2018.

[341] Baohua Sun, Lin Yang, Patrick Dong, Wenhan Zhang, Jason Dong, Charles Young, Ultra power-efficient CNN domain specific accelerator with 9.3tops/watt for mobile and embedded applications, CoRR, arXiv:1805.00361 [abs], 2018.

[342] Wonyong Sung, Kyuyeon Hwang, Resiliency of deep neural networks under quantization, CoRR, arXiv:1511.06488 [abs], 2015.

[343] G.A. Susto, A. Schirru, S. Pampuri, S. McLoone, A. Beghi, Machine learning for predictive maintenance: a multiple classifier approach, IEEE Transactions on Industrial Informatics 11 (3) (June 2015) 812–820.

[344] Takahiro Suzuki, Can existing media overcome the darkness of curation site?, http://diamond.jp/articles/-/110717, December 2016.

[345] V. Sze, Y. Chen, T. Yang, J.S. Emer, Efficient processing of deep neural networks: a tutorial and survey, Proceedings of the IEEE 105 (12) (Dec 2017) 2295–2329.

[346] So Takada, Current status of Japan's inequality, http://www.cao.go.jp/zei-cho/gijiroku/zeicho/2015/__icsFiles/afieldfile/2015/08/27/27zen17kai7.pdf, August 2015.

[347] Shigeyuki Takano, Performance scalability of adaptive processor architecture, ACM Transactions on Reconfigurable Technology and Systems 10 (2) (Apr 2017) 16:1–16:22.

[348] Shigeto Takeoka, Yasuhiro Ouchi, Yoshio Yamasaki, Data conversion and quantize noise for acoustic signals, in: Acoustical Society of Japan, Vol. 73, June 2017, pp. 585–591.

[349] Noriko Takiguchi, Uber's users and drivers are "exploited", criticism in the U.S. rises, http://diamond.jp/articles/-/123730, 2017.

[350] H. Tann, S. Hashemi, R.I. Bahar, S. Reda, Hardware-software codesign of accurate, multiplier-free deep neural networks, in: 2017 54th ACM/EDAC/IEEE Design Automation Conference (DAC), June 2017, pp. 1–6.

[351] M.B. Taylor, Is dark silicon useful? Harnessing the four horsemen of the coming dark silicon apocalypse, in: DAC Design Automation Conference 2012, June 2012, pp. 1131–1136.

[352] Oliver Temam, The rebirth of neural networks, in: Proceedings of the 37th Annual International Symposium on Computer Architecture, ISCA '10, IEEE Computer Society, 2010, pp. 49–349.

[353] R.M. Tomasulo, An efficient algorithm for exploiting multiple arithmetic units, IBM Journal of Research and Development 11 (1) (Jan 1967) 25–33.

[354] Alexander Toshev, Christian Szegedy, Deeppose: human pose estimation via deep neural networks, CoRR, arXiv:1312.4659 [abs], 2013.

[355] S.M. Trimberger, Three ages of FPGAs: a retrospective on the first thirty years of FPGA technology, Proceedings of the IEEE 103 (3) (March 2015) 318–331.

[356] Yaman Umuroglu, Nicholas J. Fraser, Giulio Gambardella, Michaela Blott, Philip Heng Wai Leong, Magnus Jahre, Kees A. Vissers, FINN: a framework for fast, scalable binarized neural network inference, CoRR, arXiv:1612.07119 [abs], 2016.

[357] G. Urgese, F. Barchi, E. Macii, A. Acquaviva, Optimizing network traffic for spiking neural network simulations on densely interconnected many-core neuromorphic platforms, IEEE Transactions on Emerging Topics in Computing 6 (3) (2018) 317–329.

[358] Harri Valpora, From neural pca to deep unsupervised learning, arXiv preprint, arXiv:1441.7783, 2014.

[359] Pascal Vincent, Hugo Larochelle, Isabelle Lajoie, Yoshua Bengio, Pierre-Antoine Manzagol, Stacked denoising autoencoders: learning useful representations in a deep network with a local denoising criterion, Journal of Machine Learning Research 11 (Dec 2010) 3371–3408.

[360] Oriol Vinyals, Alexander Toshev, Samy Bengio, Dumitru Erhan, A picture is worth a thousand (coherent) words: building a natural description of images, https://research.googleblog.com/2014/11/a-picture-is-worth-thousand-coherent.html, November 2014, Google Research Blog.

[361] Punkaj Y. Vohra, The New Era of Watson Computing, February 2014.

[362] E. Waingold, M. Taylor, D. Srikrishna, V. Sarkar, W. Lee, V. Lee, J. Kim, M. Frank, P. Finch, R. Barua, J. Babb, S. Amarasinghe, A. Agarwal, Baring it all to software: raw machines, Computer 30 (9) (Sep 1997) 86–93.

[363] Li Wan, Matthew Zeiler, Sixin Zhang, Yann Le Cun, Rob Fergus, Regularization of neural networks using dropconnect, in: Sanjoy Dasgupta, David McAllester (Eds.), Proceedings of the 30th International Conference on Machine Learning, Atlanta, Georgia, USA, in: Proceedings of Machine Learning Research, vol. 28, PMLR, 17–19 Jun 2013, pp. 1058–1066.

[364] Pete Warden, How to quantize neural networks with TensorFlow, https://petewarden.com/2016/05/03/how-to-quantize-neural-networks-with-tensorflow/, May 2016.

[365] Shlomo Weiss, James E. Smith, Instruction issue logic for pipelined supercomputers, SIGARCH Computer Architecture News 12 (3) (Jan 1984) 110–118.

[366] Paul N. Whatmough, Sae Kyu Lee, Hyunkwang Lee, Saketh Rama, David Brooks, Gu-Yeon Wei, A 28nm SoC with a 1.2GHz 568nJ/prediction sparse deep-neural-network engine with >0.1 timing error rate tolerance for IoT applications, in: 2017 IEEE International Solid-State Circuits Conference (ISSCC), February 2017.

[367] Samuel Webb Williams, Andrew Waterman, David A. Patterson, Roofline: an Insightful Visual Performance Model for Floating-Point Programs and Multicore Architectures, Technical Report UCB/EECS-2008-134, University of California at Berkeley, October 2008.

[368] F. Woergoetter, B. Porr, Reinforcement learning, Scholarpedia 3 (3) (2008) 1448, revision #91704.

[369] Michael E. Wolf, Monica S. Lam, A data locality optimizing algorithm, in: Proceedings of the ACM SIGPLAN 1991 Conference on Programming Language Design and Implementation, PLDI '91, New York, NY, USA, ACM, 1991, pp. 30–44.

[370] Bichen Wu, Alvin Wan, Xiangyu Yue, Peter H. Jin, Sicheng Zhao, Noah Golmant, Amir Gholaminejad, Joseph Gonzalez, Kurt Keutzer, Shift: a zero flop, zero parameter alternative to spatial convolutions, CoRR, arXiv:1711.08141 [abs], 2017.

[371] Jiajun Wu, Chengkai Zhang, Xiuming Zhang, Zhoutong Zhang, William T. Freeman, Joshua B. Tenenbaum, Learning 3D shape priors for shape completion and reconstruction, in: European Conference on Computer Vision (ECCV), 2018.

[372] Yu Xiang, Alexandre Alahi, Silvio Savarese, Learning to track: online multi-object tracking by decision making, in: Proceedings of the IEEE International Conference on Computer Vision, 2015, pp. 4705–4713.

[373] W. Xiong, J. Droppo, X. Huang, F. Seide, M. Seltzer, A. Stolcke, D. Yu, G. Zweig, The Microsoft 2016 conversational speech recognition system, ArXiv e-prints, Sep 2016.

[374] Keyulu Xu, Weihua Hu, Jure Leskovec, Stefanie Jegelka, How powerful are graph neural networks?, CoRR, arXiv:1810.00826 [abs], 2018.

[375] Reiko Yagi, What is the "copy and paste judgment tool" that is attracting attention in the STAP disturbance, http://itpro.nikkeibp.co.jp/pc/article/trend/20140411/1127564/, June 2014.

[376] A. Yang, Deep learning training at scale spring crest deep learning accelerator (Intel® Nervana™ NNP-T), in: 2019 IEEE Hot Chips 31 Symposium (HCS), Cupertino, CA, USA, 2019, pp. 1–20.

[377] Amir Yazdanbakhsh, Kambiz Samadi, Nam Sung Kim, Hadi Esmaeilzadeh, Ganax: a unified mimd-simd acceleration for generative adversarial networks, in: Proceedings of the 45th Annual International Symposium on Computer Architecture, ISCA '18, IEEE Press, 2018, pp. 650–661.

[378] Li Yi, Guangyao Li, Mingming Jiang, An end-to-end steel strip surface defects recognition system based on convolutional neural networks, Steel Research International 88 (2) (2017) 1600068.

[379] Alireza Zaeemzadeh, Nazanin Rahnavard, Mubarak Shah, Norm-preservation: why residual networks can become extremely deep?, CoRR, arXiv:1805.07477 [abs], 2018.

[380] Chen Zhang, Peng Li, Guangyu Sun, Yijin Guan, Bingjun Xiao, Jason Cong, Optimizing FPGA-based accelerator design for deep convolutional neural networks, in: Proceedings of the 2015 ACM/SIGDA International Symposium on Field-Programmable Gate Arrays, FPGA '15, New York, NY, USA, ACM, 2015, pp. 161–170.

[381] Sarah Zhang, Infiltrate! Fully-automated "robot full" biolab, http://wired.jp/2016/09/07/inside-robot-run-genetics-lab/, September 2016.

[382] Shijin Zhang, Zidong Du, Lei Zhang, Huiying Lan, Shaoli Liu, Ling Li, Qi Guo, Tianshi Chen, Yunji Chen, Cambricon-x: an accelerator for sparse neural networks, in: 2016 49th Annual IEEE/ACM International Symposium on Microarchitecture (MICRO), October 2016, pp. 1–12.

[383] Yongwei Zhao, Zidong Du, Qi Guo, Shaoli Liu, Ling Li, Zhiwei Xu, Tianshi Chen, Yunji Chen, Cambricon-f: machine learning computers with fractal von Neumann architecture, in: Proceedings of the 46th International Symposium on Computer Architecture, ISCA '19, New York, NY, USA, Association for Computing Machinery, 2019, pp. 788–801.

[384] Xuda Zhou, Zidong Du, Qi Guo, Shaoli Liu, Chengsi Liu, Chao Wang, Xuehai Zhou, Ling Li, Tianshi Chen, Yunji Chen, Cambricon-s: addressing irregularity in sparse neural networks through a cooperative software/hardware approach, in: Proceedings of the 51st Annual IEEE/ACM International Symposium on Microarchitecture, MICRO-51, IEEE Press, 2018, pp. 15–28.

Index

Printed in the United States
by Baker & Taylor Publisher Services